THE STAR CHAMBER OF STANFORD

THE STAR CHAMBER OF STANFORD

ON THE SECRET TRIAL AND INVISIBLE PERSECUTION OF A STANFORD LAW FELLOW

RONY GULDMANN

All facts recounted by the author are true to the best of his recollection. Some statements cannot be substantiated other than through recollection and may be disputed by other parties. Where the author does not assert firsthand knowledge of the facts alleged, he alleges them as conjecture or surmise. As discussed in the memoranda of law in appendix 2, the author and publisher are in full compliance with all applicable laws.

Editing by Polly Kummel and Ann Aubrey Hanson
Cover design by Fiona Jayde Media
Book design by Wordzworth, *www.wordzworth.com*

Published by None Spared Press
Astoria, New York
ronyguldmann.com

Publisher's Cataloging-in-Publication Data

Names: Guldmann, Rony, author.

Title: The star chamber of Stanford : on the secret trial and invisible persecution of a Stanford Law fellow / Rony Guldmann.

Description: Includes bibliographical references. | Astoria, NY: None Spared Press, 2022.

Identifiers: LCCN 2020911314 | ISBN: 978-1-7352472-0-5 (pbk.) | 978-1-7352472-1-2 (Hardcover) | 978-1-7352472-2-9 (ebook)

Subjects: LCSH Guldmann, Rony. | Stanford University. School of Law. | Stanford University–Officials and employees–Biography. | Academic freedom–United States. | Learning and scholarship–United States. | Liberalism–United States. | Conservatism–United States. | Political culture–United States. | BISAC BIOGRAPHY & AUTOBIOGRAPHY / Personal Memoirs | BIOGRAPHY & AUTOBIOGRAPHY / Educators | EDUCATION / Higher | EDUCATION / Philosophy, Theory & Social Aspect | PHILOSOPHY / Movements / Critical Theory

Classification: LCC LC72.2 .G85 2021 | DDC 378.1/213/092–dc23

In loving memory of my mother

Students at Stanford are expected to show both within and without the university such respect for order, morality, personal honor and the rights of others as is demanded of good citizens. Failure to do this will be sufficient cause for removal from the university.

—"Fundamental Standard" of Stanford University

Whoever associates with scholars knows that one occasionally wounds them to the marrow with some harmless word; one incenses one's scholarly friends just when one means to honor them, one can drive them beside themselves merely because one has been too coarse to realize with whom one was really dealing—with sufferers who refuse to admit to themselves what they are, with drugged and heedless men who fear only one thing: *regaining consciousness.*

—Friedrich Nietzsche, *On the Genealogy of Morals*

One of the classic procedures of university polemics … is to designate opponents only by allusions, insinuations, or undertones understood solely by those initiated in the code, that is to say, more often than not solely by the opponents attacked. … [This] can thus help to charge discourse with that extra violence which is added to the discreet polemics of academic hatred by the methodical erasure of all external signs of violence.

—Pierre Bourdieu, *Homo Academicus*

CONTENTS

ACKNOWLEDGMENTS

I would like to thank James C. Gaither for generously funding this research and Stanford Law School for seeing my promise and admitting me. Gratitude to all the sundry faculty and fellows at Stanford and elsewhere who provided crucial inspiration at all stages of my journey. The Federalist Society made important contributions. Stanford's Office of the General Counsel provided valuable assistance. Above all, though, I am profoundly indebted to my faculty advisers, Barbara Fried, Joe Bankman, Dick Craswell, and Larry Kramer, worthy adversaries whose ingenuity and intrepidness made this book possible.

INTRODUCTION

This is a book about the writing of a book, *Conservative Claims of Cultural Oppression*, during my time at Stanford Law School between 2006 and 2011, first as a law student and then as the law school's James C. Gaither Fellow. Such a chronicle may strike readers as rather peculiar. The making of high-budget, action-packed Hollywood blockbusters may occasionally merit documentation. But to memorialize the making of a book, and an academic treatise no less? What could there be to say of any conceivable interest to the lay reader? What were the special effects and where was the drama? I assure you, drama there was. This should come as no surprise to readers of Rousseau's *Discourse on the Sciences and the Arts*, where he observed:

> It was an old tradition, passed on from Egypt into Greece, that a god hostile to men's peace and quiet was the inventor of the sciences. What opinion, then, must the Egyptians themselves have had about the sciences, which were born among them? They could keep a close eye on the sources which produced them. In fact, whether we leaf through the annals of the world or supplement uncertain chronicles with philosophical research, we will not find an origin for human learning which corresponds to the idea we like to create for it. Astronomy was born from superstition, eloquence from ambition, hate, flattery, and lies, geometry from avarice, physics from a vain curiosity—everything,

> even morality itself, from human pride. The sciences and the arts thus owe their birth to our vices; we would have fewer doubts about their advantages if they owed their birth to our virtues.[1]

This work is a case study in Rousseau's hypothesis. Just like astronomy, geometry, and physics, my research agenda at Stanford was born of vice rather than virtue, spurred on not by any saccharine "love of learning" or "devotion to a calling" but by pride, hate, ambition, flattery, and lies. That's why there is a story to tell, the story of how these vices and their ramifications yielded the insights that would become *Conservative Claims of Cultural Oppression.*[i] Stanford Law School was where my own all-too-human vices would interface synergistically with those of my colleagues to bring this project to fruition. The project was, therefore, a collaborative enterprise that flowered amid the human relationships that nourished it. I was the author, but the inspiration came from many sources, and these pages are written to give credit where it is due.

As the subject matter of my research announces, the saga I will now recount was as much about politics as about human folly and vainglory. Like most of my Stanford colleagues, I was substantially liberal. Run down the checklist of the day's hot-button political issues and I could generally be found on the left side of the controversy. Unlike my Stanford colleagues, however, I entertained a curious academic interest in the predicament of our ideological adversaries: conservatives. The oppression of blacks, women, and gays had been studied extensively, the subject of far-reaching interdisciplinary disquisitions. *But what of the tribulations of conservatives?* I asked myself Conservatives look upon their alleged cultural oppression by liberals as a defining feature of the contemporary political landscape and lament this to all who will

---

i Interested readers can access a near-final draft of the manuscript at *www.ronyguldmann.com,* under Upcoming Work. Even uninterested readers may benefit from reading the detailed abstract. Those interested in a deep dive into this memoir's big ideas can also access an in-progress draft of its more theoretical companion volume, *The Critical Theory of Academia,* at the same location.

listen. Typifying this zeitgeist, the Claire Boothe Luce Policy Institute once distributed "conservative safe space" stickers, alerting the public that, with gays "no longer the group shunned or berated on modern college campuses," campus intolerance "has now turned on conservatives and it is the conservative students and faculty who most need a 'safe space.'"[2] Had conservatives, in fact, been deprived of a safe space?

The liberals in my midst dismissed complaints of this nature as posturing and histrionics, the politically opportunistic swiping of progressive lingo, and I understood where they were coming from. But strangely, I couldn't shake the vague yet irrepressible conviction that there was more to the story, that conservative claims of cultural oppression encased some profound truth that resisted articulation but that I would uncover. At the very least, it was apparent to me that my own milieu, liberal academia, had yet to give those claims a fair hearing. Might liberals have trespassed against conservatives in ways they won't acknowledge and perhaps cannot recognize? It is axiomatic for the Left that oppressed groups can discern social iniquities that dominant ones are privileged to paper over, and I wondered whether the relationship between conservatives and liberals in America today might be yet another variant of this phenomenon—and a most ironic one, given conservatives' reputed callousness toward the oppressed and downtrodden.

This was the question I tasked myself with answering at Stanford, first as a law student and then as a paid researcher. I would conclude that conservative claims of cultural oppression are animated by the visceral sense that liberals are institutionally privileged to indulge in sublimated and intellectualized iterations of the same moral and cognitive vices that conservatives are compelled to exhibit more crudely and openly. Some of this idea is captured by the professor and blogger Timothy Burke:

> [Jonathan] Haidt argues that liberal political dispositions, which he views (like other political dispositions) as substantially subconscious and intuitive, are unresponsive to blasphemy

> or sacrilege, that liberals do not cross-wire deep emotional responses connected to disgust or repulsion to politics, do not have strong notions about the sacred and the profane as a part of their subconscious script for reading the public sphere and political events.
>
> My colleague and friend Ben Berger pointed out during one of our discussions that this observation seemed fundamentally wrong to him—that people can hold things sacred that are not designated as religious, and that many liberals held other kinds of institutions, texts, and manners as "sacred" in the same deep-seated, pre-conscious, emotionally intense way, perhaps without even knowing that they do. Ben observed that Haidt might be missing that because many liberals and leftists did not feel deeply trespassed against in this way in their own favored institutional and social worlds, and usually looked upon a public sphere that largely aligned with their vision of civic propriety and ritual.[3]

This charmed life lies at the root of what conservative culture warriors resent as "liberal privilege." In his widely read *What's the Matter with Kansas?* Thomas Frank characterized right-wing cultural discontent as "a curious amassing of petty, unrelated beefs with the world," but the culture warriors' superficially disjointed grievances are all reactions to that privilege.[4] While liberals' notions of sacredness and corresponding capacity for disgust are every bit as robust as conservatives', these traits are less easily recognized as such in liberals. Because liberals' distinctive cultural sensibilities are more often in sync with ambient mores and practices, they can fade into the unnoticed, taken-for-granted background of things, enabling liberals to style themselves as compassionate pragmatists pursuing universal human interests. Liberals are no more "secular" than conservatives. But in their case, the secular and the sacred bleed into each other so as to obscure the latter. Conservatives feel aggrieved by the "liberal elites" because these elites bask in this rarefied privilege, routinely excoriating the default human impulses of conservatives while remaining unaccountable for their own subtler and better-concealed variants thereof. That is the "safe space" afforded to liberals but denied to conservatives.

This particular form of social inequality passes under the liberal radar because of a certain historical and cultural narrative that enjoys wide currency in educated circles. Liberals can congratulate themselves for transcending the blinkered authoritarianism of conservatives because liberals presume that their Enlightenment ideals liberate them from the anachronistic "hero-systems" to which conservatives remain captive. The anthropologist Ernest Becker explains the concept:

> The fact is that this is what society is and always has been: a symbolic action system, a structure of statuses and roles, customs and rules of behavior, designed to serve as a vehicle for earthly heroism. Each script is somewhat unique, each culture has a different hero-system. What the anthropologists call "cultural relativity" is thus really the relativity of hero-systems the world over. But each cultural system cuts out roles for earthly heroics; each system cuts out roles for performances of various degrees of heroism: from the "high" heroism of a Churchill, a Mao, or a Buddha, to the "low" heroism of the coal miner, the peasant, the simple priest, the plain, everyday, earthy heroism wrought by gnarled working hands guiding a family through hunger and disease.
>
> It doesn't matter whether the cultural hero-system is frankly magical, religious, and primitive or secular, scientific, and civilized. It is still a mythical hero-system in which people serve in order to earn a feeling of primary value, of cosmic specialness, of ultimate usefulness to creation, of unshakable meaning. They earn this feeling by carving out a place in nature, by building an edifice that reflects human value: a temple, a cathedral, a totem pole, a skyscraper, a family that lasts three generations. The hope and belief is that the things that man creates in society are of lasting worth and meaning, that they outlive or outshine death and decay,

> that man and his products count. When Norman O. Brown said that Western society since Newton, no matter how scientific or secular it claims to be, is still as "religious" as any other, this is what he meant: "civilized" society is a hopeful belief and protest that science, money and goods make man count for more than any other animal. In this sense everything that man does is religious and heroic, and yet in danger of being fictitious and fallible.[5]

Hero-systems are social teleologies, systems of collective meaning-production, and liberals intuit that conservatives' authoritarian instincts are fueled by an atavistic attraction to these relics of a benighted premodern past. Against this, conservatives remonstrate that liberalism is a hero-system that conceals itself behind a secular facade of enlightenment, pragmatism, and utilitarianism, all of which grant plausible deniability to essentially religious impulses. This plausible deniability, my research would reveal, in turn grants the liberal elites their unearned rhetorical advantages over the conservative classes, setting the stage for the latter's cultural oppression. Every hero-system spawns its own array of illiberal impulses, but these are less readily identifiable as such in the elites. Whereas the hero-systems of the Right—for instance, "God, Country, and Family"—are a "low" heroism operating nakedly in full public view, those of the Left are an intellectualized, "high" heroism operating surreptitiously within insulated institutional enclaves whose specialized discourses provide the illiberalism of the liberal elites with a benign veneer.

Stanford Law School is one such enclave, I would learn, and by becoming the target of its highbrow illiberalism I would uncover the heretofore hidden truth of conservative claims of cultural oppression. Ahead lies the story of how my strange fascination with conservatives' oppression by liberalism precipitated an improbable chain of events culminating in my own such oppression, when my very bid to expose the cultural pathologies of liberalism and academia—understood intuitively by conservatives—would eventuate in my own personal gaslighting at the hands of the elites. This ordeal would in time articulate the truth that had all along driven my research agenda. I am, therefore, indebted to those elites, who brought that agenda to life as lesser minds could not have.

These are my principal claims, and I have written what follows to defend them. To this end I offer the reader not only logic and narrative coherence but also digital evidence. Together these show that I was targeted by what the Bourdieu epigraph dubs the "discreet polemics of academic hatred" after I transgressed the elites' covert religiosity and provoked a disgust-based response to the perceived sacrilege. Those discreet polemics would, as Bourdieu says, initiate me into a code that, while invisible to the unaware bystander, generated that charge of "extra violence" that is the special hallmark of academic hatred. Hence my secret trial and invisible persecution, which were born of this violence. But by absorbing this extra violence into my being, I encountered the higher truth of conservative claims of cultural oppression. As I will explain in the pages to come, this would in due course enable me to explode the plausible deniability in which the violence was enshrouded, thus making this book possible.

My engagement with conservative claims of cultural oppression would also excavate vital truths about the life of the mind, illustrating what it can become if liberated from the prejudices of the dominant academic culture. I would come to recognize that this culture, which had oppressed me, was but one offshoot of the wider liberal culture that oppresses conservatives—and that I could therefore expose its covert illiberalism by means of the same theory. That is what I aim to achieve here.

By studying how conservative culture warriors had, for their own purposes, glommed on to, and then inverted, the critical theory of the Left, I would learn to appropriate it in the service of the foregoing enterprise, thereby liberating myself from the ideologies of academia—which I'd held in suspicion since my earliest days as a youthful philosophy grad student. Thus would I come to view "scholarliness" as one of

Becker's "secular, scientific, and civilized" hero-systems, a vehicle for a "feeling of primary value, of cosmic specialness, of ultimate usefulness to creation, of unshakable meaning." Scholarliness isn't some timeless ideal of intellectual probity but a historically contingent cultural ethos, one more outgrowth of the modern disciplinary society and its pinched vision of human flourishing. That's what conservatives ultimately protest in claiming cultural oppression by liberalism, whose official virtues are silently undergirded by a disciplinary ethos. I would repudiate that ethos, however, and this was why my predicament would come to recapitulate that of conservatives. Like them, I presented a challenge to the dominant dispensation. Like them, I was gaslighted into silence. What was superficially a clash of personalities was in fact a clash of cultures with a discernible philosophical logic. The higher truth of conservative claims of cultural oppression became articulated through that clash, releasing forces in liberal academia that until my arrival on the scene had stayed latent and disguised.

What had begun as a narrowly academic endeavor thereby spilled over into the real world, yielding a kind of truth that is won only through experience. Ideas are thought to inhabit the mind alone, but some ideas can seep into our very being and from there into our social worlds. Conservative claims of cultural oppression proved to be such an idea, after my association with Stanford Law School thrust me into a star chamber whose rules and proceedings would not be disclosed to me, a process that would in due course liberate my research agenda from the paper to which it was formerly confined. This is the story of a term paper that came to life, the paper that was written *for* Stanford before the force of its own inner logic made it become *about* Stanford.[ii] What follows is a study of that inner logic.

[ii] Actions and intentions, both known and conjectured, that I have attributed to "Stanford" are those of the various Stanford employees named. I make no allegations regarding the decisions, designs, or policies, official or otherwise, of the board of trustees, the president, or other university officials.

Because I cannot assume the reader's familiarity with this research, I reintroduce its principal arguments at various points in the narrative, where I recount my Stanford Law experience first as a bright-eyed law student, then as a rising young scholar, and finally as an outcast and dissident. Chapter 1 provides readers with background about me and the genesis of my association with Stanford. In the second chapter I begin to narrate the conflict that emerged from that association, and subsequent chapters chronicle its successive stages. I recount my actions and their settings in sometimes granular detail to acquaint readers with the milieu in which I was compelled to operate, as this was the fiery crucible of my struggle. Parts of the discussion veer in a theoretical direction, but that struggle is always at their epicenter, as the narrative bears out. As to these theoretical forays, my intention is not to paint with a totalizing brush, but I leave to thoughtful readers to fill in the needed nuances and qualifications. This is a scholarly memoir but not scholarship per se, and such a potentially endless task would lead me too far astray from my narrative purposes.

Lest I be misunderstood, nothing I've written here should be construed as a personal attack on anyone, least of all my faculty advisers. I cannot stress enough that I hold them in only the highest regard. How could I not? It was they who first divined the promise of my project and they who then brought that promise to fruition. They are eminently likable as people, and nothing in this book derogates from that opinion. This critique is not a personal attack because its subject is the *impersonal*—not my colleagues' qualities as individual actors but rather the cultural pathologies that vitiated those qualities. The pathologies of liberalism and academia—and *not* any freestanding character flaws—were what truly spawned the pride, hate, flattery, and lies that fueled the project. As outgrowths of a socially constructed hero-system, these afflictions are hardly unique to Stanford, which was merely the contingent arena in which they played out as they did, according to a logic that could not be fully grasped in real time.

The Egyptian myth cited by Rousseau thus proved to be true at least allegorically. Whether the arts and sciences are a curse cast by a hostile god or not, all of us were swept up by forces that we could neither control nor fathom.

To the extent my alma mater can be held up as unique, that would be because it boasted personalities and intellects that could give life to Rousseau's thesis, as well as to my own. That is to the great credit of Stanford Law School, which in my case more than lived up to its reputation, and I heartily recommend it to any prospective law students. Stanford gave me not only a legal education but also a life-defining experience. I am a product of Stanford. Indeed, I am its *creation.* Forged and hardened on its anvil, I am its revanchist bad conscience and cast-off shadow self.

If my colleagues were guilty of anything, it was being creatures of their place and time, agents of the dominant dispensation and civilizational identity. Their interests and prejudices were broadly those of their class, the chattering class—also known as the "New Class" or "knowledge class" or "cognitive elite"—whose clandestine illiberalism it would fall upon me to expose and chronicle. Notwithstanding this task, I do not advance a one-dimensional victim-villain narrative with me occupying the moral high ground. As will become clear, I was hardly a boy scout, and one of my principal contentions is that the conduct of all concerned was morally indeterminate. Whether the charge of "extra violence" that was visited upon me was commensurate with the nature of my own transgressions holds less interest for me than does the philosophical and psychological meaning of these events, which I interrogate here. My purpose is only to recover that meaning, not to issue moral judgments in my own favor. I leave moral judgments largely in readers' hands, should they be interested. My own instinct is that to understand all is to forgive all.

This stranger-than-fiction story poses perennial questions about when the lone wolf may defy the collective and its pieties, about when order may be sacrificed to liberty, and it would be disingenuous to pretend as though such dilemmas have cut-and-dried answers. What follows isn't a Manichean struggle between good and evil but a culture war between incompatible values that were tragicomically fated to clash. The reader will find nothing here that is black and white, only shifting shades of gray, and reductionist attempts to pigeonhole my position as simply "anti-Stanford" will prove unavailing. Should my claims prove divisive, this owes to the nature of my thesis, and the reader will recognize that I have not gone out of my way to stoke the flames. On the contrary, I have done my utmost to give the other side its due within the bounds of my worldview, to which end I scrutinize myself as vigorously as I do any other party. I do not pretend to offer unblemished objectivity, but this memoir is far from a hatchet job—in an age of hatchet jobs. To those who say that, even so, I am a disloyal alum for ventilating all this dirty laundry, I ask only whether they endorse such blinkered tribalism in any other context. Here I stand, I can do no other.

Although this memoir is first and foremost a general human interest story, I hope it can also serve as a cautionary tale for those now considering an academic career, a case study in what *not* to do lest one tempt fate. For reasons I will spell out, I have no regrets, but neither would I wish any semblance of my trials and tribulations upon unsuspecting innocents. The probability of that is infinitesimal. Still, my ordeal illuminates the dangers of a certain mind-set and ethos that can only compound the intrinsic perils of the academic enterprise, offering an extreme illustration of these. Whether that is a pox on me or on that enterprise as presently constituted is a philosophical question about which reasonable minds can disagree. Without question I reaped what I sowed. But what exactly I sowed is open to interpretation, and I put forth my own two cents for the reader's consideration and amusement. I am not a licensed mental health practitioner, but I also hope my tribulations contribute useful fodder for the academic study of gaslighting, which is perhaps still in its infancy. My odyssey is testament to the richly varied forms the phenomenon can take.

The pages to come will lay bare the meaning of all these cryptic pronouncements, with all their real-world ramifications. Stanford and its affiliates will undoubtedly dispute my telling of events, but I believe my allegations will hold up to scrutiny. Detractors may discount my argument as conspiratorial speculation, and it is that among other things. But, as the adage goes, just because you're paranoid doesn't mean they're not out to get you. The reader will find that this highbrow conspiracy theory proceeds rigorously (in no small part owing to a Stanford legal education) and will, I hope, be swayed by my interpretations.

I do not presume to have proved my allegations beyond a reasonable doubt, but I do believe the evidence is clear and convincing. No single piece of that evidence can carry the entire burden of making my case. But skeptics should resist the urge to seize upon this in order to peremptorily dismiss my argument, as each piece of evidence still has one degree or another of probative value. To draw an analogy, there may be no single study that, standing alone, proves that smoking causes cancer or that carbon emissions cause climate change. Taken in isolation, each study may be inconclusive and admit of competing interpretations. But cumulatively the entire body of research paints a clear picture. Climate change deniers obfuscate that clear picture by fetishizing the inconclusiveness of individual studies, so as to discount these before their evidentiary value can be aggregated, as though each bore the entire burden of proof. And so they dishonestly sidestep the cumulative weight of the evidence, which more scientific minds will judiciously assess. I believe that readers who approach my argument holistically in the manner of scientists, rather than piecemeal in the manner of climate change deniers, will find it compelling or at least reasonable. Skeptical readers nevertheless have my permission to read this memoir as literary fiction if they wish.

Because I am advancing my claims as a philosophical *theory*, I will scrupulously distinguish between the facts as recollected from direct sensory experience and what I argue are reasonable inferences therefrom.[iii] Some of those facts are documented in emails or the public record whereas others rest on my credibility alone, which is for readers to judge however they see fit. Regrettably, I can adduce nothing beyond personal recollection in these instances. My argument is that readers who (1) accept my account of the sensory data and (2) accept what I argue is the higher truth of conservative claims of cultural oppression will (3) conclude that my inferences are highly plausible and that I was in all likelihood gaslighted at Stanford. Correlatively, readers who accept my eyewitness account and find my inferences to be intuitively plausible should be swayed to also accept the higher truth of conservative claims of cultural oppression, as it is what explains that intuitive plausibility. It is to this argument that I now proceed.

---

iii See appendix 2, Memorandum of Law Concerning the Memoirist's Claims.

CHAPTER 1

The Beginning

Up Through August 2008

From Philosophy to Law

My clash with Stanford Law School was the culmination of a long-standing love-hate relationship with academia at large. The life of the mind held a singular attraction for me when I entered Indiana University's doctoral program in philosophy in 1996. But as with countless graduate students before and after, I soon realized that the unglamorous realities of academia bear slight resemblance to the values that first drew me to it. The free-wheeling intellectual life of the bright-eyed undergraduate and the sober ponderousness of the professional philosopher are very different animals, and I felt stultified by the regimentation and calculatedness that went hand in hand with intellectual professionalization. Professionalization offered "seriousness," but this putative virtue seemed to come at the expense of human resonance, without which the life of the mind lost its appeal for me. Many who arrive at similar conclusions leave grad school after a few years, disillusioned but, with any luck, with the consolation prize of a master's degree. That is a natural progression. Others have a talent for acquiescing to their professional deformation and sometimes flourish. Yet others are so compatible with the programming as to look past the deformation entirely. They are the ultimate insiders and may go far. I belonged to none of these camps. I saw things for what they were and didn't like them. But I was strangely persuaded that I would somehow prevail over the cultural pathologies that beleaguered me. Cursed with a headstrong disposition, I fancied that I was superior to my circumstances such that they would yield to me and not I to them.

This presumption would be tested a decade later at Stanford. Its first outward manifestation, though, was my initial, eventually abandoned, dissertation topic, titled "On Rigor: Against the Rationalization of Intellectual Life." My thinking here was inspired by Russell Jacoby's *The Last Intellectuals*, which gave voice to the alienation I was feeling. Jacoby observes:

> Intellectuals who write with vigor and clarity are as scarce as low rents in New York or San Francisco. Raised in city streets and cafes before the age of massive universities, "last" generation intellectuals wrote for the educated reader. They have been supplanted by high-tech intellectuals, consultants and professors—anonymous souls who may be competent, and more than competent, but who do not enrich public life.[1]

The ivory tower's perennial isolation from the proverbial real world is a platitude, and many academics are resigned to it as the price of intellectual seriousness. The only alternative to weltering as an anonymous soul, they assume, is a wide-eyed amateurism undisciplined by professional rigor. Mary Midgley delineates the nature and origins of this prejudice:

> Our training stresses the need to keep out of our work everything subjective or emotional, indeed, everything that is individual at all. The fear of offending against this standard can seem to

> make a totally anonymous, colourless style and choice of topics a matter of professional honor. …
>
> Nobody is likely to doubt that a musician, for instance, needs individual qualities as well as the anonymous reliability, training, industry, and so forth which make up a professional approach to music. But this individual element is just as vital in many other contexts, some of which arise in almost every profession once we get beyond the basic general demands just mentioned. …
>
> Many professionals have at present a strong impression that the only possible effect of attending to large questions, or of allowing interplay between thought and feeling, must be to produce crude ideologies. The mere existence of these ideologies shows, in their view, that feeling should never have been allowed to enter systematic thought.[2]

The "totally anonymous, colourless style and choice of topics" that academic philosophy upholds as "a matter of professional honor" was in my own estimation the symptom of unacknowledged cultural pathologies—not a reasoned conclusion but a faith in which identities had become invested. The individual element was as vital to philosophy as it was to music, I felt, and I suspected that the taken-for-granted hierarchy between the serious scholar and the starry-eyed dilettante was an ideological guise for the vices of academic professionalism. By inflating the perils of free-wheeling, unregimented thought, that ideology ratifies the prevailing vision of intellectual rigor as sacrosanct, reifying its contingent mores and pieties as reason itself. The problem wasn't that professionalization had rendered intellectual life tedious to the person on the street but that a technocratic orientation sacrifices the intellectual imagination to the performance of a parochial cultural identity that offers only a simulacrum of true intellectual virtue. The insularity Jacoby laments is taken for granted as part and parcel of a necessary trade-off between rigor and relevance.

But I suspected that the prevailing paradigm of rigor was a social illusion of sorts, the idolatrous outgrowth of a sectarian ethos that conceals or rationalizes its own costs and limitations. This wasn't to dismiss scholarly rigor as otiose—far from it—but I believed its value had been ideologically inflated to the detriment of other virtues, such as unfettered thought, which had to be traduced accordingly.

I was in a philosophy graduate program, after all, and the business of philosophy is to shine a light on just such distortions. The philosopher is a gadfly, Socrates taught us, and I earnestly assumed that role. Since my polis was academia, it was natural that I unmask its contradictions. I accepted Nietzsche's counsel that "it is very advisable to examine and dissect the men of learning themselves for once, since they for their part are quite accustomed to laying bold hands on everything in the world, even the most venerable things, and taking them to pieces."[3] This was the mission I embarked on as a fourth-year doctoral student at the tender age of twenty-six. Only much later would I finally find myself poised to execute it, however. I had the enthusiasm of my age but lacked the intellectual maturity to really see the project through, as finally hit me a few months into it. My dissertation adviser was most disappointed with this capitulation, having been persuaded that I could pull it off.

Instead, I wrote *Two Orientations Toward Human Nature*, which argues that contemporary Western culture entertains a schizophrenic view of human nature. One stream of that culture assigns a vital explanatory role to egoism, setting forth a tough-minded account of human motivation wherein self-interest only rarely yields to altruism. However, another cultural current discounts the egoism-altruism dichotomy and instead dichotomizes wholeness and alienation, authenticity and inauthenticity, or self-awareness and self-oblivion. These distinct orientations toward human nature, respectively embodied in the Anglo-American and Continental philosophical traditions, yield ostensibly incongruous portraits of the social status quo. Where the first, tough-minded, orientation highlights robust individualism, the second, more "countercultural," orientation shines a light on depersonalization by mass culture, discerning a frenzied "escape from freedom" where the first orientation sees atomistic self-absorption. I wanted to get to the bottom of this intellectual rift and determine whether these facially incongruous vocabularies were genuinely at odds or merely underscored different facets of the same human condition.

I wrote most of my dissertation on Manhattan's Upper West Side and then in Brooklyn. Bloomington was unimpeachable as a college town. But I had spent the better part of my adult life in such settings by my fourth year of the program, and the town's bucolic beauty was rapidly becoming overshadowed by the black malaise of the grad school experience that is known to many. I needed a second wind that I could find only elsewhere. Since I'd completed my coursework by then, nothing was keeping me in Bloomington. I could produce the dissertation anywhere. And so, I U-Hauled it to New York City with two chums in the summer of 2000 and would remain there for the next five years, wrapping up the dissertation after two years and then spending the next three readying it and other work for publication. All the while I worked as an adjunct philosophy instructor, taught English as a second language to Asian immigrants, and graded Graduate Record Exam essays online. I finally extricated myself from adjunct teaching in 2003 with a postdoctoral fellowship at Fordham University, where I would continue to teach and write, now with health insurance.

I would eventually publish my dissertation and a journal article, but these arrived in print too late to do me any good as I hustled for a tenure-track position in philosophy between 2002 and 2005.[i] As in most academic fields, it was a buyer's market with a long-standing glut of would-be professors. The post–World War II hiring boom in higher education was never to be reprised, despite all the sanguine forecasts.

---

i Rony Guldmann, *Two Orientations Toward Human Nature* (New York: Routledge, 2007); Rony Guldmann, "Determinism and Forbearance," *Social Theory and Practice* 32, no. 1 (January 2006): 97–135.

I was further compromised by the nature of my research interests, which didn't align well with any recognized disciplinary specialties. More than once I received personal messages from hiring committee members who applauded my work while regretting that it just didn't line up with their hiring needs that year. *Two Orientations* wasn't quite as exotic as *On Rigor* would have been, but neither respected disciplinary boundaries. Neither contributed to any ongoing scholarly debate within some esteemed coterie of mandarins. Both "attended to large questions," as Midgley says, and so could only arouse ire and suspicion among those mandarins. I had thrown caution to the winds and elected to play the maverick, compounding the challenges that were already inherent to any academic job search, even in the best of circumstances. My dissertation adviser was enamored of my iconoclastic aspirations, but hiring committees weren't so charmed, evidently.

I secured a handful of interviews at recruiting conferences and elsewhere, but my academic career was clearly stalled. The Fordham position was set to expire in the summer of 2005, and I wasn't about to step back ignominiously into adjunct teaching or wither away as a nomadic visiting professor chronically anxious about whether his contract was being renewed for another year. So I resolved upon law school. Granted, this was a rather hackneyed escape hatch for the beleaguered academic refugee, but the law drew on a skill set I possessed, and I hankered for the security of some bona fide professional qualifications. Moreover, I reasoned that this didn't foreclose the academic route, since teaching law remained a possibility. I had so far failed to slip past the gatekeepers of academia, but perhaps I'd merely lost some battles and not yet the war. I needed time, some breathing space, a little security, a new environment. With this reset I might still prevail over the forces that had to date stymied me. With these hopes in mind, I arrived at the University of Texas School of Law in fall 2005, eagerly awaiting new adventures.

Law school and philosophy grad school were starkly different animals. First-year law curricula aren't recondite stuff in comparison with the fare in philosophy graduate seminars. As one of my Texas cohorts quipped, the case law we were being assigned was surely lighter reading than Jean-Paul Sartre's eight-hundred-page *Being and Nothingness*. On the other hand, law school presented its own novel challenges for which a PhD is no preparation. An A or A– is the default grade in a graduate philosophy course, so grades were among the last things on our minds. We didn't face much day-to-day time pressure either. I would submit term papers months after the conclusion of a course, and months turned into years for some of my more lackadaisical peers. But grades, and especially first-year grades, are the end-all and be-all of law school, as these are what employers look at. With first-year classes strictly curved, only so many As were available, and whether you took one home boiled down to your performance on a single three- or four-hour exam. Texas was highly selective but not so selective that students would land on their feet no matter their grades, so this made for a competitive (though still friendly) environment. The mental gymnastics were also incommensurable. Doctoral students impress their professors by evincing the potential to contribute to an ongoing academic debate in noteworthy ways, but top grades on law school exams require insight into the minds that crafted the tests, along with the ability to apply such knowledge in real time. The exam hypotheticals were laden with mines and booby traps, and you needed to know the enemy to evade them.

This could get stressful, but mere stress was welcome relief from the angst of scholarship and publication. Gone were the gnawing doubts about whether an argument was heading anywhere at all. Gone, too, was the endless revision of works in progress. No longer did I grovel at the feet of publishers and journal editors. The rules were crystal clear: attend class, take notes, craft comprehensive outlines, convene regularly with study partners, and review old exams. I was something of a gunner in my classes and occasionally clashed horns with professors. My comments were substantive, though, so I don't imagine anyone held this against me. Like law students everywhere, most of my peers were haunted by the specter of being called on in class. But I was conversant with the travails of teaching a class and so wasn't kept awake at night by this ever-lurking bogeyman.

Law school was a far more festive experience than philosophy had been. There were parties and gatherings aplenty, prodigiously funded by white-shoe law firms eager to recruit Texas's best and brightest. This was a far cry from the annual meetings of the American Philosophical Association, where the most one could hope for was two hours of free Bud Lite before they started charging. Now, I studied hard and partied hard. Even study group sessions had a bacchanalian element, complete with whiskey, pizza, and plenty of case law. Indeed, I confess to being high a good deal of that time. Between the Mexican food and the Texas BBQ, I ate quite well in Austin. My spacious one-bedroom with a pool in the complex for $700 a month was nothing I could have dreamed of in New York. In short, 2005–2006 was a great year in every way.

Yet it was time to move on. I still clung to the dream of a second go at academia, and this could be helped considerably by transferring to the most elite law school that would have me. Texas was a top law school that produced its fair share of legal scholars, but the premier feeders for such careers were known to be Yale, Harvard, Stanford, and the University of Chicago, with Yale dominating and the other three coming in at a distant but still highly advantageous second. I carried the day on the exams, racking up a pile of four much-coveted A-pluses. With my GPA thus catapulted to the very top of the class, the ultraelite schools were now within reach, as they had not been the first time around after my lackluster LSAT performance of 165. I mailed off some transfer applications during the summer of 2006 and was admitted to all the above, save Yale.

I was in Israel, enrolled in a summer law program, when these decisions were handed down. It had been a turbulent summer, as the Second Lebanon War had broken out and the program had to be transplanted out of rocket range from Haifa to Jerusalem. Since I'd be back stateside only in mid-August, mere weeks before the start of classes, I had no time for campus visits, and my deliberations would have to proceed abstractly. But the San Francisco Bay Area had always held a mysterious allure for me, as it does for many, and Stanford was a long-awaited opportunity to put down roots there. As a transfer student I wouldn't have the social networks others had built over their formative first year. But with a brother and some old high school friends already making lives in the Bay Area, a move out west came with a ready-made social scene, which I wouldn't have in Cambridge or Chicago. Stanford was also a small law school, which would help me stand out from the crowd as a rising young scholar—my rationale for transferring. Harvard Law was lavished with more pop culture recognition, but Stanford was a lot warmer and did just fine placing grads in faculty positions. After agonizing about my options for a few days, I heeded the call to go west, loaded up my nineties-era Toyota Corolla, and hit the road for the three-day trip from the Texas Hill Country to San Francisco Bay.

Most of my social life came to revolve around San Francisco itself, where I wound up living after six months in Palo Alto. It was forty miles to Stanford, but the scenic drive down the I-280 was tolerable. I got to know some of my Stanford classmates, but as an older transfer on a second career track, I was essentially a commuter student. I paid modest heed to my coursework but knew I wasn't going to repeat my stratospheric first-year performance. Top grades would be harder to harvest at Stanford and were no longer so crucial to employers, anyway. I'd never been much of a grade grubber in college and couldn't be motivated in this pursuit beyond what had been necessary to ensure a transfer. I had better things to do than study the minutiae of professors' cognitive predilections—stimulating though this exercise had been at Texas.

The situation seemed ideal. Once an overworked and put-upon adjunct professor suffering through long commutes to teach frequently bored undergraduates at $2,200 a course, I had climbed beyond my humble station and was now enrolled at an elite law school while ensconced in the Bay Area serenity of idyllic San Francisco. Appearances were deceiving, however, and the years to follow would be marred by two traumas that still haunt me today.

The first and by far lesser of these took place after my first year at Stanford in the summer of 2007, during my stint as a summer associate in the employment law group at the Silicon Valley office of a major international law firm. Most of this was typical of the big-firm summer associateship: secretary hours, free lunches, scavenger hunts, visits to Napa wineries, and happy hours with open bars and complimentary hot appetizers—for which we were compensated at $13,000 a month. The experience was most atypical in its denouement, however, as I learned at my final performance review in August 2007, when the attorneys overseeing the employment group's summer program began by running off a long litany of errors made in the course of several recent assignments. In light of these they couldn't offer me an associate position following graduation the next year (as was customary at that kind of firm). This was nothing personal, they assured me, declaring, "We all like you," and conceding that I'd been operating at an associate level by summer's end. "Never in ten years" could they have penned the kind of cease-and-desist letter I'd recently cranked out for them, they also acknowledged.

This was all quite odd. The enumerated screwups struck me as trifling. A few of my memos were too long. Another lacked the requisite subheadings. The first iteration of a motion I'd drafted was improperly formatted. This was, I demurred, because I'd been wrongly instructed by the assigning attorney. Such was no excuse, they chided, as I should have been exercising independent judgment. This admonition smelled contrived, though. I had no special reason to second-guess the assigning attorney's competence here and wasn't going to do so willy-nilly on the off chance this would have been justified. Other criticisms were more legitimate. Still, I was confounded that they'd sufficed to tip the scales against me, given the supervisors' lavish praise of my general aptitude, which seemed more germane to the big picture long term than these minor lapses of judgment. Landing an offer at a big firm after a summer associateship wasn't supposed to be a tall order. You could forfeit it by sleeping with a partner's spouse or sloppy drunkenness at a firm social function, but nothing like that had occurred. At any rate, I wasn't going to quarrel with them about a fait accompli, so we agreed to disagree and ended the meeting cordially.

There was more to the story, however, as I was to learn a few hours later upon clearing out of my office. I stopped by each employment attorney's office to say my goodbyes. One associate was dumbfounded that I'd been no-offered and briefly commiserated with me. Others extended only a perfunctory "good luck." My last stop was the group's senior partner and godfather, who invited me to sit down and chat about the day's unpleasantness. The truth, he now divulged, was that the reasons given for my no-offer should be taken with a grain of salt. My failings were, as I'd surmised, minor missteps and oversights of the sort to be expected of a green summer associate. The real reason was that the employment law group had somehow overhired, taking on three summer associates when they needed only two. Coming on the heels of a business downturn, that meant they couldn't bring on a third new attorney the next year. The blunder couldn't be fessed up to, of course, so an alternative rationale was concocted by making mountains out of molehills. But for the firm's financial vicissitudes, I would have received an offer. Yet given them, someone had to be thrown overboard for the ship to stay afloat.

Why me? It turned out that I had inadvertently intimidated some of the younger associates intellectually. One, the partner related, had opined that I was perhaps "too smart" to be working at that firm. He and my associate mentor had broken ranks and protested my ouster but were outvoted. Even so, they were now prepared to defy firm policy and serve as my references. When interviewers asked why I'd been no-offered, I could refer them to these attorneys, who would pull back the curtain on the official lies and reassure that I'd had no genuine performance problems. Suggesting it might all be for the best, the partner hazarded that I was probably being understimulated by employment law and would be more fulfilled in a more theoretical specialty, such as intellectual property.

Blessing in disguise, perhaps, but what followed were four angst-ridden months of pounding the pavement as a no-offered third-year law student with questionable private-sector propensities in a declining legal job market. I had the two attorneys to back me up, but the no-offer was still a scarlet letter and the campus interviews were harrowing. How to explain what happened? I could state that the employment law group was downsizing and leave it at that. But then the interviewer might rightly suspect that there was more to the story than the firm's balance sheet. Alternatively, I could tell all, but then I risked coming off as arrogant, as the "too smart" candidate, notwithstanding that I was just relaying verbatim what I'd been told. There was no easy way to navigate this Scylla and Charybdis. A couple of interviewers were surprisingly receptive to the unabridged story, with one bringing me back to the office for further interviews after sizing me up as having "the personality of a litigator." But this was the exception, and that firm wound up not taking on any new associates that year. Things had been so effortless when I first arrived at Stanford a year earlier. I could send unsolicited résumés directly to big New York firms and receive fly-in invitations the next day. Now I was a beggar scrounging for leftovers. With the legal job market already in freefall in 2007, new associate openings were in short supply, and law firms invariably looked askance at no-offered third-year students.

At the same time I was hard at work on seminar papers that I hoped to eventually publish. Amid all this turmoil the dream of a second go at academia was never far from my mind. Because I was yet again on the job market, I also needed to keep my grades up. Added to this were my (then) girlfriend's protests about the prospect of uprooting to New York with me, along with her eight-year-old daughter, a future

I had informed her was more likely than my finding employment in the smaller legal market of the Bay Area, where her family lived. These protests would only intensify in November, after that prophesy was fulfilled and I at last landed an offer from one of the few New York City firms with any interest in hiring third-years that year. My no-offer in August had meant months of blood, sweat, and tears, all for something my cohorts took for granted. At least the nightmare was over. The relief that set in when the industry-standard $160,000 offer letter turned up in my mailbox was incalculable.

Legal Theory and Moral Luck

The turbulence with which my second year at Stanford had begun was now behind me. But new, as-yet darker, clouds loomed, and that year would lay the foundations for the far greater struggles still in the offing. I anticipated that I'd be toiling at a law firm for a few years after graduation. But my plan was to position myself for an eventual legal teaching career already now. Looking to cultivate faculty contacts who could have my back here, I enrolled in two courses I thought might deliver. This was where I first came upon the cast of characters who would one day vault me into headlong conflict with the prevailing ideology. The story of these associations begins later in this chapter. Next, I provide an overview of the two courses and their subject matters. This is no idle aside, though; these subject matters would eventually bleed into the real world and come to define my Stanford Law experience.

The first of these courses was the Legal Theory Workshop, team-taught by Joe Bankman, a leading authority on tax law, and Larry Kramer, a renowned constitutional theorist and the law school's dean at the time, acclaimed for overhauling the curriculum in a more practical and interdisciplinary direction, to keep up with the times. This was a two-semester course specifically designed to groom students for academic careers in law. I had tried to snag a spot my first year at Stanford, but the class was booked solid by the time I arrived. Fortunately, my bid to enroll during my second and last year at the law school had been well received. We would be convening only biweekly during the first semester, when visitors from Stanford or elsewhere would join us and present a legal theory article they had been penning, after which we would submit short-response papers. These assignments were intended to give us the lay of the land of legal academia. After the talks Joe, Larry, and whatever students had signed up would accompany our guest—often flown in from another part of the country—to an upscale Palo Alto restaurant for some casual banter. The class would then gather weekly during the second semester, when the focus would shift to the students' own papers. We would still host a few guest presenters, but this would be cut off once students were ready to present their work to the class.

This was where the saga of *Conservative Claims of Cultural Oppression* first took root. I was far from divining these claims' inner meaning at this early date, but I was fascinated by a certain posture and worldview that is just as intoxicating to some Americans as it is repugnant to others. Though written a few years later, Victor Davis Hanson's scathing indictment of Barack Obama is illustrative:

> Obama represents their utopian dreams where an anointed technocracy, exempt from the messy ramifications of its own ideology, directs from on high a socially just society—diverse, green, non-judgmental, neutral abroad, tribal at home—in which an equality of result is ensured, albeit with proper exemptions for the better educated and more sophisticated, whose perks are necessary to give them proper downtime for their exhausting work on our behalf. …

> Whom does the liberal elite detest? Not the very poor. Not the middle class. Not the conservative wealthy of like class. Mostly it is the Sarah-Palin-type grasping want-to-be's (thus the vicious David Letterman jokes or Katie Couric animus or Bill Maher venom).
>
> Those of the entrepreneurial class who own small businesses ("you didn't build that"), who send their kids to San Diego State rather than Stanford, who waste their ill-gotten gains on jet skis rather than skis and on Winnebagos rather than mountain climbing equipment, who employ 10 rather than 10,000, and who vacation at Pismo Beach rather than Carmel. The cool of Obama says to the very wealthy, "I'm one of you. See you again next summer on the Vineyard."
>
> Obama signals to the elite that he too is bothered by those non-arugula-eating greedy losers who are xenophobic and angry that the world left them behind, who are without tastes and culture, who are materialistic to the core, and who are greedy in their emphases on the individual—the tea-baggers, the clingers, the Cliven Bundy Neanderthals, the Palins in their Alaska haunts, and the Duck Dynasty freaks. These are not the sort of successful people that we want the world to associate with America, not when we have suitably green, suitably diverse zillionaires who know where to eat in Paris.[4]

As a heavily indebted law student, I was far from a zillionaire. This aside, though, it was the likes of me whom conservatives like Hanson were decrying. I went to Stanford and loved arugula. I'd never jet-skied but had spent weekends at a Tahoe ski cabin. They were also talking about the rest of the class, and especially about Joe and Larry, who as Stanford Law professors were at the pinnacle of the liberal elite. This was where we all wanted to get. Not every Stanford Law professor was machinating to direct a socially just society from on high. But a fair number were, and most supported the effort. I didn't know whether

Joe and Larry knew where to eat in Paris, but their restaurant choices in Palo Alto were unimpeachable. And while I didn't ask, I'd have been shocked to learn that they owned Winnebagos.

Conservatives such as Hanson come eagerly to the defense of "tea-baggers" and the Palins because they resent liberals for having ushered in and entrenched an unofficial social hierarchy that credentials liberals as self-aware, reflective, and cosmopolitan while stigmatizing conservatives as benighted, parochial, and authoritarian, turning them into a socially denigrated Other perennially exposed to the scorn and derision of the dominant liberal culture. In advancing this unspoken agenda, liberals contravene their own professed commitment to equality, tolerance, and openness, vilifying conservatives much as the latter stand accused of vilifying blacks, gays, and other historically disfavored minorities. The liberal elites are so privileged that they need never confront this hypocrisy, however. Having seized the reins of academia, the courts, foundations, the bureaucracies, media, Hollywood, public schools, and corporate human resources departments, liberals occupy the commanding heights of the culture, whence they malign conservative voices as mindless reaction or pathology, in supercilious contempt for the heartfelt values of authentic, salt-of-the-earth ordinary Americans, who must be discredited by any means necessary. Liberalism isn't merely a family of policies or principles but a totalistic cultural ethos that with each passing year encroaches ever further upon the lives of those ordinary Americans. As Thomas Frank wryly puts it in *What's the Matter with Kansas?*, conservatives believe liberalism is "in power whether its politicians are elected or not." Liberalism is "beyond politics, a tyrant that dominates our lives in countless ways great and small, and which is virtually incapable of being overthrown."[5]

I asked myself whether these claims of cultural oppression contained a grain of truth, sizable or otherwise, after discounting all the ad hominems about arugula and the like. Frank contends that conservative laments about a haughty liberal elite scornful of the beliefs and values of the ordinary American are hollow symbolic grievances, wedge issues cultivated by business interests to distract long-suffering proles from their rational self-interest, which lies with the Left. But something in me whispered that it was more complicated. I understood why liberals dismissed conservatives' cultural grievances as posturing and histrionics, for that is indeed the form they often take. But I suspected that conservatives' inexorable impulse to claim cultural oppression harbored some deeper layer of meaning to which liberals like Frank were insensible. Rightly or wrongly, conservatives feel perennially under the heel of the liberal jackboot, and I wanted to understand why.

Such curiosity wasn't natural for someone with my background, which had placed me within the general ambit of the liberal elite. Though I'd been whisked away to Columbus, Ohio, at the tender age of four after my father secured a professorship at Ohio State, I was born in Strasbourg, France, and spoke French and Hebrew before learning English. I came of age in Middle America but was never quite of Middle America. This much was readily apparent from my parents' social milieu, whose entrance requirements included either an advanced degree or a foreign accent—preferably both. Their dinner parties were suffused with disdain for the region's relative conservatism. Columbus, Ohio, certainly wasn't the most conservative corner of the country, yet the *Columbus Dispatch* was adjudged too benighted for the household, forcing us to drive to the store to pick up the *New York Times*. Having lived in this way for so long, I was naturally receptive to Frank's analysis as an eloquent articulation of the obvious.

And yet my chosen vocation called on me to eschew this path of least resistance. My gut instincts were on the liberal side, but perhaps that reflected my indoctrination into the blind pieties of the liberal bubble, as conservatives would have it. Maybe Frank's book was the propaganda of the powerful, the self-serving ideology of liberal domination. This domination wasn't readily apparent to the naked eye, certainly. But a mainstay of left-liberal thought is that sundry forms of white, male, or heterosexual privilege blind us to pervasive subterranean inequalities, which norms passing as neutral then naturalize as the ineluctable fabric of things. Was it not conceivable, then, that liberals were themselves blind to the social inequality from which conservatives claim to suffer? If there can be a subterranean white male privilege, why not also a subterranean liberal one? Liberals' alleged "conservaphobia" may not be as strident as right-wing polemicists make it out to be, but another mainstay of left-liberal thought is that racism, sexism, and homophobia need not be overt or conscious. These bigotries are said to operate below the threshold of awareness, on an insidious structural level that outruns the beliefs and intentions of individual actors. I couldn't discount the possibility of an anti-conservative bigotry that works along similar lines. If there can be a structural racism, why not also a structural liberalism that oppresses conservatives despite their formal political equality?

These were the questions I took up in the Legal Theory Workshop. The Left wielded a sophisticated critical theory in its ceaseless battles with racism, sexism, homophobia, and bourgeois philistinism. I aspired to propound a critical theory of the Right whose deconstruction of the Left would mirror the Left's deconstruction of the wider society, and especially conservatives, by laying out the conservative grievance with a degree of intellectual probity that liberals couldn't reflexively dismiss. Lest I be misunderstood, I was motivated in this endeavor not by conservatism but by liberalism. My aim wasn't to vindicate some litany of conservative tenets—like the evils of abortion or the wisdom of laissez-faire—but to take liberalism to its logical conclusion, to turn liberal principles against themselves and thereby expose a subterranean dimension of things infested by some fundamental contradiction.

To be sure, I had only the faintest notion of what this might all add up to. But that faintness was perhaps attributable to my own liberal privilege, against which I felt perversely compelled to rebel. Just like conservatives, I chafed under the yoke of an "anointed technocracy," as Hanson says, even as I had enrolled myself in a seminar intended to facilitate my entry into one of its higher echelons. My alienation from academia had been long in the making and was now burgeoning to encompass the liberal culture at large. Conservatives' wariness of academia was differently motivated than mine, but my instincts whispered that their alienation could illuminate my own, and these vague intimations fueled my passion for the subject.

The second course was titled Luck in Morality, Public Policy, and the Law ("Moral Luck"). It, too, was team-taught, by Barbara Fried, a specialist in contracts and legal philosophy (also married to Joe Bankman), and Josh Cohen, an academic philosopher and Rawlsian liberal holding far-flung appointments in law, philosophy, and political science. Unlike Legal Theory, the course wasn't specifically designed with academic careers in mind. It had no major paper requirement, only a series of short essays. Still, the subject matter was right up my alley, and here was another opportunity to cultivate crucial faculty contacts.

This class would commence only in winter term, but I became acquainted with Barbara already in the fall when she visited Legal Theory as a guest presenter. The first half of her talk was theoretical, with her guiding us through an article on retributivism, one of her philosophical interests.[ii] The second and more personally relevant

[ii] Retributivism is a moral theory that holds that punishment is an end in itself. Utilitarians regard punishment as an intrinsic evil that may be justified by the greater good of crime prevention, through the deterrence, incarceration, or rehabilitation of offenders or potential offenders. In contrast, retributivists hold that punishment is justified, and indeed morally desirable, irrespective of these outcomes because meting out to criminals their just deserts is an intrinsic good, not just an instrumental one. Whether retributivism is anything more than intellectual whitewashing for dubious motives like vengefulness or resentment is an ongoing controversy among philosophers.

part was career advice about crafting a marketable research agenda, indispensable for securing academic employment. It was immediately apparent that here was a true Otto von Bismarck of academic realpolitik, a consummate strategist and tactician with eagle eyes for the perils and pitfalls of a complex, ever-changing scholarly landscape. Barbara was plainly all that I was not.

The seminar was a mélange of overlapping topics, all revolving around what philosophers call "moral luck," the conundrum that, whereas our considered moral intuitions dictate that people are responsible solely for what lies in their control, our real-life moral judgments incorporate factors outside people's control. In a famous treatment of the subject, the philosopher Thomas Nagel drives this home by juxtaposing two reckless motorists. The first one is reckless but also lucky. His recklessness endangers pedestrians, but, as luck would have it, no accident occurs and no one is harmed. So while his recklessness remains blameworthy, his guilt consists of this alone. The second reckless driver is less fortunate, though, because he ends by maiming a hapless pedestrian in a preventable accident. Here we consider the driver responsible not only for his recklessness but also for its chance consequences, a maimed pedestrian.

Our moral verdicts upon these two drivers will therefore be quite different—as will their own verdicts upon themselves. But this difference is not attributable to their different intentions, the sphere of human control, for both drivers harbored the same intentions, which were reckless but not homicidal. The difference is brought about not by what they controlled but by what they did not—whether a random pedestrian happened to be at the wrong place at the wrong time. The pedestrian's bad luck became the second driver's bad *moral* luck, because chance misfortune is why we'll judge him more harshly than we will the first. The dispositive consideration won't be these motorists' characters but the chance contingencies by which their characters got beset, which will shape our assessments of their characters' content and, hence, their moral culpability. Yet these judgments are inconsistent with what we reflectively uphold as the essence of morality—intention and control. We are, therefore, in contradiction with ourselves, and this contradiction cannot be resolved even once highlighted, because our practical moral sensibilities do not control for the vicissitudes of fortune, even if our articulated moral principles tell us they should.

The foregoing is an example of what Nagel dubs resultant moral luck. Moral luck can also be circumstantial, which Nagel illustrates by juxtaposing two Germans. The first expatriates from Germany in the 1930s after being lured to some business venture in Argentina and, having stayed abroad, leads a morally blameless life. The second German isn't so lucky, however, as he remains in Germany and eventually finds himself serving as a concentration camp officer. We are tempted to say that the first was a good German whereas the second was a bad one. But we know not what would have become of the first had he also stayed put in Germany. Maybe he, too, would have been swept up by Nazi fervor and emerged as a death camp executioner. Only the good luck of having been enticed into a business venture on another continent insulated him from this risk—to which the other German, never having chanced upon this opportunity, remained fully exposed. Can any truly say how they would have turned out as citizens of Nazi Germany? Here, too, bad luck translates into bad moral luck. For here, too, we hold others responsible not only for the content of their characters but also for the chance contingencies by which their characters get tested. Our considered moral principles—that people are responsible solely for what they control—are here again belied by our actual human practices.[6]

Another famous treatment of moral luck by Bernard Williams takes up a philosophically stylized version of the impressionist painter Paul Gauguin, who notoriously abandoned his family in France in order to paint amid the natives of Tahiti. Williams's Gauguin feels this drastic step is necessary to truly realize his artistic gifts, but is his rationale defensible, given his moral obligations to wife and children? Williams argues:

> Whether he will succeed cannot, in the nature of the case, be foreseen. We are not dealing here with the removal of an external obstacle to something which, once that is removed, will fairly predictably go through. Gauguin, in our story, is putting a great deal on a possibility which has not unequivocally declared itself. I want to explore and uphold the claim that in such a situation the only thing that will justify his choice is success itself. If he fails ... then he did the wrong thing, not just in the sense in which that platitudinously follows, but in the sense that having done the wrong thing in those circumstances he has no basis for the thought that he was justified in acting as he did. If he succeeds, he does have a basis for that thought.[7]

Artistic success means Gaugin can feel justified in looking back upon his flight to Tahiti differently than he would have had to had he failed, even though he couldn't possibly have foreseen at the time how it would pan out. Hence, the moral luck. Should he fail to blossom as a great painter, all he will see in his younger self will be the arrogant self-delusion of an artist manqué and that vice's grave repercussions for others. Should he succeed, he will see the repercussions but not the arrogant self-delusion, and the moral fallout of his actions will have been mitigated in some sense that is not altogether clear. His family's grievance against him will remain defensible, but it won't define his identity, and his fateful decision will assume a different moral hue. It will then have become apparent that Gauguin's transgressions couldn't be helped if a great artist was to emerge on the scene, and that will place those transgressions in a wider context that modulates their implications for the kind of man he is *and always was*. That's pure moral luck, because his decisions were what they were when he made them.

Correlatively, failure means he will look back upon his choices as cowardice and vanity not just because he now knows better than he did then but because he'll feel that he should have known better at the time, even though he couldn't have foreseen the events that would lead him to this conclusion. His bad moral luck will be to condemn himself for failing to recognize moral vices that didn't yet exist and came into being only retroactively. In line with Nagel's first thought-experiment, the upshot is that Gauguin's morality cannot be definitively evaluated in real time, hinging as it does on the vicissitudes of fortune.

These two courses differed in both form and content, but their subject matters would eventually converge in my relationship to those instructing them. Little did Barbara suspect as I first sauntered into her classroom in winter 2008 that I was to become her bad moral luck. If the liberal elites enjoy an unearned reputation for moral superiority over a conservative underclass, that's because they enjoy the good moral luck of dictating the conditions under which their own illiberal impulses get expressed. Those impulses, sublimated and intellectualized within elite enclaves and high hero-systems, do not ordinarily assume a form that is readily recognizable as problematic. I, however, would generate conditions under which they would do so after becoming deintellectualized and desublimated. Like Nagel's hapless pedestrian and the Nazi regime, I would compel a latent amorality to turn self-conscious and explicit, thereby confronting the elites with their own will to power. For that I would never be forgiven.

A Tour de Force

All this still lay far off in the future. In the meantime things were looking up, as these seminars appeared to be furthering my designs exactly as planned. A new dawn arose on my erstwhile dampened academic aspirations, as I succeeded in drawing these faculty ever closer to me.

Already in the fall Joe and Larry were unfailingly pleased with my short-response papers, which consistently garnered top marks. By early February I had submitted a first draft of what would become *Conservative Claims of Cultural Oppression.* Joe was assigned as my workshop mentor and initiated contact with an email assessing it as "very interesting" and "lovely, in its way." We met soon thereafter, whereupon he hailed it as a "tour de force" that was "dripping with irony." It was just the kind of writing Stanford looked for in prospective hires, he noted, speculating that I could ripen into one of the legal academy's most prolific scholars. I was flattered but also befuddled, since this seventeen-page rough draft didn't seem capable of transmitting all that. Still, I was happy to defer to his judgment.

As might have been predicted, Joe greeted my musings with a curious mixture of incredulity and fascination. He was a platinum card member of the liberal elite, after all, so the moral and intellectual bankruptcy of conservatism went without saying. Even so, he couldn't discount that one of his own, and not some evangelical yahoo from Alabama, was now airing the conservative grievance. Despite his visceral disdain for conservatism and conservatives, Joe seemed intrigued by my budding sense that this grievance harbored some deeper level of meaning to which he and other liberals were insensible. My draft was inchoate and halting, but it was good enough to advertise my intuitive insight on this front, and it was this that was now drawing Joe into my orbit. Indeed, he was struck by my genuine charity toward opposing perspectives, which he lamented was rare even among seasoned scholars. Religious conservatives were an enigma to him, and he speculated that I might come to understand them better than they do themselves.

While Joe believed this draft was book material that might initiate a distinguished academic career, I still wondered whether my receptivity to conservatism could stymie my prospects in the legal academy. Joe didn't think so. My tolerant nature would shine through, he reassured, so law school audiences would get that my solicitude for conservatives and their cultural oppression was ironic and that I wasn't truly of their ilk. I went on to tell a bit about myself and noted the book I'd published, which Joe requested and I later delivered. A bond was forged and the outlook was sunny. I had taken quite a drubbing on the philosophy job market, but this exchange suggested there was still hope, maybe a good deal of it.

I would achieve a similar feat in Moral Luck within the week. Each student was charged with introducing one day's reading, and here was my chance to make a strong first impression. I noticed that the reading list included P. F. Strawson's *Freedom and Resentment*, about which I'd published a peer-reviewed article, so I volunteered to introduce the essay when we signed up for presentation assignments. Because I was intimately familiar with the piece, I would face no difficulty delivering a successful student presentation. Was I cheating here? Perhaps I was no better than the student who recycles a paper first written for another class. Would this ploy give Josh and Barbara an inflated estimation of my abilities? Or was it only natural that I put my best foot forward? Reasonable minds could disagree, I suppose. At any rate such duplicity was rather low on the ladder of conceivable academic nefariousness. Many had surely done worse to further their fortunes, and I wasn't going to throw away this secret advantage.

Strawson's essay takes up the moral implications of determinism, the thesis that, because all our actions are ultimately traceable to some earlier state of the physical universe, no one enjoys free will despite our subjective sense that we do. The scientific worldview proceeds from the premise that every event has a cause. It follows that all our choices are, at the end of the day, attributable to forces beyond our control. How, then, can we be held accountable for our actions?

Strawson tackles this problem by mediating between two warring interlocutors, whom he dubs the pessimist and the optimist. The pessimist is persuaded that the truth of determinism undermines moral judgment because moral guilt presupposes free will. The thesis of determinism denies free will, however, so it's never rational to praise or blame anyone for anything. Hence, the pessimist's pessimism. In contrast, the optimist holds that moral judgment is compatible with the truth of determinism. We mete out such judgments not because we've deduced the falsity of determinism but to rehabilitate existing offenders and deter potential ones. Our everyday moral practices have a utilitarian rationale that doesn't hinge on free will. The pessimist isn't satisfied with these apologetics, however, and retorts that the salutary effects of moral judgment and punishment don't obviate the question of whether they can be justified in a deterministic universe. He holds that they can't be, whatever their utility, and the optimist elides this crux of his argument. Prisons may deter crime, but that doesn't settle the question of whether anyone deserves to be in them once we take their childhood traumas and inherited genetic dispositions into account.

Strawson agrees with the pessimist that the optimist's utilitarian rationale for moral judgment misses something fundamental. Having overintellectualized the stakes, the optimist overlooks that moral judgment is rooted in something more primordial than utilitarian calculation, which is the very nature of human involvement. We treat others as responsible for their actions because maintaining "reactive attitudes" toward them, as Strawson says, is part and parcel of what it means to treat them as fully fledged humans. The pessimist overintellectualizes moral judgment, too, however, and in much the same way. We dispense praise and blame not because we believe others to be free in some ultimate metaphysical sense but, again, because we couldn't otherwise engage with them as human beings. Under unusual circumstances we may allow that someone isn't responsible for misdeeds attributable to mental illness. But Strawson argues that this "objective attitude" isn't theoretically motivated and rather presupposes a practical breakdown of normal human interaction, whereupon it becomes impossible to treat another as a fully functioning human agent.

That's how parents sometimes treat children and how psychiatrists sometimes treat patients. It could never constitute a regular feature of normal adult life. The optimist is, therefore, correct inasmuch as he holds that the truth of determinism doesn't undermine ordinary moral judgment, but he is mistaken as to the real grounds for optimism, which lie in human nature itself.

Whether duplicitous or not, my presentation had the desired effect. On February 13, the following day, Barbara reached out by email:

> HI Rony: That was a tour de force yesterday. Thank you. If you feel like stopping by some time, I'd love to know what you are thinking about your own professional future, whether you are academia-bound, etc. —Barbara

Josh Cohen, the coinstructor, had been copied and concurred, responding, "Just want to second that judgment: wonderful presentation of a very hard piece." I hadn't yet communicated my academic aspirations to Barbara, but my presentation had now greased the wheels, just as I'd hoped. I replied enthusiastically that we should indeed meet and that Joe and I had been hoping to involve both of them in *Conservative Claims of Cultural Oppression*, which aspired to articulate "the right-wing lament about the liberal elites' domination of courts, universities, popular culture, etc., through the kinds of analytical frameworks employed by multiculturalism, critical race theory, etc." We met soon thereafter, and Barbara was as intrigued as Joe, venturing that I might wind up teaching conservatives to wield Foucault against liberals. That was highly prescient, as Barbara's observations would often prove to be, because I would eventually be led to conclude that liberals impose a regime of disciplinary power on conservatives with affinities to those unmasked by Foucault. I, too, would fall under that yoke one day—and at the hands of Barbara, no less.

This couldn't be foreseen at the time, of course, and the better part of the discussion centered on Barbara's bailiwick, academic realpolitik.

What would it take to land a law faculty position and where might I conceivably find myself teaching? The spots at the very top law schools often went to Yale grads, Barbara lamented, but the best Stanfordians also landed them sometimes, and finding a tenure-track job in law was certainly easier than in philosophy, she reassured. What were my grades, she inquired? I apprised that while my Stanford grades were only marginally above average, my 4.14 at Texas had vaulted me to the very top of the heap there. That was good enough for any law school, she assessed. Grades had become secondary to research as entry qualifications, but they still helped reassure hiring committees that candidates had the chops to run a rambunctious first-year class. My stratospheric first-year performance at a top-twenty law school like Texas sufficed for that.

However, there were some potential pitfalls to keep in mind. I'd noted that my intellectual approach was informed by the likes of Nietzsche and Heidegger, and Barbara cautioned that "high theory is risky," meaning that European thinkers of this ilk, or at least their academic disciples, are often held in suspicion as obscurantists and charlatans. I would have to be careful to avoid fostering this impression. There was also the political dimension. I mentioned that I had some ongoing projects that, in line with *Conservative Claims of Cultural Oppression*, critiqued certain tendencies in feminism and multiculturalism, but Barbara, ever circumspect, advised that these were best postponed until after tenure. I didn't want politics landing me in trouble so early in my academic career. And I ought not delay here. I was already thirty-four, and law schools weren't keen on hiring entry-level professors much older than thirty-five, she divulged. It was still doable, but I shouldn't dither. With these and other matters hashed out, we concluded the meeting, agreeing that I would send her a more advanced iteration of the Legal Theory term paper when I had it.

In the meantime word about my performance in Moral Luck had spread, as I learned from Joe upon receiving his feedback on my latest short essay:

> Hi Rony
>
> Another nice essay. I especially liked your (undoubtedly correct) skepticism as to how important folks like Finnis are to the conservative revolution.
>
> Have you come up with a version of your paper to send to Cohen, Fried etc? I ask because I think now is the time to get faculty behind you for an eventual academic career. In this connection, I heard you were great last week in the Moral Luck class.

My plan had been executed without flaw. With Stanford faculty watching my back, the dream that had escaped me in philosophy was becoming eminently realistic, or so it appeared. Joe's and Barbara's enthusiasms were now operating synergistically, and this would carry Larry, Josh, and others along with them. All I needed was to maintain this cascading momentum.

The relationship between a faculty adviser and an academic job seeker is akin to that between a great power and a small client state. It is the academic job seeker who derives tangible material benefits from the alliance—a tenure-track job—since it's the faculty adviser's phone calls to colleagues at other schools that separate a résumé from a stack of hundreds. The faculty adviser has an interest in expending these efforts because the empowerment of the client state redounds to the prestige and prominence of the great power. The more Stanford Law graduates are teaching at law schools, and especially illustrious ones, the stronger becomes Stanford's standing in the competition with other great powers—Yale, Harvard, Chicago, and others. When Stanford wins, so does its faculty. This was the nonzero-sum game that Joe and Barbara were now proposing. I'd have sooner or later angled to broker this alliance myself if need be, but it was better that they were coming to me. Everyone wants to feel like a protagonist, and I was allowing them to act as talent spotters exercising their carefully honed judgment.

The rest of the semester went without a hitch in Legal Theory. Joe and Larry remained deeply intrigued by the project, all the while knowing that they'd never be moved to stomach conservatism, no matter the argument. At one point I summarized for the class the views of Amy Wax, a controversial conservative from Penn Law who had recently visited the law school to debate same-sex marriage with the liberal Stanford professor Pam Karlan. Wax argued that while conservatives' ill-articulated apprehensions about the perils of same-sex marriage seem unfounded to liberals, these "vague premonitions of erosion and unraveling" may be reliable indicators of the subtle shifts in mores that normalizing homosexuality could presage.[8] "Traditional values" may be illusory or subjective in some ultimate metaphysical sense; even so, they are vital to the moral identities of many everyday people. Same-sex marriage may not threaten heterosexual marriage in any direct, obvious way, but cumulatively it can erode the frameworks of moral meaning that sustain vital human conventions.

Entranced by logic and syllogism, liberals embrace same-sex marriage as a rational extension of their universalistic commitment to equality and so consign reservations about it to the same low moral dustbin as disgust with miscegenation. Conservatives are less concerned with the syllogistic entailments of universal principles, however, and are instead attuned to what cold logic fails to capture, the subtle, often irrational, springs of human motivation that precariously undergird social cooperation. These do not necessarily respect the abstractions of liberal rationalism, but they are real all the same. Larry breezily dismissed this line of argument as ridiculous, or something to that effect, thus confirming Wax's lament that liberals have no time for conservatives' sociological worldview, which is foreign to liberals' more atomistic and economistic outlook.

My term paper presentation later in the semester was also met with a certain incredulity. Folks didn't dismiss my musings as ridiculous, but Joe was mildly distressed that I should be giving so charitable a hearing to perspectives that he and the rest of the class deemed hateful. Larry seemed to feel the same way. I concluded the talk by likening my own methodology to that of Stephen Colbert, who also spoke ironically in a conservative voice. But Larry demurred that the comparison wasn't really apt. Colbert was angling to subvert conservatism whereas I was lending it intellectual credibility, which wasn't offset by my ironic tone. Such reservations aside, the class seemed readily engaged by the topic. Larry evinced optimism about its potential when he, having espied me chewing gum during my presentation, warned me not to do this in actual job talks (the paper presentations given at campus interviews). It was nicotine gum, I disclosed, whereupon he volunteered that his wife had been resorting to it as well.

The rest of the semester went smoothly in Moral Luck, too. Barbara had given me until after the end of the term to submit my final essay so I could stay focused on my term paper in Legal Theory, and her evaluations of my various submissions were consistent with the praise first lavished on my class presentation. The first of these she assessed as "trenchantly argued and beautifully written." The second was "absolutely first-rate work" and "stellar—so smart and so beautifully written." The last was "characteristically carefully reasoned and beautifully written." Unfortunately I would one day be left with no recourse but to deploy these very capabilities against her.

The Fellowship

May rolled around and school was out. Now that I had graduated from Stanford with JD in hand, I was looking forward to one long dark summer of cramming for the bar exam. I had by then cleared out of my sunny studio loft downtown and moved in with my girlfriend in the foggy western end of San Francisco. My job in New York would begin in late September, but I'd need to make a preliminary trip there in late July for the two-day examination. The move would follow soon thereafter. The plan was to sweat it out at the firm for a few years while refining my research and then hit the law-teaching market. This was a common route to legal academia, and I felt it wouldn't hurt to wet my feet in the proverbial real world.

I was on vacation in Hawaii with my girlfriend in mid-May 2008 when I received another encouraging email from Joe:

> Hi Rony,
>
> I hope your summer is going well. Your paper was terrific. When you get back in the fall, let's brainstorm ways that you might put together a writing package that would get you a top-flight job at a law school. And we can talk about more general strategy, as well. Hopefully, you're still interested in pursuing this kind of life.

At 110 pages my term paper was nearly thrice the required length, and Joe was now reiterating his long-standing position that my writing could open glittering doors. My professional strategy seemed vindicated. Joe did appear to be underestimating the extent of my interest in an academic career, though, perhaps due to the facade of passivity I had been donning. At any rate what mattered at this juncture was his interest, not his perception of my own, and interested he was. However, he had apparently forgotten that I'd been a third-year and wouldn't be returning to campus in the fall. I wrote back and, thanking him for the outreach, reminded that I had just graduated and was heading off to New York for work, so the proposed brainstorming would have to be moved forward. I would be making regular trips to campus for the bar prep class, so we could meet and confer later in the summer, I proposed. I would touch base again then.

The next ten weeks were frenetic. I would commute to the law school each weekday morning to sit through four hours of bar prep, drive home to spend a few hours reviewing notes, and then devote what remained of the afternoon to *Conservative Claims of Cultural Oppression*. I knew I wouldn't be any less busy come fall, when I might be working sweatshop hours, so here I was in a race against the clock to advance as far as possible before this grew harder. Even as I was readying to join a law firm, the academic dream was never far from mind. Indeed, while I had every realistic expectation of relocating to New York in September, I was recurrently visited by the uncanny premonition that I would somehow be involved with the project full time in the fall. This was starkly inconsistent with facts on the ground, so I dismissed the thought as idle reverie. I had to set my writing aside as the exam approached, though I'd made considerable progress, reaching 170 pages by late July when I boarded a flight to New York for the moment of truth.

At the airport I ran into another recent Stanford Law grad who was there for the same reason, and the studying took off right then and there. We managed to sit together on the flight and treated neighboring passengers to hours of conversation about salacious topics like trusts and estates in New York and the Rule Against Perpetuities, the dreaded bugaboo of every first-year property classroom.[iii] We were joined by another newly minted alum in New York and spent the next three days in coffee shops and bars reviewing material. Our anxiety was palpable. Mine jumped another notch whenever I ventured online to read harrowing accounts of would-be attorneys whose careers were derailed after they failed the bar. Would my firm let me have a second go at it if I blew it this time around, or would it all come to naught after the horrors of last year's job search as a no-offered third-year?

In truth, I was more than ready. It was rather unusual for a Stanford Law grad to drop the ball on a bar exam—though our former dean, Kathleen Sullivan, enjoyed the distinction of having done just that

---

iii At common law "the principle that no interest in property is valid unless it vests not later than twenty-one years, plus the period of gestation, after some life or lives in being which exist at the time of the creation of the interest." "Rule Against Perpetuities," *The Free Dictionary*, https://legal-dictionary.thefreedictionary.com/rule+against+perpetuities.

(in California, admittedly the hardest one in the country).[iv] Relief set in after day one. The essay questions on New York law were the most worrisome segment and I encountered no serious snags. The next day's multiple-choice component would be a walk in the park, just your meat-and-potatoes doctrine, the ABCs of contracts, torts, and all the rest. When it was all over, the debauchery commenced, beginning with a carnivorous feast at Peter Luger Steak House in Brooklyn's Williamsburg. Only the best would do after this protracted nightmare. Before leaving New York, I emailed Joe to schedule the brainstorming session he had proposed in May. I had little more than a month left in San Francisco before the move. I also sent my latest draft to Barbara, so as to confer with her as well, and eventually scheduled meetings with both on August 11.

I dropped by Barbara's office first that day and announced my intent to keep on top of the project with whatever downtime the firm job left me. After a few years it would be ripe for dissemination, and I would hit the faculty job market. This plan of action struck her as reasonable, and she ventured that if anyone could maintain a productive research agenda while toiling in a law firm, that would be me. The draft she'd finally read was brilliant, she assayed. She had spotted some redundancies, but these could be cleaned up, and the paper was free of needless jargon. I was easily competitive for a position in a top-fifteen or top-twenty law school, she prognosticated.

Turning to the substance of the project, Barbara made some astute observations that would prove to be preternaturally prescient. She distilled my driving intuition as the sense that "there is something indeterminate to liberalism," meaning that what liberals presume is the only valid application of their principles may simply be a parochial cultural preference, with another equally defensible interpretation inuring to the conservative cause. The key to the project, she advised,

---

[iv] She had passed the New York and Massachusetts bars earlier in her career and would pass California upon retaking it.

was to explain just why conservative claims of cultural oppression amount to more than hollow ad hominems against the banal human foibles of liberals. Another crucial question, she stressed, was why liberals seem less agitated than conservatives by difference and dissent. Liberals appear unconcerned with how their next-door neighbors go about their lives, whereas conservatives can feel threatened by this, perceiving phantasmal assaults on order and decency everywhere. Is this ostensible asymmetry reality or a social illusion? Like Joe, Barbara was at once incredulous of and fascinated by conservative claims of cultural oppression. Her instinct was to discount conservatives as benighted authoritarians, but she was receptive to my still-inchoate sense that the liberal consensus was one-sided and simplistic and hoped I could explain her unease to her.

These perplexities would be cleared up in due course through my association with Barbara herself, which took an unexpected turn when she abruptly asked, "How about a fellowship?" She would have to run this by Larry for the definitive go-ahead, but she believed the James C. Gaither Fellowship was still available and that she could confer it on me either now or next year (if I wanted to practice some law first). This was the first I'd heard of this fellowship, though it was perhaps the law school's most prestigious. Recently endowed by one of its more successful graduates, it was intended as a stepping-stone to a tenure-track academic career. A press release explained:

> "For years, Stanford Law School has been at the forefront of training law students for academic careers," said Barbara Fried, William W. and Gertrude H. Saunders Professor of Law. "Jim's generous and farsighted gift is the capstone to those efforts. The Gaither fellowships will enable us to do what few law schools have been able to do: provide an opportunity for some of our most promising graduates to develop as scholars and teachers before going on the academic job market. Everyone will be a winner: our graduates, the law school, and the legal academy."

The idea was that this two-year appointment would give me the time and financial freedom to position myself for success on the legal-teaching market. I would hone my research and build contacts during the first year and then hit the job market in the second. All this was a bolt from the blue, since the planned purpose of the meeting was merely to formulate long-term career strategies. But I was more than just interested. Barbara would take it up with Larry and get back to me when she knew more.

I then stopped by Joe's office and he was fully on board with the idea. He casually remarked that he had been around the previous night as Barbara was reading my paper (they were married), but I couldn't tell whether they'd collaborated on the proposal. At any rate Joe went on to laud my term paper as "forty-times longer and forty-times better" than anything else written in Legal Theory that year, adding that "everyone knew it." I should know, he stressed, that I'd reaped the highest grade there. My paper presentation, on the other hand, was lackluster and would have been calamitous as a job talk. This was readily forgivable, though, he reassured me, given my exhaustion from working so assiduously on the paper presented.

While he wanted to see the best in me, Joe then went on to voice some reservations that Barbara had not yet broached. He and Larry had discussed my work and were agreed on my potential to eventually emerge a legal luminary. But they also had certain misgivings, because they were at a loss about where the paper was heading, and this betokened a more general challenge. No law school employer would impugn my intellectual bona fides, Joe stressed. Indeed, I could forget about getting hired outside the top fifty, as those at these lesser schools would be too intimidated. But law school faculty might rightly wonder what I had to offer them as coworkers. As things stood, it was not clear how my research "fit in" with that of potential law school colleagues and what our relationship would look like. I would have to rectify this problem during the fellowship. I might well land an appointment toward the top of the law school pecking order, Joe speculated, but the crucial thing was getting hired somewhere in the top fifty. Where in particular was of slight importance, as life would be good wherever. However, this necessitated that I first surmount the intellectually insular nature of my research as it then stood. I might, he suggested, speak to Jane Schacter, another law professor and a gay rights activist, about involving myself in her litigation projects, as that might help ground me in the law school community and remedy my research agenda's problematic insularity.

Boundlessly forbearing, Joe flattered that one so brilliant as I might be tempted to pooh-pooh these concerns as pedestrian distractions from the true intellectual quest. Still, they were critical as a practical matter. Pragmatism also dictated that I wrap up *Conservative Claims of Cultural Oppression* at some point. Since I had yet to reach any definitive conclusions, I might bring it to a close by rebutting my erstwhile apologetics for conservatism, he suggested, as that would showcase my ability to argue both sides of an issue. Of course, Joe was effectively urging me to conclude the paper by exonerating liberalism, to proclaim that conservatives aren't truly oppressed all things considered, notwithstanding my charitable treatment of their grievances. The bankruptcy of conservatism was a foregone conclusion, after all.

Having heard him out, I bade Joe farewell and awaited word from Barbara that the fellowship was indeed available. Soon enough, word came in that it was, either now or next year. Office space in the law school might be in short supply, but a private library cubicle could be earmarked for me. This was a trivial consideration, of course. More important was whether I'd be teaching a class at the law school, since the fellowship came with that opportunity. Barbara advised that I hold off on this, as she didn't "think that would be the optimal use of your time at this point—much better to use it all for writing." Sixty thousand dollars a year just to write wasn't something I could pass up, or even postpone. Given the momentum I'd already built in Legal Theory and then over the summer, I wanted to accept forthwith and just notify my law firm that I would be standing them up.

Joe was out of town by this point, so I arranged to meet and confer with Barbara and Larry. I put to them the question of whether I'd be at a disadvantage on the law faculty job market without any practical legal experience. They opined that while some experience is preferable, other things being equal, it was much less important than scholarship and certainly in my case, where my research interests bore no conceivable relationship to anything I could be doing in a firm. Larry concurred that I had little to gain by teaching during the first year of the fellowship, when the focus should be writing. With these matters hashed out, I announced that I would mull it over a bit but would likely accept. In truth, I would only go through the motions of mulling it over, as the offer was simply irresistible. Given that I was already committed to the project come hell or high water, this opportunity to pursue it with a cushy Stanford gig rather than on top of a sixty-hour workweek was the answer to my prayers. Soon thereafter I issued my official acceptance by email, thanking everyone involved for the tremendous opportunity. Joe was delighted, replying, "That's great, Rony—not the least of which because we'll get you as a colleague."

What began as the fanciful premonition that I'd somehow be occupied full time with the project come fall had abruptly materialized as concrete reality. Talk about serendipity. I didn't believe in telepathy or clairvoyance qua supernatural phenomena. But my oracular prescience on this front raised some questions. I was uncannily in sync with Joe and Barbara, who had just brought my premonition to effortless fruition. To be sure, this effortlessness rode on the shoulders of blood, sweat, and tears. There was my performance at Texas that had allowed me to transfer. Then there was my performance in Legal Theory and Moral Luck that had now earned me this fellowship. Sandwiched between those feats was the abyss of my third-year job search. No doubt, the road ahead would present its own novel challenges. But the worst was now behind me, I sanguinely surmised. I had ridden out the storm of recent years, and it was going to be relative smooth sailing from here on out.

The Tacit Dimension

I could not have been more wrong. I had no inkling that I had just laid the groundwork for a trial by fire for which these earlier challenges could not have prepared me. In ways no one could have fathomed at the time, my Legal Theory term paper had released forces that would leave an indelible imprint on all my days to come. Joe was elated to have me as a colleague, but those forces would in time reduce me from a cherished colleague to a despised pariah. All too ironically, only in the wake of this fall from grace would I finally surmount the challenges he had underscored. His misgivings were incipient articulations of a conflict of visions that would bedevil the fellowship and gradually transfigure it into the concrete biographical instantiation of my research agenda. Only by way of this conflagration would the heretofore hidden essence of my collegial relations at last be clarified.

Joe thought I might be dismissive of his concerns, but I was acutely aware of where he was coming from. Notwithstanding its captivating originality, the paper as it then stood gestured foggily toward various perplexities and ambiguities without clarifying their ultimate significance. I couldn't disagree that my ruminations were missing a certain concreteness, absent which they wouldn't resonate for others, and that my research agenda wasn't well anchored in familiar academic currents. Joe's critical error, however, was to attribute these challenges to bad habits to be uprooted, when they were intrinsic to the research agenda itself. That agenda had yet to overcome the cultural pathologies by which my colleagues had been infected, and this was what was keeping me from delivering the concreteness they were demanding.

Central to my first, abandoned dissertation topic were the insights of the German sociologist Georg Simmel. Writing at the turn of the twentieth century, Simmel observed a stark discrepancy between his civilization's "objective culture," which had expanded exponentially in modern times, and its "subjective" or "individual" culture, which had grown emaciated:

> If one compares our culture with that of a hundred years ago, then one may surely say—subject to many individual exceptions—that the things that determine and surround our lives, such as tools, means of transport, the products of science, technology and art are extremely refined. Yet individual culture, at least in the higher strata, has not progressed at all to the same extent.[9]

Whereas modern tools of production have specialized functions, preindustrial ones were comparatively crude and undifferentiated. Yet this primitiveness enabled a degree of personal expressiveness that our ever-burgeoning objective culture now hampers:

> The more differentiated these means are, the more they are composed of a multitude of specialized parts, the less is the worker able to express his personality through them, and the less visible is his personal contribution to the product. The tools that the artist uses are relatively undifferentiated and thus afford the personality the widest scope for releasing all its capacities. They do not confront the artist as does the industrial machine, whose specialized complexity itself possesses a form of personal solidity and cohesiveness so that the worker is unable to imbue it with his personality as he can with other less elaborate tools. The tools of the sculptor have not changed for thousands of years in their total lack of specialization. Wherever the artistic tools have changed

> decisively, as with the piano, its character has become quite objective. It has become much too autonomous and has set a more rigid limit to the expression of subjectivity than has, for instance, the violin, which is technically much less differentiated.[10]

Examples of this lag between subjective and objective culture abound. The contrast between the idiosyncrasies of handwriting and the mass standardization of typeface is only the most obvious of these. This sacrifice of subjective culture to objective culture is tolerated as a necessary trade-off because old-fashioned craftsmanship can only hinder the historically unprecedented productivity enabled by modern specialization. Modern machine production may not "afford the personality the widest scope for releasing all its capacities." But such aspirations are deemed inessential luxuries to be pursued in the realms of leisure, religion, and family, where they won't interfere with more serious business.

Simmel observed that the life of the mind, too, has undergone this transformation and now confronts intellectuals with highly specialized discourses that resist their personal imprint:

> In the purely intellectual sphere, even the best informed and most thoughtful persons work with a growing number of ideas, concepts and statements, the exact meaning and content of which they are not fully aware. The tremendous expansion of objective, available material of knowledge allows or even enforces the use of expressions that pass from hand to hand like sealed containers without the condensed content of thought actually enclosed within them being unfolded for the individual user. Just as our everyday life is surrounded more and more by objects of which we cannot conceive how much intellectual effort is expended in their production, so our mental and social communication is filled with symbolic terms, in which a comprehensive intellectuality is accumulated, but of which the individual mind need make only minimal use.[11]

These sealed containers of condensed cogitation are readily discernible in the standardization of tone, style, and concern associated with academic professionalism, which is undergirded by an extensive conceptual scaffolding variously known as the field, the debate, or the literature. Carefully erected over time by well-credentialed experts, this apparatus is thought to channel scholars' mental energies more productively than could their own unaided lights. In the life of the mind, as in modern culture generally, Simmel observed that "cultural objects increasingly evolve into an interconnected enclosed world that has increasingly fewer points at which the subjective soul can interpose its will and feelings."[12] This is the sense in which intellectual life has become rationalized, my dissertation was to argue, by becoming increasingly subject to methods, procedures, and precedents that progressively narrow the role of individual instinct and intuition.

This constriction is celebrated as a mark of progress and precondition of further progress. A scholarly advance qualifies as such precisely because it demarcates the permissible points of subjective interposition more strictly than was formerly possible, charting a clear direction for future advances by sidelining other avenues as unprofitable distractions or redundancies. It is platitudinous that scholars should think independently within this inherited matrix, adopting one or another side of an ongoing academic controversy according to where the arguments lead them. But thinking independently of this matrix is discounted as presumptuous amateurism that self-indulgently sacrifices scholarly rigor to personal idiosyncrasy and will at best reinvent the wheel. Scholars may believe in academic freedom. But to be genuinely academic, that freedom must be circumscribed by the basic building blocks of intellectual production marked out ahead of time. These prefabricated construction materials are upheld as needful guardrails against the cognitive overexuberance that a less surgical set of intellectual tools might set loose. Perhaps the intellectual amateur's wanderlust was forgivable in some antediluvian age closer to the dawn of human thought, when we were by and large condemned to roam blindly from error to error. But with all the great leaps forward now bequeathed to us, that wanderlust is deemed an obsolete atavism.

This was the alluring ideology that I was already aspiring to overthrow as a philosophy grad student way back at Indiana. Scholarly exchanges, with their never-ending spirals of arguments and counterarguments, objections and concessions, reservations and qualifications, are seen as the hallmark of intellectual seriousness. But my twenty-six-year-old self sensed that these spirals can uproot thought from its pretheoretical moorings in lived experience, fueling an ever-widening gulf between language and life by depriving the former of its capacity for resonance, pregnancy, and evocativeness—for becoming "luminous with manifold allusion," to borrow from Emerson.[13] The dominant dispensation will discount such priorities as mere self-edification, but overreliance on Simmel's condensed, accumulated intellectuality can carry real intellectual costs. Schopenhauer articulates why:

> The man who thinks for himself becomes acquainted with the authorities for his opinions only after he has acquired them and merely as a confirmation of them, while the book-philosopher starts with his authorities, in that he constructs his opinions by collecting together the opinions of others: his mind then compares with that of the former as an automaton compares with a living man. ...
>
> A truth that has merely been learnt adheres to us only as an artificial limb, a false tooth, a wax nose does, or at most like transplanted skin; but a truth won by thinking for ourselves is like a natural limb: it alone really belongs to us. This is what determines the difference between a thinker and a mere scholar.[14]

Schopenhauer's sharp dichotomy between the self-propelled sovereign intellect of the thinker and the slavish book-learning of the scholar surely oversimplifies. Even so, it highlights a vital difference between a purely academic or scholarly intelligence and an embodied one that develops organically in meaningful interaction with the whole human being. This is precisely what the ideologies of academia must discount. The semantic and logical discipline they enforce is not without its virtues, certainly. But that discipline can be a Faustian bargain that is secured only by first uprooting thought from its lived moorings, so that it devolves into "expressions that pass from hand to hand like sealed containers without the condensed content of thought actually enclosed within them being unfolded for the individual user," as Simmel says. That condensed content can unfold only through the murky flux of lived experience. But scholarly discipline is frequently won not through the difficult task of ordering that experience but by the easy expedient of excommunicating it. Graduate school is a training ground in these pathologies, the sacrifice of the living human being to the scholar.

Scholarly seriousness can undermine our attunement to what the philosopher Michael Polanyi calls the tacit dimension:

> It appears, then, that to know that a statement is true is to know more than we can tell and that hence, when a discovery solves a problem, it is itself fraught with further intimations of an indeterminate range, and that furthermore, when we accept the discovery as true, we commit ourselves to a belief in all these as yet undisclosed, perhaps as yet unthinkable, consequences.
>
> Yet, looking *forward* before the event, the act of discovery appears personal and indeterminate. It starts with the solitary intimations of a problem of bits and pieces here and there which seem to offer clues to something hidden. They look like fragments of a yet unknown coherent whole. This tentative vision must turn into a personal obsession; for a problem that does not worry us is no problem: there is no drive in it, it does not exist. This obsession, which spurs and guides us, is about something

> that no one can tell; its content is undefinable, indeterminate, strictly personal. Indeed, the process by which it will be brought to light will be acknowledged as a discovery precisely because it could not have been achieved by any persistence in applying explicit rules to given facts.[15]

The tacit dimension opens us to realms of meaning of which we are not presently the masters. We are operating along it whenever we find ourselves viscerally gripped by an intuition that we cannot readily verbalize but that nonetheless resonates as the portal to some ineffable intellectual vista. The rationalization of intellectual life holds out the allure of total self-control and self-possession by suppressing this kind of deep intuitive perplexity, whose intrinsic confusions and ambiguities can leave one disoriented, unable to proceed as a highly focused, productive scholar circulating sealed containers of condensed thought in an unwavering commitment to advancing the field. This social imperative encourages academics to unduly inflate the value of conscious cogitation in relation to unconscious processes and, correspondingly, to discount our ability to be intellectually productive without knowing what the productivity consists of. Mistaking our articulated intelligence for the entirety of our mental life, academia's prevailing technocratic vision prejudices its devotees against all that is merely unconscious, semiconscious, intuitive, and visceral, which is subtly anathematized as a departure from scholarly seriousness and sign of ingratitude for the contributions of scholarly forebears. Inveterately hostile to the tacit dimension, the dominant dispensation leaves its devotees insensible to the mind's ability to create order out of chaos and, indeed, to generate chaos for the very purpose of imposing order on it. This process won't add many lines to a CV and cannot be neatly outlined in a research prospectus, for it resides in the tacit dimension, where our still-unconscious wits may be percolating unostentatiously.

Dominant Enlightenment narratives associate modernity with the explosion of knowledge and critical reflection. But in *Conservative Claims of Cultural Oppression* I argue that modernity also springs from what Charles Taylor calls the building of "renunciation into ordinary life," the transposing of the medieval world's renunciatory asceticism away from its original religious settings into secular ones, where it comes to shape a host of everyday practices and attitudes.[16] Modernity is not a brute lopping-off of religion but the secularization of the religious, the melding of the religious and the secular into what Taylor calls a "spiritual-secular whole," which infuses various features of ordinary life with a spiritual meaning that was once cordoned off in the sacred and otherworldly as the specialized purview of a priestly class.[17] With modernity the masses internalize priestly sensibilities and adapt these to secular pursuits, giving rise to what we now celebrate as the autonomous individual.

This secularized asceticism is readily apparent within the political Right, most obviously in authoritarian sexual moralities, where its religious origins are undisguised, but also in free-market fundamentalism and distrust of the welfare state, where those origins are less obvious. Richard Hofstadter observes that "insofar as economic life is regarded as a sphere for the fulfillment of the ascetic Protestant virtues, Christian moralism has worked for right-wing discontent."[18] However, this historical legacy is also in play more subtly in the rationalization of intellectual life. The cognitive regimentation I have just decried has a religious appeal notwithstanding its secular rationales—and that appeal artificially amplifies the convincingness of those rationales. Seamlessly camouflaged as no-nonsense, postideological professionalism, the secularized asceticism of the liberal elites quietly fuels academia's ingrained chariness of the autonomous mind unmoored from the strictures of field and literature, which are revered as moral guardrails against the wanton self-indulgence and potential degeneracy of the undisciplined intellect guided solely by its own inner lights. The sociologist Alvin

Gouldner observes that the cosmopolitan New Class of well-schooled, left-leaning knowledge workers is predisposed "toward an unhealthy self-consciousness, toward stilted convoluted speech, an inhibition of play, imagination and passion, and continual pressure for expressive discipline."[19] That continual pressure is most fundamentally the secularization of an age-old religious drive, an intellectualized variant of the traditional spiritual aspiration to rise above animal impulse toward a purified state of heightened self-possession and self-control.

Hence, my claim in the introduction that scholarliness is no less a hero-system than the cruder and more transparent ideologies of the Right. The elites despise the vulgar traditionalism of social conservatives. But their own, more rarefied, traditionalism leaves them implacably hostile to the unregulated freedom of the tacit dimension, whose indeterminate and inarticulate nature occupies a place analogous to the sexual libertinism that offends the Right. The tacit dimension is a libertinism of the intellect, a realm of uninhibited personal impulse unfettered by the exogenous strictures of academic professionalism, whose renunciatory impulses are what dictate "a totally anonymous style and choice of topics as a matter of professional honor," as Midgley says. This aspiration to impersonality harbors a religious meaning, promising redemption from the original sin of intellectual idiosyncrasy as expressed in the solitary intimations of the tacit dimension. That is the "secular, scientific, and civilized" hero-system of academia, and Nietzsche was on to it in observing that "it will take an unspeakable amount of effort to exchange the fundamental idea behind our present system of education, which has its roots in the Middle Ages and the idea of which is actually the production of the medieval scholar, for a new fundamental idea." The New Class of liberal elites is our contemporary clerisy, the legatee of the medieval priestly class, now charged with enforcing good manners and morals within the populace, including in academia.[20]

The pathologies of academia are also pathologies of liberalism because the ascetic ethos I'm here exposing is deeply at odds with the emancipatory ideals that the elites would foist upon society at large. Midgely observes:

> Officially, we can enquire about anything. In fact, in any academic area, current traditions ensure that only certain quite limited tropes and methods will be accepted. Officially, the reasons for these limitations are impersonal, rational, clearly statable, and ready to be changed at any time if good reason is given. Actually, they have all kinds of other sources as well as these acknowledged ones—a background web of obscure and complex historical causes, involving notably clashes of personality and feuds with neighbouring studies. They are very resistant to deliberate attempts to change. Much of this rigidity, too, is certainly not impersonal because it results from the individual temperaments of the people involved. … Much academic conceptual apparatus is designed to insulate specialties from outside interference.[21]

The liberal elites will dismiss the "low" hero-systems of the Right—God, country, and family—as the atavistic residue of a benighted past. Tradition as such has no normative weight, they insist, so conservatives have no legitimate grievance against liberal interventions targeting it. But, as Midgley observes and my own experience would confirm, the elites attach great weight to *their* traditions even as they are contemptuous of traditionalism in the abstract, enshrining the contingent outcomes of historical accident as reason itself. Conservative worries about threats to the moral fiber of society seem quaint. But the elites, too, are subject to Amy Wax's "vague premonitions of erosion or unraveling" when confronted with threats to the rationalization of intellectual life, which spawns its own distinctive pieties. Being readily apparent to the naked eye, the moralism of conservatives is exposed to unremitting ridicule, critique, and intervention. Being sublimated and intellectualized, that of elites is readily camouflaged in the "impersonal, rational, clearly statable." The elites may disdain the "traditional values" of the old, crudely materialistic, bourgeosie as repressive and retrograde. But, as Gouldner recognizes, such contempt is possible only because the New Class is "a new cultural bourgeoisie whose capital is not its money but its control over valuable cultures."[22] The elites' own, subtler and more covert, moralism serves to maintain that control and the privilege that invisibilizes it.

Scholarly discipline is not without its virtues, as I've acknowledged and should be obvious. No one can think in a vacuum, and all profit from the wisdom of forebears and the scrutiny of peers. As this memoir proves, I do not deny scholarly citations their rightful place. But otherwise liberal academics leverage these platitudes ideologically to rationalize the essentially conservative sensibilities of academia's ruling class, whose sublimated and intellectualized authoritarianism lies happily disguised in ostensibly neutral technocratic commitments, such as hard-won mastery of the field or the vital advances being made thereto.[v]

---

[v] The cognitive scientist George Lakoff argues that progressives' "Nurturant Parent" morality and conservatives' "Strict Father" morality are general neural structures that compete to become concretely instantiated in particular spheres of concern, achieving this when they neurally bind such spheres to the general structure they represent and thereby inhibit the influence of the opposing system. There is no centrist morality because centrists are actually "biconceptuals" in whom the progressive and conservative systems have variously established themselves in distinct spheres—for example, domestic versus foreign policy—or in whom the two systems operate diffusely without having securely colonized the synaptic connections correlated with specific spheres of political controversy. Hence, the swing voter. Just as one may be biconceptual between different areas of political concern, so one may be biconceptual between politics generally and other realms of life. Lakoff observes that this describes most academics, who are liberal politically but conceptualize academic scholarship "metaphorically as a version of Strict Father morality," adhering to such precepts as "Mature Scholars Are Strict Fathers," "Intellectual Authority is Moral Authority," "Scholarliness is Morality," "Unscholarliness is Immorality," "Scholarly Rigor is Moral Strength," "Lack of Scholarly Rigor is Moral Weakness," "Scholarly Discipline is Moral Discipline," and "Scholarly Standards are Moral Standards." George Lakoff, *Moral Politics: How Liberals and Conservatives Think* (Chicago: University of Chicago Press, 2002), 297.

"Even as it subverts old inequities, the New Class silently inaugurates a new hierarchy of the knowing, the knowledgeable, the reflexive and insightful," Gouldner observes. Like other features of the elite culture, the rationalization of intellectual life conceals that hierarchy in a cloak of unadulterated epistemic virtue, and this dissimulation sires the elites' manifold contradictions and hypocrisies. The New Class's "culture of critical discourse" is "the grounding for a critique of established forms of domination and provides an escape from tradition," Gouldner acknowledges. But as "a lumbering machinery of argumentation that can wither imagination, discourage play, and curb expressivity," that culture also "bears the seeds of a new domination."[22] As will become clear in the pages to come, my fellowship at Stanford would become a struggle against that new domination, the consummation of which would be my relegation to the bottom of the New Class hierarchy and all the enlightenment springing therefrom.

The New Class's lumbering machinery of argumentation may seem validated by the fact that its stewards do generally exhibit greater argumentative sophistication than is commonly found among intellectual freewheelers personally invested in big questions—who may indeed just reinvent the wheel without knowing it. But every status quo manages to generate evidence in its own support. As Foucault observes, "Each society has its regime of truth, its 'general politics' of truth," discourses that it "accepts and makes function as true."[23] The ideologies of academia are made to function as true because, as with any artificial social hierarchy, scholarly supremacy acts to systemically debilitate all who would challenge it. Just as white supremacy manufactures black criminality by curtailing black economic opportunity, and male supremacy manufactures stereotypical femininity by enforcing female dependency, so scholarly supremacy maintains social and material conditions under which a competing paradigm can never come to its own and will appear discredited in even the attempt.

This was precisely the challenge presented by the fellowship. Joe's unease about my academic marketability wasn't unfounded, as will become clear, but it nonetheless illustrated Jonah Goldberg's central insight in *Liberal Fascism*:

> The unique threat of today's left-wing political religions is precisely that they claim to be free of dogma. Instead, they profess to be champions of liberty and pragmatism, which in their view are self-evident goods. They eschew "ideological" concerns. Therefore they make it impossible to argue with their most basic ideas and exceedingly difficult to expose the totalitarian temptations residing in their hearts.[24]

Joe, along with Larry and Barbara, could "claim to be free of dogma" inasmuch as they weren't straightforwardly hostile to my sympathetic treatment of a worldview they abhorred. Joe doubtless saw his enthusiasm for the project as testament to his ecumenical tolerance, which was limited only by hard-nosed concerns about my professional viability. But this Janus-faced pragmatism concealed an ideology—the rationalization of intellectual life as nourished by the renunciatory asceticism of the liberal elites. That's why he diagnosed the difficulties then afflicting my research agenda as he did, as a deficit of professional maturity, overlooking that the pragmatic obstacles occupying his attention were inevitable by-products of New Class hegemony at Stanford and kindred institutions. Joe's misgivings were reasonable. But that hegemony was what had made them reasonable, and he was upholding this status quo by harboring expectations that could be met only by acquiescing to it.

What struck Joe as a certain navel-gazing was in point of fact my immersion in the solitary intimations of the tacit dimension. The higher truth of conservative claims of cultural oppression could be accessed only therein because those claims express and affirm human drives that liberalism suppresses without acknowledgment, making the loss resistant to verbal articulation. This voicelessness is what places conservatives at a perennial rhetorical disadvantage, explaining why their grievances may seem ludicrous when taken literally and apart from the larger system of social meaning they protest. But considered in this wider context, their agitation vents a primordial alienation from the intellectualized asceticism of the liberal culture, manifesting a clash of hero-systems that is "beyond politics," as Frank says, and to which existing political vocabularies therefore cannot do justice. I couldn't explain where the project was headed because I approached conservative claims of cultural oppression as Polanyi's "bits and pieces here and there which seem to offer clues to something hidden," as mere "fragments of a yet unknown coherent whole." I hadn't yet worked out a language to articulate this obscure vision by my August tête-à-tête with Joe, even as I was gripped by a visceral conviction that such awaited discovery, and this disjunction between primordial instinct and available vocabulary was why I knew more than I could tell, as Polanyi says.

The conservative author and screenwriter Andrew Klavan aptly evokes the nature and origins of this surfeit in his reminiscences of his student days at Berkeley:

> [Leftism] was the atmosphere you breathed, was the water you swam. I was always a disgruntled liberal. I always knew something was wrong and I can pick out things along the way that just drove me crazy. I mean, I remember affirmative action, just thinking this is a dead end in terms of thought, in terms of the ability to think. But it never occurred to me that the air I was breathing was wrong. … It was like being in the matrix. Remember the movie *The Matrix*? It was like a complete imitation of reality that you really had to start to hook your finger through and start to see outside that there was another reality that you could have.[25]

The subject of *Conservative Claims of Cultural Oppression* was indeed the Matrix itself. I wasn't looking to discredit affirmative action or weigh in on any other such controversy (where my views were largely liberal). Rather, I hankered to expose liberalism as a system of cultural oppression, liberalism in its surreptitious performative dimension. I knew "the air I was breathing was wrong." But having yet to plumb the murky depths of this miasma, I could only "hook my finger" through its benign veneer. My driving intuition was that the liberal culture's official facade of outward tolerance is informally circumscribed by a subterranean background of clandestine coercions, threats, and stigmas that cumulatively enshrine certain parochial mores as bedrock reality. But giving real life to these words required deprogramming myself from that culture, as I couldn't expose that in which I was myself implicated. The covert sectarianism of the liberal elites would be visible only from the outside, and I wasn't yet standing there.

Joe had been struck by my prodigious ability to entertain foreign perspectives. Hence, his prediction that I'd one day come to understand religious conservatives better than they do themselves. But that would require me to encounter the oppressiveness of the elite culture firsthand, at the visceral level that grips conservative culture warriors, which I could not yet do. My mind was still too tethered to my upbringing and milieu, and these had encumbered me with blind spots that could be chipped away only incrementally. The enigma of conservative claims of cultural oppression did not offer an organized literature designating the questions, lingoes, and arguments through which I could position myself as a rising young scholar making valuable contributions to his field. There were no academic grandees to flatter in an endless procession of timely citations advertising my scholarly pertinence. Others had taken up some of the same questions, certainly, but usually in a sanitized fashion that didn't speak to the adversarial impulses animating me. The challenge I faced, then, was intrinsic to my subject matter. My scholarly milieu had yet to take up the problem of its own liberal privilege, so I was condemned to operate in a vacuum without the usual guideposts. Hence, the aloof and self-enclosed tenor of my research agenda as it then stood.

My intellectual eccentricities had once fascinated Joe. They were why he could read so much into an inchoate draft of my term paper when we first met in winter 2008. But he had lost patience now that I was formally on the professorial track and operating on the law school's dime. I, however, had not, and that meant I would have to persist in my facially rudderless ways, no matter how long it took, following one solitary intimation after another, articulating each as best I could in the hope that they would one day congeal into whatever it was I was seeking. That was where the argument "was heading" and something that could not be delineated ahead of time. It demanded a leap of faith, which Joe was unprepared to take with me. He had enough acumen to divine the project's potential but not enough to appreciate what realizing it would require. Intrigued though he'd been by my capacious treatment of conservatives' cultural grievances, his full-fledged membership in the liberal elite curtailed his sympathy for the thought that they encased some deep truth to which we were all insensible. Yet this faith was the entirety of what captivated me, the lifeblood of my research agenda.

Though Joe was ostensibly concerned with style and method rather than ideology, the last could not but creep into his impression of the first. My methods had to strike acolytes of the prevailing vision as dilatory wandering, wanton self-indulgence, proof that I'd exhausted my topic. Hence, Joe's advice to close out the paper by exonerating liberalism, which merely articulated the structural forces I was already confronting implicitly. He was entreating me to recast my sympathetic treatment of the conservative grievance as an idle intellectual excursion, just food for thought and nothing too serious. We were at Stanford, after all, and therefore sophisticated enough to grasp the bottom-line fatuity of that grievance. So why not end this dalliance and move on to more important things—like rubbing elbows with the academic gatekeepers whose favor I would need to curry on the job market next year?

There was a method to my madness but no way to assure Joe of it. And so began a pattern of half-conscious dissimulation as I proceeded to hijack the fellowship for my own purposes. Through a series of feints, I would find myself machinating to deceive my advisers that we were on the same wavelength, deceiving myself as necessary along the way, all in order to buy the time I needed to achieve my true ends—which spurred me on even as I couldn't state their nature. Conservative claims of cultural oppression had become a personal obsession whose inner meaning would be clarified only by its future reverberations.

CHAPTER 2

A Gathering Storm

September 2008–August 2009

The Very Opposite of Sarah Palin

The first fallout of the fellowship was a precipitous breakup with my girlfriend. As a single mother, she turned out to be rather invested in the financial security of a white-shoe legal career, which the fellowship didn't offer. I expected that it would transition me to a tenure-track job somewhere. But nothing was guaranteed at this point. Already problematic in its own right, this abrupt turnabout then doused gasoline on other tensions, and it was all over by early September. We had been cohabitating for four months by then. Now homeless, I crashed at my brother's place in the Mission District for a few weeks as I underwent the tribulations of a San Francisco apartment search on a fellow's salary. I finally found a spacious studio in the Inner Sunset neighborhood, with a balcony overlooking Golden Gate Park. The building was a nondescript, East Berlin–style behemoth, and I would have preferred quaint, but the rest was agreeable. Now I could finally get to work. My research agenda beckoned.

Unlike other law school fellows, I had no teaching or administrative responsibilities, and my newly assigned office was in the law school annex, a solitary building devoted to alternative dispute resolution. I saw no reason to commute to campus daily just to languish in these boondocks. Those two hours on the road could be better spent working from home. There was nothing to gain by so interrupting my workflow, to which my San Francisco lair was much more congenial. I would have liked greater cause to head on down, but aside from biweekly meetings of the fellows group, I saw no solid rationale for the trip.

Still, I ran into Joe twice in the early fall. The first encounter was in the coffee dispensary adjacent to the faculty lounge, where the fellows group was then congregating. After some small talk he remarked out of the blue that I was the very opposite of Sarah Palin. Given the great contempt in which he held the Republican Party's poorly spoken 2008 vice presidential nominee, I knew this was the highest praise the man had to offer. My fascination with conservatism notwithstanding, Joe had always taken me for a good liberal who was basically on his team when all is said and done. This tribute was the latest expression of that confidence.

The observation had a suprapolitical dimension, too. Despite his misgivings, Joe appreciated at some intuitive level that *Conservative Claims of Cultural Oppression* was becoming Polanyi's "undefinable, indeterminate, strictly personal" obsession "about something that no one can tell." And it was this resolve to uncover an as yet unnamed truth, not liberal politics, that truly distinguished me as Sarah Palin's antipode. Whether Joe could stomach the full implications of his own insight was an open question, however, and one that would eventually be answered in the negative.

This problem was first articulated in our August conferral, and it would reappear in my second encounter with Joe that fall, when he joined the fellows group to dispense career wisdom. He issued his usual cautions about the perils of perfectionism, voiced many times over in Legal Theory, and advised us not to worry about where exactly we land jobs. Just get hired somewhere and the good life would be ours. Nor should we fret about making original contributions to our fields at this early stage of our careers. Even someplace like Stanford had no expectation that entry-level hires would have made one and was looking only for this potential. Indeed, not once had a new hire made an original contribution when first retained by the law school. To my surprise Joe also downplayed publication. What mattered was the quality of our job-talk papers, not whether they'd already been accepted for publication somewhere, he stressed.[i] This was so unimportant that he had no recollection of whether successful entry-level candidates at Stanford had published their papers.

Though facially sound, Joe's counsels once again betrayed the intellectualized illiberalism against which my research agenda now pitted me. The powers that be weren't expecting original contributions so much as the potential thereof. But that meant our intellectual paths would be dictated by the preestablished matrix to which we would eventually be contributing. Joe might have instead remarked that no entry-level hire had ever put forward any genuinely original *ideas* when first brought on board. If he preferred to speak of contributions, this was in reflection of the technocratic prism I've been denouncing.

I didn't articulate these critiques contemporaneously, but they were silently germinating in my lived attitude and therefore in the clash of attitudes this provoked. Joe and I had no direct, one-on-one engagement during that fellows meeting. But the first hint of our emerging estrangement surfaced when I introduced myself during the round of introductions, in response to which he reminded me that he knew my name. The introductions were ostensibly for the

---

i Job-talk papers are the papers that candidates for academic positions present to an audience of their prospective colleagues when visiting a campus for a series of interviews. Candidates will be invited on such visits only if they first make a suitably strong impression at an off-campus screening interview.

benefit of the whole group, not him specifically, so he had no logical basis for inferring that I believed him unaware of my name. Nevertheless his strange pique made sense as a muted expression of the temperamental and ideological chasm that had always separated us notwithstanding the strong first impression I had managed to produce.

Unbeknown to us, we were both reacting to what Bourdieu calls the "imperceptible cues of bodily *hexis*." Bodily hexis is "political mythology realized, *em-bodied*, turned into a permanent disposition, a durable manner of standing, speaking, and thereby of *feeling* and *thinking*." It constitutes a "pattern of postures that is both individual and systematic" and that, "charged with a host of social meanings and values," permits these "to pass from practice to practice without going through discourse or consciousness."[1] Bodily dispositions can play this role because some ideas aren't just theoretical constructs but also emanations of our biological temperament and way of being that needn't be enunciated theoretically to be communicated viscerally. My battle against the prevailing ideology would proceed on this plane during the first year of the fellowship.

I contributed little to that meeting, but my demeanor already signaled my repudiation of the political mythology implicit in Joe's own bodily hexis. This was the rationalization of intellectual life, and Joe grasped on some level that something within me resisted all rationalization; his irritation was a visceral, semiconscious reaction to this primordial recalcitrance, the depth of which he had yet to fully appreciate. My ever-deepening engrossment by conservative claims of cultural oppression had to go hand in hand with a burgeoning alienation from my academic milieu and its "secular, scientific, and civilized" hero-system, whose self-congratulatory Kool-Aid was becoming harder and harder to drink. Joe was not wrong to peg me as a man of the Left, all things considered. But having overlooked that "there is something indeterminate to liberalism," as Barbara put it, he could not see that, as the opposite of Sarah Palin, I would feel compelled to set my crosshairs on the sublimated and intellectualized conservatism of the liberal elites. Our discord that day was still too subtle and understated to permit any clear recognition, let alone resolution, of the substratal schism taking root beneath, with the result that I would continue to fill up a powder keg that could be detonated by the slightest spark by year's end.

One Level Up

Come early November I realized I should touch base with Joe and Barbara notwithstanding that I didn't have much new to report. I had written prolifically, but the draft remained rough, and I hadn't yet unpacked the meaning of it all. Still, I had had only fleeting contact with Joe, and no contact with Barbara, since the fellowship began more than two months earlier. So an appearance seemed in order. I initiated contact by email and advised that I'd sequestered myself from the world to maximize progress. My draft still required revision but had advanced considerably. Were they around to chat sometime? They happily consented to meet. After sundry delays we finally convened in the faculty lounge about a month later, in mid-December right before the winter break.

I related some of the formulations I'd been wrestling with. But given the project's ongoing inchoateness, I really didn't have that much new to impart beyond the manuscript's length, now at about 250 pages. These were still unpolished, I advised. Their initial reaction was auspicious. "No one works harder than Rony," Barbara declared. Even so, she feared my efforts were going to waste and, citing her own experience with contract theory, counseled against the futility of writing on and on in the absence of a clear thesis, as I now appeared to be doing. Much better to break the tome into articles, post these on SSRN—an online database of academic works in progress—and promote myself thusly, she advised. I could also involve myself in an ongoing interdisciplinary workshop sponsored by Stanford's Humanities Center, which was now bringing together scholars from sundry fields, such as philosophy, political science, economics, and law, in order to apply the latest empirical research to "foundational issues in the study of normative ethics," as an email she later forwarded explained. Barbara was hoping this would focus me, since my research would then become suitably enmeshed with these recognizable academic currents.

I may have been hard at work, but this hadn't positioned me to explain what the hell I was trying to accomplish. On the contrary, my assiduity had plunged me ever further into the opaque inarticulacy of the tacit dimension. Barbara's budding disenchantment was confirmed when she abruptly confessed to having forgotten whether I had a PhD and asked to be reminded. The question took me by surprise, as those six years of my life had been a topic of earlier conversations, and her unprompted request for clarification betrayed that they hadn't been entirely forgotten. This amnesia about my credentials was a roundabout way of venting frustration with the glacial pace of things. PhD or not, my autonomous judgment hadn't yielded a coherent research agenda. With that autonomy seemingly discredited, Barbara would now seek to impose the order I appeared incapable of generating myself.

This was the query's undeclared subtext. As I was socially constrained to acknowledge only its official text, I brushed aside the microaggression and reminded Barbara that I did happen to have a PhD. Indeed, I had published a peer-reviewed article on Strawson's *Freedom and Resentment* (the subject of the class presentation by which I had first wooed her). I furthermore had a book on human nature, whose findings I was now applying to conservative claims of cultural oppression, I also noted (I'd gifted a copy to Joe, a $99 value on Amazon at the time). This wasn't a massive record of scholarly accomplishment, granted, but I felt it bespoke the wherewithal to carry a project through to completion. No matter, the damage was done. Barbara now wanted more influence and suggested I could rack up another publication with a book review for the prestigious *Journal of Philosophy and Public Affairs*, where she was the review editor. I had nothing to show for myself, and she was trying to do me a favor, so I could not refuse, and I gestured that I would be turning my attention to this.

Joe was equally dispirited by my seemingly rudderless ways. With facetious forbearance he groused that, as a "mad genius," I had probably dismissed my colleagues as imbeciles but that this didn't obviate the need to concretize my musings by explaining their connection to the law and my colleagues' work. Whatever I'd been doing hadn't helped in this regard. I noted in passing that I was pondering the writings of Robert Bork, on whom I had seized as a paradigmatic conservative culture warrior. But Joe dismissed this focus as unworthy of me, declaring that Bork was an imbecile whereas I was brilliant. So why burn daylight on him? Why not instead turn my efforts to, say, law and economics? Some of my short-response papers in Legal Theory had been on the subject and were of nearly publishable quality, Joe assayed, so I might audit Professor Polinsky's law and economics seminar and take my research in that direction. The moral and intellectual bankruptcy of conservatism was a foregone conclusion, and it was time to get serious.

Joe also floated the thought of attending the Wednesday faculty luncheon, where professors would be presenting their latest research. Most speakers were invitees from other law schools, and that presented an opportunity to network. I could make a practice of dispatching ingratiating emails to our weekly visitors, which might get their ears and strengthen my hand next year on the job market. This would also be helped, Joe further advised, by turning my focus to law and religion. The faculty had enjoyed hearing a guest speaker who advocated for a new, more rigorous, standard of Establishment Clause review that would more seamlessly invalidate religiously motivated legislation. I should follow suit, Joe urged, as this kind of thing tends to engage law school audiences.[ii]

Since the goal was to make my work more relatable to potential colleagues, I might also tie it in to conflict of laws to win the attention of conflict-of-laws specialists, Joe added, ignoring that the First

---

[ii] The Establishment Clause is the first clause of the First Amendment, which in its entirety reads, "Congress shall make no law respecting an establishment of religion, nor prohibiting the free exercise thereof; or abridging the freedom of speech, or of the press; or the right of the people peaceably to assemble, and to petition the Government for a redress of grievances." Legal scholars of all stripes agree that the Establishment Clause restrains the state from establishing a national religion, promulgating official interpretations of religious texts, mandating regular church attendance, or making financial contributions to preferred faith groups. However, liberals tend to interpret the Establishment Clause more expansively as commanding a "wall of separation" between church and state, so as to ensure that laws have a secular legislative purpose and remain neutral as to religion, which the state may neither advance nor inhibit. Accordingly, liberal legal scholars will oppose organized prayer sessions in public schools, religious holiday displays on public property, and public funding for parochial schools as unconstitutional violations of the Establishment Clause.

Against this, conservative scholars and jurists argue that the Establishment Clause permits the state to support religion in ways they contend are noncoercive and nondiscriminatory. Although the state may not favor specific creeds or sects, it can promote religion generally as a public good or at least acknowledge religion's significance in the lives of citizens and in shaping American history. So conservatives may defend a Ten Commandments monument in a public building as a nonsectarian acknowledgment of the nation's monotheistic heritage. Conservatives often stress the founding generation's consensus that religion is a necessary bulwark of morality and civic virtue. They also highlight that the Supreme Court did not apply the Establishment Clause to restrict the activities of state governments until the 1940s, reflecting the Founders' intent only to prevent federal encroachments on state religious establishments through a national church, not to cleanse the public sphere of religion generally.

Liberals argue that the conservative position is a slippery slope to theocracy. Conservatives rejoin that this very apprehension betrays antireligious animus. Both sides can find historical evidence to support their rival interpretations of the Establishment Clause, and the Supreme Court's frequent attempts to split the difference between these has led to considerable doctrinal confusion that remains unresolved to this day.

Amendment is federal constitutional law that cannot be neutralized by any other law—no conflict of laws could conceivably arise. Joe had surely heard of the Supremacy Clause. His odd suggestion was another circuitous expression of his ongoing frustration with me, one more objection to my seemingly fanatical insularity. It was a portent of the conflict to-be, when what began as simple chagrin would metastasize into something more interesting.

As the meeting was winding down, Barbara tried to sum things up by confessing her trepidation that my job-talk paper just wouldn't be ready in time for early circulation. She wanted to spread the word about me to folks at other law schools and hopefully drum up interest. But that required some presentable work to pass on. This was vital in my case, she stressed. With law and philosophy representing a rarefied and nonessential niche area in law school hiring, appointments committees would seek assurances that they were bringing on "the best" law and philosophy candidate before splurging on such an extravagant hire. So I needed to be marketed proactively.

All this was wise and sensible. More baffling were the two cryptic warnings with which Barbara then concluded the meeting. The first was her strenuous insistence that mastering the religion case law was vital, especially as I operated "one level up." Someone like Pam Karlan, a Stanford colleague, would accept no less, she added in passing. That it behooved me to learn the case law made sense enough, but what did that have to do with operating "one level up," and what did this even mean? Building on these words of warning, Barbara next cautioned me to check my tendency to "make specimens" of people. Instead, I should convey that "we're all absurd." What was this all about? Yes, I made specimens of people inasmuch as I situated their beliefs and values within cultural or historical currents of which they might be unaware, but this style of argument wasn't unique to me and didn't amount to an ad hominem attack. So where, exactly, did my transgression lie, and how was acknowledging our collective absurdity the remedy? I didn't ask. These tenebrous admonitions were offered as food for thought, and Barbara clearly intended that I find their meaning within myself.

My advisers' other concerns were less opaque. Indeed, Joe's grumble that I was posturing as a "mad genius" dismissive of his colleagues' intelligence was just a more poignant formulation of the nagging doubts first aired in August, which now seemed vindicated by the record of recent months. With their technocratic hostility to the tacit dimension and my own inability to articulate any semblance of a clear thesis, my advisers were left to conclude that I was chasing some chimera, driven by hubris to ascend a ladder of outsized abstractions that could never be reconnected with anything a normal human being might be brought to care about or even understand. I was flying too close to the sun, and they wanted me back on Earth.

Against all the empirical evidence that I was floundering, I had nothing beyond the tacit dimension and its "intimations of an indeterminate range," only a visceral faith that conservative claims of cultural oppression harbored some profound truth that I would one day excavate. In my mind this quest obviated all my mentors' advice. Barbara's admonition about the futility of writing on and on without a clear thesis was reasonable on its face, but this insight arose from her own work of secondary literature on a subject that had already received significant commentary. In contrast, conservative claims of cultural oppression presented a singular problem, which was to enter the lived experience whence they issue. We were fated to talk past one another at every turn, because our philosophical visions were fundamentally at odds.

Joe's insistence that Bork was an imbecile unworthy of my attention was similarly misbegotten. What mattered wasn't Bork's IQ—surely higher than Joe gave him credit for—but whether his formulations could gain me access to the standpoint of conservative claims of cultural oppression, by offering "bits and pieces" of the unknown whole toward which I was half-blindly clambering. As in our August consultation, a challenge intrinsic to the project was misread as a sign of poor judgment and professional immaturity. My advisers hoped the guidance of more seasoned scholars would rescue me from my meandering confusion. But the real stumbling block wasn't confusion; it was the liberal culture, of which the confusion was just a symptom. Those scholars' vaster experience would be unavailing because it did not touch on this problem.

Moreover, I was wary of such assistance as an insidious distraction from the task at hand. Penning a book review for Barbara's journal was appealing in the abstract. Another publication never hurts. But whether I had this additional line on my résumé wasn't going to make or break me. I already had two publications more substantive than a book review, even one written for none less than Barbara. If having published one's job-talk paper was inessential, as Joe had stressed at the fellows meeting earlier in the fall, then a three-page book review wouldn't be a game changer either. Nor was I really going to take up Joe's suggestion about auditing Polinsky's law and economics seminar. There was surely much to learn there, but that was even more true of *teaching* a class. If the writing was important enough to justify foregoing this—as Larry and Barbara had both advised in August—then it was important enough to justify not attending a class as a student. All else had to take a backseat to the momentum I was now building—that my advisers were doing their utmost to derail.

I had to thwart these efforts while dissembling compliance. So I contrived an attitude of open-minded receptivity throughout our meeting, feigning that I was being moved by nostrums at which I balked in my heart of hearts. I didn't relish this dissimulation or the self-deception it necessitated. But the ends justified the means, in my mind. Anything else would fall short of the mandate I had assumed when I ascended to the fellowship to become the law school's latest James C. Gaither Fellow.

Such was the curious logic by which I justified my obstinacy. Rational prudence dictated that I cease and desist from my navel-gazing and kowtow unreservedly to my mentors. At stake was my one shot at a tenure-track position in a good law school, a private sector–level salary without the specter of private sector–level tedium. Since my prospects rode on the strings that Joe, Barbara, and others could pull for me, wholesale capitulation would have been in order. But, alas, rational prudence wasn't my strong suit. On the contrary, I was being spurred on by a quasi-religious yearning to expose liberalism's heart of darkness and wasn't about to let anything get in my way. Whatever problems this policy spawned would be cured by that date with destiny, when my obstinacy would stand vindicated, I reassured myself.

While the warnings about operating one level up and my tendency to make specimens of people seemed cryptic, nothing that left Barbara's mouth was gratuitous. Here, as elsewhere, her words were pregnant with an oracular profundity that would unfold only gradually in the fullness of time. I was operating one level up because I was harnessing the power of conservative claims of cultural oppression to transcend the academic ideology in which Barbara was well steeped, and this trajectory had made her feel like a specimen. My "imperceptible cues of bodily *hexis*" intimated that her academic realpolitik disguised technocratic false consciousness, her unwitting enslavement to the cultural pathologies of the chattering class, which her words of advice that day were unconsciously reproducing. Barbara admonished me as she did because she could already intuit that my immersion in the tacit dimension had these pathologies in its undeclared crosshairs. Since this telos was still confined to that dimension, manifesting itself only indistinctly in the turn now taken by our relationship, she could protest it only metaphorically. Hence the elliptical warnings, which reverberated events on this plane and uncannily hinted at the conflict to come, when we would vie to operate one level up in a struggle to make specimens of each other—the true future genesis of *Conservative Claims of Cultural Oppression*.

A Downward Spiral

My advisers and I were ostensibly on opposing wavelengths, but our relations had always been Janus-faced if not downright schizophrenic, and there was another level on which we were uncannily in sync. They would never have proposed the fellowship had it been otherwise. So, while I balked at most of their suggestions as untimely distractions, I did take up Joe's to turn the focus to law and religion. The idea wasn't just sound but supremely wise. Beyond yielding a theory of religious neutrality, turning to the Establishment Clause would provide a clearly delineated context wherein to erect the entire edifice of *Conservative Claims of Cultural Oppression*. Though offered up casually as just a thought, the suggestion was profoundly attuned to the needs of the hour.

The agreement ended there, however. Joe and Barbara were surely hoping I'd go on to pen a secularist screed. But I intended to argue that "secular humanism" isn't the paranoid conspiracy theory of benighted fundamentalists but rather a surreptitious form of religiosity that has insinuated itself into the public schools and other putatively neutral institutions. Secular liberals hold that the state stays religiously neutral so long as it neither advocates nor denigrates religion. A public school's mere refusal to actively organize voluntary prayer sessions for students doesn't qualify as antireligious because the topic of religion just isn't being taken up one way or the other. But where liberals see benign neglect, religious conservatives detect an affirmative slight, not a mere bracketing of theological questions but subterranean undertones of antireligious animus that liberals will not forthrightly acknowledge. Here, as elsewhere, the elites operate with plausible deniability, enshrouding their parochial cultural preferences in a cloak of universalism that makes it, as Goldberg warns, "impossible to argue with their most basic ideas and exceedingly difficult to expose the totalitarian temptations residing in their hearts."[2]

Were these suspicions just sectarian paranoia, as liberals were wont to believe, or did they harbor undertheorized understandings that the liberal culture must peremptorily dismiss? The liberal logic was straightforward, but perhaps this common sense was part and parcel of the liberal Matrix. I couldn't rid myself of the thought that, because conservatives stand outside this Matrix, they are attuned to something that the liberals stuck within it must overlook. The elites discount conservative anxieties about secular humanist encroachment as unsophisticated and muddleheaded. But my contrarian intuitions whispered that these anxieties were too sophisticated for liberals to understand or for conservatives to properly articulate, making them seem muddleheaded. That's because the liberal vision of religious neutrality is a covert, secularized expression of the traditional religious drive to expose and chastise idolatry. This surreptitious secularization of an age-old monotheistic impulse is elided by conventional, Enlightenment-inspired interpretations of modernity. But move past this received wisdom and conservatives' ostensible paranoia begins to make sense, because we can then recognize that the antagonism between secular liberals and conservative evangelicals recapitulates the historical one between morally stern Christian missionaries and headstrong pagans clinging to their sinful ways.

I would spend the winter, spring, and summer of 2009 occupied with this driving intuition. Joe's suggestion would focus my energies but also meant that I'd be starting from scratch in some respects. I had taken a class on the religion clauses at Texas with the renowned Douglas Laycock and so knew the general lay of the land, but I still had to revisit the case law through the prism of conservative claims of cultural oppression. This became my all-consuming focus, so the book review Barbara had solicited would never materialize. I had momentum, a limited time in which to capitalize on it, and so would not be distracted by things that would have captured my interest under less exigent circumstances.

I wasn't initially aware of how far the religious neutrality problem would draw me in, however. Fancying that I was tackling a question of smaller scope, I dropped by Barbara's office in early February 2009 to touch base, advising that my focus had turned to whether state subsidies for religious drug and alcohol rehabilitation programs are consistent with religious neutrality. This narrow question was intimately bound up with the entire theoretical edifice of *Conservative Claims of Cultural Oppression*, but I had little inkling of this at the time. Supposing the issue to be self-contained and easily manageable, I pitched it to Barbara as the solution to the desultoriness that had so disquieted her in December. To my relief, she was delighted with what she lauded as a wonderful idea. I should get her an outline or summary in the next few weeks, she urged, so she could pass it on to a law-and-religion maven she knew at Georgetown. She also entreated me to write on atheism. She and Joe were firm atheists, inexhaustibly bewildered by the religious beguilement of lesser minds, and she was hoping I'd validate the sentiment.

Leaving her office with me to head off somewhere, Barbara then remarked that she hadn't seen me around much. I responded that this was natural seeing as I'd been stationed in the law school annex until only recently, when office space had finally opened up in the law school proper just down the hall. I had apprised her about the annex earlier in the fall. Even so, she was alarmed at this absenteeism and urged that I be in my office more, so she and Joe could keep an eye on me. I intimated consent, naturally.

Part of me was pleased with the new office space, as I was in principle eager to integrate into the legal academic community. At the same time I hadn't yet excavated the enlightenment buried in the depths of conservative claims of cultural oppression and believed that end was better served by not commuting to Stanford daily. I did take up Joe's idea about attending the Wednesday faculty luncheons and indeed made a point of reading the papers and asking questions. But as I had no responsibilities beyond writing, I had nothing to gain from many further interruptions. This logic had seemed impeccable all through my tenure in the annex. Although the new office on the mainland somewhat undermined it, I had formed some habits by then. Only a logistical fluke had now domiciled me in the main building, and why should I be at the mercy of logistical flukes? Barbara wanted to supervise me more closely, but this would have been impossible but for that fluke, so how vital could her supervision be?

Moreover, I feared such oversight as an insidious threat to my research agenda. As in December, I remained persuaded that conservative claims of cultural oppression sheathed some deep profundity that it was my solemn task to uncover. But with my ongoing inability to defend that conviction rationally, my advisers' skepticism had even more rhetorical force now that another two months had elapsed. Their patience was surely wearing thinner by the day, with my credibility evaporating accordingly. Yet I was bound to the same course, and so the synopsis Barbara awaited would also never materialize. The untethered mission creep that had set in that fall—and, really, over the summer—did not abate. Again and again I would be impelled to extend my argument, so that what was supposed to be a short summary over the following months became many hundreds of pages of jumbled notes—most of which would have been unintelligible to anyone but me (if even that).

By spring 2009, I was the proverbial hamster on a treadmill. Enslaved by my own momentum, I despaired of arriving at that magical turning point where it would all finally come together. With my rhetorical position vis-à-vis my advisers deteriorating further with each passing day, I was propelled into a downward spiral of apprehension and evasiveness. I would make my way down to Stanford for the luncheon and fellows meetings and occasionally on a lark. I needed to exhibit my membership in the law school community. At the same time I hoped to head off a run-in where I might be compelled to give an account of myself under unfavorable rhetorical conditions. So I took evasive measures to minimize that threat, leaving my office door ajar to signal my presence but not so ajar as to invite scrutiny.

This comical furtiveness was the logical consequence of my willingness to exploit the amorphousness of my role as the James C. Gaither Fellow. I was a Stanford employee and ultimately answerable to it. But unlike other law school fellowships, mine involved no teaching or administrative duties, so considerable flexibility was built into it. I was expected to involve myself with the law school community, but I had no obligation to be physically present on the premises at all times. I was also supposed to heed Joe's and Barbara's broad guidance, but they had no expectation that I hang on to their every word and swallow every counsel wholesale. I was on a long leash, and this latitude enabled me to miss the forest for the trees. Ideating each of my decisions in isolation from the others, I gave short shrift to the broader pattern they were forming, compartmentalizing my deteriorating relations with my mentors in the periphery of my consciousness, where they wouldn't distract from my all-consuming ruminations.

My faith in the higher truth of conservative claims of cultural oppression was growing ever more visceral as I fell ever further into the murky depths of the tacit dimension, still unable to translate this conviction into any communicable propositions. The resulting dissonance only aggravated my mounting alienation from the ambient culture, my solipsistic retreat into a self-enclosed conceptual universe, a black hole from which no light escaped. What Joe had feared most was now coming to pass. I would manage to overlook my descent into insularity and obsession, however, as this vortex would take shape in small increments, each of which I could readily minimize. Even so, the cumulative truth of my steadily percolating estrangement and anomie would be communicated to me from myriad directions during the winter and spring of 2009. Like my advisers' disquietude in December, these incidents were subtle portents of things to come, incipient materializations of institutional headwinds that would in time place me in intractable conflict with the might of Stanford itself.

The first of these contretemps erupted at the fellows group when Joe Grundfest, a corporate law professor, arrived at our February 19 meeting to dispense career advice. True to his wheelhouse, Grundfest brought a hard-nosed, no-nonsense CEO style to the discussion. His objective was to gauge where our job-talk papers stood, and the bottom line in his mind was our ability to encapsulate them in three sentences explaining the problem we were tackling, the question we were posing, and the answer we were giving. This proved challenging but also helpful for all present. Submerged as I was in the tacit dimension, my own performance was a mixed bag. I managed to boil down the project to the mandated three sentences but strained to do so, with my halting formulations betraying my ongoing disorientation and hesitancy. Signaling his vexation, Grundfest sniped that "it's probably not really that complicated" after I tried to elaborate on my answers. Given the project's lofty ambitions, he was surely irked by the gap between these and my actual ability to explain and defend, which remained modest.

Disinterested third parties would later attest that my thesis was indeed complicated. But Grundfest's reflexes here were a natural expression of the regnant ideology. Midgley observes:

> It is an awkward fact, often overlooked in this concentration on clarity, that familiar, accepted ideas always tend to seem clearer than unfamiliar ones, whether they actually are so or not. The clarity of an argument depends on its relation to the relevant premises. But in real life (as opposed to mathematics) most of

> the premises of an argument are unstated, and many of them have never even been made explicit. The real need is somehow to become conscious of this mass of hidden premises, and to pick out for attention the ones that matter most. But this process takes time, during which things seem to become more confused. If clarity is one's sole aim, it can be reached much faster by refusing to consider any premises except those that have already occurred to one as leading to one's chosen conclusions. This simplifying of the premises is what many people think of as a "rational" approach, and it is just what gives the notion of rationality such a bad name that people are quite happy to say that they prefer to be irrational. In philosophy teaching, it leads to a flat, dogmatic insistence on the current fashionable approach as the only possible professional path.[3]

Grundfest's agenda that day illustrated how an enlightened ideal such as clarity can be weaponized to serve the intellectual status quo. Clarity is indeed a virtue, other things being equal. But Midgley highlights why they never are. If I couldn't offer up the mandated clarity that day, it was because I was still unearthing the "mass of hidden premises" that undergirded the liberal vision of religious neutrality. I was excavating the unsaid of liberalism, a form of oppression that as yet had no name. This required cultivating my visceral sense of the conservative condition, which I would have to develop intensively before any clarity could be reaped. Until then, it was easy to write off the entire enterprise as confusion, obscurantism, or affectation. Grundfest's not-so-subtle dig was just such an indictment and one that flowed directly from his professional and civilizational identity. He treated clarity as a superlative ideal not only for its intrinsic value but also to reinforce the social virtues of productivity and communicability, the foundation of his New Class (chattering class) identity as a serious scholar. In slighting clarity I slighted that identity, and the retribution followed swiftly.

Foucault's deconstruction of "the examination" lays bare the logic of Grundfest's microaggression that day:

> The examination combines the techniques of an observing hierarchy and those of a normalizing judgment. It is a normalizing gaze, a surveillance that makes it possible to qualify, to classify, and to punish. It establishes over individuals a visibility through which one differentiates them and judges them. That is why, in all the mechanisms of discipline, the examination is highly ritualized. In it are combined the ceremony of power and the form of the experiment, the deployment of force and the establishment of truth. At the heart of the procedures of discipline, it manifests the subjection of those who are perceived as objects and the objectification of those who are subjected. The superimposition of the power relations and knowledge assumes in the examination all its visible brilliance.[4]

Grundfest's three-sentence test was one man's version of this wider cultural practice, endemic to the modern disciplinary society. Its purpose was nothing less than to impose on the fellows "a visibility through which one differentiates and judges them." Grundfest knew the day's performances would be placed within "a field of comparison" and "space of differentiation" that would serve to "[hierarchize] in terms of value and abilities, the level, the 'nature' of individuals," as Foucault says.[5] He had rolled out his examination to smoke out resistors to the New Class's lumbering machinery of argumentation, who, unaided by that apparatus, would be at a natural disadvantage. The exercise thus reinforced that class's dominion, defiance of which would invite Grundfest's "normalizing gaze," his "subjection of those who are perceived as objects and [his] objectification of those who are subjected." This was the fate that befell me at that meeting when I became the public target of his chafing skepticism, whose disciplinary function was to uphold the established universe of discourse through "the ceremony of power and form of the experiment"—the brass tacks of that day's exercise.

I would go on to attract some normalizing gazes from the fellows themselves at another meeting in late April. I had distributed a short outline of my project to the group, and David Ball, its fearless leader, was taken aback that Hegel was the only writer cited, echoing Joe's concern that I was dismissing the contributions of contemporary colleagues. Echoing Barbara, he also remarked that I was rarely around the law school, thereby impugning my work ethic. As with Grundfest, my ruminations impressed him as pie-in-the-sky obscurantism. "High theory is risky," Barbara had warned early on, and her Delphic prescience was now being confirmed from all sides. One fellow alerted that the working title of my job-talk paper, "The Impossibility of the Establishment Clause," could be off-putting. Another admonished that irony would gain me nothing. Someone else offered to send me some pertinent scholarly literature. In a follow-up email, another fellow, Teneille Brown, volunteered to read any future drafts and cautioned: "It's great to be provocative in a job talk, but you do want to make sure that your tone does not come off as insulting some % of the audience. I think you can strike that balance by making your arguments very strong, but by not being too heavy-handed." I thanked her for her thoughts and noted that I had replaced "The Impossibility of the Establishment Clause" with "The Relativity of the Establishment Clause." These were just alternative framings of the same thesis. But *relativity* sounded more humble than *impossibility*, and I hoped this stylistic concession to local mores would mitigate the potential offense.

That was a Band-Aid solution, obviously. The underlying problem ran much deeper. Jacoby observes in *The Last Intellectuals*:

> Universities encourage a definite intellectual form. They do not shoot, they simply do not hire those who are unable or unwilling to fit in. Even Henry Luce of the *Time* magazine empire, often denounced as a master propagandist, employed and even liked

> mavericks and dissenters. Universities, on the other hand, hire by committee: one needs degrees, references, the proper deference, a pleasant demeanor. To win over a committee that recommends to a department which counsels a chairman who advises a dean who suggests to a college president takes a talent very different from gaining the assent of a single individual. It is almost ludicrous to imagine "Professor Edmund Wilson" or "Professor H. L. Mencken."[6]

Universities encourage a definite intellectual form because academics seek out colleagues whose variety of intelligence validates their own. Providing that validation takes a reflexive, quasi-instinctual attunement to the panoply of subtle ways in which one's intellectual style, temper, and interests can either affirm or upset others in their rarefied scholarly identities. Teneille's foreboding sense that my tone might come off as insulting betrayed the dense webs of social meaning operating surreptitiously beneath the surface of what may present itself as disembodied intellectual inquiry. Jacoby's "proper deference" and "pleasant demeanor" aren't just quotidian social etiquette, like knowing when to extend a handshake or address someone formally, but the heedful cues signaling one's commitment to fostering those dense webs. This performative dimension is intrinsic to the academic enterprise at the unspoken level of undertone and intimation—that is, bodily hexis—and must be conveyed as convincingly as an argument's substance. Proper deference and pleasant demeanor position one as an insider or prospective insider who affirms the superior wisdom and virtue of the insider. Substantive dissent on discrete points of controversy is generally brooked, but all such schisms must be authorized by the hegemonic meta-orthodoxy of the au courant, which demands an unwavering animal faith. That's the crux of so-called academic professionalism, the sublimated and intellectualized conservatism of the liberal elites, which can blur the line between intellectual virtues and social ones. As Gouldner observes, colleges and universities are the "finishing schools" of the New Class.[7]

This latest fellows meeting confirmed that I lacked the good breeding to properly rub elbows. It could not be otherwise when I was wrestling with the solitary intimations of the tacit dimension. As Polanyi says, this is to gather "bits and pieces here and there which seem to offer clues to something hidden," an obsession "about something that no one can tell."[8] Such obsessions invariably violate ordinary conventions of academic sociability. The bits and pieces harvested cannot inure to the social identities of colleagues as serious, productive scholars making valuable contributions to their specialties. Hence, Joe's allegation that I'd dismissed my colleagues as imbeciles. This was a misinterpretation, as my submersion in the tacit dimension was a confession of ignorance, not intellectual preening. But those discounting that dimension had to register this brand of humility as pretense and affectation—the message repeatedly conveyed to me from every quarter during the first half of 2009. Ryan Calo, a fellow who hadn't attended my pillorying by the others, drew the point explicitly when we met up a few weeks later to kick around the project, gauging that while he was personally fascinated, I risked being mistaken for a charlatan.

Ryan's insight would be confirmed a few weeks later when I met with Josh Cohen, my other Moral Luck instructor. Josh had recently team-taught a seminar on the religion clauses with Kathleen Sullivan, a renowned First Amendment maven and the law school's former dean. Since we now occupied adjacent offices, I suggested we set a time to discuss our shared interest, as he, too, was now dabbling in the Establishment Clause. We exchanged drafts and planned to get together after reviewing them.

Resplendent with proper deference and pleasant demeanor, Josh was a well-adjusted member of the academy. Just like Barbara, he was all that I was not. As a graduate student at Harvard, he had shrewdly placed himself under the wings of John Rawls, from there emerging as one of the nation's preeminent theorists of liberalism. His devotion to carrying on his august mentor's legacy was confirmed by the draft he was now penning, which defended Justice Sandra Day O'Connor's "endorsement test" as the constitutional derivation of Rawls's concept of public reason. Public reason was Rawls's answer to the perennial dilemma of political deliberation:

> Those who insist, when fundamental political questions are at stake, on what they take as true but others do not, seem to others simply to insist on their own beliefs when they have the political power to do so. Of course, those who insist on their beliefs also insist that their beliefs alone are true: they impose their beliefs because, they say, their beliefs are true and not because they are their beliefs. But this is a claim that all equally could make; it is also a claim that cannot be made good by anyone to citizens generally.[9]

Our ideological divisions may seem intractable, but we can palliate them by striving to be reasonable rather than right, and that means restricting the terms of political debate to premises that can resonate across a society's entire spectrum of reasonable conceptions of the good. Thus, to regulate alcohol because its consumption offends God is to violate public reason. This rationale is inaccessible not only to atheists but also to any religious believers who think differently. Those making such appeals are thuggishly imposing their wills on others in a rejection of genuine democratic deliberation, even if they go through the motions of such. In contrast, regulating alcohol out of public health concerns complies with public reason. Whatever our theological leanings or lack thereof, drunk driving and liver disease are indisputably bad things. People may not see eye to eye on the appropriate interventions. But such disagreements proceed within an "overlapping consensus" of beliefs and values shared by all reasonable conceptions of the good.

What did this have to do with Justice O'Connor's endorsement test, the other prong of Josh's analysis? This test provides that a state action violates the Establishment Clause when it designates certain groups as "outsiders, not full members of the political community."[10] Thus a publicly sponsored nativity scene will usually violate the Establishment Clause because its message marginalizes those refusing Jesus Christ as their savior. In contrast, a Santa's sleigh will pass constitutional muster because it acknowledges Christmas only in its secular aspect, excluding none from the political community. A Ten Commandments monument standing in grand isolation constitutes an unconstitutional endorsement of monotheism, but one displayed alongside tributes to Plato and Confucius creates no such religious entanglements, as it would then be promoting the ecumenical values of law, wisdom, and truth-seeking. Josh was arguing that the endorsement test instantiates public reason because nonexclusion and the overlapping consensus are different facets of the same principle. These ideas were nothing new, but their affinities had yet to be canvassed, and this was where Josh was now hanging his hat.

As a committed liberal, Josh proved to be a useful sounding board for my sundry musings when we eventually met. We concurred that while religious conservatives and secular liberals hold each other in mutual suspicion, only the former feel genuinely denigrated and bullied by the other side. Liberals may believe themselves oppressed by conservatives as women, gays, racial minorities, union members, creative artists, or just freedom-loving Americans. But they don't ordinarily feel oppressed *as liberals*, in the way conservatives feel oppressed *as conservatives*. This asymmetry lay at the heart of my research agenda, and Josh had now validated it. The cool-headed, mild-mannered Josh exemplified everything anathema to the conservative culture warrior, so his reactions were noteworthy. And his vexation with me and my project was betrayed when he sized up my announced goal—making sense of why religious conservatives and secular liberals talk past one another—by advising that understanding why people do this is "what philosophy is," thereby insinuating that I didn't know what philosophy is, which I felt was a pretty low bar to miss. The insinuation persisted into his closing admonition that I "work for it," which was to imply that I hadn't been doing so and was rather looking to get something for nothing.

Just as Barbara had forgotten about my PhD, so Josh was now forgetting that I knew what philosophy is. This low opinion of me was something new. After all, I had scooped up a 4.1 in his own philosophy class, where he had joined Barbara in lauding my presentation, calling it "a wonderful presentation of a very hard piece." He had also solicited my feedback on his own work in progress, which likewise suggested he had once thought more highly of me. There may be a philosophically interesting sense in which no one really knows what philosophy is, in which case Josh was technically justified in alluding to my ignorance. But then I was being singled out for what is our universal predicament, which I felt was discriminatory. To be fair, Josh could not but grow suspicious upon encountering my ever-deepening inarticulacy. His was just another in the chorus of skeptical voices I'd been hearing for months from fellows and faculty alike, starting with Joe and Barbara back in December. I was in fact "working for it." But the *it* at this juncture consisted of hundreds upon hundreds of pages of disjointed notes, a byzantine mental labyrinth that only proliferated with every attempt at containment. As a living rebuke to the prevailing ideology, my immersion in the tacit dimension could only draw ire and suspicion.

This latest tangle with the powers that be once more illustrated how the virtue of clarity may be weaponized to serve the intellectual status quo. Josh's thesis was clear because nonexclusion is uncontroversial on its face. I, on the other hand, was trying to wrap my mind around why conservative evangelicals won't be moved by carefully honed arguments like Josh's and feel marginalized in ways secular liberals are unprepared to credit as lucid or even sincere. Stupidity, sectarianism, and self-pity were all clear explanations for this disdain of liberal eloquence, but they were also shallow ones. Pursuing this topic had to come at the expense of clarity, leaving me haplessly exposed to Josh's innuendo. Having arrogated the power to define the rhetorical rules of serious or responsible intellectual discourse, the elites can discredit dissent before it can come to its own and become articulate, leaving it stillborn and dumb. This new friction with Josh was but another instance of the structural liberalism under which I labored, one more battering by the subtle microaggressions through which the boundaries of the Matrix were being policed at Stanford.

A Disembodied Fellowship

In the meantime my credibility with Joe and Barbara was steadily dwindling. I imposed enough order on my stack of notes to cobble together an untidy twenty-one-page essay by the end of April. Hoping to reestablish a rapport, I emailed it to them and explained:

> Hi Joe and Barbara,
>
> I was hoping you guys might have some time over the next several weeks to read what will be my job talk paper. It concerns the Establishment Clause and is 21 pages so far. I think I figured out how to translate philosophy into doctrine, though I have yet to integrate a lot of case law and scholarship. What I have so far just sets up the agenda. I'm attaching the draft, though we could go over it when the year is out if that's more convenient.
>
> Best,
>
> Rony

They had always replied to my emails dutifully. But day after day no response came. A normal postgraduate fellow might have been profoundly distraught by this silence, but, absorbed as I was in my mental labyrinth, I remained nonplussed, at least consciously. The matter was out of my hands. There was no starting afresh in another direction at this late hour, in the few months that remained before the start of the hiring season in early August. I had staked my future to this paper, and it was either do or die. With the much-needed breakthrough still unattained, I didn't really have all that much to impart, much as the situation had been in December. So the cold shoulder was tolerable. I had reached out to them but couldn't compel reciprocity, so I shrugged it off and plowed on.

Then I ran into the two about two weeks later, in mid-May at the weekly faculty luncheon, which had been temporarily relocated to a lecture room after a recent fire in the faculty lounge. Exuding surliness, Joe walked right on past me without acknowledgment. His bodily hexis said it all. Barbara, on the other hand, took a seat beside me. Jockeying to set the tone of the conversation, I straightaway asked whether she'd received the draft I'd dispatched two weeks earlier. Indeed, she had. Sensing her anxiety here, I reiterated that I had a lot more material to integrate into what she'd seen, as noted in the email. With my question having highlighted her failure to reply to that email, these reassurances left her rhetorically ill-positioned to then underscore my own more all-encompassing derelictions. Still, her unease remained evident, further fueling my own indeterminate apprehensiveness.

It could not have been otherwise. It had been five months since our December 2008 meeting and more than eight since the fellowship began, and all I had to show for it was an anemic twenty-one pages of disjointed draft. That stood in stark contrast with my 110-page Legal Theory term paper, written in less time amid a full course load. True enough, I had to start afresh after taking up Joe's suggestion about law and religion. But with all the time in the world to produce, my progress seemed glacial. So Barbara's worries couldn't have been much assuaged by promises she had heard before. Joe's passive-aggressiveness was now undisguised, which meant it was festering not far beneath the surface in Barbara.

This state of affairs was a logical outgrowth of my willingness to exploit the ambiguity of my role and station. I wasn't my advisers' equal statuswise. They were tenured Stanford professors, bona fide elites, whereas I was only an elite in the making. Still, I was no mere student or acolyte, given the esteem in which they held my writing. Given this balance of power, they could opine, suggest, urge, and entreat but not order. They had reckoned their gentle nudging sufficient to gain my compliance—as it would have been with a less wayward fellow—and I had repeatedly frustrated that ostensibly reasonable expectation. My amorphous status, moreover, frustrated the expression of this frustration, because my advisers couldn't point to any clear-cut rules that I'd unambiguously flouted. This second-order frustration only compounded the first-order one, which then metastasized into passive-aggressive pique as they felt increasingly put-upon. I picked up on all this at some primal level but employed a host of defense mechanisms to hold this awareness at bay, in the periphery of my consciousness where it wouldn't affect my focus.

The rest of the summer was a race against the clock. With the fellows group disbanded for the recess, I had even less reason to make the drive down to Palo Alto and stayed holed up in my San Francisco crib, always on the cusp of the mythologized breakthrough lying just around the corner. The anxiety grew deeper. But having been repressed, it manifested itself only symbolically and allegorically. I found myself recurrently haunted by the thought that I would be arrested on some felony by overzealous law enforcement, only to be swiftly exonerated of what would be revealed as preposterous allegations. As with the previous summer's premonitions that I'd be pursuing my research agenda full time that fall, I dismissed the notion as peculiar and outlandish even as I remained haunted by it.

I still made it down to the law school for a few Wednesday luncheons, which were more sparsely attended in the summer. In June I had my last encounter with Barbara there before the conflagration that was soon to erupt. As in May, she took a seat beside me. Once again I angled to take control of the conversation and head off any troublesome scrutiny, right away calling her attention to the thesis of my job-talk paper, that religious conservatives are being discriminated against on the basis of their premodern consciousness. By steering the conversation toward the paper's content, I circumvented the issue of its status, of how far along it really was a mere two months before the dawn of the hiring season. Barbara responded with a curt, almost brusque, "Good," suggesting that I was as much the target of her hostile impatience as these retrograde conservatives. Trying to assuage her worries, I made known that I was crafting my Stanford Law profile (which really should have been online earlier in the year) in preparation for the hiring season. Could I send her and Joe a draft for feedback? She consented with what seemed like a modicum of enthusiasm. The threat was ever so momentarily contained.

Soon thereafter, another fellow from across the table introduced herself and asked under whom I was working. I responded that I worked under no one because mine was a "disembodied fellowship," as that was indeed what it had become. Barbara voiced no objection, but the turn of phrase encapsulated the sum of her fears. This had never been my goal. From the outset I had been striving to attain the requisite breakthrough, emerge from my cloistered solipsism, and then reintegrate into the law school on a new footing. Joe and Barbara were never far from mind, as I was struggling to vindicate the faith they'd placed in me and contribute to the glory of Stanford. But by imperceptible increments, the prospect of reintegration had steadily receded ever further into the horizon until it simply vanished from view. Hours turned into days, days into weeks, weeks into months, and those months into nearly a year now. And I was still inside my own head. Joe had been alert to this tendency from the outset but gambled that it could be contained and had lost.

My extreme aloofness was further confirmed after Barbara overheard me introduce myself to the other fellow and realized that she'd been mispronouncing my name. She had been pronouncing Rony with a long *o*, as in Tony, when it was properly pronounced with a short one, as in Johnny. The mistake was common and understandable, I assured her, since the short *o* pronunciation is normally accompanied by a second *n* in the spelling—as in Ronny or Ronnie. The long pronunciation, I elaborated, was proper in the lands of my conception and birth, Israel and France, respectively, but I had adopted the short one to anglicize myself and jump into the melting pot after immigrating to the United States as a child. Hence the discrepancy between spelling and pronunciation, which Barbara hadn't detected till now. While trivial this oversight crystalized the profound rift that silently frayed our relationship, a rift that, having emerged gradually and imperceptibly, could no longer be acknowledged without embarrassment.

This dysfunctionality reared its head anew when Joe and Barbara failed to respond to the law school profile I later emailed them pursuant to the foregoing conversation. The profile listed my credentials, work history, and publications, and announced my interest in "applying continental philosophy to the analysis of constitutional doctrine" along with my focus on "conservative victimology in law and culture." The profile summarized my two ongoing book projects. The first, *Conservative Claims of Cultural Oppression*, examined conservatism's penchant for "incorporating the relativistic intellectual temper of the left into its critiques of the left." The second project, I went on, argued that religious neutrality is a social fiction and that "the deep structure of Establishment Clause doctrine is ultimately *theological*, because secular modernity arises out of religious dispositions that become concealed but do not disappear." These two projects would eventually coalesce into one and then provide the intellectual foundations for this memoir. But little of this existed in June 2009. So the most salient feature of the proposed profile must have been the profound disjunction between my self-presentation and the year's meager output. Yet I had no choice but to soldier on in search of the longed-for breakthrough, when my efforts would begin paying some much-deserved dividends. One might call into question the entire train of judgments that had brought me to my Sisyphean labors. But that was neither here nor there, because I had long ago passed all the exit ramps.

The Epiphany

The situation began to shift rapidly in late July and early August, however, just as the faculty recruiting season was taking off. I began to glimpse what I'd been reaching for half-blindly all along. My thinking on religious neutrality was finally gelling as my formulations reached a new maturity. I didn't yet have a viable job-talk paper. But I found myself enveloped by a new hopefulness, as my previous self-doubt rapidly dissipated, supplanted by a new alacrity. Clearly, I was in the zone.

Such was the great redemption for which I'd been pining. Less expected, however, was the existential transfiguration that accompanied the theoretical advances. The future remained salient inasmuch as the law-teaching market remained the ostensible raison d'être of the fellowship. But at another level time stood still. The present became infused with a new self-sufficiency, as my consciousness grew increasingly attuned to the simple being of things, their bare "thatness" as it were. This Zen-like attunement was accompanied by a pronounced surge of physical energy. I'd always kept fit, but this improved markedly in the span of a few weeks, as I discovered I could stay awake for twenty-four hours or longer before recuperating on a few hours of sleep. My requirements varied from day to day, but the overall change was pronounced, and this was on a much-reduced diet, sometimes fewer than a thousand daily calories. As my optometrist would later confirm, my eyesight had also improved, and my back pains disappeared entirely. I usually channeled this new exuberance into my research, but I was sometimes propelled to traipse energetically through Golden Gate Park for several hours on end. All this was initially attended by unusual levels of perspiration, especially while I was typing the project into existence, but that soon enough subsided.

This new condition was rather akin to a low-intensity LSD trip, involving as it did the loosening of my social conditioning and disruption of the corresponding social reality. Maybe this had something to do with the prodigious quantities of acid I'd absorbed years earlier as an intrepid undergraduate. Regardless, I felt I had retrogressed to a state of nature unencumbered by the strictures and inhibitions of the civilized order. Nietzsche writes:

> I regard the bad conscience as the serious illness that man was bound to contract under the stress of the most fundamental change he ever experienced—that change which occurred when he found himself finally enclosed within the walls of society and of peace. The situation that faced sea animals when they were compelled to become land animals or perish was the same as that which faced these semi-animals, well adapted to the wilderness, to war, to prowling, to adventure: suddenly all their instincts were disvalued and "suspended." From now on they had to walk on their feet and "bear themselves" whereas hitherto they had been borne by the water: a dreadful heaviness lay upon them. They felt unable to cope with the simplest undertakings; in this new world they no longer possessed their former guides, their regulating, unconscious and infallible drives: they were reduced to thinking, inferring, reckoning, co-ordinating cause and effect, these unfortunate creatures: they were reduced to their "consciousness," their weakest and most fallible organ! I believe there has never been such a feeling of misery on earth, such a leaden discomfort.[11]

By surrendering to unconscious drives heretofore suppressed by the surrounding order, I was now overcoming precisely these disabilities, with the "leaden discomfort" by which I'd been unwittingly burdened supplanted by a sure-footed animal faith. Casting off the deformations of civilized life, I had awoken as Nietzsche's semi-animal returned to the wilderness, where I would be guided by forces that transcended the shallow reach of the conscious mind. The last had been dislodged from the helm of my identity, revealing itself as a mask and social adaptation behind which a higher, more primeval, intelligence machinated. I was becoming desocialized, liberated from the culture that had been obstructing this hidden telos. I could still hew to that culture's norms and conventions, but their social and historical contingency became increasingly salient to me, revealed as part and parcel of an alien ethos with which I had ceased to identify. Now extruded from my primal reflexes, that ethos could no longer guarantee the automatic, quasi-instinctual acquiescence appropriate to properly socialized human agents.

All this was a bolt from the blue. But I wasn't so shocked or disoriented upon reflection, because this evolution was weirdly intelligible as the logical consummation of my research agenda. These physiological changes were fully consistent with the central thrust of *Conservative Claims of Cultural Oppression*: my vitality had increased so in such short order because I had transcended the secularized asceticism of the liberal culture and the academic ethos it supports.

I had posited that contemporary liberalism represents the apex of the disciplinary impulses that shaped modernity. Those impulses originate not in Enlightenment pure and simple but in the secularization of religious asceticism and democratization of courtly sociability, medieval outgrowths that gradually mutated into the modern disciplinary society, discarding their original legitimations as they assumed a modern secular sheen. These origins can go undetected by that order's vanguard, the liberal elites, because the disciplines and repressions of liberalism—of which the ideologies of academia are one instance—have been culturally sanctified as a state of heightened self-possession, self-control, and self-transparency, the liberation of essential human faculties from the teleological illusions and moralistic strictures of a benighted premodern past. Against this interpretation, conservative claims of cultural oppression manifest a visceral conviction that liberalism's self-congratulatory Enlightenment narrative conceals a murkier story. What the elites tout as our newly won autonomy and self-possession are, in fact, the internalized repressions of what Norbert Elias calls the civilizing process, the progressive historical suppression of our embodied, animal nature by the new social disciplines of the modern order.[12] Conservative culture warriors grasp this intuitively, and they are resisting precisely those disciplines in claiming cultural oppression. Hence their refusal to accept liberal enlightenment—and liberals themselves—at face value.

These were the thoughts that had all along animated my research agenda, which aimed to deflate liberalism's putative universalism by properly theorizing conservatives' raw sense that liberalism is a parochial ethos that reifies a historically constructed way of being as timeless human nature. It was now apparent that in pursuing this thesis I had unwittingly rewired my own way of being. I had known early on that a merely academic treatment of conservative claims of cultural oppression wouldn't do, because I would have to extricate myself from the liberal culture to truly understand them. And this epiphany of August 2009 was now effecting that exit by undoing my own socialization into the modern order and civilizational identity.

Joe and Barbara had pleaded with me to make my abstract musings concrete. And that was now happening, it seemed. Wherever I turned, concepts that had engrossed me throughout the year began to color my world. What had started as a mere thesis or, even less, a hodgepodge of hazy intuitions masquerading as a thesis, had now filtered into my lebenswelt. My argument had been that liberalism's concealed repressiveness can pass under the radar because liberalism is a hero-system disguised as the transcendence of all hero-systems, and I was now casting off these blinders. What had once been ideas on paper now operated in all three dimensions, with the social world of my San Francisco taking on a new sheen. Where others beheld a mecca of liberty and enlightenment, I saw the disciplinary impulses of the liberal culture that were lying concealed beneath all the self-congratulatory Enlightenment narratives. By identifying the historical forces that have molded our present, I transcended that present, positioning myself to discern a heretofore invisible layer of human meaning that I had always intuited but could only now begin to articulate. The veil of illusion had been lifted. The Matrix had been exited. I was often tripping when writing my senior thesis on Heidegger, which earned high honors, so I was never one to discount the fecundity of altered states.

These reflections yielded fresh insight into the path of the fellowship to date. Marred as it was by recurring delays, false starts, and detours, my research had been downright shambolic by conventional metrics of academic productivity. After a year I had hundreds upon hundreds of pages of scattered intuitions that had yet to be subsumed within any clear theses and arguments. But I could see in retrospect that this profligacy had been necessary to exit the Matrix and enter the consciousness whence conservative claims of cultural oppression issue. My research strategy was rudderless and slipshod when judged according to what the cognitive scientist George Lakoff calls the "Old Enlightenment" paradigm of reason as conscious, articulate, logical, linear, and disembodied.[13] But it now registered that my fly-by-the-seat-of-my-pants ethos had been guided by an ineffable attunement to the specific sequence of neural pathways that would have to be carved out and traversed in order to flip the switch and check out of the ambient culture. That sequence didn't make obvious sense when translated into linear argument, which was why I had voluminous notes but only twenty-one pages of actual draft. Yet it was by dint of those notes that I attained this epiphany, when a truth that had been steadily percolating throughout the year revealed itself holistically.

Lakoff observes that many who acknowledge the mind's nature as an embodied physiological organ when speaking abstractly may struggle to draw out that embodiment's concrete moral and political implications:

> It should come as no surprise then that the ideas that our embodied brains come up with depend in large measure on the peculiarities of human anatomy in general and on the way we, as human beings, function on our planet and with each other. This is not surprising when discussed in vague abstractions, but it is remarkable in detail: even our ideas of morality and politics are embodied in this rich way—those ideas are created and carried out not merely by the neural anatomy and connectivity of our brains, but also by the ways we function bodily in the physical and social world.[14]

This embodiment explains how my engagement with conservative claims of cultural oppression could have gone hand in hand with the new awakening I've described. Those claims are most profoundly understood as an inarticulate, unconscious, and ultimately physiological protest against the secularized asceticism of the modern disciplinary society. That asceticism reaches its apex in the "expressive discipline" of the liberal, New Class culture, whose mores and pieties mold how we "function bodily in the physical and social world" in ways many find oppressive. In pursuing this intuition I had overcome the expressive discipline in myself and thereby liberated some portion of Nietzsche's semi-animal man from the New Class strictures by which I, too, had been oppressed. That was the hitherto hidden meaning of my submersion in the tacit dimension, which had now ripened into this epiphany.

For a year I had played the prophet, absconding from ordered society to wander in a mental wilderness of my own making, and that trek had now been redeemed by this new dispensation of meaning. All this was thanks to Joe. His law-and-religion suggestion had set me on my road to Damascus by forcing me to grapple with the historical forces against which religious conservatives' sense of besiegement makes sense, allowing me to recognize modern secularism as part and parcel of a disciplinary regime hostile to human nature's ancestral default settings. Conservative claims of cultural oppression weren't mere posturing and histrionics but flawed articulations of this truth, in whose light I now walked. I wasn't privy to the full implications of these realizations. But it was clear that, in pursuing the truth of those claims, I had also been pursuing the truth of myself, wrestling to liberate something that had been suppressed by the dominant order but yearned to live. With my mind now decolonized, I was gripped by a powerful yet ill-understood sense of mission. I had always counted myself as among modernity's discontents, and my system was now in full-on rebellion in a bid to fully actualize my formerly latent neurodivergence.

Yet this Promethean fervor was eerily qualified by an emerging sense of peril lurking on the periphery of consciousness. My earlier premonitions about being arrested for some felony and then swiftly exonerated had receded from my mind, replaced by a vague sense that I would be set upon by the forces of liberalism and that they would be congregating at Stanford. I didn't know what that concretely portended, but this state of play followed logically from the nature of my research agenda. If I now stood in an adversarial relationship to the elite culture and liberal hero-system, then their devotees would perforce stand in the same relationship to me. And who could these be but the liberal elites who had strangely volunteered to subsidize a research agenda that had always had them in its crosshairs?

CHAPTER 3

A Conspiracy Is Born

August–September 2009

What's the Story?

Danger began to materialize when I was recalled to the world of men on August 27, 2009, after I logged in to my email for the first time in several days and found a three-day-old message from Larry Kramer with "what's the story?" in the subject line:

> Hi Rony:
>
> I got an email from Amy Applebaum saying that you have not sent your resume to be listed in the book we send to all schools. Is that because you are not, in fact, going on the market this year? Either way, you should reply to Amy so she knows your status. What's the story?
>
> Best,
>
> Larry

The story was precisely as I have told it here; I was flying high thanks to the aforedescribed epiphany. But that wasn't the story that interested Larry, and the more mundane matters to which he had just drawn my attention were now catching up to me. I would soon learn just how much I had sacrificed on the altar of my higher calling.

Preliminary interviews for law school faculty positions were to take place in early November at the annual recruitment conference of the Association of American Law Schools (AALS) in Washington, D.C. Would-be law professors could apply for these jobs in three ways: the résumé book referenced by Larry that showcased the law school's graduates and fellows to hiring committees; direct mailings for openings advertised in AALS bulletins, to be published four times during the hiring season; and the AALS's online databank of résumés, which included a one-page résumé distributed to every law school and a full-length CV that committees could then download if suitably intrigued by the short résumé.

I was now reminded that I had neglected nearly all of this in my rapturous abandon. I had entirely overlooked the direct mailings and the Stanford résumé book, of whose existence I was unaware until apprised by Larry. An email had surely gone out. But my attention to emails had become fleeting and sporadic in the wake of recent events. I did at least submit the AALS short résumé in time for the first distribution on August 5, but I had then neglected to produce and upload a full-length CV for interested parties to download and peruse. All this radically understates my delinquency. While the recruiting officially began on August 5 with the first distribution of the short résumés, the informal but equally vital networking component of the process had been in play much earlier. Hence Barbara's concern in December that my job-talk paper wouldn't be ready for early circulation. Her anxiety on this front had proved justified. Even had everything else been timely, that my job-talk paper was only now truly taking shape was enough to kneecap my job search.

I responded to Larry and apologized for my dereliction, pleading that I was indeed on the market and was unaware of the Stanford résumé book. I would get in touch with Amy Applebaum (who would inform me it had already gone out). Updating him on the state of my research, I suggested I could use his feedback at some point. He replied that while he was "happy to look at stuff," he was "not sure how useful I'll be" and recommended that I consult Josh Cohen and Michael McConnell (arguably the American doyen of law and religion, who would be joining the faculty shortly). I should, he directed, get a full package out to schools, including a CV and writing sample, and speak to Barbara and Dick Craswell (the law school's placement adviser that year) about good target schools for me.

And so I emailed Dick, Barbara, and Joe the next day, Friday, August 28, writing:

> Hi Dick, Barbara, and Joe,
>
> I am getting my materials together to send out to target schools and was hoping I could meet with you guys, perhaps next week or the following week, to discuss strategy and so forth. I'll have my CV ready in a few days and will send it to you then.
>
> But the basic deal is that I've got two books in the works, *Conservative Claims of Cultural Oppression*, which takes off from the original paper, and *The Impossibility of the Establishment Clause*, which focuses on religion specifically. Both are over halfway done, though the latter is at a much more advanced stage: I basically have all the ideas written down and only need to stitch it all together and fill in a few holes. I should have a decent initial version complete in about 2 months, which is what I will be presenting at job talks (without the expectation that it will have been read, of course!).
>
> Anyway, I'll send more info with my resume. Let me know about availability to meet. Thanks.
>
> Rony

As usual, this latest update was a complex amalgam of truth and falsehood. My progress on these projects had been considerable in that I had voluminous notes awaiting the clearer articulation that my exit from the liberal culture now enabled. That I could get by on a few hours of sleep most nights meant I could achieve much in short order. On the other hand, the naive observer just glancing at my stack of notes wouldn't necessarily appreciate this milestone, whose nature remained ineffable.

Also as usual, neither Joe nor Barbara replied. But Dick, with whom I was only passingly acquainted in his capacity as faculty adviser to the fellows group, did so. He was happy to meet, but the priority, he stressed, was to send off my materials to target schools posthaste. I also needed to get a full-length résumé uploaded to the AALS database. The first distribution of short résumés had gone out three weeks earlier, and many schools were already deciding whom to interview. The sooner my materials fell in their laps, the better. My religious neutrality paper wasn't yet presentable, so we agreed I would instead submit my article on Strawson's *Freedom and Resentment*, a few chapters from my book, and a favorable review thereof in *The Review of Metaphysics*. I could distribute the religious neutrality paper later to whoever was keen on reading it. I also needed to submit a description of my research interests. Dick counseled: "The main question the schools will be interested in is, 'What is this guy's future research going to look like?' so what you send them should be designed to shed light on that question."

The next few days were a whirlwind of work. Dick had recommended that the research descriptions be two to four pages. But, enthralled by the philosophical vision now gripping me, I seized on the occasion as an opportunity to programmatically articulate its nature. Taking up everything I'd written over the years in various Stanford classes and before, I reimagined these projects in light of my recent exit from the ambient culture, in the process generating a seventeen-page CV, fourteen pages of which consisted of elaborate synopses of two publications, two book projects, and five article projects. I could now recognize the demiurge driving me all these years, a primordial will to expose the elites that had galvanized not only my Legal Theory term paper but also much that predated it.

I wrapped this up by Wednesday, September 2, and emailed the CV to my advisers. Everything was now in order, I advised, as the materials were ready for distribution. Should we now meet? Once again it was crickets from Joe. This was my fourth unanswered email to him in recent months. But Barbara, to my surprise and relief, finally decided to join the mix, responding:

> Hi Rony— I'm on leave for the year, up at the Center for Advanced Studies. I'll take a look at the material, and we should try to get together soon, as you are starting the process somewhat late and will have to push to get yourself on everyone's radar screen. If you have not already, you should definitely get in touch with Dick Craswell, who is chairing the teaching placement committee this year in my absence. Dick is key, as schools will be calling him to get his view on whom they should talk to. Best, Barbara

I was fully cognizant of my lateness. But that would turn out to be only the most prosaic of my problems in the weeks and months to come. Barbara's abrupt decision to respond illustrated the schizophrenic character of our relationship as it had by then evolved. The pique stoked by my research habits didn't suddenly disappear. But since her true sentiments had never been formally aired but only vented passive-aggressively through sullen looks and unanswered emails, she now had no choice but to concede something to the official pretense that our relations were something other than dysfunctional. She had to reply at this stage because the faculty recruitment process was the entire raison d'être of the fellowship (or so it appeared at the time), so she no longer enjoyed the luxury of giving me the cold shoulder.

As was my wont I responded with exaggerated optimism about impending progress. Acknowledging my late arrival on the scene, I explained that "everything finally came together only in the latter half of this summer." This was perfectly true from where I sat, as the epiphany had now positioned me to deliver the goods my advisers had long awaited. This was nothing I could have expected them to appreciate, though. I had only recently extricated myself from the elite culture and so was less than fully cognizant of the distance now separating me from my milieu, which would soon widen to previously unimaginable proportions.

Barbara hadn't yet reviewed my materials when she replied. But Larry apparently had. Later that day I received an email from him directing that I "be sure to talk to Dick Craswell about this," giving me a queasy feeling that perhaps all was not well, despite my recent scramble to jump-start my candidacy. So I emailed Dick and relayed Larry's directive, asking him to have a look at the CV before I distributed it. Dick responded that "Larry is right," suggesting they'd perhaps been in touch. The various research summaries were too long, he explained. Readers needed to take in my research agenda at a glance. My references were also a problem, as they were listed at the bottom of the lengthy résumé, requiring readers to plod through too much before reaching them. I had a "rich and complex intellectual agenda," he acknowledged, but appointments committees were full of busy people sifting through hundreds of CVs, so it had to be made more digestible. I should drastically shorten the summaries and discard those of research not related to law.

This was all sensible. Even so, those summaries were my programmatic vision for the future, articulating the anticipated apotheosis of my work to date, which I felt compelled to announce. So I undertook to split the difference by tailoring the CV to Dick's specifications (short summaries) while incorporating the original longer summaries into a separate document, the "Overview of Publications and Works in Progress," which prospective interviewers could read if interested and ignore if not. These two documents—which I initially distributed to my advisers as a single document—are in appendix 1 as exhibits A and B.

I emailed these to Dick and Barbara the next day, Thursday, September 3, advising of the revisions. Barbara didn't respond right away, but Dick replied the next day with his stamp of approval: "This looks MUCH better. Good job." That was welcome relief, and I spent the rest of that Friday mailing off applications for positions advertised in the AALS bulletin. My car had been towed, as I'd parked in an off-limits space after my own was illicitly occupied, so everything was rushed that day, with several hours spent retrieving the vehicle. I wrapped everything up just in time to head off with a band of friends to Sonoma County, where we had rented some seaside cabins for a long weekend of Labor Day merriment.

The Knockout Email

It would be my last carefree weekend in memory, as the forces of liberalism and academia would commence their assault the following week. On Tuesday, September 8, I emailed Dick a list of seventeen schools to which I'd applied and suggested that we at last meet to hash things out in greater depth. Dick had previously replied to my emails speedily, but no response came that day. Later that evening I logged in to my email again to notice a new, deeply unsettling, message from Barbara:

> Hi Rony—I read over the materials. I don't know where you are in the process—if you have sent your materials out already—but if changes are still timely, here are my thoughts, for what they're worth. I'm copying Dick and Joe, in case they disagree with any of this.
>
> On the CV: I corrected a number of typos on the attached copy, and suggested one deletion. Otherwise, the main change I'd suggest concerns presentation of WIPs [works in progress]. First, I'd indicate which (if any) are in draft form that is available for circulation. If you have submitted any for publication, I would indicate that as well.

Secondly, I'd strongly urge an introductory paragraph that locates your general intellectual interests for committees—both as to subject areas and intellectual approach. There are obviously a lot of commonalities among these projects, and it would be a good idea to spell them out, briefly.

On the Overview of scholarship: I'd suggest making the same changes as on the description of scholarship on the CV—Start with an intro parag that gives an overview of your scholarly interests and work to date. Here would be a good place to state, for example, that while the published book was written before law school, its intellectual framework has informed much of the law-related writing you are doing now (explaining how). Then indicate the status of each of the works in progress (in draft; submitted for publication; contemplated future work, etc.).

Those are relatively easy changes. I have a more general concern that will be harder to address. I worry that the description of scholarly projects will make you very appealing to a handful of schools that have a critical mass of people doing critical theory/cultural critique of law, but knock you out of contention everywhere else. The concern is that your interests will sound too tangential to law, and your approach too indebted to the sort of continental, critical theory that many, many law faculty are allergic to, for a variety of reasons. I think there are ways to mitigate these dangers without misrepresenting who you are or trying to change yourself into a different person.

First, be more explicit about the legal implications of various projects. You did this for the 1st A piece [first article], but in a flatfooted way that, to my ear, trivializes your analysis and vastly understates the difficulty of fashioning a legal "remedy" for the disease you diagnose. Second, shorten your descriptions of the projects significantly, and avoid all critical jargon. Your descriptions are written for people who already understand and are sold on the kind of work you are doing, and are ready to luxuriate in it; you need to write them for people who are clueless or deeply skeptical about the approach you are taking and short on time.

> Give me a call if you want to talk about any of this. My number at the Center is [number redacted].
>
> Best, Barbara

Barbara had warned early on that "high theory is risky," so her worry that "many, many" readers would blanch at the tone and tenor of my research agenda was perhaps unsurprising. Even so, she had volunteered to subsidize that high theory with the fellowship, knowing full well where my interests lay. That this contradiction hadn't been resolved more than a year later was merely another testament to the yawning yet undeclared chasm that had stealthily crept between us.

I began to suspect that there was more afoot here than Barbara was letting on. She urged that I shorten my descriptions for people who were "short on time." But I had already done so in response to Dick's feedback. The CV summaries were of reasonable length, and no one uninterested in reading any further was compelled to plod through the longer Overview, which she did not advise me to discard. Taken in itself, this logical lapse was trivial, but it reinforced my intuitive sense that Barbara was throwing in the kitchen sink to buttress the foregone conclusion that my candidacy was a train wreck. She introduced her message with "I don't know where you are in the process," but I had informed her the previous week that everything was ready to be mailed off. This, too, was of no great moment when taken in isolation, but I detected a certain feigned ignorance and detachment, reinforcing my intuitive sense that undisclosed considerations were at play.

This suspicion was further fortified by her having copied Dick and Joe, as though to suggest that this was the first they were hearing of all this. Since she and Joe lived under the same roof, it beggared belief that they hadn't already discussed these matters ahead of this email. Barbara had seen fit to apprise Joe of my tour de force performance in Moral Luck, and the career disaster now looming seemed at least as consequential. Surely it was serious enough for them to have a conversation about it, rather than hold it at arm's length with a parenthetical cc, especially when she saw Joe daily. It wasn't unduly narcissistic of me to imagine that this crisis, and hence the fate of the law school's $120,000 investment in me, would warrant such attention. Dick did not live with Barbara, of course, so it was a tad more plausible that this was the first he was learning of her misgivings. Still, it was unlikely. Professors are a loquacious bunch, and two professors so intimately involved in the academic fortunes of the law school's graduates and fellows could be expected to communicate on such matters more directly. Barbara was feigning a certain independence from Dick and Joe in order to obfuscate what was probably a collaborative consensus.

So what was going on here? Barbara was positioning herself as on my side, offering ostensibly well-intentioned constructive criticism in order to advance our mutual interest in the timely progression of my academic career. But "the truth of euphemism," Bourdieu notes, "is revealed in the use made of it by professorial rhetoric any time that an unfavorable judgment has to be delivered within the limits of academic etiquette and/or prudence."[1] And here was that professorial rhetoric in all its subtlety and circumspection—as was to be expected of Barbara, whose prognosis was just as disingenuous as it was accurate. It was accurate inasmuch as it correctly gauged how the market would respond to my résumé. It was disingenuous, however, inasmuch as Barbara held herself out as merely tendering a prognosis, when what she was passing off as just educated guesses about others' hostile reactions also constituted her own reaction, which was identical to those from which she was distancing herself rhetorically.

Hence, her word choices and insinuations—the likelihood that I'd be "knocked out of contention," the "flatfooted" character of my argument, the "allergic" reactions the Overview would elicit, the importunity of asking busy people to "luxuriate" in it. These microaggressions gave the lie to the official persona Barbara had donned. Her talk of my being knocked out of contention carried echoes of my summer associate experience two years earlier, and I began to feel some vague affinity between that episode in my life and the one now under way. The criticisms leveled during my final performance review at the firm contained some grains of truth while concealing what was a larger, more complicated, story. Something like that was being reprised here in this latest performance review.

Indeed, it seemed that our relations were now being legalized to an extent. Barbara had set out to establish an email record to document the issuance of an adverse professional judgment. That record was, moreover, designed to elicit peer assent by default, as Joe and Dick would be signaling that they did not "disagree with any of this" through an ambiguous silence, without having to affirmatively defend that position or even engage with me. Barbara had deftly engineered semantic conditions under which Joe and Dick could condemn me in unison through mere inaction. The chasm sundering the official and unofficial narratives of our relationship had been steadily widening throughout the year. It was now on full display in this most dispiriting missive.

What of the substance of the feedback? This, too, could not be taken at face value. Barbara worried that my research would be dismissed as "too tangential to the law," but that seemed implausible given my Establishment Clause focus and the summaries' references to a number of legal theorists and jurists. I had, after all, initiated most of the works in progress in law school courses. My research descriptions were also too laden with "critical jargon" for her taste, but I was in truth little acquainted with the critical theorists with whom I was being lumped. I wasn't name-dropping Derrida or Judith Butler, who were among the last people on my mind as I was crafting what became the Overview, the aim of which was to articulate the epiphany as a programmatic intellectual vision, as I've explained. The summaries introduced some terms of art. But these weren't tantamount to jargon in my book, since they'd been introduced as suggestive images and metaphors, not professional cant. I certainly wasn't contriving to peer-signal my membership in some elite coterie of critical theory Brahmins, as Barbara seemed to be reading my motives.

So, Barbara's chosen formulation of the problem was debatable to my mind. And yet her gut was on to something real: my application materials' implicit repudiation of academia's dominant technocratic prejudices. The Overview was the brainchild of the epiphany, which had merely amplified the conflict of visions that had always bedeviled my relations with my advisers and academia at large. If recruitment committees were going to have allergic reactions to my materials, as Barbara predicted, that was because those materials lacked a "pleasant demeanor" and "proper deference" and failed to uphold Midgley's "totally anonymous, colourless style and choice of topics" as the hallmark of "professional honor." Barbara was ultimately reacting to these transgressions, and this gravamen was why more was afoot than met the eye.

Recall the distant origins of the crisis at hand. Speaking for both himself and Larry, Joe had relayed that while they agreed I might one day emerge as a luminary of the legal academy, they were confounded as to my project's direction and disconcerted that it didn't resonate with my colleagues' work. Like everything in my fellowship experience, those misgivings were multilayered and ambiguous. On one level Joe was underscoring the uncontested fact that the project as it then stood was wanting in direction and concreteness, leaving readers confused about what I was really hawking and why they should care. Joe's frustration here was also my own, because I was pursuing, without having yet found, that elusive concreteness.

At the same time, these facially reasonable worries disguised deeply problematic ideological commitments, which I've already begun to diagnose. Dissecting the core values of *Homo academicus*, Bourdieu highlights the sublimated and intellectualized conservatism of academia's gatekeepers, the liberal elites:

> There is no acknowledged master who does not recognize a master and, through him, the intellectual magistrature of the sacred college of masters who acknowledge him. In short, there is no master who does not recognize the value of the institution and institutional values which are all rooted in the institutionalized refusal of any non-institutional thought, in the exaltation of academic "reliability," that instrument of normalization which has all appearances on its side, those of learning and those of morality, although it is often only the instrument of the transformation of individual and collective limits into the choice of scientific virtuousness.[2]

In discerning my potential to become an eminent legal scholar, Joe was holding out the prospect that I might eventually ascend to the rank of "acknowledged master." But in insisting that my research first be tied in with that of colleagues, he was also reminding me, with Bourdieu, that "there is no acknowledged master who does not recognize a master and, through him, the intellectual magistrature of the sacred college of masters who acknowledge him." The knockout email was the culmination of my repeated refusals to bow before this magistrature. Joe's and Barbara's guidance had always been advice for doing so, for exhibiting "academic 'reliability.'" If their respect-cum-fascination had now deteriorated into suspicion and ire, this was owing to the ingratitude with which I had discounted their Janus-faced counsels.

What would heeding them have required of me? Barbara's reaction to the Overview would have been rather more sanguine had my summaries read something like this:

> Professor X has recently introduced a fascinating new framework through which to address Problem A in an effort to replace the approach that has been most famously defended by Professor Y, arguing that this not only provides fresh, multidisciplinary insight into Problem A but also sheds a new and intriguing light

> on Problem B, which Professor Z first brought to our attention in his rigorously argued and thoroughly researched book C. But Professor Z's book, C, in fact anticipated, and raised serious reservations about, the approach now being defended by Professor X in response to Professor Y.
>
> This article argues that while Professor Z's reservations have substantial merit, the force of those concerns is attenuated to the extent we (plausibly) interpret Professor X as supplementing rather than supplanting the analysis of Professor Y. Thus conceived, the questions introduced by Professor X promise not only to enrich our understanding of Problem A but also to open up new avenues of interdisciplinary research into Problem B that build on those painstakingly developed by Professor Z, because Problem B, properly understood, is just another facet of Problem A.

In pleading with me to acknowledge the intellectual magistrature of the sacred college of masters, Joe was saying that I could eventually become Professor X but only if I first attended to him in this genteelly interstitial manner, because that was how he got to where he was. I would have to first bend the knee if I ever wanted it bended to me. And that meant bending to the New Class's lumbering machinery of argumentation—to which I myself was allergic.

David Brooks nicely translates Bourdieu's ponderous prose into plain English, as the insight that intellectuals "compete to gain a monopoly over the power to consecrate": "Certain people and institutions at the top of each specialty have the power to confer prestige and honor on favored individuals, subjects, and styles of discourse. Those who hold this power of consecration influence taste, favor certain methodologies, and define the boundary of their discipline. To be the chief consecrator is the intellectual's dream."[3] Joe was saying I could make this dream come true, that I had it in me to become a chief consecrator, but that I wouldn't begin to accrue consecratory authority without first submitting to such authority. My research needed to mesh better with that of potential colleagues because the latter embodied the subjects, styles, and methodologies to which I'd have to acquiesce if I was to one day ascend to the rank of chief consecrator.

Yet the dream Joe had been hoping to facilitate was anathema to the task at hand—to uncover the higher, heretofore hidden, truth of conservative claims of cultural oppression. Brooks identifies the crux of my dilemma:

> The aspiring intellectual must perform a delicate balancing act in determining her subject niche: If there are ten thousand young intellectuals setting out to write books about communitarianism and the theory of civil society, does she want to be another? Here she must be subtle, because in the intellectual arena sometimes it's best to follow the crowd. The more people are specializing in civil society, the more civil society conferences will be organized. More civil society arguments will be put forward and therefore there will be more demand for people to comment on or to rebut them. Because each person in the field will read (slightly) more than he writes, each new errant in this specialty increases the demand for critics and panelists. That's Say's Law. The more people are saying, the more there is to be said.[4]

Joe was upholding Say's law back in December when he recommended that the law and religion focus he'd urged also delve into conflict of laws. The idea was senseless jurisprudentially, as I have explained, but it symbolically affirmed the political economy of Say's law: People were already saying things about conflict of laws. Ergo, there was more to be said about it. I couldn't emerge as a chief consecrator without first submitting to Say's law, an article of faith of the chattering class. Yet my research agenda dictated the antipodal principle that the *less* people are saying, the more there is to be said. Conservative claims of cultural oppression are a reaction to the unacknowledged performative dimension of liberalism, a sectarian ethos that goes without saying but shapes what is said. And so my subject matter could not but submerge me in the murky intimations of the tacit dimension, where the aspiring intellectual's delicate balancing act became impossible. That meant I could never hope to be consecrated as a theorist of conservative claims of cultural oppression the way someone like Josh had been consecrated a theorist of liberalism, by Rawls and others. Instead, I would have to consecrate myself through those very claims.

That was the undeclared counterideology of the Overview, the reason it stood beyond the pale, and precisely what Barbara's hermeneutics failed to tease out. My outré application materials were destined to alienate "many, many" readers because my texts radiated a holistic vision that, emanating from my engagement with conservative claims of cultural oppression, proceeded in blithe disregard of any clearly delineated academic specialties, including the critical theory to which all were allergic. I wasn't dismissing Professors X, Y, and Z per se; I wasn't affecting to think in a vacuum. But my framework of relevance originated in the nature of my subject, not these luminaries' seminal insights and the resultant "state of the field." The Overview addressed itself not to any ongoing debate within some esteemed commentariat but to a driving *idea*—to which all such debates had become subsidiary.

In so relegating them, my research summaries transgressed the New Class hierarchy of "the knowing, the knowledgeable, the reflexive and insightful." Gouldner observes:

> The special privileges and powers of the New Class are grounded in their *individual* control of special cultures, languages, techniques, and the skills resulting from these. The New Class is a cultural bourgeoisie who appropriates privately the advantages of a historically and collectively produced cultural capital. …
>
> The New Class, then, is prepared to be egalitarian so far as the privileges of the *old* class are concerned. That is, under certain conditions it is prepared to remove or restrict the special

> incomes of the old class: profits, rents, interest. The New Class is anti-egalitarian, however, in that it seeks special guild advantages—political powers and incomes—on the basis of its possession of cultural capital.[5]

The elites are willing to attack existing distributions of economic and political power in the name of greater equality and general human welfare. But, as a cultural bourgeoisie, they treat unequal divisions of *cultural* capital as sacrosanct and will repress any who would attempt to accrue it in disregard of the distributive status quo. Discourse that respects that status quo—by acquiescing to the lingos, conceptualizations, and lines of inquiry that define "the field"—is serious. Discourse that slights it by proceeding from a different set of starting points and perplexities is not. My project summaries were just such a discourse. They overflowed with palpable hostility to what David Gelernter describes as the elites' ambition to "convert as much of the landscape as possible into fenced-off, neatly tended, carefully patrolled academic preserves," which I had eschewed as part and parcel of modern liberalism's disciplinary agenda and civilizing project.[6] With my mind now decolonized, I preferred to roam away from these preserves in a wild expanse of untamed impulse, and that was what the Overview signaled above all. As she had noted in an earlier email, Barbara was sojourning at Stanford's Center for Advanced Studies in the Behavioral Sciences (CASBS), and this very appellation affirmed the rationalization of intellectual life and its aspiration toward ever-progressing cumulative knowledge. In contrast, I had repudiated the liberal idolatry of progress and retrogressed to an intellectual state of nature, where I wandered in the wilderness of the tacit dimension. Having thrown off all shackles, I would be neither master nor slave, neither consecrator nor consecrated, but only self-consecrating and free.

Therein lay the essence of my transgression, an effrontery that Barbara sensed but could not readily verbalize. My wanderlust was an affront to the academic asceticism I examined in chapter 1 and the true subterranean wellspring of Barbara's latest misgivings about me. Bourdieu observes:

> In fact, since the positions of power are hierarchized and separated in time, reproduction of the hierarchy presupposes a respect for distances, that is respect for the *order of succession*. It is this very order which threatens the *celeritas* of those who want to "cut corners" (for example, by importing into the university field properties or powers acquired on other terrains), as against *gravitas*, the healthy slowness which people like to feel is in itself a guarantee of reliability (in writing a thesis, for instance) and which is really the most authentic proof of *obsequium*, unconditional respect for the fundamental principles of the established order.[7]

In warning that readers had no time to "luxuriate" in the Overview, Barbara was insinuating that it exuded self-indulgent *celeritas* at the expense of hard-won *gravitas*.[i] Eschewing the circumspect stolidity of the latter, the Overview resonated with her as bumptious grandiloquence unschooled by New Class expressive discipline. She advised that "there are ways to mitigate these dangers without misrepresenting who you are or trying to change yourself into a different person" because she processed the Overview's self-consecratory tenor as tawdry *celeritas*, mere self-expression to be discounted by those imbued with ascetic *gravitas*. These silent judgments vented an identitarian

---

i *Gravitas* ordinarily carries positive connotations, suggesting dignity and seriousness. However, Bourdieu is taking this putative virtue with a grain of salt, casting it as an affectation that sacrifices intellectual freedom to respectability. What Bourdieu calls *celeritas* is the opposite of *gravitas* as seen through the inauthentic lens of *gravitas*. Academics who eschew *gravitas* will be seen as having surrendered to shallow, impatient ostentation in a bid for unearned celebrity. But this judgment may be unfair insofar as the perspective from which it issues is distorted. I follow Bourdieu in italicizing *gravitas* and *celeritas* to signal my adoption of his critical valences.

imperative to abjure the intuitive, unregimented cognition harbored by the tacit dimension, embodied in conservative claims of cultural oppression, and then carried forth into my application materials.

Hiring committees were scouring those materials for "the most authentic proof of *obsequium*" that I could not tender. In the epiphany's wake I was "importing into the university field properties or powers acquired on other terrains," and Barbara was telling me that such contraband would not be well received. Refusing the vassalage of academic realpolitik and the monastic virtues that undergird it, I had broken ranks with the normal reproduction of the academic hierarchy, the order of succession that had scaffolded my colleagues' professional ascents. In broadcasting this emancipatory project, the Overview subtly communicated that the "roles for earthly heroics" cut out by the academic hero-system were mere social constructions, asseverations of social identity rather than unadulterated intellectual virtue. As Gouldner observes, "professionalism is one of the public *ideologies* of the New Class."[8] Triggered by this message, Barbara succumbed to Wax's "vague premonitions of erosion or unraveling" and acted to neutralize the ideological threat.[9]

Barbara's epistle encapsulated the contradiction dogging me from the outset. Joe had extolled my first draft, all seventeen pages, as a tour de force, and it could have been that only because it was animated by the unregimented cognition of the tacit dimension, the will to think outside the "carefully patrolled academic preserves" demarcated by the elites. These elites were at once fascinated and put off by this obstreperousness. So they incongruously eulogized my tour de force while also demanding that it submit to the jurisdiction of the intellectual magistrature of the sacred college of masters, whose conventions disguise "the transformation of individual and collective limits into the choice of scientific virtuousness." My own contradictions were merely reflections upon this one, the driving force of my advisers' perennial ambivalence about me. My deceptions and evasions were essentially stratagems for managing that ambivalence, for circumventing the magistrature's jurisdiction within the limits prescribed by an asymmetrical power relationship.

But these manipulations had now caught up with me in this latest feedback from Barbara, and I began to appreciate that the drama unfolding before me was also the unfolding of my research agenda and the light it shined on the elites. Once a neural labyrinth confined to my cranium, that agenda was now becoming instantiated three-dimensionally in the real world, with Simmel's sealed containers of condensed cogitation at last unsealing themselves as they bled forth into my predicament as an academic job seeker. Such was the true arc of the fellowship, which events were now disclosing to me. The hero-systems of the Left operate within elite enclaves, where they enjoy a plausible deniability that is inaccessible to those of the Right. And Barbara had now confirmed just this, betraying the sublimated and intellectualized conservatism of the liberal elites. On the surface her feedback was narrowly pragmatic. Beneath it she was standing guard as a New Class gatekeeper, upholding the consecratory authority of the magistrature against my own bid for self-consecration, to which the logic of my research agenda had ineluctably led me.

The Call

Per her invitation I phoned Barbara at CASBS the next day, hoping to do a little advanced behavioral science of my own. She was initially away from her office, so I left a message and followed up with an email asking when best to reach her. She replied in a friendly tone, "HI Rony: I'm back in the office now. (I was at the law school for lunch, and hoping to snag you there ...) Should be here until 4:30 at least. —Barbara." I called again later that afternoon.

Angling to seize the reins of the narrative and exploit the situation's ambiguities in my favor, I began the call by announcing that

I had things to say "that should assuage your worries." "Oh, please do," Barbara replied with evident exasperation. With this invitation I went on to explain that "I have accepted your and Joe's advice and I have implemented it." They had urged in December that I turn to law and religion, and that was precisely what I'd done, I advised. Her concern that nonspecialists would be unreceptive to my research agenda, I continued, was belied by Dick's reaction. His expertise was business law, far removed from my own, yet he endorsed that agenda as "rich and complex." He had some issues with the length and format of the original CV, but those had been addressed to his ostensible satisfaction.

Barbara responded by clarifying that I'd misunderstood her concerns. She was scarcely worried about the reactions of learned and worldly nonspecialists like Dick but rather those of interviewers at lower-ranked schools, like Boston College, for instance, who might prove insensible to my work's merits. Others, however, would take notice. Indeed, Stanford had already received several inquiries about me. Reiterating the previous day's email, she stressed that she wasn't objecting to my expressing my individuality but merely underscoring the realities of the job market.

With this new concord established, I went on to ask whether more schools would be advertising in subsequent bulletins of the AALS. I had found only about seventeen openings with a conceivable fit, which didn't seem like many. Barbara reassured me that whether a law school advertised in the bulletin was of no moment. All the law schools would be making an appearance at the recruiting conference in November, if only to make an appearance, including those that hadn't advertised and were relying exclusively on the AALS résumé databank. There was just no way to tell at this juncture who was serious about hiring. I expressed relief, confessing that these nuances had been lost on me. Barbara circled back to her reassuring flattery, declaring that anyone as reasonable as I couldn't fairly be expected to understand anything as unreasonable as the law faculty hiring process.

After discussing sundry logistical matters for a few minutes in a friendly, conciliatory tone, Barbara popped a most unforeseen question: "How much of your works in progress have you actually written?" "Some people," she went on, "write next to nothing and then call that a work in progress." She had introduced the question casually, almost as an afterthought, toward what seemed like the close of the conversation. Indeed, she hadn't really made an issue of this in the previous day's email. She had recommended that I make note of where projects were in the pipeline, but she presented this as a helpful formatting suggestion, not one of the graver concerns broached in her last two paragraphs. I therefore treated the question as a casual afterthought in my response, going on at some length about the revision the book projects still required but without providing a comprehensive answer. Work that couldn't be circulated wouldn't cut it, Barbara replied, thus changing the official subject from the projects' existence to their condition. I assured her that I could have some of the religious neutrality project suitably revised in short order, which I would then send to her and to the schools, as a supplement to my original mailings. This plan of action seemed acceptable to her. Yet her anxiety, palpable at the conversation's outset before receding into the background, had resurfaced. I asked whether we should now meet to discuss things in greater depth. Sounding eager to end the conversation and get off the phone, Barbara answered with a terse, committed no. I should be in touch with Dick, as he was the placement adviser that year. So the call ended.

As with the previous day's email, I could take little here at face value, as most of this was rank historical revisionism. Barbara was recasting the email's grave concern—that well-nigh every law school in the country would dismiss me as a charlatan—as the less serious and more flattering worry that my ruminations were just too deep for hiring committees at middling institutions, who, unlike Dick, lacked the humanistic breadth to truly appreciate me. That was patently absurd, as Barbara well knew. Maybe Dick was at Stanford rather than Boston College because he'd written a seminal paper that transformed antitrust law. Maybe he was just cited a lot generally. Maybe it was something else. Whatever the explanation it had nothing to do with his ability to appreciate the Overview, which was a function of intellectual temperament much more than academic stature. Some professors begin their careers at places like Boston College before climbing their way to the likes of Stanford, and that's not because they've demonstrated a sensitivity for someone's humanistic breadth. If this was perfectly obvious to me, then it was also clear to Barbara, who also knew that Boston College is a perfectly respectable law school typically ranked in the top thirty.

Even more incredible was the news that Stanford was already receiving a groundswell of interest in me, as such glad tidings contradicted both the letter and spirit of the previous day's email, according to which my career was careening toward disaster. Had everything somehow changed just in the last twenty-four hours? I had sent the direct mailings only two business days earlier, right before Labor Day weekend, so they likely hadn't even reached anyone's desk, let alone been perused. My materials had been available online slightly earlier. Still, it strained credulity that things could have moved along so swiftly since then, especially given my late start. Only a week earlier Barbara was warning that I'd have to "push to get yourself on everyone's radar screen" to offset this. Now she was telling me I was already on those radars and flying high.

Barbara's estimation of my reasonableness also didn't hold water. The frequent arbitrariness of academic hiring decisions is a platitude. As will later become apparent, the suggestion that anyone as reasonable as I couldn't be expected to grasp anything as irrational as law school hiring was another of Barbara's many acute observations and premonitions, laden with multiple layers of profundity that could not be properly appreciated when first uttered. I will return to this in due course. Yet Barbara had not thus far judged my course of conduct to be reasonable. Why would it have suddenly become that, especially when the sum of her fears—a belated job-talk paper—had now materialized? Perhaps I was reasonable in some higher philosophical sense but certainly not in the pragmatic sense that concerned her at the moment.

Her declining to meet was equally peculiar. Yes, Dick was serving as the official placement adviser that year, but that didn't mean no one else was involved in the process. On the contrary, ensuring the law school's success here called for far-reaching faculty engagement. Barbara had always involved herself energetically in the law school's placement efforts, whether in an official capacity or otherwise. Only a week earlier she had urged that "we should try to get together soon." Why the sudden change of heart?

All these bizarre pivots reinforced my initial sense that the knockout email camouflaged undisclosed considerations, and what those might be now dawned on me. What Barbara had gone out of her way to spin as a tangential afterthought—whether I'd even written anything at all—was in fact at the front of her mind. The misgivings of the knockout email were not unfounded—I was genuinely unmarketable. Still, they served as a smoke screen for suspicions Barbara didn't want put to writing: that I'd falsified my qualifications by fabricating summaries of projects that didn't exist. Barbara had casually noted that "some people" write next to nothing before touting this as a bona fide work in progress, but the impersonal framing was pure euphemism, more of Barbara's "professorial rhetoric" in action, because "some people" in fact referred to *me*. Hence the tone and tenor of the knockout email, which had allowed Barbara to document the existence of an adverse professional judgment for future reference. She wasn't going to call me out as a liar and a fraud, but that conclusion was running beneath what purported to be neutral speculation about my résumé's reception.

Barbara's suspicions were erroneous. The works in progress were all substantially under way. But her hunches were understandable, and perhaps inevitable, under the circumstances. My publications were a matter of public record. But aside from the Legal Theory term paper and the meager twenty-one pages I had delivered to her in April, she hadn't seen any of the many works in progress that the Overview summarized. I had mentioned some of them to her in passing about eighteen months earlier, but she wouldn't have recalled that. Added to this were my consistently evanescent appearances at the law school. I had furthermore discounted the better part of my advisers' counsels while giving mendacious indications that I had taken them to heart. If all that weren't bad enough, it then took Larry to wake me from my philosophical reverie and send me off belatedly into the hiring season. Against this backdrop the fourteen pages of elaborate summaries in the Overview must have impressed Barbara as a bill of goods fabricated to conceal a truth to which the facts on the ground now pointed. If I had cobbled together a fourteen-page research agenda when two to four pages were in order, I must have done so in the hopes of hustling my colleagues, engaging in a rearguard action to shore up a crumbling facade and naively expecting that they would be none the wiser. Joe had already accused me of dismissing my colleagues as imbeciles in December, and the situation at hand must have struck him and Barbara as further confirmation of this alleged contempt.

Certain stylistic peculiarities of the Overview must have further fanned Barbara's incredulity. As I explained earlier, I had crafted it as a programmatic vision over a long weekend during which I circled back to my sundry projects to reimagine them in light of the epiphany, my newly achieved extrication from the elite culture. I had therefore summarized my projects not as they then existed but as I envisioned they would appear upon being revised pursuant to this newfound transcendence, whose deepest implications I hadn't yet fathomed, let alone absorbed. This approach imbued the summaries with a certain impatiently exuberant, free-wheeling, and effervescent quality that Barbara surely had the acumen to discern. Lacking a "totally anonymous, colorless style," the Overview scandalized her standards of professional honor, as Midgley says. In light of the credibility gap begat by my yearlong deviance, it wasn't a big leap to conclude that I might have flouted those standards in other ways as well, perhaps through outright fraud. After all, I was pursuing "the *celeritas* of those who want to 'cut corners.'"

Enough stood behind the Overview. The projects needed substantial revision, but they were hardly incipient, and no reasonable reader of academic CVs could conclude that labeling them "works in progress" was misleading. Just as crucially, the Overview betokened my exit from the liberal culture, the sine qua non of endowing the project with the concreteness, direction, and coherence being demanded of me. I would have ideally attained that end while spinning out a salable job-talk paper in the process. But given the limits of human endurance, I was prepared to cut myself some slack. This wasn't the logic of your typical law school fellowship, admittedly, but it was the logic of my research agenda, which had earned the fellowship. Barbara was unacquainted with that logic, however. Given her technocratic prejudices, the misapprehension that I must have been idling away was perhaps natural. This outcome might have been averted had my earlier emails met with an invitation to meet and confer. But they had not, and the situation was as it was.

Barbara's equivocations on the phone stemmed from the fact that her suspicions—to which all the evidence pointed—stood in stark conflict with what she and Joe had once imagined they knew of me. Barbara had gone out of her way to recruit me to the academic track, with Joe speculating at our first tête-à-tête that I would one day emerge as one of the legal academy's most prolific denizens. Both had been impressed with my doggedness. Were they now to accept that I was a ne'er-do-well and grifter living high off purloined fellowship funds? That conclusion was incongruous with everything that had led them to propose the Gaither fellowship, and their egos were invested in the soundness of their judgments. But they couldn't brush aside this nightmare scenario, because it seemed like the most straightforward explanation of my conduct all through the year (as seen through the philosophical filters dissected earlier).

The ensuing disorientation was what had spurred all the backpedaling, including the hyperbolic flattery with which Barbara periodically showered me during the call. As everyone knows from personal experience, it's much easier to vent resentments and frustrations in an email than in face-to-face conversation or even a phone call, where we are confronted with the concrete humanity of the offender rather than a mental mock-up. A conversation is liable to expose the unjust caricature feeding our paroxysm of indignation, leading to a provisional about-face. Unsure of how distortedly one-sided our judgments may have been, we may momentarily repudiate the better part of our rancor. That was exactly what happened during the call. Barbara's resultant ambivalence and vacillation drove both the implausible flattery and the undertones of uneasiness that permeated the entire conversation. My deviance had propelled Barbara into cognitive dissonance. The knockout email gave vent to one side of that dissonance and the flattery gave vent to the other. Concomitantly, her blandishments served a strategic function, as she was also trying to cajole me into lowering my guard and confessing to what part of her believed had to be the case.

I was now navigating troubled waters. The situation was dire. Yet it felt eminently fitting as the progressive realization of the premonition that had first gripped me in August, that I'd be falsely accused of a felony, the real-life instantiation of which was this attack by the forces of liberalism and academia. The focal point of Barbara's consternation—the suspected fraudulence of the works in progress—was empirical, not ideological. But her suspicions had been fueled by my broader pattern of conduct, which in turn bespoke my progressive alienation from the intellectual magistrature of the sacred college of masters, of which the Overview was the final repudiation. In ways I couldn't yet articulate, the substance of my research agenda and my predicament as an academic job seeker were melding into a single experiential universe as theory bled into praxis. Barbara was operating under the cover of plausible deniability, and it was likewise thereunder that the liberal elites maintain their cultural preeminence generally. So it was fitting that the one problem had delivered me straight into the jaws of the other.

How this would all shake out I couldn't say. For now I was left to revise the paper posthaste and dispatch it to Barbara and the law schools. I gave myself a week and buckled down. The plot thickened on Sunday, September 13, when Dick finally responded to my email of five days earlier. I had urged that we meet, and he now assented:

> Hi, Rony. Yes, let's get together. I have some of the same concerns that Barbara Fried expressed in her message. I can meet tomorrow (Monday) any time between 1:30 and 4:00 pm. I'm also available on Tuesday between 1:30 to 3:30, or on Wednesday morning from 10:00 to noon. Do any of those times work for you?
>
> — Dick Craswell

Dick had previously replied to my emails without much delay. That it took him so long this time around suggested that he and Barbara were working in tandem and that he had held off at her behest. She had been hoping to get to the bottom of things, maybe by extracting a confession that my synopses were a bill of goods. Having failed to wring this out of me over the phone but still lacking a definitive account of the facts, she must have been left flummoxed and unnerved by my caginess. It had been only four days since our call, but she had yet to receive anything from me. Exhausted, exasperated, and at wit's end, she was now handing the torch to Dick, who would renew the inquest in his office.

Did Dick in fact share Barbara's concerns? Perhaps. But she had fostered any such concurrence. My intellectual agenda had impressed him as "rich and complex," and he had given the revised CV the unequivocal go-ahead. Set against Barbara's assurances that he was *not* the sort of interviewer who concerned her, Dick's new reservations cemented my budding sense that the factual question of whether I'd done any work at all stood at the center of this unfolding imbroglio. Since I wasn't rhetorically positioned to articulate this, I responded that I had already conferred with Barbara, who had "qualified the scope" of her concerns, but that these still merited discussion. We arranged to chat in his office on Wednesday morning, shortly before the faculty luncheon.

The paper was far from polished by Tuesday, the eve of that meeting. No matter. Time was up and I had to get something out the door. My relations with Barbara hung in limbo. A definitive audit of their status was premature, but my instincts told me I had crossed a Rubicon and we were now locked in irreversible conflict. The ire and frustration steadily built up over the year were on the verge of combustion. Barbara's immediate concern was the suspected fraudulence of my works-in-progress summaries. But she had been driven to her suspicions by factors that predated the summaries' distribution and now enjoyed a momentum that any apologia I might tender could not readily arrest. My one meaningful achievement that year, my exit from the ambient culture, was precisely what Barbara could not be counted upon to appreciate.

Since fortune favors the bold, I embraced this fate and decided to reciprocate Barbara's microaggressions with my own and let the chips fall where they may. I attached the paper to my email and wrote:

> Hi Barbara,
>
> I have attached the introductory chapter. Sorry it took me a while to edit. I will send hard copies to schools. The next nine chapters, which is what I have pretty well organized by now and would need in order to present, are listed in the Table of Contents. Almost all of these are shorter and less in need of editing than the one I'm now sending you.

> I will try to get them wrapped up ASAP—hopefully by around the end of the month.
>
> I became distracted last week from completing my response to your question about the works in progress. I started writing the two strictly philosophy articles before law school. One of them is nearly publishable. The three more law-related ones were written in law school through various classes and independent writings. True Merit: Employment Discrimination Law. Radical Feminism: Gender in Public Policy and the Law. Multiculturalism: Race and Religion Seminar + independ. writing. True Merit is 30 pages long and needs a lot of work. Radical Feminism and Multiculturalism are around 75 and 110 pages and are nearly publishable. But I now need to go back and revise all three papers to integrate them with the framework of the books. The summaries in the CV and the overview are summaries of these papers as they will appear upon being thus revised.
>
> Last Jan. or Feb., you requested that I write about atheism. I discuss atheism in this and later chapters.
>
> Best,
>
> Rony

Barbara had subtly legalized our relations with the knockout email. I was now responding in kind by memorializing the existence of a factual controversy concerning the veracity of my representations. I didn't directly enunciate the nature of that controversy but conveyed it by implication when I submitted the proof of the works in progress. Because copies of seminar papers at the law school were filed with the registrar, Barbara was given to understand that the exculpatory evidence was readily available for inspection. In advising that my summaries described the works in progress as they would appear upon being revised—and not as they then existed—I offered, also by implication, a partial explanation for her fallacious inferences, again highlighting the seriousness of something she had been casting as peripheral and documenting what she preferred to leave undocumented, should some conflict later arise. Anyone who doubts Barbara's ability to parse this out is plainly unfamiliar with her cunning, shrewdness, and subtlety of discernment—qualities with which I would become all too well acquainted in the months to come. She understood the factual background and she understood me, so she could have encountered no difficulty extrapolating the subtext.

In retrospect I could see that I had displayed my own wiles on the phone, when I played the trusting, semihapless naif looking up to a wise and compassionate adviser for light and solace, taking her every word to heart. These histrionics only exacerbated the cognitive dissonance into which my heterodox behaviors had already plunged Barbara, causing her to disavow both the tone and substance of the knockout email and then present her suspicions in the casual, friendly fashion in which I subsequently took them up. In this way I engineered a social context that then enabled me to generate a contemporaneous record of the controversy. My email wasn't incontrovertible proof of Barbara's suspicions. She could always disclaim them and I'd have only my say-so. But none could say that I'd simply confabulated the whole thing months or years after the fact, and that was the most I could realistically accomplish.

How, exactly, I could parlay this novel chaos to my advantage remained unclear. But I was gripped by a powerful intuitive sense that this improbable situation, and not the draft I had just sent off, represented the culmination of my now twenty-month investigation of elite tyranny. For most fellows a research agenda is a means to career progression. But the normal order of things had now been stood on its head, with my career ambitions becoming vessels for a research agenda whose experimental component lay plainly before me. Barbara's enumerated reservations seemed just as hard-nosed as Joe's a year earlier, in August 2008. But now as then, the pragmatism aimed to suppress a budding insurrection against New Class hegemony, precisely the plight of conservative culture warriors. By the time Barbara fired off the knockout email, I had already been tried in secret, with no opportunity to confront the full indictment. Only the vagaries of human conversation had brought it to the fore. Just like conservatives, I had been targeted by the liberal elites and then oppressed by the plausible deniability in which the attack was ensconced.

I was obviously the underdog here. Whereas I was merely a would-be elite, Barbara was a full-fledged one on whom my prospects depended. But underdog was the role I had voluntarily assumed when I took up the problem of conservative claims of cultural oppression at one of the great citadels of American liberalism, Stanford Law School. Stanford had all the terrestrial might, but I had the higher truth of those claims, my abiding demiurge. The collision of these forces now seemed foreordained, with my professional future serving as the battleground.

The Meeting

I drove down to Stanford the next morning for my scheduled interrogation, ready for another big day in this new drama. My intermittent contact with Dick during the year had always been in a group setting, so this was our first tête-à-tête. All I knew going in was that he was perhaps the most mild-mannered and even-keeled human being I would ever chance to meet. Following a perfunctory exchange of greetings, I inquired whether Barbara had relayed to him that my works in progress still required revision. Dick responded in the affirmative, thus confirming that they were indeed working in tandem and that she'd tipped him off about the new facts on the ground in anticipation of this inquest. Both circumstantial evidence and an uncoerced confession now supported the inference of an unofficial reality playing out beyond the four corners of the email record.

With this confirmed, I went on to apologize for dropping the ball on the Stanford résumé book. I was doing my utmost to make my research accessible to nonspecialists but had hit some snags along the way, I pleaded. Things were now under control, but these challenges had distracted me from the exigencies to which he and others had recently called my attention. Dick responded forbearingly and dismissed the résumé book as unimportant. Stanford, he averred, would have been proud to have my résumé in it, and the loss was more its than mine. This aside, my conduct to date had been reasonable, he reassured. As in my dialogue with Barbara a week afore, what had begun as acute concerns about my career prospects had mysteriously transmuted into hyperbolic yet soothing flattery.

Moving on to the project's substance, it became apparent that Dick had a strong, intuitive grasp of its purport. Notwithstanding that he'd read nothing beyond the Overview, he could anticipate points that I was only then beginning to formulate. As the theoretical exchange was winding down, Dick changed gears and admonished that, since I could "read minds," I would do well to take any interviewers "where they're at," elaborating that "it's kind of like this" as he gestured toward his copy of the Overview.

What to make of these cryptic pronouncements? Since I'd never had the pleasure of playing poker with Dick, his advertence to my mind-reading powers could have referred only to my ability to see past the official text of the emails, as evidenced in my last email to Barbara and his answer to my information request about their correspondences. This mind reading was no supernatural feat but the simple by-product of transcending the liberal culture. Having attained the vantage point of conservative claims of cultural oppression, I was now operating "one level up," just as Barbara had prophesied in December 2008, and so could see through the intellectual magistrature and its manifold machinations. It was no longer the silent, taken-for-granted backdrop of things but a contingent, socially constructed, hero-system drawing on the sublimated, intellectualized conservatism of the liberal elites. Now attuned to Barbara's ideological drives, I could readily detect the disingenuity of the knockout email and, with it, the unofficial reality of my collegial relations—which Dick had now acknowledged allusively.

As to Dick's advice about taking prospective interviewers "where they're at," I responded that I would also try to "nudge them a little from where they're at." As I would later learn but had every reason to know at the time, even this little bit would be too much in the hallowed halls of academe. Dick already had grasped the danger fully, however, and was alerting me to it. In designating the Overview as the framework by which to make sense of interviewers' likely wariness and skepticism, Dick astutely gauged that my research agenda would be culturally oppressive to academia—just as academia was culturally oppressive to it and to me. I was already entertaining such thoughts, as discussed earlier, and was pleased to have them confirmed by Dick's own observations. Dick was, in fact, the only person to have ever drawn an analogy between the substance of my research agenda and the nature of my predicament as an academic job seeker. A disinterested party had now confirmed my budding sense that this predicament was channeling the logic of conservative claims of cultural oppression.

The conversation concluded with sundry logistical matters. Dick confirmed a point first introduced by Barbara, that schools that weren't serious about hiring that year might still be conducting interviews at the recruitment conference, just to make an appearance and network. He also assured me that having a serviceable job-talk paper was immaterial at this juncture, since most interviewers had no patience to read anything beyond a CV and would be looking only at papers of candidates they were inviting back to campus after the conference.

I let it be known that I was nevertheless positioned to mail off the first chapter of the religious neutrality project to law schools, but Dick advised me to hold off on this and instead distribute a longer, more advanced, iteration nearer the dates of the conference in early November, which could be helpful if I received, say, only two or three interview invitations. He had no reason to expect such an outcome, he stressed. But should it come to pass, sending off a stronger paper on the eve of the conference might help rekindle interest.

As in my conversation with Barbara, I knew better than to take these words at face value. If Dick wasn't worried about a paucity of interviews, why did the thought cross his mind? In fact he had every reason to fear that eventuality, including the seemingly arcane nature of my research agenda and the culturally alien format of my application materials; my belated entry into the hiring process and failure to network with faculty at Sanford and elsewhere during the year; and now the new "X factor" that materialized after I smoked out Barbara's disingenuity in the previous night's email about the works in progress. What all this portended I couldn't yet say. My clairvoyance faltered here. But this silent backstory to the day's meeting could not be discounted.

Moreover, Dick's suggestion was at odds with his previous assurances that hiring committees wouldn't be reading anything longer than a CV prior to the conference. If he nevertheless entertained hope that a stronger paper might resuscitate my prospects at the eleventh hour, this was testament to my dire straits, his sense that it would take something dramatic to offset all the forces now converging against me. And yet, in light of recent events, those forces could no longer be acknowledged. Dick could not cite the off-puttingly arcane nature of my research or my general waywardness as his reasons for anticipating a dearth of interviews because these problems had become entwined with Barbara's disingenuity and his complicity in it—which were now a source of furtive embarrassment.

The Death Stare

Not long after this meeting, I headed off to the faculty lounge for the Wednesday afternoon luncheon and speaker series. As usual, lunch was served buffet style, and I ran into Dick, who said nothing but threw me a knowing look of consternation and foreboding, as though to suggest I shouldn't be there. I inferred that this bore some relation to recent events but nonchalantly concluded that I had nothing to fear, as I'd clarified the facts to his ostensible satisfaction. I helped myself to some food and headed off to the dining area, where I spotted a table around which three professors were standing, just about to seat themselves.

These were Marcus Cole, whom I didn't know; Robert Daines, who had taught me corporations two years before; and Bob Weisberg, a criminal law specialist and pal of Joe and Barbara's. Indeed, Joe had suggested early on in Legal Theory that I have Weisberg take a look at my paper, which I characteristically neglected to do. I didn't know Weisberg well, but he had once visited my white-collar crime class to offer some insights on quid pro quos, if I remember right. Over the year we had engaged in occasional banter at the Wednesday luncheon, where I had given him a copy of my Strawson article after he gave a talk on a related topic. I also recall his dismissing Judge David Bazelon's reputed arrogance as a distraction. Conservative jeremiads about liberal arrogance are neither here nor there, he insisted. Arrogance is a human universal evenly distributed across the political spectrum and has no political significance.

I approached the table, greeting all with a friendly hello, at which point Weisberg reciprocated with a look the likes of which I had never encountered before or since. To call it a scowl would be a gross understatement, because his entire being became apoplectically gripped by a venomous hatred and profound loathing that were being directed at me in a most unambiguous fashion. His face at once became contorted with jaws extended in an animal-like attack mode, his eyes consumed by a piercing intensity that eclipsed the rest of the world, designating me with laser precision as a villain and evildoer without peer.

Thinking I had just exonerated myself regarding the presumable source of this biblical anger, I instinctively brushed it aside and responded, "Should we sit down?" with solicitous aplomb. Weisberg's silent yet incandescent rage dissolved instantly as he replied that indeed we should. He then proceeded to rather spiritedly introduce me to the other professors present. Soon the conversation turned to the dictatorial tendencies of one of the university's wealthy donors, whom Weisberg accused of self-indulgently micromanaging his projects heedless of university priorities. I didn't know enough to form an opinion, but giving Weisberg the benefit of the doubt, I ventured that this philanthropist had gone so far as to "deify his own whims." This formulation apparently captured the crux of Weisberg's grievance, as it was accepted with enthusiasm and gratitude.

The conversation then turned to sports, in which I had no interest or conversational aptitude. Eventually the group subdivided, and I found myself chatting with Robert Daines, who knew he remembered me from somewhere. I reminded him that I'd taken his corporations course, which jogged his memory, though he guessed it had been four years back when it had been only two. Daines recalled me because I had participated in class discussions rather energetically and was sometimes called upon to liven things up. We then went on to discuss my religious neutrality project, which was rather far removed from shareholder derivative actions, but he seemed intrigued.

Soon enough, that day's speaker was introduced and the room quieted down. Not long thereafter Weisberg left the table and took another position, leaning back on a nearby counter. Maybe that was just his way. But I suspected that his earlier loathing had resurfaced and he was trying to generate some physical distance between himself and the devil's spawn. This was consistent with something I had noticed earlier in the hour, right upon arriving in the room, when I espied Larry, originally seated on one of the sofa chairs along the wall, storming out of the room in an enraged gait, never to return. Dick's look of foreboding had evidently been in anticipation of just such eventualities. I was persona non grata at Stanford.

I raced home to San Francisco after the luncheon to take stock of the new facts on the ground. A few things were clear. First, Joe and Barbara had been gnashing their teeth about me before Weisberg. My limited contacts with him had always been cordial or friendly up to that point. I had never inflicted any injury upon him capable of inciting the visceral antipathy with which I was first greeted. That his apoplexy should have been quickly subdued was hardly surprising. Weisberg's death stare was premised on hearsay, not firsthand interaction with me, which had always been positive or neutral. I felt innocent, acted innocent, and made a deliberate effort to stay cool, calm, and collected. This was a public setting, moreover. There were at least two other people at that table and dozens more scattered about the room. So Weisberg wasn't going to rake me over the coals about whatever Joe and Barbara had told him, especially when they hadn't ever done so. Given these social constraints, he managed the cognitive dissonance between his hearsay knowledge and the unflappable persona I was presenting by just defaulting to his customary friendliness—much like Barbara over the phone the other week.

And what exactly had they told Weisberg? Plainly, it was not what Barbara had told me over the phone—that anyone as reasonable as I couldn't be expected to understand law school hiring, that I was just too deep for the country bumpkins of Boston College, or that the law school was already receiving torrents of inquiries about me a mere two business days after I belatedly mailed off my hastily crafted CV. It also wasn't the ostensibly well-intentioned constructive criticisms of the knockout email. Standing alone, these couldn't have drawn the odium I'd just encountered. Barbara warned that recruiting committees were allergic to critical theory, but Weisberg had just exhibited an allergic reaction to me personally.

My advisers had by now accumulated a suite of unaired grievances against me, so they doubtless had fulminated on multiple fronts. But the alleged fraudulence of the works in progress was likely at the epicenter of the vitriol. Sullying Stanford's reputation in the eyes of peers, news of such chicanery would have easily sufficed to blow Weisberg's gasket. So, too, would the thought that I'd been loafing about all year, pocketing my $60,000 salary to subsidize an extended vacation. It had been less than twenty-four hours since I'd sought to disabuse Barbara of such inferences. Word of my claimed innocence had reached Dick in the interim because she knew we were meeting the next day. But it evidently hadn't gotten to Weisberg (and probably Larry). Barbara had no reason to treat this as an emergency, after all, and she was surely waiting to debrief Dick about the morning meeting before revisiting the situation. Hence, his consternation upon my arrival, which portended that reactions to my presence would be informed by Barbara's earlier suspicions rather than my recent bid to quell them.

My legal instincts now kicked in, as I wondered whether I had been defamed. Joe and Barbara had a First Amendment right to their opinions. But false factual assertions damaging to my professional reputation were another matter, and any statements concerning the fraudulence of the works in progress might well qualify as such. Whether I had a bona fide cause of action depended on the precise details of the communication, to which I wasn't privy. Was the alleged falsification presented as a certainty, a likelihood, or just a possibility? Had they disclosed the factual bases for their allegations, allowing Weisberg to make up his own mind? The biblical anger I had just witnessed suggested that the verdict upon me had been disseminated as ascertained fact, not mere surmise, but I couldn't be sure. The charges were false, but whether they had been leveled negligently was another matter, given my deviant conduct that year. The strength of any claim also depended on the nuances of California law, of which I was likewise ignorant. Perhaps any communications between Stanford colleagues was privileged.

I didn't know and didn't really care, as I was far more interested in my research agenda than traveling down this dark, disagreeable road. And yet the question could not but come to mind in a law school setting, which my advisers understood just as well as I. The legalization of our relations had commenced with the knockout email, was then ramped up by me in the works-in-progress email, and had now been cemented by the situation at hand. The existence of a controversy concerning the veracity of my dossier had been entered into the email record only the previous night. With the day's events coming right on the heels of that deed, the question naturally presented itself. Nothing was certain beyond Barbara's disingenuity, which was a by-product of my own disingenuity and not unlawful. But an inference of defamation was scarcely capricious on a stylized Law School 101 kind of level. Indeed, it was quintessential LSAT reasoning in action. Everyone involved had more than enough schooling to put two and two together.

Equally clear was that no one would speak of what everyone understood. I wasn't going to shout my innocence from the rooftops when I had no direct evidence that it had ever been impugned. As importantly, railing against the injustice suffered would have been rather awkward and unpleasant. My advisers wouldn't say a word either, both because that might be self-incriminating and because broaching this new third rail of our relationship would have been awkward and unpleasant for them, too. Since normal academic etiquette had to be observed, everyone would maintain an attitude of strategic ambiguity, with this recent turn of events becoming the silent subtext, and not the official text, of future communications—which would therefore have to proceed through the tacit dimension, just like my research agenda. My immersion therein had reached new depths, seeping from my academic pursuits into my professional relationships. The fissure between the official and unofficial realities of these associations had been growing all year and now manifested itself in unambiguous terms. Even so, this new self-censorship meant that no one would address this most improbable, unprecedented, and delicate of situations directly.

The reader might wonder whether any of this mattered, now that I had cleared my name of Barbara's false (though scarcely capricious) inferences. But whether I had in fact cleared my name was still an open question. I hadn't misrepresented myself in the crudest, most transparently unethical, sense of just inventing works in progress on the fly in a cynical ploy to beguile prospective employers and the Stanford professoriate. Dick now appreciated that I'd been burning the midnight oil, engrossed in the project to the point of obsession. Still, there was a case to be made that I had misrepresented myself in some more ambiguous and less calculated fashion. Notwithstanding my recent bid for exoneration, my output during the year had been exceedingly modest. I had, moreover, been a phantasmal presence at the law school and brushed aside most of Joe's and Barbara's counsels, all while issuing misleadingly optimistic forecasts of impending progress in an unremitting gambit to buy time.

This had all been in service of the tacit dimension, which I had to traverse to access the higher truth of conservative claims of cultural oppression. But the intellectual magistrature of the sacred college of masters did not acknowledge that dimension. All my transgressions during the year had been transgressions against the magistrature—the linchpin of my colleagues' professional identities. That was the backdrop for the Overview's reception and why Barbara's conclusions resonated with her. These were merely the effect, and not the cause, of the underlying crisis of confidence, which had been long in the making, having been set in motion by my youthful contempt for the New Class and its lumbering machinery of argumentation. Events could have unfolded as they did only because I was already living under a cloud of suspicion. The Overview was just the final straw. That had become evident, both logically and viscerally, when Joe's and Barbara's vituperation was conveyed to me vicariously through the medium of Bob Weisberg. The truth about the works in progress might now modulate that vituperation, but modulated vituperation is still no pretty sight.

Moreover, my recent one-upmanship was probably an outrage in its own right, spawning another still-nascent fault line. Barbara had felt hoodwinked by me all year and was doubtless savoring the prospect of hoodwinking me in turn through her professorial rhetoric. I had now deprived her of the satisfaction. Having discerned at our December 2008 meeting that I operated "one level up," she had been hoping to clarify that it was she, not I, who would now be doing so. However, I had just foiled her first foray on this front after I outflanked her considerable wiles to uncover and then document the unofficial reality of my status. I had no inclination to actually escalate matters legally—because this was distasteful, because the case would be exceedingly difficult to prove, and because my deepest interests lay elsewhere. Nonetheless, Barbara had supposably emerged from the imbroglio as a tortfeasor—on a simplified Law School 101 level—and in consequence of inferences that flowed naturally from her handle on the facts. This most unexpected twist of fate could only have stoked her ire as an insult to her lawyerly pride. Whatever the truth of the works in progress, I had most surely crossed a Rubicon.

Barbara had zeroed in on my tendency to "make specimens" of people back in December, and this was precisely what had now come to pass. I had bested her tactically when I anticipated her movements more deftly than she did mine, making me the subject and her the object. Barbara *wanted* to operate "one level up," but it was I who wound up doing so this time around. Barbara's oracular prescience—a concomitant of her ability to intuitively discern subtle structural tendencies in the minutiae of personalities and relationships—has never ceased to astonish me and would be further confirmed in the months to come.

Great Work

Barbara replied to the previous night's email two days later, on Friday, September 18. Predictably passing over the body of the email about the works in progress, she broached only the draft I'd attached, reporting a situational sea change since her last missive:

> Rony—I read the intro ch. This is not my field, to put it mildly, and so I cannot really comment on how this fits into the academic lit. With that caveat, I thought sections 1-4 of the chapter were fantastic—subtle, iconoclastic in the best way, and really, really interesting. Sections 5 and 6 could use some work, I think. They are hard to follow, largely because they veer into critical-theory-speak. I also had trouble seeing how they related to the first 4 parts. Often, they seemed to be making the same points in different jargon. If you've already sent out the ch as is, don't worry about it. The first 4 sections are good enough to carry you, I think. If you haven't, I'd suggest doing some work on sections 5 and 6—getting rid of jargon and redundancies, and making the connections with the rest of the ch. clearer.
>
> If you have not already done this, someone it would be really good for you to show this to is Mike McConnell. I think he'll appreciate the subtlety, and will give you the perspective of a smart non-secularist.
>
> Great work.
>
> Best, Barbara

Here again was that curious mélange of truth and falsehood of which Barbara was uniquely capable. That the paper's intellectual core was indeed "fantastic—subtle, iconoclastic in the best way, and really, really interesting" would later be confirmed by disinterested third parties reading a much-improved version of the draft to which Barbara was reacting. McConnell would in fact go out of his way to profess his considerable interest in the project. I will take this up in due course. But its intellectual core notwithstanding, the paper as it then stood did not merit the plaudits Barbara was showering on it. The first four sections were indeed in better shape than the last two, but they, too, were disjointed and inchoate. The draft was a mere thirty-eight double-spaced pages, rather short for a job-talk paper. Even taking Barbara's assessment at face value, it was doubtful that the "first 4 sections are good enough to carry you." Do we read an initially engaging novel with an uninspired ending and then conclude that the first part was good enough to carry it? Last impressions count as much as first ones.

Barbara disclaimed that the Establishment Clause was "not my field," for which reason she couldn't assay how the paper "fits into the academic lit." But her false modesty was scarcely credible. Barbara may not have been the American doyenne of law and religion, but she had more than enough general academic acumen to tell that the project did *not* in fact "fit into the academic lit." She didn't need to keep up with the latest Establishment Clause work then circulating to see that the draft before her was only minimally footnoted and bereft of meaningful references to ongoing debates within any esteemed commentariat of Establishment Clause scholars. Jacoby observes:

> Like any quantitative study of reputation, the [citation] index is circular. It measures not the quality of work but clout and connections. If used to evaluate careers, however, the lessons for the striving professor are clear: cast a wide net, establish as many mutual relations as possible, do not isolate yourself from the mainstream. It pays not simply to footnote but to design research to mesh smoothly with the contributions of others: they refer to you as you refer to them. Everyone prospers from the saccharine scholarship.[10]

Whatever else might be said of my paper, it wasn't saccharine scholarship. Far from casting a wide net to cultivate mutual relations, I had cut all such tethers in singular pursuit of the higher truth of conservative claims of cultural oppression. That was the problem with the Overview, the reason it would stimulate allergic reactions. So what had changed in the last ten days? Barbara did not explain how her newfound sanguinity was now supposed to moot the misgivings she'd aired not so long ago in the knockout email. Why would any appointments committee blanching at my research descriptions then proceed to read what these described? And if they weren't going to read my paper, how could it be "good enough to carry you"?

Barbara understood all this just as well as I. If she advertised a Pollyannaish optimism about my prospects and signed off with "Great work," that was in consideration of the week's vicissitudes, of which she had doubtlessly been apprised, having been deeply implicated in their genesis. She understood that I'd been falsely accused, at least on the narrow question of premeditated fraud, and that this was looming large in my mind, with Bob Weisberg's visceral reflexes having raised troubling new questions about the status of our relations. Barbara also grasped that those relations' already ambiguous subtext had now been ambiguously legalized. So her instincts were to play dumb, keep the peace, and defuse simmering tensions through what was designed to look like a conciliatory gesture. Hence her fulsome praise, which, though perhaps defensible at the higher rungs of philosophical reflection, remained wildly undeserved in the real world, given the pragmatic concerns of the moment. The sincerity of the conciliatory gesture was therefore open to doubt. Were the events of late water under the bridge, with Barbara now striving to see the best in me? Or was she still livid and just angling to encourage such inferences in a calculated bid to mollify me? Did she even know? No one could broach these pressing questions because the schism giving rise to them was now an elephant in the room that would have to be skirted for reasons of both law and academic etiquette.

I wrote back to thank her for her feedback and acceded to her criticisms, once more anticipating impending progress in my research. I also relayed Dick's suggestion that I hold off distributing the paper until the eve of the recruiting conference, to rekindle interest should I confront a shortage of interviews. Did that make sense to her? Given her original directive to mail something off as soon as possible, it was natural that I solicit her response to Dick's alternative strategy before deciding how to proceed. As I had predicted, I once again got crickets from Barbara. That I would have few if any interviews at the conference was overdetermined. The disrepair into which my collegial relations had now fallen was only one of myriad factors. Yet the matter of my career prospects and the week's events were deeply intertwined, both causally and conceptually. Barbara didn't want to touch on anything that conceivably could speak to this turbulence, so she exercised her right to remain silent, declining to answer a facially innocuous question that she could have been reasonably expected to answer were our interests as squarely aligned as her reassuring email was calibrated to suggest.

CHAPTER 4

A Policy of Allusion, Intimation, and Ambiguation

October–November 2009

The Moot Interview

My moot interview (to prepare for any real ones at the conference) was originally set for the following Wednesday, September 23. But events had taken their toll on my system, so I called it off at the last minute to let my frayed nerves recuperate before returning to the site of my trauma. I had now been plunged into existential limbo. It was too soon to ascertain the precise nature of the fallout, but I was no longer just another Stanford Law fellow on the teaching market. My career prospects were dead if I was persona non grata with faculty. Legal academia is a small, incestuous world, and the merits of what Barbara lauded as my "great work" would be of no avail with the might of Stanford pitted against me. No one had to cast aspersions. A merely lukewarm recommendation would torpedo my prospects once translated from academese into the vernacular. I would plow on, revising the paper until it truly was "fantastic—subtle, iconoclastic in the best way, and really, really interesting," not only at its intellectual core but in its presentation, too. Yet this endeavor would be permeated by a recurring despair, vitiated by the inexorable awareness that my death warrant might already have been signed, so that all would come to naught despite my eleventh-hour scramble to get my house in order.

At the same time I viewed the sword of Damocles overhead as a crucial intellectual milestone, perverse though it sounds. That I had generated, and then sniffed out, a liberal conspiracy only fortified my steadfast conviction that my research had always been on the right track, despite the inevitable detours, delays, and false starts. This wasn't an argument I could make to the conspirators arrayed against me, though, who as such wouldn't acknowledge the existence of their enterprise—Stanford's unofficial reality. Even so, I was left with an inner sense of accomplishment that tempered the recurring despair. Andrew Klavan's insight that an alternative reality cannot be imagined from within the Matrix now had a concrete meaning that I could never have divined, as I was now a denizen of that alternative reality. This real-life rabbit hole resonated as the consummation of the intellectual journey I'd always been on, which had now culminated in a fully immersive experience. So while I was profoundly distraught by my fall from grace, I didn't really begrudge this new albatross around my neck. Buoyed by my strange sense of accomplishment, I couldn't help but feel that I would somehow land on my feet at the end of the day.

Amid this turmoil I'd neglected to check my voicemail for a time. When I finally got around to it in late September, I discovered that the University of Colorado Law School was keen to interview me at the recruiting conference in November. Hoping it wasn't too late to arrange something, I got back to them and pleaded that my research had distracted me from certain practical exigencies that would now have my undivided attention. Fortunately, they were still game for the interview. That was small consolation, though, given my general despair and that a single interview is statistically unlikely to yield a job offer—especially when the candidate is despondent.

The practice interview was rescheduled for October 7. With the departure of David Ball for a job at nearby Santa Clara Law, Ryan Calo had taken charge of the fellows group and rounded up a few professors to conduct it, with the other fellows observing. The professors would be Dick Craswell (the law school placement adviser), Hank Greely, and Josh Cohen. Ryan had also invited Barbara, copying me in the email. She predictably declined to respond. Given the deteriorated state of our relations, her attendance would have been discomfiting to both of us. She might have concocted some excuse for absenting herself, but keeping up the fiction of the official reality was surely trying for her as well. Dick was the first professor to arrive, and he seemed gratified to learn of my Colorado interview, which made this practice run more meaningful. Once all arrived, the exercise began.

The subsequent feedback bespoke a decidedly mixed performance. Ryan remarked that my analysis of the issues was impeccable and that he could largely follow the argument. But Dick observed, and others confirmed, that I was waxing on for too long without giving my interlocutors an opportunity to follow up. Dick also complained that I was operating "at thirty thousand feet." This was a meaningful improvement over my yearlong philosophical reverie, when I was fluttering at a still higher altitude. But it was still problematic.

Josh Cohen then took the megaphone. Josh was the practice interview's resident philosopher, so his words carried special weight. He began by saying something about my working through the night. I hadn't advertised my long hours or the minimal sleep requirements enabling them, but maybe he could tell I was wired. Did Josh know what was up? Was he aware of the yawning yet unnamed chasm that now sundered the official and unofficial realities of my collegial relations? I couldn't say with certainty. But my gut told me he knew, as did logic. Josh had had no hand in the watershed events of September so far as I could tell, but he had cotaught the course that had led me to Barbara and hence to those events. I had conferred with him in May, and his skepticism about the project might have fed into Barbara's exasperation with me. I had, moreover, listed him as a reference on my CV despite his skepticism. Faculty members discuss the doings of their fellows from time to time, and the palace intrigue now afoot at the law school was surely peculiar enough to warrant some gossip.

Josh then proceeded to probe whether I was religious and all this was personal, if I didn't mind his asking. I answered tersely in the negative on both counts. This wasn't the unequivocally correct answer, but any other response was rhetorically impracticable in the social context at hand. I was now religious only in the attenuated sense of viewing modern secularism askance as the secularization of certain inherited religious drives, a social construction of the disciplinary society rather than Enlightenment pure and simple. This was personal inasmuch as these realizations arose from the epiphany that had freed me from that social construction. Josh's intuitions weren't entirely off base, then, but I wasn't going to delve into why right there, so I had to brush these probing questions aside. I also sensed derogatory undertones in the suggestion that my research was personal, as this could also be to insinuate that it was less than rigorous. Since insinuations cannot be argued with, I acted to sidestep this line of inquiry and move on.

Substantively, though, Josh's feedback that day was quite helpful. I had been dissecting the Supreme Court's decision in *County of Allegheny v. ACLU* in order to argue that whether judicial proscriptions of publicly sponsored Nativity scenes constitute what the dissent bemoaned as a "religion of secularism" turns on whether those rulings are set against a modern or premodern conception of the relationship between the religious and the secular.[i] Josh found it remarkable that I could find anything novel to say on so hackneyed a

---

[i] In this decision, a majority of the justices agreed that a nativity scene in a county courthouse accompanied by a banner proclaiming "Glory to God in the Highest" in Latin was unconstitutional. The court held that while the "government may acknowledge Christmas as a cultural phenomenon," the Establishment Clause prohibits it from observing "it as a Christian holy day by suggesting that people praise God for the birth of Jesus." 492 U.S. 573, 601 (1989).

topic as the constitutionality of Nativity scenes. He also underscored the pertinence of Justice David Souter's concurring opinion in *Lee v. Weisman*, which I had cited but failed to spotlight.[ii] The observation was invaluable, as the Souter concurrence was more central to the thrust of my argument than I'd first appreciated. Josh had noticed my blind spot and alerted me to it.

Whereas Josh seemed to take a modicum of genuine interest in my musings, not all faculty present were so impressed. I could tell I had rubbed Hank Greely the wrong way when he pointed out a typo in my CV at the close of the exercise and, extending his arm to return it, flung it toward me while my hand was still a few inches away, as though he couldn't bear to hold it for a second longer. As I was leaving the lounge with Dick after the group had disbanded, I groaned that I had but one interview lined up. Reverting to the flattery first dispensed at our September meeting, he attributed this paucity to the strength of my philosophy credentials. Two publications, including a book, weren't

---

ii Writing for the Supreme Court majority, Justice Kennedy argued that a voluntary nonsectarian benediction at a public middle school graduation ceremony violated the Establishment Clause. While attendance at the ceremony may not have been "required by official decree," it was "apparent that a student is not free to absent herself from the graduation exercise in any real sense of the term 'voluntary,' for absence would require forfeiture of those intangible benefits which have motivated the student through youth and all her high school years." 505 U.S. 577, 595 (1992). In his concurring opinion, Justice Souter advanced a different rationale for the outcome, arguing that because religious students could "express their religious feelings" about their graduation on their own time before or after the ceremony, they had "no need for the machinery of the State to affirm their beliefs." Accordingly, "the government's sponsorship of prayer at the graduation ceremony is most reasonably understood as an official endorsement of religion and, in this instance, of theistic religion." Ibid., 630. Because the ceremony could not reasonably be construed as a neutral accommodation of religion, it counted as an unconstitutional endorsement. As I explained in a footnote in chapter 2, whereas conservatives interpret the Establishment Clause as prohibiting only religious coercion, liberals interpret it more expansively as prohibiting any endorsement of religion, whether coercive or not. This case illustrates how these competing paradigms can sometimes yield the same outcome.

bad for an entry-level hire, and a PhD was a selling point. But I wasn't trying to break into fast food, so the suggestion that I was somehow overqualified strained credulity, as Dick well knew. As the placement adviser, he had to tender a diagnosis of my meager results. Like Barbara in our last email exchange, he wasn't going to offer one that touched on why I might have gotten crosswise with faculty.

I later received some feedback by email. Ryan remarked to the group that the exercise had been "tremendously instructive." Elizabeth Pollman, another fellow who coincidentally knew my brother from Jew camp when they were teens, wrote: "Just wanted to say thank you for letting us other fellows come to watch your moot interview this week. Your work sounds very interesting and you did a nice job, especially with all of us in the peanut gallery watching." Josh also followed up, writing:

> rony:
>
> enjoyed the conversation earlier. the thing to keep in mind is this: you have something VERY interesting to say. other people are going to be interested in it and want to talk about it. make sure you give them an intuitive sense of what it is about, invite them into the argument, and make it personal—this theory is a response to your own sense of disquiet about a kind of dismissiveness that you see in people who you spend time with. Don't hide that: get it right out there.
>
> good luck,
>
> Josh

The problems that had marred our May conversation had apparently been overcome, as Josh now seemed better attuned to my motives and trajectory. The "people who you spend time with" were, of course, the liberals in my Stanford orbit, and the dismissiveness I had detected in them was their contempt for conservative claims of cultural oppression, which I was arguing betrayed liberalism's undeclared sectarianism. Dick had already noted the interrelationship of my thesis and my professional environs, and now Josh was further confirming the entanglement. What he characterized as my "sense of disquiet" with the prevailing ideology had once been strictly theoretical, but now it was personal and interpersonal.

I wrote back to thank him for the feedback and asked whether he was available to read and chat about my paper. I heard nothing for eleven days, when he finally answered that he was "just overwhelmed with stuff right now" and suggested that I submit my project to a paper competition, the Law & Humanities Junior Scholars Workshop, to be held at Columbia Law School in June. The forwarded notice advised that selected papers would "serve as the basis for a larger conversation among all the participants about the evolving standards by which we judge excellence and creativity in interdisciplinary scholarship, as well as about the nature of interdisciplinarity itself." Very meta indeed, one level up, certainly. The only thing missing was a larger conversation about whether our judgments concerning the excellence and creativity of our conversations about interdisciplinarity can themselves be interdisciplinary—but that would have been too dizzying.

Professors are nearly always "just overwhelmed with stuff right now," but they're usually able to make time when they wish to. By reading my draft and meeting with me, Josh would have been positioning himself to help move along the career of a Stanford Law fellow and graduate amid the hiring season. That was something that he, as Stanford Law faculty, would presumably be interested in doing under normal circumstances, especially if he believed I had something "VERY interesting" to say. Circumstances were far from normal, however. Maybe he really was busy in some extraordinary sense. But his acts and omissions were strongly redolent of Barbara's policy of flattery-cum-avoidance, initiated after I uncovered her machinations, suggesting that he was indeed in the loop about recent events and that, as with Barbara, our true interests perhaps dovetailed less fully than his official declarations were calculated to suggest.

Hiring at Stanford

NYU Law School reached out to me on the morning of Wednesday, October 21, with a request for my job-talk paper, relaying that its appointments committee was "seriously considering" my application for an entry-level position. This wasn't going to lead anywhere, since the draft was still in a state of disrepair. Still, this show of interest by a premier law school was mildly reassuring. I would send them the paper later in the day, as I was heading down to campus that morning for the weekly faculty luncheon and speaker series, which would prove eventful.

I happened to be standing at the buffet table right across from Bob Weisberg—the professor I'd so enraged at a previous luncheon—when another professor, Lawrence Friedman, I believe, greeted him and asked something like, "So how is it going as appointments committee chair?" After hesitating for a few seconds Weisberg haltingly replied something to the effect of "we're not doing any hiring; we don't have any money." I knew that to be false, however, as I distinctly recalled Larry telling the fellows at a February get-together that the law school would be making every effort to bring in new blood, despite the budget shortfalls left by the financial meltdown. Indeed, they were hoping to hire at the entry level, as they preferred homegrown scholars. Subsequent research confirmed my recollections, as part of Larry's update had been repeated to the *Stanford Daily* as recently as June. In an article on looming cutbacks to faculty growth at the university, Larry was quoted as reassuring the Stanford community that the law school would "not reduce hiring efforts" despite tightening purse strings. Stressing that it was keeping up with the recruitment efforts of peer schools, which were "doing the same thing," he vowed to not let "opportunities go to waste."[1]

As chair of the appointments committee, Weisberg had to know this. So why mislead another professor, who probably knew it, too, and could easily learn of it if he didn't? All I could conclude was that I, tarrying across the buffet table and well within earshot, was the proximate cause of the misstatement. Weisberg replied to Friedman as he did for the same reason Barbara sized up my paper as "Great work," not to mislead Friedman but to avoid stoking tensions wrought not so long ago in that very room. Aware that I had a rational basis for surmising some sort of slander, or at least bad faith, he didn't want to pour salt in the wound by letting it be known that Stanford would be hiring but that I wouldn't be granted so much as an interview.

Taken in the abstract, the possibility of interviewing with Stanford had never been farfetched. After all, that mine was just the kind of writing they looked for in entry-level candidates was one of the first things Joe had said to me. He had also opined that I was poised to land a "top-flight" job in a law school when he reached out to me right after graduation. Speaking for Larry as well, he would later speculate that I might one day emerge a luminary of legal academia, provided I remedied my problematic intellectual aloofness. It was in the same vein that Barbara lauded *Conservative Claims of Cultural Oppression* as brilliant, gauging that I was easily competitive for a top law faculty job before going on to offer me a fellowship for which I hadn't even applied. Certainly, I was qualified to teach a serious class at the law school, since the Gaither fellowship itself offered that opportunity (which I passed on, following Larry's and Barbara's advice that I devote all my time to writing).

But while interviewing with Stanford was consonant with my advisers' earliest hopes and aspirations for me, all that had come to pass since those halcyon days of hope, trust, and innocence had irreversibly altered the situation. I had just generated, and then smoked out, a liberal conspiracy, arguably turning Barbara into an unwitting tortfeasor in the process. Surely that changed things. While Barbara's effusive praise for my job-talk paper as "fantastic—subtle, iconoclastic in the best way, and really, really interesting" accurately summed up its promise, the draft as it then stood was still just a diamond in the rough. In my mind that was a temporary hitch, now that I was coming to grasp the socially constructed character of the modern liberal identity on the visceral level that grips conservative culture warriors. But my advisers might not have appreciated this milestone, coming as it did at the high cost of flouting ambient mores. I knew I had fallen from grace and knew the true state of my paper, so I was hardly expecting to be interviewed by Stanford and would have been neither shocked nor chagrined to hear Weisberg apprising Friedman that they had the cash and hoped to use it. All the same, cold logic left me to conclude that my inconvenient proximity had prompted Weisberg's fabrication to the contrary.

My inference was corroborated moments later when Dick seated himself by me at a table colonized by fellows, which was uncharacteristic for faculty (though not unheard of). After the usual greetings, I updated him that NYU had just asked to see my job-talk paper. Rather than celebrating the glad tidings, Dick intoned, "Remember that just because they're interviewing doesn't mean they're hiring" and then fell silent. This was factually accurate. As both he and Barbara had clarified to me, schools that weren't serious about hiring that year still liked to network at the conference, so NYU might just be going through the motions. But Dick's reiteration of this general truth seemed gratuitous seeing as he had no reason to believe it would apply to NYU specifically. His reaction to news of my Colorado interview had been markedly more sanguine. The remark was also technically inapposite. NYU had merely solicited my paper, not extended an interview invitation. It would have been more apropos to caution that "just because they want to see your paper doesn't mean they're so interested as to interview you." That would have been both true *and* on point—though it, too, could go without saying. Dick had noted that schools might be interviewing without intending to hire as part of his general briefing to me about the ins and outs of the recruiting process. There was no obvious reason to now belabor this fairly tangential and entirely nonactionable observation.

Because Dick was by no means an irrational man given to superfluous statements, some other explanation was in order. I surmised that he was endeavoring to reinforce the message Weisberg had sought to convey minutes earlier by the buffet. His generic *they're* referred neither to NYU nor to some general (and pragmatically useless) truth about law school hiring practices but to Stanford. He was saying that Stanford's having an appointments committee that would be interviewing didn't mean they intended to hire anyone. Ergo, I wasn't necessarily missing out on anything in not being interviewed, because the interviews could be charades foreordained to lead nowhere.

Why didn't Dick just say "Stanford" if that was what he meant? Any such remark about Stanford would have been pertinent only when set against the unstated background understandings—the unofficial reality—that had sprung into being in September. It would have been intelligible only by reference to Weisberg's announcement that the law school was strapped for cash, which in turn made sense only by reference to the events of September—that is, my theorized slander. Yet this silent backstory was precisely what no one could officially acknowledge, even as all understood it unofficially, so Dick evoked it allusively with his facially pointless reminder.

An explicit reference to Stanford wouldn't have been an admission of wrongdoing, but it would have confirmed that any suspicions thereof were grounded in some underlying reality—the unofficial reality that now enveloped me. I wasn't demanding such a confession, and Dick had no interest in volunteering it, so he acknowledged the situation by way of logical implication within the confines of the tacit dimension. Just like me when I fired off the works-in-progress email, Dick was resorting to allusion, intimation, and ambiguation (the willful creation of ambiguity) to communicate a clandestine meaning inaccessible to the casual bystander not privy to the situation's subterranean background. For reasons of both law and academic etiquette, his real meaning had to be histrionically encrypted in conversational irregularities that could then be decrypted into the actual message by those in the know.

Later that day I bumped into Joe on the stairwell as I was leaving the law school. The awkward encounter caught both of us off guard. We both grasped the state of play—his collusion with Barbara, the logical inference of my defamation, and hence his imaginable legal involvement. Because the conceit that all was well—the official reality—had to be upheld, I tried to generate some semblance of small talk by casually mentioning my forthcoming interview with Colorado. Would I, he inquired, be flying out to Boulder? I replied that the interview would be in Washington, DC, where the AALS faculty recruiting conference was held annually.

Joe knew this perfectly well. The conference hadn't taken place yet, and only afterward would select candidates be invited for campus visits with extended interviews, so it was well-nigh inconceivable that I'd have lined up a trip to Boulder at this early date. If Joe was feigning ignorance, that was because feigning ignorance had become the new modus operandi with respect to me. He needed to say something to fill in a few seconds of time and drive the conversation forward just enough to maintain a thin patina of normalcy, after which it became socially permissible to disengage with a perfunctory "Keep me posted." Joe had made no contribution to the email exchanges of August and September. But his silence then was speaking louder than words now. We both knew that I'd reached out to him and that he and Barbara were joined at the hip, yet we haltingly kept up the fiction of the official reality, even as there was nothing and no one in that deathly silent stairwell to distract us from the unofficial one.

Two weeks remained before the conference on November 6–7, and these were largely uneventful. David Ball, our former fellows group leader now tenure-tracked at Santa Clara, had been invited to drop by his old haunt and share his thoughts on the hiring process and teaching; he made some worthwhile points on both. As Ryan later summed them up in a group email, the key takeaways were

1. Don't write much in the first year; focus on teaching.
2. Don't reinvent the wheel. Use a popular book and syllabus.
3. For your job talk, pick something "teachable."
4. PowerPoint is ok in a job talk; it's also ok to give something already accepted for publication.
5. Your abstract should answer a) what your paper is about b) why it's important and c) what do you say that's novel.
6. Ask for faculty support early, to get your name to the top of the pile.
7. Your questions at call backs should be as specific as possible and convey your interest in the school and geographic area.

Whether my research agenda was at all teachable was still an open question, as I was only beginning to fathom its full implications myself. Certainly, it wasn't something readily put to PowerPoint. That my name was not at "the top of the pile" for faculty backing was a foregone conclusion. Not only had I failed to enlist such support early but my attempts to do so belatedly had met with public relations disaster, ending in a liberal conspiracy and my detection thereof. We were all sitting in the same room listening to David, but I inhabited an alternative world bereft of the comforts of ordinariness.

David also stressed making the most use of the time afforded by our fellowships, whereupon he turned to me and chided, "And Rony, you've got no excuse," to which I cheekily riposted that I'd made none. He then walked back his belligerence, flattering me that as smart as I was, I should have no problem on the market. If only he knew. David's admonition was an allusion to the fact that my fellowship involved no teaching or administrative responsibilities. His insinuation that I had spent the year on Easy Street reiterated his long-standing doubts about my work ethic, first voiced in April, when the fellows group had gathered to interrogate my project. Like most everyone else, he hadn't seen much of me and assumed the worst. Though of no great moment, this latest microaggression was further evidence of the reputational toll exacted by my deviant research methods. Later in the hour Joe made a brief appearance in the faculty lounge, where we'd gathered, in order to greet us but restricted himself to issuing general expressions of affection for the group from a distance.

That evening I opened an email from Larry's assistant, Amy Applebaum, sent to undisclosed recipients, presumably any Stanford affiliate who was heading off to the recruiting conference in just a week's time. It read:

> Stanford Law School will be having a hospitality suite during the AALS Faculty Recruitment Conference in Washington on Friday, November 6. We will be in the main building, suite 4066. It will be open from 9:00 to 5:00 (closed for lunch from 12:30 to 1:30). We will not be interviewing on Saturday, so the suite will just be open on Friday. Refreshments will be available. Professors David Engstrom, Jane Schacter and Bob Weisberg will be interviewing at the conference.
>
> We hope to see you there.
>
> Amy

The decision not to interview on Saturday seemed inconsistent with Larry's public commitment to not "reduce hiring efforts" or let "opportunities go to waste." Plainly, taking Saturday off was a reduction in hiring efforts that might allow opportunities to go to waste, as it could cut the pool of prospective candidates in half. Larry had stressed keeping up with the hiring efforts of other law schools, which were "doing the same thing" as Stanford. But I doubted that many appointments committees elsewhere were taking Saturday off, too. Interviewing both days was the norm, so far as I knew, because this was the one time in the year when everyone on the market was gathered under the same roof. Indeed, Applebaum would make no such announcement when she would dispatch an otherwise similar communiqué the following year. Granted the interviewing could get tiresome and tiring, but most hiring committees had the stamina to persevere through two days of it, and there was no reason to think that Engstrom, Schacter, and Weisberg were uniquely frail on this front. Maybe they were pining to visit the Smithsonian on Saturday, but one would think recruiting for Stanford would take priority.

The decision to interview on one day only was, however, consistent with the priorities of a law school that was, as Dick had reminded me can happen, only going through the motions of recruiting. I couldn't divine their true intentions or actual plans for Saturday, but the logical inference was that they maybe weren't so intent on hiring that year. And the natural effect of that inference was to reinforce the message conveyed earlier by Bob Weisberg and then by Dick—that I wasn't missing out on anything in not being interviewed because none would be hired in any event. The message was a group email sent to all the relevant Stanford affiliates. But I suspected that part of its content was a tailored response to my troubled relationship with the law school—a bid to mollify me, just like Dick's gratuitous reminder and Barbara's implausible flattery. For everyone else the notice meant only that they'd be ponying up for their coffee and donuts on Saturday. But viewed through the lens of the unofficial reality, it was evidence of Dick's sincerity—and was intended as such, I believed. In reinforcing his earlier message, the communiqué also reinforced that which had enabled it, the policy of allusion, intimation, and ambiguation that was now standard protocol.

The Interview

The Colorado interview went as well as I could have hoped, given my frazzled state. Ryan had already put me in touch with one of the interviewers, a former Stanford Law fellow himself, who wrote to me a bit about Colorado Law and Boulder, likening the latter to my undergraduate stomping ground of Ann Arbor. Everyone was nice enough, but I was left slightly disoriented and taken aback when one of my interviewers chose to introduce himself as "Dean David Getches." The others had simply introduced themselves by their first and last names, omitting *professor*, so I could simply respond, "Nice to meet you, Harry," or "Nice to meet you, Paul." It was fine by me if Getches wanted his title acknowledged, but then he should have introduced himself as "Dean Getches," and I would have known to call him that. If he preferred to be on a first-name basis and only wished it known that he was dean, then he should have announced himself as "David Getches, the dean," and I could have greeted him as David with cognizance of his rank. But having introduced himself as he did, he was asserting a claim to distinction without assuming responsibility for it, instead burdening me with the decision of whether to omit either the *Dean* or the *David* in addressing him. "Nice to meet you, Dean David Getches" would have been stilted and prolix. I don't recall how I managed this catch-22, but only that there was no satisfactory solution. He was a nice guy but was evidently torn between aristocratic and egalitarian tendencies, an inner conflict that I'd been inappropriately called upon to mediate.

Substantively, though, the interview went a lot smoother than did the dry run six weeks earlier. My intellectual contacts with the law school had been sparse during the year, so I was working through some major questions for the first time right then and there. Still, the Colorado folks were readily engaged by the subject matter and raised good questions. At the same time I was aware that my distraction and demoralization had to be apparent. I left the room hopeful because this single interview was sadly the only hope in sight, all the while knowing it was statistically unlikely to go anywhere.

The rest of my time in Washington that weekend was uneventful. With only one interview—not even Dick's speculated two or three—I had plenty of spare time. The National Zoo was walking distance from the Marriot Wardman Hotel, the site of the recruiting conference, so I stopped by. The conference was a zoo in its own right, and I now preferred the company of nonhuman animals. Back at the hotel I ran into and had drinks with some other fellows, who had the nonnegligible interview itineraries to be expected of those hailing from Stanford. I summarized my project and they surmised that it must have drawn a lot of interest, presuming I had a full schedule, too.

I spent my evenings catching up with two old chums then living in D.C., one from high school and another from college, to whom I related my tribulations. Their sharply divergent reactions were harbingers of the range of responses I would draw from others in the future. The more analytically cautious their temperament, the more prepared were they to credit my version of events as plausible. To the extent they remained skeptical, that was to get a solid handle on the facts and my reasoning. The less analytically inclined, in contrast, were most strongly impressed by the facial outlandishness of it all and were correspondingly disposed to brush it all aside as overwrought conspiratorial thinking. This instinctive incredulity was self-reinforcing, as it amplified the rhetorical challenges of delineating the complex interlocking considerations that underlay my inferences. My dystopian predicament was fast becoming an intellectual challenge as well as an existential one, as it dawned on me that only by rising to the first would I rise to the second.

CHAPTER 5

The Quid Pro Quo

November–December 2009

The Stanford Law Home Page: Set 1

My challenges would grow exponentially soon after my return to San Francisco on Sunday, November 8. Relieved that the conference was over, I set about revising my paper, as I had a practice job talk scheduled for the following week. At about this time the policy of allusion, intimation, and ambiguation took an audacious new turn. Now I would come face to face with the toxic heart of the elites' unofficial cognitive hierarchy and find myself subordinated to their covert, intellectualized illiberalism. Readers, please bear with me and suspend judgment until I have set forth all my reasons for the most peculiar conclusions to which events would now lead me.

Whereas the images on some academic home pages revolve around specific announcements (e.g., an upcoming symposium), those at Stanford Law at the time revolved around people and the law school itself and would consist of a random assortment of professors, students, and miscellaneous law- or law school–related objects (such as the building or a stack of law books). The home page would greet visitors with one slide randomly selected from a set of eight or so. After a while the set was rotated, and visitors would now land upon different slides randomly drawn from a new haphazard selection of professors, students, and law school miscellany. In this way pictures of all faculty members would rotate in from time to time. At universities or departments whose home page images are tied to events or announcements, the lifespan of images will vary according to what is being publicized. But those on the Stanford Law home page served no such purpose. These uncaptioned images existed only to highlight such things as the bushy-tailed enthusiasm of students, the Elysian serenity of the Stanford campus, and the unwavering commitment of the law school professoriate. So their selection was inherently arbitrary, and they accordingly were rotated with a fair degree of regularity.

Various reasons took me to the home page during the week after the conference, and I came to notice that the images were drawn from the following set, which I'll call set 1 (see exhibit C in appendix 1).

Slide 1

Dean Larry Kramer lecturing	Close-up of Dean Larry Kramer lecturing

Slide 2

Professor Joe Bankman chatting with a student	Random students in class

Slide 3

Random students in class	Professor Mark Kelman lecturing

Slide 4

Professor Jayashri Srikantiah counseling students	Former dean Kathleen Sullivan lecturing

Slide 5

Professor Norman Spaulding chatting with students	Different angle of Professor Norman Spaulding chatting with the same students

Slide 6

Professor Norman Spaulding lecturing	Random students in class

Slide 7

Random students chatting	Random students chatting

Slide 8

Random students in the library

At first blush nothing was unusual or noteworthy about set 1. However, its appearance would mark the beginning of a change of policy in the management of the law school's home page. As I have just explained, the standing policy had been to rotate the sets with some frequency, every few weeks or so, as I recall, because there was no special reason why one particular grouping of professors should be in the limelight at any given time. But these customary rotations would now cease, so that the visitor would continue to land upon the very same seemingly arbitrary selection of professors (and students) for the next eighteen or so months. This select coterie of law professors would now be granted an unprecedented oligopoly over the home page, depriving the law school's other scholars of the exposure they would otherwise enjoy.

This didn't make sense on its face. It wouldn't be out of place for a law school's home page to exhibit the same image of its academic building month after month or even year after year, since a building is the physical embodiment of, and hence a fitting symbol for, the institution at large. That couldn't be said of the ostensibly haphazard selection of professors domiciled by set 1, however. Their contributions were beyond dispute, but so, too, were those of an entire pantheon of top-flight scholars, most of whom would be deprived of the limelight in the wake of the new oligopoly. Though hardly uncomely, the denizens of set 1 weren't so exceptionally photogenic as to justify sidelining every other face on the faculty. With due respect, neither did they embody the law school's spirit and ideals so much more robustly than would any other grouping of professors. Set 1 was also problematic internally. The three images featuring Norman Spaulding suggested that he was three times as important as Joe Bankman, Mark Kelman, and Kathleen Sullivan, who were featured only once each, and the two slides housing these three Spaulding images suggested that he was twice as important as Larry, the dean of the law school, who was featured in two images on a single slide. Was it really necessary to incorporate two Spaulding images that were essentially the same photo shot from slightly different angles (slide 5)? Again, Spaulding's achievements cannot be gainsaid, but he was only one of many similarly accomplished professors at the law school and less senior than most other faculty on set 1.

Spaulding's outsized presence on the home page would have been trivial were he rotated out after a few weeks, as would have been customary and fitting. But it became problematic with the abrupt end to the rotations. If the object was to showcase the rich diversity of the Stanford Law experience, why let him occupy so much valuable real estate on a permanent basis? Why not feature a few black faces or another woman instead? The new entrenchment of set 1 was deeply at odds with the law school's long-standing commitment to diversity. Sure, there were Ashkenazi Jews aplenty—Larry Kramer, Joe Bankman, and Mark Kelman—who indeed outnumbered the more Nordic stock, Kathleen Sullivan and Norman Spaulding. But the new oligopoly meant that, for well more than a year, the home page would feature no black professors and only one professor of color, Jayashri Srikantiah (who still happened to be Caucasoid, likely with Aryan admixture). There was also a profound gender disparity. Of the nine images of professors, only two, or 22 percent, were of women—at a time when half the country's law school enrollment was female.

Might the tech staff in charge have collectively forgotten to rotate the images for an entire eighteen months or just wearied of the task and thrown in the towel? That was conceivable but highly unlikely. There was no reason to suspect that those responsible for curating the home page were anything less than professional, and rotating digital images every now and then doesn't seem unduly onerous. Someone had gone to the trouble of tracking down and photographing the entire law school faculty, so actually putting the photographs to use couldn't have been seen as a bothersome distraction. The oddity of it all may seem trifling. But institutions have their reasons for attending to a whole bevy of arguable trifles. Go to any academic or corporate brochure and there will almost always be a few black faces. That's no accident, because someone was thinking about it. The Stanford Law home page was essentially a digital brochure and had always been treated with the care appropriate to one.[i] I rather doubt that Stanford's new protocol would tempt many other law schools, especially at such cost to diversity. Indeed, a number of universities have been embarrassed after being caught Photoshopping their promotional images in a gambit to deceptively augment minority representation.[ii] Yet Stanford Law, which had its fair share of brilliant black, Hispanic, and East Asian professors, was now electing never to showcase them in order to maintain an inordinate white male presence.

As I will later argue, compelling evidence would emerge that the oligopoly was no oversight or accident. But the human artifice was already apparent to me early on. Computer glitches happen, sure, but they're usually fixed by the tech staff employed for that purpose,

---

i OHO Interactive, a digital marketing consultancy whose clientele includes a number of elite American universities, cautions academic webmasters: "Be attentive in how you compose photos and videos and select subjects. Students pick up on environmental details in photos and will notice someone in a wheelchair or wearing a hijab in the background, a gender-inclusive sign on a restroom door, or adult students in a classroom scene." Notwithstanding the need to showcase diversity, websites should accurately represent the campus, since they "can't in good conscience reflect something that you are not, even if it is something you aspire to be. If you … publish photos inauthentically representing the diversity of your campus, the truth will surface easily enough." Georgy Cohen, "Communicating About Diversity on Your Website," OHO Interactive, March 30, 2016, https://www.oho.com/blog/communicating-about-diversity-your-website.

Nielsen Norman Group, another digital marketing consultancy, tells universities: "Visitors make value judgments about your school based on the images that you use. A few photos of sporting events: users see an emphasis on athletics. A video gallery with thumbnails of people that all look the same: users see a lack of diversity. When selecting images, be conscious of what each one communicates individually and as part of the whole." Katie Sherwin, "University Websites: Top 10 Design Guidelines," Nielsen Norman Group, April 23, 2016, https://www.nngroup.com/articles/university-sites/.

ii Nancy Leong, "Fake Diversity and Racial Capitalism," *Medium*, November 23, 2014, https://medium.com/@nancyleong/racial-photoshop-and-faking-diversity-b880e7bc5e7a; Josh Jaschik, "When Colleges Seek Diversity Through Photoshop," *Inside Higher Ed*, February 4, 2019, https://www.insidehighered.com/admissions/article/2019/02/04/york-college-pennsylvania-illustrates-issues-when-colleges-change.

which is why they don't ordinarily last eighteen months. Academic departments' inexplicably forgetting about the existence of their websites is not a regular feature of the world as we know it. It might happen with a lone blogger or a Facebook page but not at a well-run institution like Stanford Law. The home page's textual content, such as announcements about upcoming events, continued to be updated, so its existence hadn't just slipped everyone's mind.

Given all the foregoing, I formulated the alternative hypothesis that set 1 was the latest chapter in the game of allusion, intimation, and ambiguation first initiated in September. That is, I posited that the ostensibly haphazard contents of set 1 weren't haphazard at all and that its anomalous longevity therefore wasn't gratuitous. Set 1's makeup and duration were both explicable by reference to the unofficial reality of my predicament, to which this concatenation of images was a further subterranean allusion. There was a reason for the anomaly at hand, and he was right there, staring at the screen.

I have already chronicled the roles of Joe and Larry in this saga. Mark Kelman was connected because I had cited him in one of the research summaries that provoked the knockout email of September 8. Kathleen Sullivan, the law school's former dean and a First Amendment scholar, was connected because I had cited her in the Establishment Clause paper, so long in coming, that I delivered to Barbara with the works-in-progress email of September 15, the eve of my run-in with the silent yet incandescent rage of Bob Weisberg. These were the two communications by way of which my collegial relations initially became legalized. The first sparked Barbara's suspicions about the veracity of my summaries, while the second then exposed and documented those suspicions, setting the stage for my subsequent inferences about the genesis and meaning of Weisberg's biblical fury.

The images of Kelman and Sullivan, along with those of Larry and Joe, thus alluded to the entire chain of events that had brought me to my present straits. Those of Larry and Joe—slides 1 and 2—harkened back to Legal Theory and the fellowship, while those of Kelman and Sullivan—slides 3 and 4—evoked the seminal events of September 2009. If these images were a symbolic allusion to the origins and nature of the problem, then those of Norman Spaulding—slides 5 and 6—were a symbolic allusion to a potential solution. I had no personal or academic connection to him, but he was approximately my age—maybe a few years older. And the reason he alone appeared on two slides was, I surmised, that the second of his appearances was serving as a symbolic proxy for me. His role in set 1 was to allude to the possibility of a continued presence at Stanford, which would certainly solve my employment problem. Thus did the home page narrate my past, my present, and my conceivable future.

Set 1, I posited, was a response to the conundrum of how to negotiate a problem whose very existence none could openly acknowledge. The events of September 2009 had conceivably left me with a cause of action against my advisers. Did that development cement their now incurable enmity toward me, or was it water under the bridge, an absurd imbroglio and comedy of errors? I could get no answer because I couldn't even ask the question. How, then, were we to handle this impasse? Clearly, by relying on the very protocols that had generated it in the first instance, through a policy of allusion, intimation, and ambiguation, the histrionic deployment of symbols whose clandestine meaning was clarified by the semantic context of the unofficial reality, to which only the conspirators and I were privy. This, I submit, was why a facially arbitrary configuration of images remained undisturbed for well more than a year, in defiance of precedent, good sense, and professorial equity. Set 1's diversity deficit was attributable not to any resurgent racism or misogyny but to a higher purpose to which diversity was being sacrificed. Call my hypothesis strange, but it was in fact that which *dissolved* strangeness, demystifying anomalies that weren't less real for being inconspicuous or appearing trivial.

The message of set 1 was "We know we were wrong about you. So, don't think about suing. Just sit tight and we'll take care of you when we can." Joe, Larry, Barbara, Dick, and whoever else was involved didn't know that I wanted to sue them. I *didn't*, in fact, as I have explained. Yet intellectual honesty recognized that this avenue was nonetheless among the logical possibilities springing from the moral, semantic, and existential ambiguities of September 2009—one of their "penumbras, formed by emanations," as Larry surely appreciated.[iii] Set 1 was another such logical penumbra, a further reverberation of September 2009, and the proposal it clandestinely conveyed had the ambiguities of those events as its subterranean frame of reference. They were being alluded to under a cloak of plausible deniability, enabled by the fact that my inferences rested on background knowledge that could be readily disclaimed. To acknowledge this legal dimension of things wasn't to admit actual liability. Still, any such acknowledgment could be construed as guilty knowledge, which the conspirators were unwilling to evince except with plausible deniability, the quintessential lawyer's craft. The suggestion was that a settlement with no admission of liability could be arranged—a concept every lawyer likewise understands.

My advisers had no assurance of the scheme's success, certainly. There was always the chance that I'd simply overlook the images or fail to connect the dots. Still, they could surmise a reasonable likelihood that sundry contingencies would take me to my employer's home page often enough that I would sooner or later take notice of an anomalous state of affairs and draw out its subterranean logic on the basis of the portentous precedents set by earlier developments. The matter of my continued presence at the law school had already been the subject of earlier allusions, as detailed in chapter 4, so set 1 was a natural extension of an ongoing conversation.

[iii] Griswold v. Connecticut, 381 U.S. 479, 484 (1965).

The other elements of set 1 had been introduced to augment the plausible deniability by ambiguously contravening the home page's driving logic. On the one hand the random students could be discounted from the equation as mere background, with the coded message inhering in the more important professors. On the other they could be trotted out to kneecap my argument with the objection that I was ignoring countervailing data points in order to cherry-pick those elements of set 1 that suited my theory. The same could be said of Jayashri Srikantiah. She was a law professor, but a clinical practice-focused teaching professor rather than a research-focused tenured/tenure-track one, the kind of position for which the fellowship was intended to groom me. So, whether she formed part of the relevant data set was open to interpretation. Likewise, Norman Spaulding appeared on two different slides but in three different images. So one could argue that he appeared thrice rather than twice and that my inference that the second of his two appearances was serving as a symbolic stand-in for my own career aspirations rested on a false premise. On one level these outliers were an exception to the core logic of the home page. But on another they were an extension of it, the logic of plausible deniability. Their presence was consistent with my hypothesis but could also be marshaled to discredit it as ad hoc and unrigorous. Embodying an intricate cost-benefit analysis, set 1 was imbued with enough logical structure to lead me to certain designated conclusions but not enough that I could readily sway anyone else to them.

Whether the message was sincere was another matter. Its plausible—more than plausible—deniability bespoke the possibility that it was not, that the conspirators had no intentions of salvaging my prospects and were just dangling this carrot to buy time and/or toy with me. Given the moral ambiguities of September 2009, it wasn't a given that they had truly recanted their former enmity and were now willing to resolve the situation amicably.

This indeterminacy had been logically baked into set 1. But as masters of cost-benefit analysis, my advisers had rightly calculated that the risk of their insincerity only partially discounted the value that set 1 might hold for me. Whereas any allegations regarding Barbara's suspicions or Weisberg's apoplexy rested on my credibility alone, set 1 was in full public view. Its incontrovertible presence on the home page wasn't an admission of wrongdoing. But it was an unofficial acknowledgment of the unofficial reality, confirming that any suspicions of wrongdoing were grounded in something real—the inflection point of September 2009. Set 1 therefore generated a new, nonlegal form of exposure, because, properly understood, it betrayed that one of the nation's premier law schools had elected to tinker with its home page in response to the improbable cascade of events I am chronicling here.

Whether or not my rights had actually been violated, the public revelation that set 1 had been instituted to address what might have been my inference to that effect could be deeply problematic for Stanford. Although perfectly legal, such shenanigans were incongruous with the *gravitas* of Stanford Law School and, if exposed, might be looked upon in some quarters as unbecoming the supreme dignity of so august an institution. Stanford's vulnerability on this front was therefore being held out as surety for the uncertainty that attached to the offer. The specter of insincerity didn't eviscerate the value of set 1 because set 1 constituted publicly accessible evidence of our byzantine power struggle, a potential counterweight to the might of Stanford that I might then parlay to my advantage should the message prove insincere. Set 1 offered up Stanford's social and cultural capital as a hedge against that eventuality, by enabling me to then lob these bombshell accusations and hoist the conspirators with their own petard.

This hedge meant that their latest outreach was in fact sincere at base. Here was a multilayered surreptitious quid pro quo arrangement according to which I would sit tight and not sue in exchange for either (1) a job of some sort or (2) some modicum of publicly accessible evidence for the existence of an underlying controversy, one interpretation of which might have moved Stanford to give me a job through a clandestine quid pro quo—but ultimately would not. The contractual "consideration" for my inaction might consist in continued employment, but it might also consist in just the home page itself as an allusion to that unrealized possibility, with the conspirators' true intentions remaining undisclosed and for me to ponder. They astutely reckoned that this proposal would survive my own cost-benefit analysis because the risk of public exposure via the home page turned the quid pro quo proposal into its own guarantor and collateral.

Of course, the realizable value of this insurance policy turned on my ability to persuade the public of its nature, as the burden of authenticating the evidence for it as evidence would be entirely my own. That presented a logical conundrum. I was arguing that the anomalous set 1 constituted evidence for the events of September 2009. But its probative value on this front in turn presupposed those events. So my argument could be readily dismissed as question begging, and the challenge would be to surmount this logical circularity by bootstrapping each half of the equation to the other. Set 1 therefore threw down the gauntlet with a challenge to my intellectual vanity. Barbara had been roiled by my deviance, discounting it as vain presumption and bravado, and set 1 begged the question of whether I'd been unduly cocksure when distributing my self-consecratory application materials back in September.

I was operating one level up during the conflict's infancy, when Barbara mistook my exit from the ambient culture for *celeritas* and unsuspectingly fired off the knockout email. Caught unaware by epistemic advantages I had recently accrued and incredulous of my ability to import "into the university field properties or powers acquired on other terrains," she found herself epistemically outflanked after Weisberg's biblical anger validated the inferences alluded to in the previous night's email. But the conceptual pyrotechnics announced by the home page signaled that Barbara, too, was now operating one level up. Whereas my hedge was Stanford's vulnerability to public exposure, Stanford's hedge was that I'd be dismissed as a lunatic simply for making this argument. That meant I would have to operate two levels up if I was to one-up Barbara anew by persuading whatever audience I could find that the ostensible crackpot was really a lone crusader for truth. How to do that? I didn't really know. But I was convinced the solution lay in conservative claims of cultural oppression, whose inner truth the Stanford Law home page was now beginning to articulate.

Observant readers will note that I couldn't have ascertained set 1's unusual longevity in autumn 2009, when I first formulated my heterodox hypothesis. Accordingly, that hypothesis was initially tentative, just a hunch at first. I appreciated that I might be projecting my own problems onto facts bearing no real relationship to them. But it was equally possible that my advisers had, knowing those problems and their origins, structured an image configuration calibrated to spur certain logically natural inferences. I had no direct evidence on this point one way or the other, but my theory had testable consequences. I would simply submit it to the scientific method, the outcome of which could allay these doubts. The question wasn't whether the theory resonated with me subjectively but whether it could withstand the test of a falsifiable prediction.

Suppose I was deluded as to either set 1 in particular or the whole chain of inferences that had led me to interpret it as I did, making its special resonance for me fortuitous. In that case I could reasonably expect set 1 to disappear in a few weeks' time, to be supplanted by a new random mélange of professors, students, and law school miscellany. The regular rotation of home page images was the custom. It was what made sense, given that the images weren't synchronized with special events, issues, or announcements. Since their only function was to exhibit an array of Stanford Law vignettes, they would soon enough be dislodged by other vignettes.

But if I was right, then it followed that set 1 would remain on the home page for much longer than was customary. I had conjectured that set 1's images had been assembled not only to clandestinely broadcast the quid pro quo but also to stand as surety for the uncertainty that perforce accompanied it—by generating a novel, nonlegal but still problematic font of exposure. Set 1 couldn't serve that function if it was to be, per the custom, removed after the usual few weeks. The anomalousness would then vanish, making it not only challenging but downright impossible to plead that set 1 bore the subterranean meaning I was ascribing to it. The quid pro quo would accordingly unravel, and there would then have been no sense in proposing it in the first place. The hazard of subjective delusion therefore didn't trouble me. Whatever my confirmation bias, the question would soon be settled by events over which I could exercise no influence or interpretive license. Set 1 would either remain up against all precedent or it wouldn't, and the outcome couldn't be attributed to subjective projection.

I will discuss the epistemic force of my falsifiable prediction in greater depth in chapter 6. Suffice it to say for present purposes that it was not in fact falsified. So, yes, I am purveying a conspiracy theory here. But my predictive prowess on this front would set that conspiracy theory apart from the rest, as would the other anomalies I would continue to encounter at Stanford. I reiterate that readers should evaluate my evidence cumulatively in the manner of scientists rather than piecemeal in the manner of climate change deniers, as I urged in the introduction. Kneejerk reactions to the facial outlandishness of my hypothesis are understandable, but I ask readers to resist these reflexes and keep their focus squarely on the totality of my argument, which I have only just begun to make.

Out of the Loop

Set 1 was still up the following week, too early for me to reach any definitive conclusions. Still, I wanted to touch base with Barbara and, with any luck, suss out more information. On Tuesday, November 17, I wrote her:

> Hi Barbara,
>
> I haven't thus far received a call-back from Colorado. I think the interview went well, but it's safe to say at this point that I'm not at the very top of their list. I'll remain on the lookout for new openings. But

> since these will probably be few in number, I would like to apply for an extension of my fellowship contract into the 2010-11 academic year and try again then. Please apprise me of the process.
>
> Best,
>
> Rony

In line with the policy of allusion, intimation, and ambiguation that was now standard protocol, I used a visual metaphor—"remain[ing] on the lookout for new openings"—to allude to the home page and my expectation that it would remain in its present configuration despite customary practice. In speaking of the new openings as being few in number, I was alluding to the specific opening at Stanford that I believed that configuration was intimating. In asking to be apprised of the process, I was soliciting a more concrete sense of the proposal and its implementation. I asked about renewing the fellowship both as a plausible context for these allusions and for its own sake. Whatever was to become of my tenure-track job search, I had to bring the project to completion, to which end I might require another year of fellowship.

Barbara's response the next day again betrayed the profound rift sundering the official and unofficial realities of our relations:

> Hi Rony: Let me talk to Larry about where we are on the fellowship for next year. I'm kind of out of the loop, as a result of being on leave and away from the law school. Can you update me on what transpired this fall? Did you interview w/Colorado at AALS? Did you interview with other schools there? If not, what's your take on why more schools didn't respond? And have you enlisted the help of Dick, Larry, Joe or others in drumming up interest at Colorado or elsewhere? -Barbara

Like her fulsome praise for my "great work," this debriefing could not be taken at face value. Barbara confessed to being "kind of out of the loop" by virtue of "being on leave and away from the law school." But that was an anachronistic excuse, since the internet had been with us for well more than a decade by then, and the telephone and automobile for even longer. The Center for Advanced Studies in the Behavioral Sciences (CASBS) was on the Stanford campus, moreover. As recently as September Barbara had made known her attempt to snag me when back at the law school for lunch. A sabbatical at CASBS wasn't an expedition to the Arctic. The fiction that it left her out of the loop was the latest chapter in her policy of feigned ignorance and detachment, once again enacted to maintain the unofficial reality's cloak of plausible deniability.

Barbara was indeed kind of out of the loop. But that was because she had kind of taken herself out of it when she declined my invitation to meet at the close of our September 8 phone conversation; failed to respond to my September 18 email asking for her take on Dick's idea to hold off on distributing the job-talk paper; and then failed to so much as acknowledge Ryan's invitation to participate in my moot interview. Barbara asked about my efforts to enlist her colleagues' assistance, but in this she was rather brazenly skirting the more immediate question about my efforts to enlist her own. I had also sought out Josh's assistance, but he was almost as elusive as she and, I suspected, for the same reasons. As when she copied Joe on the knockout email, Barbara's putative ignorance concerning her spouse's involvement could not be credited. Joe did not, in fact, appear overeager to assist me when we crossed paths in October, as I've related. Her putative ignorance regarding Larry also wasn't credible. Sure, they didn't cohabitate, but they worked for the same law school and had collaborated to bestow the fellowship. So one might think they'd occasionally correspond about the fruits of their investment.

Barbara was trying to elicit evidence of my culpability for the hiring season's disastrous denouement. Given my manifold derelictions, such evidence wasn't in short supply. However, she was constrained to seek out only the kind of evidence that was admissible within the official narrative of quotidian faculty-fellow collegiality, without hinting at the unofficial shadow world of deceit, enmity, and theorized slander. She couldn't just reiterate the verdict of the knockout email and, in a "see, I told you so" fashion, chide that the Overview's shortcomings had now caught up with me. That would have been inconsistent with the post–Weisberg death stare sanguinity of September 18, when she praised my "great work," sizing it up as good enough to sustain my candidacy, warts and all. The contradiction would have taken us to the toxic heart of the unofficial reality, the untouchable third rail of our relations. So, estopped from issuing any global indictment of my job performance, Barbara was restricted to underscoring discrete derelictions, like a failure to timely enlist faculty support—notwithstanding that this was well-nigh impossible under the circumstances, as evidenced by her own aloofness. If enlisting faculty assistance to drum up interest at Colorado was what truly concerned her, why not volunteer to drum it up herself, especially when my work was "fantastic—subtle, iconoclastic in the best way, and really, really interesting"? It had been only a week since the conference, so she conceivably could still exert some influence. If the thought didn't cross her mind, that was because the singular purpose of her probing was to histrionically prop up the facade of the official reality.

Barbara was out of the loop not because she was away at CASBS but because there had never been any loop to begin with. My recalcitrance since December 2008 had meant that the authenticity of our relationship would be undermined by the moral, semantic, and existential indeterminacy that first precipitated, and was then entrenched by, the tsunami of September 2009. With the ensuing bifurcation of the two realities, "the loop" had been running along two distinct tracks, making communication a rather burdensome and sometimes futile affair. The bifurcation couldn't be acknowledged, however, since its causes had to be elided for reasons of both law and academic etiquette.

Further information about my future would have to wait. In the meantime, I responded to this debriefing with a reminder of the facts, writing back the same day:

> Hi Barbara,
>
> I emailed Joe in late August hoping to meet and thereby enlist his help. But he hasn't gotten back to me yet. If you happen to run into him sometime, please remind him about it. I also emailed Larry at about the same time, hoping to enlist his interest in the Establishment Clause book, but he thought there were others more qualified to comment on that subject. I have talked with Dick on a number of occasions during the process, submitting to his advice and informing him of my actions and other developments. Since helping place fellows is part of his official job, I assumed that formally enlisting his services would be redundant. Was I mistaken?
>
> As to the process as a whole, let's just say that I have adopted an objective, as opposed to reactive, attitude toward it. Do you think that imperative can be universalized? I hope you're having an interesting time at CASBS. Human behavior is rich subject matter, particularly, I think, in connection with the problem of moral luck, both constitutive and outcome.
>
> Rony

Joe had remarked that my term paper was "dripping with irony." So, too, was this email. Of course, Barbara was going to run into Joe sometime. They lived under the same roof, making her feigned ignorance unconvincing. Barbara's efforts to coax evidence of my culpability moreover compelled me to remind her that agreement can be implied from circumstances, which she as a scholar of contracts understood as well as anyone. By intimating that any failure to enlist faculty support couldn't fully account for the hiring season's dismal outcome, my facetious ripostes to Barbara's inquest alluded to the unofficial reality, which contained the unabridged story.

Because I was rhetorically barred from tendering the comprehensive self-assessment that she was also trying to wring out of me, I addressed the situation at large philosophically, drawing Barbara's attention to certain affinities between it and the academic subject matter that had first entwined our paths in the primeval past of the moral luck class. In averring my adoption of an objective attitude, I was of course alluding to Strawson's *Freedom and Resentment* and, therefore, the class presentation that had once seduced her interest and earned her favor. As Strawson argues, the objective attitude is precipitated not by the theoretical embrace of determinism but by a practical breakdown in normal human engagement. This descent into dysfunctionality was precisely what had transpired that fall. And the point was that I wasn't taking things personally and rather aspired to a dispassionate, scientific understanding of a complicated state of play. In asking whether that "imperative could be universalized," I was urging Barbara to follow suit, our only hope of reconciliation.

The reference to moral luck touched on a related point that I was only then beginning to formulate: Though hardly an intrinsic evildoer, Barbara had had the bad moral luck of encountering circumstances (precipitated by me) that compelled the latent illiberalism of the liberal elites to surface (as it usually doesn't in our culture). Barbara's incredulity of the works in progress was a natural by-product of her devotion to no-nonsense academic realpolitik. Yet this incredulity culminated in my arguable defamation. I was, therefore, Barbara's bad moral luck, because I had generated conditions under which impulses that ordinarily pass as unproblematic were abruptly transmuted into imaginable legal exposure.

"Liberal fascists," Jonah Goldberg writes, conceal the latent "totalitarian temptations in their hearts." And my deviance had smoked out those temptations by compelling Barbara to more openly express the academic ideology that routinely passes under the radar as the natural order of things. She and Joe had initially sought to enforce their pinched technocratic paradigm more subtly, with well-meaning counsels and admonitions. In resisting these, I induced a steady buildup of pent-up frustration that later metastasized into bitter hatred, becoming physiologically embodied in Weisberg's biblical anger and hence my arguable cause of action, which henceforth stood as a symbolic rebuke to the prevailing ideology. Barbara had dismissed the Overview as mere *celeritas*. But this verdict redounded to her embarrassment when her machinations became subsumed by my own. Other professors at Stanford and elsewhere had never faced such misfortune, for they'd never faced the bad moral luck of a tangle with me. I wasn't expecting to communicate these precise thoughts, which were only then crystallizing in my own mind. But the subject of moral luck had become eminently germane to the situation. And Barbara, who had taught a class on the subject, was amply qualified to reflect on why.

The Moot Job Talk

I had a moot job talk to give that same day, Wednesday, November 18, to which I'd invited Josh, Marcus Cole, and Dick, along with the fellows. Marcus, who hadn't RSVP'd, nonetheless showed up. But Josh, who had accepted the invite, did not and later emailed me to apologize, pleading that he was occupied with an undisclosed emergency. Emergencies do happen, but it was at least as likely that I was now radioactive and he was maneuvering to minimize contact. At any rate I at last had a version of the paper that could pass muster. It wasn't yet what it would become, but I had cleaned up the major weaknesses Barbara had discerned, and I was in command of the material. In the feedback session Dick remarked that I faced a real challenge presenting material of such richness in a mere twenty minutes. Ryan seconded the observation, noting that the thesis had "so many threads" while alerting me to my tendency to utter "of course" too much.

Marcus had been at the table with Weisberg on September 16, but I hadn't yet had the pleasure of an extended conversation with him.

As a burly black conservative law professor, complete with dreadlocks and a street-savvy, street-tough attitude, he was a peculiar character who confounded all the usual categories. His observations were no less interesting. The first was that I was maldistributing my glances at various audience members. I hadn't noticed, but others confirmed the insight. I promised to watch for this in the future.

My talk noted that the first "war on Christmas" had been waged not by the secular liberals of the ACLU but by a different group of "East Coast elites," the New England Puritans who denounced public celebrations of Christmas as papal corruptions of the true faith, relics of paganism rather than Christianity proper. And, moving on to the talk's substance, Marcus now corrected me, admonishing that the first war on Christmas had been instigated in England, not New England. That stood to reason, since the Puritans hailed from there. Even so, this pedantic objection wasn't germane intellectually, as my subject was religious neutrality, not English history. The latter would have been topical were we debating, say, the original understanding of the Establishment Clause, which had the Anglican Church as a negative reference point.[iv] However, the Puritans' hewing to the same theology

---

[iv] Established national religions have been the norm in the West going back at least to Emperor Theodosius, who instituted Christianity as the official religion of the Roman Empire. The official state religion gave divine legitimacy to the state's secular authority, while that authority in turn helped enforce church orthodoxy. England's official state religion has been the Anglican Church since Henry VIII's break with Roman Catholicism (aside from a brief Catholic restoration), and Americans of the Revolutionary period balked at an established national church as part and parcel of the royal oppression against which they were rebelling. In the years following the Revolution, Thomas Jefferson and James Madison famously succeeded in dislodging the Anglican Church from its place of privilege as the official religion of their native Virginia. Until then the Anglican Church had been the sole religious recipient of public funds. While some Virginians advocated that citizens instead be permitted to direct their tax dollars to the religious denomination of their choosing, Jefferson and Madison insisted that mandatory religious tithing of any kind violated liberty of conscience. Their view prevailed, and many scholars credit their campaign in Virginia as an important precursor to the Establishment Clause, which would be ratified a few years later.

in England as they later took with them to the New World didn't seem particularly noteworthy. Given that the "war on Christmas" was an American meme, I felt justified in restricting my attention to the American context, and Marcus's gratuitous reproof in no way detracted from the irony I was highlighting—or from my thesis that American secularism isn't religiously neutral insofar as it is a historical offshoot of Protestantism's ascetic hostility to embodied forms of religiosity revolving around sacred times, places, and things. At any rate I wasn't going to cavil about relevance. He had scored his point, and I wasn't one to try to take it away from him.

Marcus next protested that just as he didn't, as a black American, appreciate broad generalizations about blacks, neither did he as a conservative look kindly upon such treatments of conservatives. My paper was contrasting different kinds of people, but the focus should be their arguments, he admonished. This was a serious point. Even so, I remonstrated that my perhaps counterintuitive approach was commanded by my very thesis, according to which competing paradigms of religious neutrality spring from differences in our prerational makeup. As Norbert Elias observes, "Civilization, and therefore rationalization, for example, is not a process within a separate sphere of 'ideas' or 'thought.' It does not involve solely changes of 'knowledge,' transformations of 'ideologies,' in short alterations of the content of consciousness, but changes in the whole human make-up, within which ideas and habits of thought are only a single sector."[1] I was addressing conservatives (and liberals) as people and not just as opinion holders because I had posited that our conceptions of religious neutrality bespeak "the whole human make-up," reflecting the degree to which the disciplines and repressions of the liberal culture have molded consciousness. That is why conservative culture warriors treat liberalism as "beyond politics," as Thomas Frank observes. The discussion's ad hominem tenor wasn't gratuitous but part and parcel of that thesis.

Marcus acknowledged my rationale but stressed that it still ran afoul of customary faculty expectations, which I would have to figure out how to appease. He then probed whether my argument spoke to the idea that environmentalism constitutes a secular religion, to which he appeared sympathetic. Without endorsing this, I answered that it might well follow from my broader argument that secularism secularizes certain historically bequeathed religious impulses that are no longer recognized as such.

Marcus's final question concerned my argument's affinities to the work of Thomas Sowell, the famed black conservative economist and social thinker. The question was facially serious and profitable. But Marcus did not see fit to disclose what part of Sowell's vast corpus he was referencing and thus clarify exactly what he was getting at. As luck would have it, I was familiar enough with Sowell to extemporize that while a counter-Enlightenment thinker like Nietzsche doesn't share Sowell's overall normative worldview, Nietzsche would probably endorse Sowell's nonrationalistic take on human motivation as expounded in his "constrained vision" of the human condition.

This response seemed to satisfy Marcus. But my familiarity with Sowell, and hence my ability to take up Marcus's deliberately vague question on the fly, had been fortuitous. Sowell wasn't known for his commentary on the Establishment Clause, and this wasn't a question that would naturally pop into the mind of someone who had that as their focus. Although serious in its substance, the question was a trap in its function, which I had the good fortune to elude. Its purpose wasn't to stimulate thought or satisfy curiosity but to expose ignorance and, ideally, embarrass. Barbara was warning me about these shark-infested waters back in December 2008, when she stressed that it behooved me to master the Establishment Clause case law. She foresaw that anything less would leave me exposed to such onslaughts, haplessly peppered by a barrage of gratuitous questions about random cases, my ignorance of which would be embarrassing and discrediting even if intellectually tangential to the topic at hand.

The exercise concluded without further incident. I hadn't emailed Marcus the paper, now sixty-five pages, as he hadn't confirmed his attendance. But he was interested in possessing it, so Dick donated his copy. As the audience disbanded, I updated Dick that I hadn't received any word from Colorado but had applied to renew the Gaither fellowship. He responded with nebulous expressions of confidence about my future and then threw me a wink and a nod—the universal symbol of plausible deniability—thus dog whistling to the unofficial reality in whose long shadow I now operated.

The Informal Route

I made a visit to my hometown of Columbus, Ohio, for Thanksgiving but was back in San Francisco by December 9, when I received the following email from Barbara:

> Rony—The answer on extending the fellowship is, alas, no. We've got a strict two-year limit. I'm happy to talk about where to go from here if you want. The answer, I imagine, will depend a lot on what you think went wrong this year. It would probably be a good idea to triangulate your own impressions with others' (Dick and Joe, maybe). If you ultimately decide that reapplying next year [for a tenure-track job], with another fellowship next year [to hold you over], is the way you want to go, there are now a ton of options out there for fellowships. The most comprehensive list I know of is posted on Paul Caron's website.
>
> Here's the link:
>
> http://taxprof.typepad.com/taxprof_blog/2008/03/teaching-fellow.html
>
> But new ones pop up all the time. Many of the deadlines are in Jan or Feb, so you should start thinking about it now. In addition, many schools will do a one-off arrangement if they have the money, you can fill temporary teaching needs they have, etc. The informal route requires persistence and often some in, to get the relevant administrator to pay attention to you. Best, Barbara

I had been awaiting some further allusion to the possibility intimated by set 1. And Barbara was now delivering this in her speculations about a "one-off arrangement" through an "informal route" helped along by "some in." The referent was "many schools," not Stanford in particular. Nor was Stanford specifically excluded, however. As with Dick's facially gratuitous reminder that "just because they're interviewing doesn't meaning they're hiring," the delicate nature of the situation called for the use of generic terms whose concrete referents would be laid bare inside the shadow world of the unofficial reality. I needed "some in," but what law school fit that bill other than Stanford? Was I supposed to first procure that place of privilege elsewhere? Was the suggestion that I, say, drive across the Bay to Berkeley, walk into the law school, locate the "relevant administrator," and then petition her to "pay attention" to me? Should I, in that show of persistence Barbara stressed would be necessary, then proceed to periodically pester this as-yet-unidentified power broker about a job on the off chance that some unspecified teaching need had cropped up? This would have to be an opening that I was qualified to fill but couldn't be filled by anyone in Berkeley's large Rolodex of trusted research professors, visiting professors, fellows, and adjunct lecturers, a most implausible scenario that couldn't be taken at face value.

The "relevant administrator" was Barbara herself, and the events of September 2009 were the reason she might now pay attention to me. She advised that I might "fill temporary teaching needs they have, etc." The *etc.* could, of course, have referred to some unspecified possibilities that Barbara hadn't the time or inclination to contemplate but didn't want to rule out. But the policy of allusion, intimation, and ambiguation that was the order of the day called for a more rigorous parsing. *Etc.* placed after "temporary teaching needs" meant "something other than temporary," and what isn't temporary is ipso facto permanent, or at least long term. Who was in any position to deliver that? Was I going to importune the "relevant administrator" at Berkeley or elsewhere for a permanent job? Barbara appreciated the semantic ambiguity of *etc.* and exploited it to further intimate at the proposal already outlined by set 1.

Barbara stated that the Gaither fellowship was not renewable owing to a "strict two-year limit." But why had it taken her three weeks to respond that, "alas," she had no discretion in the matter? Why, given what she suggested was a fixed administrative regulation, did she have to consult with Larry about "where we are on the fellowship for next year"? If a strict two-year limit was really built into the fellowship's charter, she could have declined my petition off the top of her head without further ado, whether "out of the loop" at CASBS or not. Barbara had dispensed the fellowship to me and been involved in its endowment, so such a stricture couldn't have slipped from mind.

The fellowship did not in fact have a "strict two-year limit," as the law school's own web pages revealed. Two postings, one quoting Barbara and the other referencing Dick, divulged that it would ordinarily span two years but could also be shorter or longer according to individual circumstances.[2] There was a flexible two-year general expectation, not a "strict two-year limit." Whereas I'd been awarded the fellowship without even applying—moments after Barbara declared my Legal Theory term paper brilliant—I was now barred from so much as applying for its renewal, when the fellowship's publicly posted charter clearly allowed for that possibility. Notwithstanding her *alas*, Barbara had made a decision that was inconsistent with her earlier plaudits for my job-talk paper. I subsequently sat rotting on the faculty hiring market, but Barbara had predicted a different outcome when she reassured in that same email that the paper was "good enough to carry you." By her own lights, then, I had simply run into some bad luck, and it didn't make moral or institutional sense to punish mere bad luck in this manner.

So Barbara's decision here was at odds with the official narrative of healthy faculty-fellow collegiality being spun in her emails. What, then, did it all mean unofficially? As with set 1 and everything else by that point, this latest correspondence allowed for two competing interpretations:

Interpretation 1—Having realized that she'd misjudged me and my research agenda, Barbara wanted a cessation of hostilities. She could now see that I was indeed the person whom she and Joe believed they knew, despite the heterodox methods necessitated by my heterodox subject matter. My advisers, furthermore, appreciated the rich irony that a term paper whose thesis concerned liberal hypocrisy—and specifically the academic elites'—should have received empirical confirmation in their own rush to judgment. As the "relevant administrator," Barbara would provide the "in" whereby to access some form of continued employment at what was now looking like my only option, Stanford, where I would continue to do "great work" that was "fantastic—subtle, iconoclastic in the best way, and really, really interesting." My fellowship hadn't been renewed because such was unnecessary when I'd be landing something better. The declination would, moreover, belie the existence of a quid pro quo, since plausible deniability had to be maintained. If Barbara was resorting to a procedural falsehood rather than substantive grounds to rebuff my petition, that was to avoid saying anything disparaging of me. She had taken three weeks and consulted with Larry before coming back with an answer that, had it been true, would have been available to her immediately because the gratuitous delay was intended to convey the utter unreality of the official reality.

Interpretation 2—Interpretation 1 was indeed the message, but it was insincere. Barbara had written off the fellowship as an embarrassing boondoggle for which she reproached herself and despised me. My death warrant had already been signed, and she wanted me out of the law school before her repatriation from CASBS next year. She had generously conferred the fellowship, but with singular ingratitude I then declined to play by her rules and metastasized into her bad moral luck, generating conditions under which a sequence of good faith inferences grounded in the available evidence eventuated in conceivable legal exposure. Not only had she backed the wrong horse; this beast was now biting the hand that fed it. Barbara was hoping I'd buy into interpretation 1 so she could avenge these wrongs by fostering an expectation that she could later both dash and deny ever having fostered. In this manner she would imbue my fall from grace with that "extra violence" that Bourdieu observes "is added to the discreet polemics of academic hatred by the methodical erasure of all external signs of violence," thus doubling her revenge. Simply put, she and my other advisers were conspiring to reduce me to a conspiracy theorist.

As a collateral benefit, such gaslighting would also stave off any legal reprisals on my part, should that avenue tempt me. That I could ever prove defamation by a preponderance of the evidence was rather doubtful, as was my ability to proselytize a jury of average learning and intellect to the subterranean significance of set 1. But the preemptive quashing of my fellowship renewal request gave me a firmer legal footing. It was a two-year contract and I wasn't entitled to an extension. But I could make a nonfrivolous case that I was owed a good faith *review* of my request for one—rather than a bad faith averment of a provably nonexistent "strict two-year limit." Whatever this claim's ultimate legal merits, my advisers were "the relevant administrators," and academic administrators crave peace and quiet above all. Fostering the hope of interpretation 1 would promote precisely these goods by giving me an incentive to tread lightly.

Whereas interpretation 1 operated one level up from the official reality, interpretation 2 operated one level up from interpretation 1 itself, which is to say two levels up from the official reality. The risk that interpretation 2 might prove correct did not destroy the value that this game of smoke and mirrors held for me because these new lines concerning an "informal route" and the contradiction between Barbara's averment of a "strict two-year limit" and the publicly accessible truth would in any event serve as further evidence of the unofficial reality. These were two more pieces of a puzzle that I might cobble into a credible argument that would inure to my advantage by exposing my employer's metalevel machinations.

The truth of interpretation 1 was exponentially preferable to the alternative, which was merely the possibility of proving the truth of interpretation 2. But that opportunity was still better than nothing, which was exactly what I'd be left with if I failed to engage with the palace intrigue. I might still have a contractual claim against Stanford. But, given my aversion to all the hassles, uncertainty, and other ordeals the legal route entailed, it held much less appeal than the prospect of exposing the policy of allusion, intimation, and ambiguation that was fast becoming an extension of my research agenda.

The conspirators grasped my position perfectly well. As masters of cost-benefit analysis, they had adroitly reckoned that set 1, along with other indicia of the unofficial reality, would placate me at this juncture, inducing me to sit tight in acceptance of the terms of the quid pro quo. This wasn't a lasting peace treaty but only a fragile armistice, and I acceded to it only because I fancied I could exploit its terms to somehow neutralize the might of Stanford, if it came to that. Barbara, in contrast, was confident that any such gambit was futile and accordingly felt secure in her plausible deniability. Her policy of allusion, intimation, and ambiguation thus posed a challenge to my intellectual vanity, and that was what made it effective. Precisely because we disagreed about the nature of my capabilities, the surety held out by the home page could facilitate a new modus vivendi. Barbara thought me too clever by half. But, unaware of my lasting interest in the critical theory of academia, she failed to appreciate that I was in my element, far better equipped to navigate these uncharted waters than the typical fellow lacking such expertise.

Whatever the Overview's merits as a set of summaries, it was a great success as a set of prophesies. That document observed that conservatives' cultural subordination to liberals places them in a Kafkaesque predicament. The conservative understands himself, like Kafka's Josef K. in *The Trial*, as a man "who wakes up to find himself hounded by the Court for a crime the nature of which he cannot be given to understand." This had now become my own predicament.

The system of allusion, intimation, and ambiguation now oppressing me had its origins in the controversy of September 2009. But "the Court"—that is, Stanford Law School—would not divulge its own interpretation of that controversy, turning my guilt before it into a black box.

I hadn't misrepresented myself in the crudest, most transparently unethical, sense of simply inventing works in progress from whole cloth. But was that the gravamen of the indictment, or had I also been charged with some broader, more philosophically debatable, transgressions? My conduct during the year flouted industry-standard expectations, and I had launched into the hiring season belatedly and shambolically. On the other hand, Dick had hailed my research agenda as "rich and complex." Josh had gone out of his way to praise it for raising new and important questions that would draw widespread interest. And Barbara had lauded my paper as "fantastic—subtle, iconoclastic in the best way, and really, really interesting." That draft was still in disarray at the time, but she had aptly sized up its intellectual core and potential. So how did it all add up and where did I now stand? I was no boy scout, admittedly, but what exactly was I guilty of? I knew not. My guilt was just as indeterminate as set 1 and the situation generally, placing me in a Kafkaesque relationship to a star chamber that would not publicize the nature of the charges lodged.

Now mired in semantic and existential indeterminacy, I was being plunged into an ever-deepening spiral of angst, nihilism, and exhaustion as my future hung in the balance. Would I one day be released from this weltering limbo with some sort of reprieve after I'd done my penance? Or was the penance to be everlasting, as it became clear that my alma mater was grinding me down for sport? What would it take to sate Barbara's sublime vengefulness? I couldn't assess the severity of the sentencing because I wasn't privy to the nature of the charges. The question was whether I was temporarily in purgatory or permanently in hell, and my ignorance of my sentence was a hell in its own right. My punishment, just like my crime, operated one level up.

The nature of my predicament was clear in its broad outlines. But I wanted to know more. However, I wasn't terribly inclined to meet with Joe or Barbara now to "triangulate" impressions of what went wrong, given their elusiveness in the fall before my job search went sideways. This outcome was overdetermined, and their elusiveness was scarcely the only factor. Their elusiveness was, moreover, forgivable under the circumstances, seeing as the recent legalization of our already frayed relations had made things exceedingly awkward for all concerned. So I didn't begrudge them their inaccessibility, which was just the mirror image of my own during the preceding year. Still, my tolerance for the charade also had its limits, and such a conversation now would have been too much to bear. I replied to Barbara's email by saying that I would first touch base with Dick, with whom I'd already been in consultation, to "get his take on the two routes you've suggested and on strategies for pursuing them."

My relationship with Dick was also a farce. But it had been that from the start and therefore felt more natural. I wrote to him on Friday, December 11:

> Hi Dick,
>
> No word still from Colorado, which probably means no good word may be expected. It turns out that my fellowship isn't renewable. But Barbara suggested some other possible avenues, such as pursuing other fellowships and informal networking. Are you available sometime next week to discuss these ideas and where to go from here?
>
> Best,
>
> Rony

The manipulation of the home page images had alerted me to some kind of proposal from Stanford, and Barbara's invocation of an informal "one-off arrangement" facilitated by the right contacts gave me a somewhat more concrete sense of how it might be implemented But I needed to ferret out more, and this email was intended to prime Dick for a deep dive into "informal networking." Naturally, this briefing would have to proceed according to precedent, in keeping with the policy of allusion, intimation, and ambiguation that was now standard protocol. A lawyer of Dick's caliber would face no difficulty operating in that key. He had already displayed his talents on this front back in October, and I looked forward to an informative chat.

We scheduled a meeting for the following Wednesday, December 16, after what would be the last faculty luncheon of the fall term. This would be in Dick's office, but he already seated himself beside me at the luncheon. He was the conspiracy's liaison to me, after all, tasked with reassuring me that the powers that be were monitoring my situation, and here was another gesture to that effect. We later reconvened in his office for the official conferral, and his first words after our exchange of greetings were "So I didn't know your fellowship couldn't be renewed." The histrionics of feigned ignorance were in high gear. The web posting inviting fellowship applications, where the absence of a strict two-year limit was expressly disclosed, listed Dick as the contact person. Was he asking me to believe that he was ill acquainted with the very fellowship he administered? Hardly. The point, rather, was that his utterances weren't to be taken at face value.

Feigning resignation to the facts on the ground, I reiterated Barbara's proposed solutions to my present misfortune, another fellowship and informal networking, noting in passing that David Ball, the former fellow now at Santa Clara, had been helped along by informal networking, as I recalled his having some contacts there before being hired on the tenure track. I intended the remark as anodyne small talk, but Dick took umbrage and chided that Ball's contacts weren't the only reason he was hired. And so I was compelled to articulate the disclaimer I had assumed could go without saying, that I'd never meant to suggest otherwise. Relationships are no substitute for merit but merely a way to offset the frequent randomness of academic hiring. I wouldn't be insinuating that exploiting these was somehow dishonorable when I was now hoping to do so myself. No doubt, much academic hiring proceeds in this fashion. Dick probably discerned a modicum of chagrin in my voice as I invoked David Ball. But that had nothing to do with his scholarly qualifications and everything to do with his habit of publicly impugning my work ethic, as I have discussed. My modicum of chagrin was a more than measured response, I felt.

Moving past this contretemps to serious matters, I invited Dick to elaborate on how, exactly, Barbara's suggestion about informal networking might play out, putting the question in a knowing tone. He advised, also knowingly, that informal networking might "at some point in the year" place my CV in the hands of an appointments committee somewhere that needed someone to teach, say, constitutional law on short notice and so couldn't conduct a full search. "Would such a position pay like a visiting professorship?" I probed.

"Or a first-year law professor," he clarified sanguinely.

Dick's hypothetical scenario was undoubtedly possible, both logically and physically. But it was so improbable on its face that one could be forgiven for wondering why this piece of ostensibly free-floating speculation had crossed his mind in the first place. How often do teaching requirements arise on such short notice that a full search isn't possible? Such a contingency probably wouldn't be handled by an appointments committee anyway but by whoever administered the Rolodex of the relevant law school's known and trusted adjuncts or visiting lecturers. Thus a full search would likely be unnecessary even if possible. And what was the practical value of such speculation, given that there was no way to pound the pavement in search of whichever law school out there was going to find itself in this opportune predicament? Even granting that such things happen once in a blue moon, why did Dick feel the need to gratuitously embellish the envisioned prospect by tying it to what my résumé listed as my top teaching preference, constitutional law—making it doubly improbable?

That such a position might pay like a first-year law professor was also outlandish on its face. Visiting assistant professorships—temporary positions for folks who aren't already affiliated with another institution—are just fellowships with teaching loads and pay about the same. That is, substantially less than a first-year tenure-track law professor. Why would the informality of Dick's conjured arrangement upend that industry-standard remuneration? Why would a law school pay someone they don't know, and who isn't established at another law school, so much more than their own fellows, adjuncts, and lecturers? Nothing in the record suggested I had that kind of bargaining power.

Hiring me to teach constitutional law also made little sense, as I had no real expertise in the subject. I had wrested a Dean's Achievement Award for my first-year performance in it at Texas but had never taught it or published in it, and my "iconoclastic" thoughts on the Establishment Clause weren't the sort of thing that's on the menu in first-year constitutional law courses. This inexperience wouldn't be a deal breaker in the context of an entry-level tenure-track position. Given that tenure-track law professors often instruct a first-year or other bread-and-butter course as part of their teaching load, they will often spend their first year on the job developing expertise in a mainstay subject that lies outside their niche research interests. A specialist in law and philosophy, for instance, might have to hit the evidence books her first year, if that was her assigned bread-and-butter course. Indeed, Barbara had once counseled me not to fret about cultivating any specialized teaching competence, since I'd be afforded a chance to do so on the job. However, a law school seeking to retain an interim instructor to fill in some one-off vacancy would be looking for someone with demonstrable competence in the subject—because they're paying him only to run a single class, not investing in his long-term value for the institution.

Given the fanciful nature of the scenario, I asked Dick how I might bring it about. He replied that I need only inform my recommenders of my interest. That is, he did not say something like "maybe you could attend talks at Berkeley or elsewhere and make contacts that way." The informal networking opportunity, if it came, would be through my recommenders, one of whom, Barbara, was at the origin of the idea.

All this confirmed my surmise that the appointments committee Dick was conjuring wasn't generic at all but rather denoted Stanford's appointments committee. These were the éminences grises to whom my recommenders—the conduits of my informal networking—could hand off my CV. Some last-minute emergency "at some point in the year"—when I was the only one around to teach what just happened to be my preferred subject—would be the pretext whereby to fulfill the home page's intimations of continued employment at the law school. The point of the ostensible hypothetical was to suggest that I might be insulated from the usual vagaries of the academic marketplace. Where could that insulation come from except Stanford, to which I was already connected?

What kind of post was being proposed? I wasn't sure, and just about anything would have sufficed, given the impending expiration of the fellowship in August. But "first-year law professor" suggested it could lead to a second year, implying something long term (which confirmed my reading of Barbara's *etc.*). Dick's reference to the salary of a "first-year law professor" was outlandish in the ostensible conversational context but cogent within the unofficial backstory that undergirded it. This was Stanford, which had already been the subtext of a previous conversation. Only Stanford and the unofficial reality endowed Dick's musings with the cogency they were superficially lacking. The home page's subterranean intimations of a job were the true semantic background for those musings, decrypting what seemed like a fanciful hypothetical about my good fortune with some unknown appointments committee into a concrete proposal concerning the terms on which our months-old standoff could be resolved. This was the "one-off" arrangement referenced in Barbara's email.

Sure, you could argue that Dick's hypothetical didn't make sense on its own terms only because he was speaking off the cuff, without having put much thought into it. But I had come to know Dick well enough to appreciate that he was not a thoughtless man given to gratuitous, ill-conceived utterances. These superficially risible lapses of logic and good sense were calculated semantic manipulations of background understandings springing from the unofficial reality. As before, he had engaged in these manipulations to intimate what had to be left unsaid, confined to the tacit dimension where my advisers had now joined me.

As with the home page itself, the sincerity of Dick's assurances that afternoon was an open question. The ostensible message was "We shouldn't have leaped to conclude that you were slacking and falsifying the record. Now that we know better and see your commitment, we want to make it up to you." But, as I've stressed, the moral topography of September 2009 was exponentially murkier than a child's morality tale. Barbara had been too quick to discount my works in progress, and the knockout email was less than forthright about the true scope of her concerns. Even so, her inferences proceeded in good faith and were reasonable, given how the available data had to appear through her professionalized epistemic prism. She couldn't have foreseen that my deviant ways would lead me to check out of the liberal culture and that such would prove indispensable to my research agenda. I myself came to this realization only late in the day, and that exit had yet to bear any tangible fruits, so it wasn't a given that we were truly on the same page. While I hadn't been slacking in my primordial commitments, these had led me to violate ambient cultural norms when I treated the relative freedom of the fellowship as carte blanche to dwell in the tacit dimension and then sacrificed collegiality on the altar of legal advantage. Against this backdrop Dick's sincerity was very much up in the air. The moral and intellectual ambiguities of September 2009 weren't dead history but rather lived on in the semantic ambiguities enveloping Dick's strange pronouncements that afternoon in mid-December.

The conversation concluded with some chitchat about applying for other fellowships, as this formed part of the total context in which Barbara had couched her thoughts about the "informal route." I told Dick that I would apply to whatever was out there, and he asked to be kept abreast of any bites. As a counterweight to his earlier intimations, he suggested that, unless I was independently wealthy, it would behoove me to seek out private-sector employment to keep me going next year, should it come to that. I threw out the idea of a foundation grant, but Dick advised that these were mostly restricted to tenured professors.

Winding things down, Dick turned to the big picture and tried to console me with the thought that success on the law faculty market could be highly random and frequently turned on luck. I shouldn't read too much into my single interview, since I might well line up fifteen the next time around. Dick's reassurances contained a grain of truth. The frequent arbitrariness of academic hiring is a platitude. None less than Max Weber observed:

> Certainly, chance does not rule alone, but it rules to an unusually high degree. I know of hardly any career on earth where chance plays such a role. I may say so all the more since I personally owe it to some mere accidents that during my very early years I was appointed to a full professorship in a discipline in which men of my generation undoubtedly achieved more than I had. And indeed, I fancy, on the basis of this experience, that I have a sharp eye for the undeserved fate of the many whom accident has cast in the opposite direction and who within this selective apparatus in spite of all their ability do not attain the positions that are due them.[3]

Be this as it may, the kernel of truth in Dick's solace was still only that. As even Weber would have to concede, the process wasn't as random as Dick was suggesting. Bad luck might explain why a candidate landed one interview rather than two or three, or ten rather than fifteen, and such vicissitudes could have ramifications for a career. But chance alone couldn't account for why I wound up with a single interview instead of fifteen. Dick's services as placement adviser would be pointless were things truly so random.

The calamity at hand had a complicated explanation, and Dick was pretending otherwise because that explanation was inextricably entwined with the unofficial reality. That it was Dick, the seasoned placement adviser, rather than I, the rookie job seeker, who appeared to be indulging in wishful thinking was another testament to the fellowship's convoluted course, the profound rupture between its official and unofficial realities. Dick's unbounded optimism was cold comfort, as his bromides about impending good luck were a poor substitute for renewing my fellowship or even a good faith review of my request thereof. That I'd be hitting the market ignominiously next year as a former Stanford fellow alone ruled out fifteen interviews, as he well knew.

The Stanford Law Home Page: Set 2

Winter break 2009 was upon us, and set 1 was removed from the home page to make room for holiday imagery announcing the law school's closure for the recess. It would be reinstated a few weeks later when classes reconvened. I had by then learned of another change to the home page system. It had been digitally bifurcated, so that the set from which images were randomly drawn now varied according to the connection through which one accessed it. It appeared that most off-campus connections displayed set 1, but all the campus connections (such as library computer terminals) were now linked to set 2, configured as follows (see exhibit D in appendix 1):

Slide 1

Dean Larry Kramer lecturing

Slide 2

Former dean Kathleen Sullivan lecturing

Slide 3

Deceased chief justice of the U.S. Supreme Court William Rehnquist, an alumnus of Stanford Law

Slide 4

Random students chatting outside the law school

Slide 5

Cyclists riding by the law school

Slide 6

Random students in the library

Slide 7

A stack of law books

Slide 8

Random students chatting

This was peculiar, as I didn't think such a bifurcation was standard practice at other law schools (or any academic departments, for that matter). It had no obvious rationale, and Stanford Law hadn't done this in the past, as far as I knew. The explanation was plain enough to me, though. Set 1 was, after all, unseemly. As I have explained, there was no obvious reason why Joe, Larry, Kathleen Sullivan, Mark Kelman, and Norman Spaulding (twice)—and not some other assortment of professors—should be paraded on the home page in perpetuity. Their selection raised no questions within a system of ongoing rotations, because one random grouping of professors soon would be supplanted by another. But it became odder by the day now that set 1 was a permanent fixture of the home page.

Naive onlookers would never divine set 1's subterranean meaning, of course, and no one was likely to raise a stink about the new policy. Images on law school home pages are among the last things on the minds of right-thinking citizens. Still, the new dispensation had a certain weirdness that might have slightly unnerved the conspirators, who as masters of cost-benefit analysis decided to mitigate that weirdness through set 2. Since most of the day-to-day home page viewing was likely taking place on campus by students, the conspirators determined that set 2 would appear there. Unlike set 1, set 2 made sense as a permanent fixture of the home page. Its denizens weren't just rank-and-file professors but Stanford Law notables—a dean, a former dean, and an alum who rose to chief justice of the Supreme Court. As fitting icons for the law school's collective identity, they endowed set 2 with a conceptual coherence that wasn't apparent in set 1. They also enjoyed a certain aesthetic coherence likewise absent in set 1, as all the luminaries were in black and white. This congruity could justify instituting set 2 on the on-campus connections. At the same time, set 2 shared a nucleus with set 1, Larry Kramer and Kathleen Sullivan, enabling me to argue that set 2 had been derived from set 1 and therefore was consonant with the unofficial reality.

This common nucleus was the conspiracy's paltry concession to my need for evidence of an underlying controversy, the bedrock requirement of the quid pro quo agreed upon. The bifurcation was a quick and dirty solution inasmuch as the facially arbitrary set 1 would remain on off-campus connections. Still, this awkward compromise was a creative response to a delicate problem, splitting the difference between my need for evidence and the conspiracy's need for normalcy and plausible deniability. Set 2 belied the suggestion that the powers that be had better things to worry about than home page images and their logical relationship to each other. If they could be bothered with ensuring the internal coherence of set 2, then they could devote the same care and attention to set 1. However trivial home page images may seem, clearly someone had contemplated them long enough to somehow arrive at the conclusion that the system should be bifurcated.

CHAPTER 6

Theoretical Excursus

A Falsifiable Hypothesis

Who could have been at the origin of all these machinations? I was guessing, obviously. Joe, Larry, Barbara, and Dick all had the requisite genius to rise to such Machiavellian heights. But the singular sublimity of the pyrotechnics pointed to Barbara as the architect, evincing her signature penchant for blurring the line between truth and falsehood. She was also a theoretician of contracts, and the quid pro quo was masterfully crafted to operate at the very edges of the law without crossing the line into any conceivable illegality. The arrangement was inherently indeterminate, premised on mere conjectures about the other party's thought process, which in turn rested on its own set of conjectures. As I've stressed, set 1 in no way promised a job. That was merely one of two possibilities; the other was that set 1 promised only itself as evidence of an underlying controversy. Feeling secure in their plausible deniability, the conspirators didn't imagine they were transacting a "thing of value" in offering up these images. Absent this mens rea, no quid pro quo took place in any legally problematic sense.

Despite her own insight that I operated one level up, Barbara had rather sloppily underestimated me in September when she fancied that I wouldn't see past the four corners of the knockout email. Caught unaware by the epistemic advantages I had accrued upon exiting the elite culture and decolonizing my mind, she presumed she was manipulating me throughout our subsequent phone conversation, when all along I was manipulating her into acquiring precisely that misapprehension—a source of considerable embarrassment. But as this renewed bid to operate one level up now confirmed, Barbara had learned some lessons from her earlier missteps. The home page was truly inspired, psychological warfare of the first order. The advanced studies in the behavioral sciences being pursued at CASBS had evidently borne fruit.

No matter who had masterminded the scheme, it was being orchestrated collaboratively, given the conspirators' mutual involvement in both the fellowship and the whirlwind events of September 2009. They could proceed as they did because they rested secure in the knowledge that their own cognitive powers towered above those of the general public and that this edge allowed them a plausible deniability that couldn't readily be disabled. Charged with training the next generation of elite lawyers, they were keenly aware that deep reflection and disciplined analysis don't come naturally, even to the highly gifted. So they presumed their stealth and subterfuge would not register for most. Because I had studied at their feet, I had soaked up enough of their brilliance that I could be counted on to read between the lines and deduce the logical intricacies that now mediated our relations. Whether I could persuade anyone else of our byzantine power struggle was another matter, however, especially in an age of popular anti-intellectualism. Lacking the conspirators' capacity for abstraction and integrative complexity, the masses would chafe at my seemingly recondite interpretations, even if they accepted my account of the underlying data points, part of which rested on my credibility alone. The conspirators understood their theoretical exposure. But they presumed that I'd never manage to articulate my plight cogently and would only beclown myself in the attempt. My rhetorical liabilities were their ring of Gyges, so the risk of public exposure seemed minimal, if not entirely negligible.[i]

The conspiracy's calculations were borne out by subsequent experience. One acquaintance to whom I later related my tribulations was rather unimpressed by the suspension of home page rotations. This was no great mystery, he opined. People are always neglecting to take down obsolete web content. As a plaintiff's lawyer, he had once prevailed in a sex discrimination case because the defendant-employer had lost sight of an old website posting that would later incriminate him. These things just happen and don't have to mean anything, he insisted.

There was ample reason to think that the home page oligopoly was no oversight. That set 1 had been removed to make room for the holiday greetings, only to be reinstated a fortnight later, already proved as much. Moreover, the comparison was simply inapt. Yes,

---

[i] The ring of Gyges is known to us from Plato's *Republic*, where Socrates's interlocutor Glaucon advances the argument that people act solely for selfish ends, not for the love of justice, which has no intrinsic value to human beings such as they are. Glaucon contends that inflicting injustice is by nature good while suffering it is by nature evil. So we would gladly inflict it on others if assured that they would not respond in kind. That usually isn't possible, however, and we discover that the harms of suffering injustice outweigh the benefits of inflicting it. Accordingly, we mutually agree to refrain from inflicting it on one another, and that arrangement becomes known as "justice." Justice is not a virtue but an imperfect compromise born of weakness.

Glaucon illustrates these points with the story of Gyges, a Greek shepherd who one day happens upon a ring that makes him invisible when turned on his finger. Gyges then uses this newfound power to seduce the queen and overthrow the king. Glaucon argues that the reputedly just and the reputedly unjust would act alike if granted this power, taking what they pleased heedless of others' interests. Both would use the ring to lead lives of complete injustice while cultivating reputations for complete justice. The ring of Gyges reveals our true natures, showing that no one acts justly for its own sake.

obsolete website content often slips from mind. But there is a genuine difference between that kind of thing and neglecting to rotate a law school's home page imagery for eighteen months (minus winter holidays), when precedent and good sense dictated that they be alternated regularly. It's easy to forget about some obsolete posting lodged deep in the dim bowels of a website. But the Stanford Law home page isn't going to slip from mind so easily. As the world's portal to a highly prominent and well-endowed institution, it must be attended to regularly for a gamut of reasons—such as updating announcements about upcoming events or posting course schedules, to name a few. I'm confident my intuitions here could be confirmed empirically, as I doubt Stanford's new practice has been widely adopted elsewhere. This lawyer's alternative explanation, then, was only superficially plausible, because he was glibly comparing apples to oranges.

If that explanation nevertheless resonated with him as obviously superior to my own, it was because "people forgetting to take down web content" was consonant with the day-to-day heuristics through which we reflexively impose a semblance of order on the world around us. In contrast, "law professors manipulating home page to send coded message to conceivably slandered fellow" assuredly wasn't. The law professors in question understood this perfectly well. They could brazenly allude to the conceivable slander in broad daylight because they knew some commonplace cognitive heuristic would readily camouflage the anomalousness of the home page oligopoly, even if that heuristic didn't hold up to rational scrutiny, and that any audience hearing of my tribulations would therefore remain reliably incredulous. Without question, they were operating one level up. Another naysayer said I couldn't rule out that the tech staff in charge might have been a bunch of stoners too high to do their jobs. This was a rather cartoonish sitcom scenario, as it defies reason that Stanford (or any law school) could have been hoodwinked into hiring drug-addled ne'er-do-wells to oversee its technical infrastructure. Yet the tropes of the stoned techie slacker and the dysfunctional office have cultural familiarity, so they resonated more strongly with this critic than my own explanation, which lacks that familiarity. Here as elsewhere, it was cultural factors rather than strict logic that fueled the tendentious skepticism.

I couldn't proselytize these particular skeptics to my outlook, but others proved more receptive. In the end people's reactions frequently turned on temperament. Feeling themselves experienced and worldwise, some folks are highly invested in their hard-earned acumen about the ways of the world and are accordingly reluctant to suspend their ingrained cognitive heuristics even where they are inapposite, as in the instant case. These interlocutors would predictably object that I was "reading too much into things." But that's another threadbare heuristic that can be relied upon quite lazily. As readers can surely recognize from personal experience, the ostensibly trifling minutiae of language—word choices, awkward pauses, turns of phrase, and the like—can assume great significance in socially complex situations. Those attuned to these minutiae are easily dismissed as overly sensitive. Yet their deep read of things may be highly accurate, even if they're hard put to explain why. The more intricate the interpersonal background, the greater the challenge of articulating their implicit rationality—to both themselves and others.

This was precisely my predicament. I was operating in a cognitively complex social ecosystem against adversaries of great learning and intellect, and that made the relevant background understandings inherently resistant to verbal articulation. But they weren't on that account unreal. Researchers in the field widely recognize that the better part of human communication is nonverbal, consisting of vocal cues, gestures, facial expressions, and so forth rather than words per se. Granted: these general truths are no guarantee that my readings of Dick's knowing undertones were on point, but they are reason enough not to peremptorily dismiss the possibility that much could have been communicated in this fashion.

The policy of allusion, intimation, and ambiguation was fully consonant with the ethos of my academic milieu. Investigating "how professors think" in the context of academic panels superintending prestigious interdisciplinary grants, the Harvard sociologist Michèle Lamont observes:

> In this context, a muted expression of enthusiasm can signal disapproval, and any more damning criticisms may be made allusively. Frowning, rolling one's eyes, sighing, blushing, and talking through clenched teeth are certainly actions that can be as powerful as words. And objections that are not fully articulated dampen debate because they are not amenable to contestation. Fortunately, such behaviors are much more easily controlled in the context of a two-day panel than they can be in, say, departmental deliberations, which occur regularly, have a history, and can be shaped by folk stories about past conflicts, interpersonal hatreds, and the like.[1]

Like Lamont's sighing and frowning, set 1 carried a rich meaning shaped by a folk story about past conflicts and interpersonal hatreds. I have been narrating that story here to underscore how set 1 embodied tensions that had been latent in my collegial relations from the outset. Exasperated by my cloistered immersion in the tacit dimension, my advisers had now determined to engage me on that very plane, taking my principles to their logical conclusion by disembodying my already disembodied fellowship experience to a previously unimaginable degree. They had protested my navel-gazing solipsism without effect, and the home page would now entrap me in it. Set 1's indeterminacy foregrounded the question mark first broached by Joe at the fellowship's outset, whether the nature of my collegial relations was consistent with future academic employment.

That incertitude was now embodied in the tension between the two interpretations of the unofficial reality. A few months later I was accused of dismissing my colleagues as imbeciles. And the home page begged the question of who was the true imbecile—and who, conversely, was operating one level up. Were my advisers fools for taking on this exposure? Or was I the sucker for fancying that I could somehow capitalize on it?

The rupture between the official and unofficial realities and between interpretations 1 and 2 of the latter weren't arbitrary mental constructs but the logical consummation of a conflict long in the making, phenomena presaged by latent centrifugal forces that had been noticed and felt much earlier. The conspirators felt securely cloaked in plausible deniability because they didn't think our rather convoluted academic folk story could be situated within a broader cultural narrative that might lend it resonance for a wider audience. The unofficial reality originated in my attempted self-consecration as it collided with the pieties of the New Class culture, the secularized asceticism of the scholarly hero-system. And outsiders who were generally unacquainted with these two essential ingredients wouldn't fathom how their violent interaction could have touched off the conspiracy. The psychological subtleties would be utterly lost on those with schematic conceptions of academia as solely about "the pursuit of knowledge." Unpacking those subtleties for culturally uninitiated parties would be like detailing the chromatic nuances of Impressionist painting for the colorblind. The casual onlooker espying the departmental deliberations evoked by Lamont might notice all the frowning and eye-rolling and register that something was off. But these would still be disconnected data points, whose overarching significance will escape the naive observer. The conspirators expected that the same would hold of the unofficial reality, whose murky dots I would be unable to connect cogently. Such was their elitism, which it would become my calling to deflate.

⚖

Reasonable readers may object that, notwithstanding all this, I enjoyed no direct sensory access to the unofficial reality. I wasn't around to overhear what precisely Joe and Barbara imparted to Weisberg during the gnashing of teeth, just as I was no fly on the wall in the smoke-filled room where the home page conspiracy was supposedly hatched. True enough, but it's also true that no physicist has ever directly apprehended a proton with her own two eyes, yet we still accept protons as scientific fact. The nature of scientific proof has been hotly debated by scientists and philosophers, but the most stringent standard, formulated by Karl Popper, dictates that a theory is scientifically confirmed only upon delivering falsifiable yet unfalsified predictions. Popper explains:

1. It is easy to obtain confirmations, or verifications, for nearly every theory—if we look for confirmations.
2. Confirmations should count only if they are the result of risky predictions; that is to say, if, unenlightened by the theory in question, we should have expected an event which was incompatible with the theory—an event which would have refuted the theory.
3. Every "good" scientific theory is a prohibition: it forbids certain things to happen. The more a theory forbids, the better it is.
4. A theory which is not refutable by any conceivable event is non-scientific. Irrefutability is not a virtue of a theory (as people often think) but a vice.[2]

These parameters were why Popper dismissed Freudianism and Marxism as pseudoscience. These theories could always be verified. Their defenders could always validate their biases by superimposing their ideological lens on the available facts. But they could never be falsified, because Freudians and Marxists couldn't specify in advance the conditions under which their ideas would stand refuted. That communist revolution took root in semiagrarian Russia rather than in the more greatly industrialized West, where Marx predicted it would first erupt, wasn't acknowledged as debunking the Marxist theory of history but instead seized upon as evidence that mass culture had blinded Western proletariats to their true class interests. Whatever happened, Marxists could find a way to rationalize it. Unfalsifiability isn't a strength but a weakness, betraying that a theory doesn't truly traffic in empirical data. In contrast, Einstein's theory of relativity enabled scientists to anticipate astronomical measurements that prior theories would not have suggested. The theory was confirmed as the result of a "risky prediction," and that was what made it genuinely scientific.

The theory of the unofficial reality was highly scientific by this exacting standard, as it yielded a falsifiable yet unfalsified prediction that no one not in my position would have thought to make or considered sensible (other than the conspirators themselves, of course). As I began to explain earlier, my hypothesis entailed that set 1 would not be dislodged by some other seemingly random amalgamation of professors, students, and Stanford Law miscellany in a few weeks' time, as had been the custom. This followed from what I had posited as set 1's purpose, to clandestinely facilitate a quid pro quo according to which I would be receiving either some job or some modicum of publicly accessible evidence for the existence of an underlying controversy, one interpretation of which might have moved Stanford to give me a job but ultimately wouldn't. Because the public revelation of this arrangement could erode popular faith in Stanford's *gravitas*, the quid pro quo carried a built-in incentive for Stanford to renew my employment somehow. Accordingly, set 1 would have to remain entrenched on the home page to maintain that incentive structure and ensure the accompanying holding pattern. Its displacement by some other selection of images would therefore have falsified this conjecture by revealing that set 1 wasn't serving its ascribed function as collateral for the indeterminacy of the quid pro quo. My theory was therefore falsifiable. But it was not in fact falsified, because set 1 would remain up for about eighteen months longer than the official reality dictated—a mere few weeks.

Imagine a hypothetical region that saw no snowfall in each of the preceding seventy-five winters. A rational layperson would reasonably gather that the local climate was adverse to snowfall and on this basis predict that there would be none in year 76 as well. How, then, should this layperson respond to a maverick climatologist who nevertheless predicts snowfall that year and is proved right? The fair inference, I submit, is that there is probably some truth in whatever theory enabled him to foresee this improbable turn of events. The snowfall might not be mathematical proof of the theory. But this maverick's confidence in it couldn't be pooh-poohed as unfounded. He couldn't be accused of reading his theory into the data because the data had been afforded an opportunity to refute the theory yet didn't.

My argument here is analogous. During the three years of my association with Stanford Law School to date, the home page had rotated with a fair degree of frequency. Let's say every two weeks for the sake of this argument; the exact schedule is unimportant. Ergo, there were approximately seventy-five sets over that period, each of which was soon replaced by another. And yet I predicted ahead of time that one particular set—set 1—would not be rotated out like the rest and was then vindicated. Mine was a "risky prediction," as Popper says. The official reality militated against it, so its success substantiated the unofficial one.

As with my climate analogy, this prediction didn't confer absolute certainty. But my hypothesis was and remains no less rational than our climatologist's. He demonstrated that nature can give rise to certain anomalies that his theory alone explained. And I'm here claiming something like that about human nature specifically. Sure, people tend to care more about the weather than about website images, but that has no logical bearing on the force of my argument. Admittedly, I could not subject the theory of the unofficial reality to a wide range of replicable experiments, the scientific ideal. But this shortcoming bedevils a lot of social science and was scarcely unique to my own research. As social science goes, my falsifiable yet unfalsified prediction was nothing to sneeze at, if I may be so immodest.

So why did my success on this front often fail to satisfy the skeptics? In *Conservative Claims of Cultural Oppression* I review Chris Mooney's contention in *The Republican Brain* that conservatives are disposed to seize on whatever isolated bits of information confirm their preconceptions and then freeze their thought process to shield it from countervailing evidence.[3] The truth, though, is that we all freeze according to how our identities interface with the specific contingencies before us. Liberals are not categorically more open-minded than conservatives. Both are subject to distinctive identity-affirmation requirements, which are what precipitate the freezing. To the extent conservatives appear more cognitively rigid, that is owing to circumstance, not inherent disposition.

This essential symmetry was borne out in my experience. I had met up with an old high school chum and our former high school history teacher over the Thanksgiving break. As conservatives wary of academia, they had little difficulty accepting my report of the shenanigans transpiring at Stanford. Though peculiar and improbable, the shenanigans were congruous with the arrogance and duplicity that they associated with the liberal elites. The uncanniness of it all wasn't lost on them, but that uncanniness resonated with their ordinary sense of things at some deep level. In contrast, the liberals in my midst harbored greater reverence for prestigious institutions like Stanford, which they admired as embodiments of their own highest virtues. As a result, they would respond not just with skepticism but by pathologizing my beliefs as symptoms of some mental disturbance.

This was fully consistent with my thesis, according to which liberals will discard their reputed tolerance and critical thinking whenever these virtues conflict with their "secular, scientific, and civilized" hero-system, as Becker would say. Liberalism is a particularistic cultural dispensation that celebrates certain human types as civilized, reflective, and rational while stigmatizing others as barbarous, unthinking, and fearful. This was the lens through which liberals routinely viewed my situation. "Stanford Law professor = humanistic and enlightened" and "people who think websites are transmitting coded messages to them = nuts" were these skeptics' axioms of thought, in whose light my cool and dispassionate dialectic had to be dismissed as hollow mental gymnastics. I held to my claims only because they survived the test of falsifiability. But having caricatured my devotion to scientific rigor as paranoia and conspiracism, these interlocutors were not buying my findings and would wave away my talk of falsifiability as highfalutin gibberish, a mere castle in the air, one more sign that I had taken leave of my senses.

I had reason on my side, but faith—the *social* faith that such things just can't happen—would override the reason of others. These San Francisco liberals could no more envisage Stanford professors machinating as alleged than could a medieval peasant envisage the village friar molesting the choirboys. They couldn't question Stanford because that would be to question themselves and their value system. Entranced by the facial outlandishness of it all and my attendant disorientation, they reflexively discounted my arguments as the rantings of a tinfoil hat conspiracy theorist. I may as well have been contending that the moon landings were faked or that the World Bank had been infiltrated by an alien race of reptilian shape-shifters. Gone were the high hopes of making vital contributions to Establishment Clause jurisprudence. Instead all my intellectual energies might now be occupied with the daunting task of defending my own sanity, a low bar for most.

The conspirators knew full well the nature of my epistemic oppression, for they had engineered the latent discursive violence that enforced it. The dazzling cunning of their enterprise was to dangle a patina of hope that my lifelong dream might somehow be salvaged while gaslighting me ever further into a self-enclosed conceptual vortex whose rational foundations were invisible to the naked eye. And just to make this argument was already to expose myself to a panoply of uncharitable imputations, from loose thinking to narcissism to resentment about career setbacks, and from there to outright lunacy. I could state unequivocally that I was not trying to slough off responsibility for the hiring season's dispiriting outcome, but this first-person report of my own motivations would not dispel the impression that I was doing just that, with the rest an elaborate rationalization for the pedestrian grievances of a disgruntled former employee.

The conservative culture warrior Angelo Codevilla laments that "the notion that the common people's words are, like grunts, mere signs of pain, pleasure, and frustration, is now axiomatic among our Ruling Class."[4] And this would now be my own lowly status within liberalism's hierarchy "of the knowing, the knowledgeable, the reflexive and insightful," to whose bottom I'd sunk precipitously. Having pursued the meaning of conservatives' cultural oppression to its logical conclusion, I had been vaulted into a kindred predicament, like them targeted for identity annihilation. Elite opinion would dismiss my advocacy much as Lionel Trilling dismissed 1950s conservatism, as "irritable mental gestures that seek to resemble ideas," or as another illustration of what Richard Hofstadter dubbed "the paranoid style in American politics."[5] Now myself oppressed by the elites, I was becoming versed in the conservative pathos firsthand—on a more highly intellectualized and individuated level, perhaps, but the existential nub of it was the same. The shadow world of the unofficial reality meant that I, too, would now look upon liberalism as "beyond politics, a tyrant that dominates our lives in countless ways great and small, and which is virtually incapable of being overthrown"—the conservative weltanschauung according to Thomas Frank.

The Academic Habitus

But what, readers will ask, could have spurred my advisers to oppress me so? There was the situation's legal dimension, certainly. Proving defamation by a preponderance of the evidence in a court of law would be a real long shot, but my fellowship renewal request was another matter. I had not combed the case law or conferred with an expert, but to think that I'd been unfairly deprived of a good faith review of that request was not crazy. Whatever the case's merits, the "relevant administrators" wanted peace and quiet, and that sufficed to drive the unofficial reality forward. However minimal their legal exposure may have been, their efforts on this front were more minimal still—a little tinkering with the home page, a few lines in an email, some chitchat about informal networking. The sheer unpleasantness of litigating against a current fellow and former student sufficed to justify their efforts here, as would the negative publicity of a law school lawsuit. The statute of limitations for defamation in California was only a year. The more time elapsed between the underlying events and any legal reprisals, the weaker my position became. Dragging things out served the conspirators' legal interests well. They had a professional duty to minimize the law school's exposure—legal or otherwise, real or conceivable—and the quid pro quo was how they discharged that duty under these most unusual of circumstances.

Events could not be reduced to their unsavory legal dimension, however. That dimension—which commenced with the knockout email before I took it up and escalated it—was the linchpin of it all *conceptually*, because all the smoke and mirrors made logical sense only against a legal backdrop. But I remain persuaded that this indispensable logical scaffolding formed a subsidiary motivation that, standing alone, could not have catalyzed this conspiracy to reduce me to a conspiracy theorist. As I have explained, the more powerful motive was to mete out a double revenge—to dash an expectation that the conspirators could then deny ever having fostered. I had managed to outflank Barbara in September by virtue of the epistemic advantages I had accrued upon exiting the liberal culture in August. Conscious of this defeat and pining to now redeem her performance, she hoped to establish conclusively that it was she and not I who operated one level up. I had bested the conspiracy in the fall when I nipped its first iteration in the bud. But Barbara expected that the impetus to truly expose it would be a double-edged sword that in the end would leave me stranded with grievances that I could not so much as articulate to outside parties—allowing her to gaslight with impunity.

Though its proximate causes were many, this vengefulness was at base roused by my transgressions against the intellectual magistrature of the sacred college of masters, the secular religion of *Homo academicus*. The home page was at its core a reassertion of that secular religion, a restatement of the magistrature's consecratory authority in the face of my ideological insubordination. Bourdieu distills the ideology's driving logic:

> There are no doubt few worlds [outside academia] which provide so much scope, or even so much institutional support, for the game of self-deceit and for the gap between the representation experienced and the true position occupied in a social field or space; the tolerance granted to this gap doubtlessly reveals the inner truth of a milieu which authorizes and encourages all forms of *splitting the ego*, in other words all ways of making the confusedly perceived objective truth coexist with its negation, thus permitting those most lacking in symbolic capital to survive in the struggle of each against all, where everyone depends on everyone else, at once his competitor and client, his opponent and judge, for the determination of his own truth and value, that is, of his own symbolic life and death.[6]

I transgressed against the magistrature when I subverted this most cardinal of principles by declining to be consecrated and resolving to consecrate myself. This, I have argued, was the subterranean counterideology and social meaning of the Overview. With Napoleonic arrogance, I attempted to snatch up the crown that my advisers would have bestowed upon me, placing it on my own brow. In doing so, I materially breached the social contract of academia, usurping the magistrature's consecratory authority in a repudiation of Bourdieu's law that "everyone depends on everyone else, at once his competitor and client, his opponent and judge, for the determination of his own truth and value, that is, of his own symbolic life and death."

With my recent fall from grace, I was now among "those most lacking in symbolic capital," as Bourdieu says. Having given short shrift to Joe's and Barbara's nostrums at the behest of my demiurge, I no longer operated under the aegis of influential allies ready to tout me as a brilliant young scholar. My stock had plummeted not innocently but culpably, not because I hadn't the wherewithal to grow it but because I had repudiated exogenous consecration as a value. My advisers, therefore, had to reaffirm that value in the face of my defiance. Before it was a legal strategy, the home page was an act of ideological self-assertion by the intellectual magistrature, a purification ritual to resanctify the once-hallowed ground now profaned by my deviance.

This would be achieved by providing "institutional support" for "the game of self-deceit and for the gap between the representation experienced and the true position occupied in a social field or space." My "true position" was the dismal outcome of my job search, the impending expiration of the fellowship in August 2010, and the state of general despair that followed. But the "representation experienced" was the promise held out by set 1, the possibility that my advisers would see fit to salvage my hopes after recognizing the error of their ways. Torn between interpretations 1 and 2, I would undergo Bourdieu's "splitting of the ego," a split between the possibility of realizing a lifelong dream and the possibility that I was vainly wallowing in false hope as the world moved on—sidelined yet again by the powers that be, once more sentenced to live in the shadows despite my successes of recent years. It was being versus nothingness, and I was straddling the two. Having thus far declined to play the petitioner to any judge, I had now been reduced to precisely that, left abjectly dependent on the forces lying inscrutably behind the home page for the determination of my fate—the determination of my truth and value, my symbolic life and death.

This indeterminacy facilitated my gaslighting on multiple levels: the indeterminacy between interpretations 1 and 2 and the indeterminacy between different conceivable outcomes of the truth of interpretation 2. Would that truth condemn me to silence, voicelessness, and alienation, with the world incredulous of my claims? Or would I prove equal to my task and somehow surmount the skepticism, expose Stanford, and vindicate what had now become my human subjects research? A third, nethermost layer of indeterminacy was spawned by the threshold question of whether the unofficial reality was a figment of my imagination. Although I had checked out of the ambient culture, remnants of my former acculturation remained intact at some level. Torn between my rational cognition, which validated the unofficial reality, and my residual cultural cognition, which endeavored to disabuse me of that reality, I had to struggle not to succumb to self-doubt lest I internalize my epistemic oppression.

The intellectual magistrature of the sacred college of masters propagates itself not as an articulated worldview—the way fundamentalists promote Scripture—but rather as an unspoken, largely unconscious, ethos. It is what Bourdieu calls a *habitus*, an "immanent law of the social body which, having become immanent in biological bodies, causes the individual agent to realize the law of the social body without intentionally or consciously obeying it."[7] The habitus is a socially and culturally acquired style of thinking, feeling, and behaving that comes to feel natural and self-justifying, allowing human conduct to be socially regulated without conscious adherence to explicit rules. The habitus explains why certain preferences in music can be found to correlate with certain preferences in food or with certain professional paths. The rules governing these different spheres of life seem unrelated, yet they may express the same habitus, a social glue that operates on us and through us without ever being expressed in formal precepts. Someone coming from a working-class habitus in a rough neighborhood may feel oppressed in a university setting not because of any discriminatory rules but because her inherited habitus is out of sync with that of her new milieu. She may be intellectually qualified, but she will find herself unable to navigate the complex social and cultural signaling in which intellectual pursuits are embedded. Forced to operate in a foreign habitus, she will feel out of her element or like a fish out of water. Such expressions manifest our intuitive awareness of the habitus.

Different classes and professions have their own habitus, which may be transmitted from parent to child, from teacher to student, or from peer to peer. The habitus determines whether it is more important to look tough, look good, or look smart, explaining not only tastes and mannerisms but also how we respond to stress. While the nature of a particular habitus can be sociologically articulated in terms of ideas, it is not reproduced through ideas but rather through a way of being whose intellectual presuppositions usually escape conscious awareness (bodily hexis, as discussed in chapter 2). Liam Gillespie explains that "subjects of (or in) the *habitus* internalize dominant social and cultural ideas, and the modes of being made available therein." In doing so they "support, reinforce and ultimately reproduce the *habitus* itself by subscribing to and propagating its dominant ideas and socio-cultural modes of being."[8] This process of sociocultural reproduction need never be recognized as such because the habitus has been internalized in the very structure of our lived experience, where it reveals itself only obscurely in our taken-for-granted gut feelings about things. The habitus is what Karl Maton calls the "the tempo, rhythms and unwritten rules of the game," our "unconscious sense of the possible, the probable and, crucially, desirable for us."[9]

Bourdieu characterizes the habitus as a system of "durable, transposable *dispositions*" to underscore that it can reproduce itself across a wide range of situations.[10] Habits are largely mechanical responses to specific stimuli. In contrast, the habitus is an adaptive skill set, what Bourdieu calls "the durably installed generative principle of regulated improvisations" that enables "a transfer of schemes ... on the basis of acquired equivalences, facilitating the substitutability of one reaction for another and enabling the agent to master all problems of a similar form that may arise in new situations."[11] Knowingly or not, we are always carrying forth an old habitus into a new situation. What may superficially present themselves as our unique responses to unique contingencies are in fact strategies for transposing the habitus to these contingencies, with the result that ostensibly unrelated spheres of activity wind up being encoded with the same ethos. Thus the acculturation students receive in university settings will eventually influence corporate mores notwithstanding that universities and corporations operate by different rules and with different aims, because graduates will carry the baggage of their habitus with them wherever they go. Dylan Riley calls the habitus "a preconscious framework or 'generative mechanism' that operates in an analogous way in a wide variety of different contexts." Mathieu Hilgers observes that it "generates an infinite number of behaviors from a limited number of principles." Robert St. Clair and his associates note that by "create[ing] evolving patterns of behavior that reproduce themselves," the habitus "generate[s] variations of a theme."[12] Our autonomy as individuals consists only in how these transpositions are effected, the subjective manner in which we have internalized the unspoken social imperatives that lie beneath the surface of all our ostensibly autonomous judgments.

It follows that human behavior cannot be explained through conventional notions of rational self-interest, because the drive to reproduce the habitus will determine the shape our perceived self-interest assumes. What may appear as hard-nosed calculations of costs and benefits are in fact unwitting transpositions of impersonal sociocultural meanings to novel contexts. Bourdieu explains:

> Even when they appear as the realization of the explicit, and explicitly stated, purposes of a project or plan, the practices produced by the habitus, as the strategy-generating principle enabling agents to cope with unforeseen and ever-changing situations, are only apparently determined by the future. If they seem determined by anticipation of their own consequences, thereby encouraging the finalist illusion, the fact is that, always tending to reproduce the objective structures of which they are the product, they are determined by the past conditions which have produced the principle of their production. ...
>
> Each agent, wittingly or unwittingly, willy nilly, is a producer and reproducer of objective meaning. Because his actions and works are the product of a *modus operandi* of which he is not the producer and has no conscious mastery, they contain an "objective intention," as the Scholastics put it, which always outruns his conscious intentions. ... It is because subjects do not, strictly speaking, know what they are doing that what they do has more meaning than they know.[13]

One cannot understand the home page without first understanding this. The conspirators' legal gymnastics appeared "determined by the anticipation of their own consequences," which were, as I have just explained, to curb any inclination I might have to sue while effecting a double revenge. But this cloak-and-dagger operation "had more meaning than they knew," as Bourdieu says. Unbeknown to the conspirators, it channeled the academic habitus, that prereflective sense of order and propriety that can shape events without ever announcing itself to consciousness. Outlandish though the conspiracy may seem at first blush, it was intelligible as an unwitting channeling of academia's unconscious hive mind spurred by the same organizing social principles that are elsewhere expressed more conventionally. Though seemingly sui generis, the home page was really a "variation of a theme," a "transfer of schemes."

The habitus explains why the logic of the home page could so seamlessly embody the gaslighting that Bourdieu observes is endemic to academia at large—"the inner truth of a milieu which authorizes and encourages all forms of *splitting the ego*." Only superficially was the home page a departure from received academic norms. Seen from one level up, it crystallized those norms as nothing else could, communicating in its own rarefied way that "everyone depends on everyone else, at once his competitor and client, his opponent and judge, for the determination of his own truth and value, that is, of his own symbolic life and death." In making explicit what usually remains implicit, the home page revealed *Homo academicus* in his naked quintessence. Here was one of Bourdieu's regulated improvisations, the manifestation of a transposable disposition, a jaw-droppingly innovative variant on what was, after all, a "classic procedure of university polemics"—violence accompanied "by the methodical erasure of all external signs of violence," violence invisible to all but its target and perpetrator. The true wellspring of the conspiracy was the academic habitus, for which my advisers were unwitting conduits. "Agents are possessed by their habitus more than they possess it," Bourdieu observes, and my advisers' machinations had now confirmed exactly that.[14]

And so intellectual honesty prevents me from laying ultimate responsibility on them. At its core the conspiracy was the fallout of my own refractory tendencies, which had frustrated the routine reproduction of the academic habitus by foregrounding the contingent, socially constructed, nature of the dominant hero-system. In declining to play my part in the time-honored social script as a well-adjusted "rising young scholar" eager to contribute to "the field," I had upset my advisers' performances as wise and benevolent mentors dispensing hard-earned sagacity to a tabula rasa. That obstructed the habitus's usual channels, compelling it to seek unconventional outlets. The habitus normally stays "immanent in biological bodies," where it is tacit and instinctive, expressing itself in unarticulated cues. But in brushing aside these cues all through the year, I had forced a buildup of passive-aggressive rancor that finally burst into the open in September, causing the ambient habitus to express itself ever more openly and stridently when it became transposed to the home page and the saga surrounding it.

Relative to everyday human communication, the home page traded on understandings that were exceedingly subtle. But relative to the normal modus operandi of the academic habitus, it betokened the near opposite, the transposition of certain "immanent laws of the social body" to a digital medium lying beyond the "biological bodies" where they normally inhere. These were the biological bodies of Joe and Barbara, and the home page served to channel their "durable, transposable dispositions" after those dispositions proved incapable of reproducing themselves through their customary vessels—Joe's and Barbara's advice. Inspired by what Barbara spurned as my glib and opportunistic citations to Kathleen Sullivan and Mark Kelman, set 1 helped restore balance to the universe by asserting my colleagues as intellectual magistrates of the sacred college of masters, before which I now lay prostrate, abjectly dependent on them for the determination of my truth and value. Set 1 had "all appearances on its side, those of learning and those of morality," as Bourdieu would say. But its true function was to ritually vindicate the magistrature by driving home the futility of my attempted self-consecration. My recalcitrance compelled the academic habitus to assume a calculatedness that is unnecessary vis-à-vis successfully socialized Stanford fellows, who, having pliantly internalized that habitus, didn't require the special measures through which it was being instilled in me now.

As I wrote Barbara back in November, I had adopted an "objective attitude" toward the situation. So viewed, my gaslighting was pure social causality, not personal malice, the direct outcome of how my heterodox behaviors were bound to collide with the ambient culture. Hence, my vague premonition in August that I would be imminently set upon by the forces of liberalism. I couldn't fathom the details of the assault at the time, but I understood intuitively that the habitus I was subverting would reassert itself in some fashion or other. For every action there is an equal and opposite reaction, and it was only a matter of time before the details came to light. "High theory is risky," as Barbara wisely cautioned.

The Art of Making Someone Wait

My own calculations at this juncture were just as indeterminate as the situation itself. I knew interpretation 1 was doubtful. Even so, it could carry a modicum of plausibility because it harkened back to Joe's, Larry's, and Barbara's earliest estimations of my promise, during the halcyon days of Legal Theory and Moral Luck and up through the fellowship's infancy in the fall of 2008. Superficially my deviance from there on out was a betrayal of their high hopes. But at one level up, it consummated those hopes. I didn't heed the better part of their enumerated counsels. But I took their concerns to heart in the higher philosophical sense when I checked out of their culture to attain the vantage point of conservative claims of cultural oppression, whereupon Simmel's sealed containers of condensed intellection would become unsealed and unfold into worldly plenitude—the sine qua non of delivering the concreteness, direction, and relevance being demanded of me.

I was no paragon of stolid scholarly virtue. But the "exaltation of academic 'reliability'" in whose light I stood condemned is, as Bourdieu observes, "often only the instrument of the transformation of individual and collective limits into the choice of scientific virtuousness." And the looming question was whether the conspirators had gotten wind that the principles by which I'd been tried and convicted were a rationalizing ideology disguising the cultural pathologies of academia—its ingrained antipathy to autonomous self-consecration, to thought for thought's sake, to ideas as against "contributions," and to the liberty of the tacit dimension as against the iron cage of Say's law (the more people are saying, the more there is to be said).

As Barbara astutely proffered moments before proposing the fellowship, "there is something indeterminate to liberalism," and that indeterminacy now stood unveiled by recent events. Yes, it was my deviance that had provoked the conspiracy, but such was necessary to unmask that which had made the provocation possible, the sublimated and intellectualized conservatism of the liberal elites, which went to the heart of my research agenda. Whether my advisers appreciated this achievement was most uncertain, however, and only by first recognizing their covert conservatism could they then be brought to recognize the virtuousness of my own conduct as my resistance to that conservatism. Barbara entreated me to tamp down my tendency to "make specimens" of people and instead acknowledge our collective absurdity—that "we're all absurd." Well, there could be no better acknowledgment than the situation at hand, and the question was whether Barbara would take this on board and bring me back into the fold. She wanted to operate one level up, after all, and was already doing so in some ways.

Beyond all this I wondered why the conspirators would have instituted set 1 if they weren't going to make good on interpretation 1 in some fashion. The home page oligopoly wasn't unlawful. They were perfectly within their rights to ordain it. But surely they preferred that its subterranean significance be kept under wraps. I personally admired the sublimity of it all, but sublimity isn't equivalent to *gravitas*, and the phenomenon could scandalize certain sensibilities as unbecoming the supreme dignity of Stanford Law School. It simply didn't make sense to me that they would trade their merely theorized legal exposure for the more tangible exposure of the home page. At worst, any lawsuit could be settled for a sum that would be less than a rounding error for Stanford and its $12.6 billion endowment (after the $4.6 billion hit of the financial crisis). Sure, it would be bad press. But no one likes a whiner, which I'd surely be pigeonholed as, so it would be easy psychologically to side with Stanford against a disgruntled former employee, and the unpleasantness would soon fade from memory.

In contrast, the home page and the drama surrounding it were the apotheosis of my research agenda, an inexhaustible cornucopia of psychophilosophical intrigue that could stimulate and entertain without end. Those pictures were worth more than a thousand words because they offered a prime outlet for what Alasdair MacIntyre calls "one of the most characteristically modern of activities," the unmasking of the "unacknowledged motives of arbitrary will and desire which sustain the moral masks of modernity."[15] The unofficial reality left me with plenty to unmask, and this embarrassment of riches gave me a decided home field advantage by enabling me to incorporate our undeclared cold war into what Dick sized up as a "rich and complex" research agenda. Such exposure simply dwarfed that of any conceivable lawsuit, as far as I could tell. So why would they take it on without eventually giving me an incentive to keep quiet? Interpretation 2 of the quid pro quo would be a devil's bargain, it seemed to me.

The truth, I must now confess, was that I had at this juncture gravely underestimated the challenges of making my case. I knew it would elicit some eye-rolling skepticism, for reasons that have been explored. But with the rationalistic naïvêté of a philosopher, I imagined that these predictable gut reactions would soon enough yield to sweet reason, my faith in which remained intact. This callow optimism was abetted by my recent exit from the ambient culture in August. Not yet fully acclimated to this new condition and still grappling with its implications, I was projecting my own critical distance onto others who didn't necessarily share it. As Barbara aptly noted during our September 9 phone conversation, one so reasonable as I couldn't be expected to get his head around anything as irrational as law faculty hiring. The conspirators understood this better than did I, so they didn't believe they were handing me the home field advantage and remained self-assured in their brinkmanship. From where they were sitting, it was I who had made a devil's bargain.

All this aside, the bottom line was that I had no good options, such that just waiting became my choice by default. Sure, I could sue or threaten as much. But what would it earn me, even if my contractual argument was on solid legal footing? If I was in it for the lucre I wouldn't have accepted the impecunious fellowship but rather stayed on course for the white-shoe firm. Should I have then alerted Dick and Barbara to something they already knew, namely, that there was no "strict two-year limit" on the fellowship? But they were either for or against me. If for, they would eventually make good on interpretation 1, and there was no point rocking the boat about the fellowship. If against, then doing so could reignite tensions and precipitate a conflict culminating in the retirement of set 1, depriving me of paramount evidence for the conspiracy's machinations. So I just let sleeping dogs lie and acquiesced to our new holding pattern.

My advisers could readily anticipate these calculations. In doing their own math accordingly, they channeled another feature of the academic habitus. Bourdieu observes:

> The establishment of *durable* relations of authority and dependency is based on *waiting*, that is, the selfish expectation of a future goal, which lastingly modifies—that is, for the whole period that the expectation lasts—the behavior of the person who counts on the thing expected; and is based also on the art of *making someone wait*, in the dual sense of stimulating, encouraging, or maintaining hope, through promises or skill in not disappointing, denying or discouraging expectations, at the same time as through an ability to inhibit and restrain impatience, to get people to put up with and accept delay, the continuing

> frustration of hopes, of anticipated satisfactions intrinsically suggested behind the promises or encouraging words of the guarantor, but indefinitely postponed, deferred, suspended.[16]

Barbara's caveat that the "informal route requires persistence" and Dick's speculation that my CV might "at some point in the year" opportunely fall in the lap of just the right appointments committee were both instantiations of these principles. Both bespoke "the art of *making someone wait.*" Too restive to plot a slow, strategic ascent up the ranks of the New Class by immersing myself in its lumbering machinery of argumentation, I presumed to consecrate myself rather than waiting to be consecrated. Having failed to show Bourdieu's "respect for distances, that is respect for the *order of succession,*" I would now be disciplined by a despotic regime of sitting and waiting. The employment intimated by set 1 was the satisfaction "intrinsically suggested behind the promises or encouraging words of the guarantor." But that satisfaction would have to be "indefinitely postponed, deferred, suspended." And my advisers expected that this indefinite chasm between hope and satisfaction would instill me with the *obsequium*—"unconditional respect for the fundamental principles of the established order"—that the system had so far failed to inculcate. They had vainly sought to establish "*durable* relations of authority and dependency" with me, and the home page was now going to deliver these goods as nothing else could.

This waiting left me with plenty of time to ponder my straits philosophically, and it bears emphasis that these were rapidly becoming the focal point of my research agenda. It seemed like fate that this agenda should have landed me in my dystopian predicament, which was therefore key to its success—giving me exactly what Legal Theory and the first year of the fellowship could not. My persecution seemed to speak to something larger than me, disclosing a higher truth for whose revelation I had become a vessel.

Conservative culture warriors feel oppressed by the liberal elites because the latter are privileged to disguise and intellectualize the hierarchical and authoritarian impulses that they would prefer to pin on conservatives exclusively. Conservatives are readily accused of *obsequium*. But being at the helm of academia and other opinion-shaping institutions, the elites can disguise their own *obsequium* in virtues of their own devising. They would contrapose their hard-won enlightenment against the unreflective mores and pieties of hidebound traditionalists. But that so-called enlightenment is defined by its own distinctive mores and pieties, which have been cloaked in the putative virtues of "academic 'reliability'" and *gravitas*. Institutionalized in elite enclaves, such values are insulated from the exogenous scrutiny routinely meted out to the conservative classes. The ideological self-affirmation of liberals—unlike that of conservatives but just like the home page—"has all appearances on its side, those of learning and those of morality." The conspiracy's plausible deniability was merely a local iteration of this broader cultural veneer, which it had become my task to upend, in both theory and practice.

The home page had planted the seeds of my future, even in the event that interpretation 2 proved correct. Paraphrasing Bourdieu, Brooks explains that "young intellectuals will have to know how to invest their capital to derive maximum 'profit,' and they will have to devise strategies for ascent—whom to kiss up to and whom to criticize and climb over."[17] I had now cut myself off from these conventional avenues of ascent. I didn't kowtow to the powers that be after December 2008, and it was too late to start genuflecting now. I might criticize rival theories of religious neutrality, my paper topic. But emanating from a déclassé former fellow with no prospects, any such criticisms would be unfunded, void of the symbolic capital required to ascend the academic pecking order—even if they were, or would soon become, "fantastic—subtle, iconoclastic in the best way, and really, really interesting."

There was, then, but one way to wiggle my way out of my subaltern status as one "most lacking in symbolic capital," and that was to mint symbolic capital out of my very oppression, a tried-and-true strategy in modern America. This would be my strategy for ascent, the true mechanism of my self-consecration, of which the Overview was only an early harbinger. Stanford had reduced me to the ultimate petitioner compelled to sit and wait. But it could have done so only by mortgaging its own symbolic capital as a hedge against the risk of insincerity, the risk of interpretation 2. It now sunk in that I might one day have to avail myself of that hedge in order to speak truth to power and expose Stanford, a logical possibility baked into set 1. The prospect of going public with my allegations was intimidating, given the backlash that might come my way, but also deeply seductive, if not intoxicating. Only by blowing the whistle on my own gaslighting could I rescue myself from the professional and intellectual oblivion to which my alma mater might seek to consign me. I would have to criticize and climb over the university itself by latching on to its symbolic capital in a gambit to appropriate some of it as my own. Elite opinion would denounce me as a parasite and bottom-feeder. But the New Class liberals of Stanford were avid to tax the ill-gotten gains of old class business plutocrats, so I had no qualms about for once redistributing a few scraps of what mattered most to them.

Such a heist was an audacious David-and-Goliath kind of proposition, given the vastly asymmetrical power relationship and risk of total beclownment. Yet I would be left with only the nuclear option should Stanford fail to give me an out. My research agenda would move forward one way or another. Stanford could put the kibosh on an academic career but not the great equalizers of reason, free speech, and the internet, and this trifecta might be all I truly needed. It would be an uphill battle, but my fringe ideas could conceivably gain traction, if not with the unwashed masses and bien-pensants, then at least in some circles, perhaps among the similarly marginalized and disaffected. My advocacy might not sway the skeptics, but it could give them pause. The conspiracy had myopically handed me the means to punch above my weight. Set 1 was the sling with which I might get the drop on a lumbering Philistine giant, if skillfully aimed. With a little grit and some luck, I might yet secure a fresh infusion of symbolic capital from my alma mater. Whatever the odds, I had to mount some form of resistance. With the apogee of my research agenda now in sight, I couldn't just go quietly into the night, lest I be consumed by self-recrimination for all time. I had to rewrite the rules to win the game, and desperate times called for desperate measures.

Moreover, it was readily apparent that everything I had stood for over the years pointed ineluctably toward this Promethean feat. As I related in chapter 1, my first, abandoned dissertation topic took up Nietzsche's counsel "to examine and dissect the men of learning themselves for once, since they for their part are quite accustomed to laying bold hands on everything in the world, even the most venerable things, and taking them to pieces." Here was an opportunity to do just that, to fulfill a now-manifest destiny that had been lying in abeyance for a decade until crystallizing before me like a long-forgotten revenant. The home page was a microcosm, indeed a Platonic embodiment, of the cultural pathologies I had first diagnosed as an overexuberant, still-unscarred graduate student, and I was now poised to ventilate them as I once was not. Stanford was awash in both plausible deniability and cultural authority, but I had a liberal arts education, which I could at long last put to good use. Joe had been persuaded from day one that I was destined for some kind of eminence. But I was now willing to settle for notoriety, and perhaps this endgame was how I'd someday make my mark.

CHAPTER 7

A String of Curious Irregularities

January–May 2010

School was back in session in January, and set 1 was back up after the brief hiatus of the winter break, just as expected. My job-talk paper was now much improved, but it wasn't looking like I'd ever have the opportunity to present it in an actual campus interview. I did, however, submit it to the Law & Humanities Junior Scholars Workshop paper competition at Columbia, as Josh had suggested back in October. Events had left me rather gloomy about my chances, but there was no harm in trying. I made it down to Stanford only once that month, for lunch with the fellows, where a visiting Harvard professor who had joined us got intrigued by the project. I had a stronger command of my subject by now and could more readily engage others with it.

These developments all transpired within the official reality. Of far greater note, however, were those within the unofficial one, which would manifest itself through a string of curious irregularities during the months to come, infusing otherwise forgettable banalities with a subterranean significance. This succession of incidents would be guided by the elemental logic first ordained in the fall, further marinating me in semantic and existential indeterminacy as I fell ever deeper into an abyss of angst, nihilism, and despair. Yet this descent would be my true training ground as a philosopher, the rite of passage I needed to truly understand the elites and, with this, the higher, previously hidden, truth of conservative claims of cultural oppression.

The Recommendation

Given the collective pretense that the fellowship had a "strict two-year limit," I began applying for whatever other fellowships were available at other law schools, touching base with Barbara on January 13 to update her on this and gauge her reaction. I knew I might one day have to pull back the curtain on her stealth and subterfuge, so I needed to sniff out what evidence I could, to discover those wrinkles in the official reality that betrayed the impingements of the unofficial one. My email read:

> Hi Barbara,
>
> Just to update you on my progress, I've already applied to a bunch of fellowships from the list you sent me. I'm also thinking about applying for positions outside of law, such as temporary slots in philosophy departments or teaching/TAing in core curricula and the like—not ideal, but not bad ways to hold me over if necessary. Is there anything else you think I need to be working on at this point in time?
>
> Best,
>
> Rony

Barbara replied:

> HI Rony: That all sounds good. I would be more than happy to write a letter of rec for any of the fellowships, if you would like. I can't recall

> if legal research and writing positions are on Solum's list.[i] If not, you might want to consider select ones that have historically served as launching pads for academics. Chicago's Bigelow Fellowship is the best known of these. Best, Barbara

I accepted Barbara's offer and also solicited letters from Josh and Dick, who were similarly obliging. My original "launching pad for academics" had collapsed under the weight of my wayward research agenda, and I now needed a replacement platform. In line with the official reality Barbara was once more casting herself as on my side, as in the knockout email. Hence her offer, which was intended to generate a digital evidence trail bespeaking earnest solicitude for my welfare, thus fortifying the conspiracy in its plausible deniability. Even so, the irony of Barbara's offer compromised that deniability. Although "more than happy" to recommend me to other law schools, she was also less than willing to disclose that the fellowship at her own law school could be extended beyond two years. Otherwise, she could have just sent that letter off to herself and persuaded herself to renew the Gaither.

This incongruity was merely the latest manifestation of the larger contradiction I had been living since September and earlier. I was in revolt against the intellectual magistrature of the sacred college of masters. But because I had never announced that insurgency in express terms, its suppression proceeded tacitly as well, in the tension between the official and unofficial realities. That explained the contradiction between the knockout email and Barbara's flattery on the phone and rave review of my paper. This latest inconsistency was another iteration of the same schizophrenic logic. Such wouldn't be apparent to the casual onlooker glancing at these email exchanges.

---

i I believe the list Barbara was referencing belonged to Paul Carron, not Larry Solum, as that was the link she had forwarded to me in her December email (see chapter 5). She likely confused the two because Larry Solum was particularly well known for his interest in the law faculty placement process. I return to him in the next section.

But that was because our relationship was unfolding at one level up, as in truth it always had.

And yet the deeper meaning of this truth remained murky. Enmeshed in ambiguity and indeterminacy, our relationship occupied a gray zone that straddled the line between truth and falsehood. The situation was as nebulous morally as it was empirically. I couldn't rule out that Barbara was justified in her sublime vengefulness, her quest for a double revenge, as my manipulations had perhaps left her with no choice but to seek to so redeem her honor as a law professor. And maybe she was dispensing pure Kantian justice in simply confronting me with the consequences of principles that I had espoused when I escalated the surreptitious legalization of our relationship in September. The knockout email had legalized things to a modest extent, but the gamesmanship reached a tipping point only after I retaliated with the works-in-progress email the next week. The cognitive dissonance now being visited upon me was just an outgrowth of that which I had first foisted upon my advisers in September, and really all through the preceding year, so maybe I lived in a glass house and couldn't throw stones. I was the architect of my own oppression at some level.

Whether that oppression had a utilitarian justification was also a thorny question. On its face the torment brought on by my gaslighting seemed to dwarf whatever satisfaction it could have offered its perpetrators. But the final calculus might turn on how many law professors beyond the core conspirators were in the loop. With enough such voyeurs, my gaslighting could have been contributing to a net increase of happiness in the world. Mill excluded vulgar pleasures from his utilitarian calculus—"better to be a human being dissatisfied than a pig satisfied"—but it wasn't obvious to me that this species of schadenfreude qualified as a vulgar pleasure. And what would Rawls have said? Would a rational agent deliberating under a veil of ignorance concerning the circumstances of his birth countenance a social order under which one born with my nature could find himself in the situation at hand? Perhaps Josh had some thoughts on that.

I had taught introductory ethics many times over the years and had a generalist's command of the subject, but nothing in my graduate training had equipped me to tackle these real-life moral complexities. Having contributed to the semantic and existential indeterminacy from which I now suffered, I had unclean hands. But that suffering seemed exponentially greater than whatever uncertainty, worry, or offense I conceivably might have inflicted. Whatever my culpability, my gaslighting more than evened the scales, I felt. Given my trespasses, my treatment was hardly capricious. On the other hand, my descent into deviance merely amplified tendencies that were apparent to all from the outset and, indeed, were part of my je ne sais quoi charm in Legal Theory and Moral Luck. However problematic, these tendencies could not be decoupled from the intellectual promise my advisers had discerned. They fancied they could stamp out my deviance without thwarting that promise, and this was their fundamental miscalculation. As Manichean liberals, they couldn't envision vice and virtue as complementary outgrowths of each other, so they also couldn't appreciate how my roguery was the long-awaited fulfillment of my deepest commitments to them.

The Entry-Level Hiring Survey

Come February, I was periodically visiting the website of Professor Larry Solum. Solum was a law professor, then at the University of Illinois, who maintained a well-trafficked blog for legal academics, the *Legal Theory Blog*. Every year the site would publish the Entry-Level Hiring Survey, where law schools that had placed their graduates in tenure-track positions could report their successes. Solum would then tally and publish the results to give everyone the scoop on each school's performance. His practice was to issue a preliminary report early in the year and then update it regularly during the following months to report on new developments (often labeling new iterations as, for example, Version 5.0). At some point in May or early June, presumably when the hiring was over, he would finalize the survey, which would later be archived.

What sports statistics are to sports fans, so the Entry-Level Hiring Survey was to law professors and others with an ego investment in the prestige of their law school. The survey offered its devotees a veritable horse race, complete with returning champions and scrappy underdogs. None could hold a candle to Yale, which would predictably dominate, at least relative to its small class size. But what of the Harvard-Stanford rivalry? With Harvard's law school enrollment nearly three times Stanford's, it would doubtless place more alums in faculty positions. But Stanford might well prevail on a per capita basis, as it had in some years. Some law professors esteemed Stanford as Harvard's equal while others didn't, and the outcome reported by the survey would speak to this controversy. How would the University of Chicago fare? Chicago labored under the indignity of being classed in lay circles as a mere "top six" rather than "top three" law school (Harvard, Yale, Stanford—aka HYS). Yet Chicago's per capita numbers of academic placements and clerkships were generally comparable to Harvard's and Stanford's. What of the NYU-Columbia rivalry? NYU hadn't always been a major player, but it was making great strides in faculty placement, telling Columbia it no longer owned the town. Would Michigan retain its historically strong showing, or would it be ceding ground to up-and-comers as it pined wistfully for the old days when it stood closer to the pinnacle of the rankings? Might Texas—my first-year alma mater—outperform the runts of the so-called top fourteen, such as Cornell or Georgetown, and thereby give the lie to the popular prejudice that it belonged in a lower tier of law schools? And how would the placements in the top-fifteen or -twenty law schools add up? Yale would dominate the field but by exactly how much?

Such questions weighed heavily on the legal academic community as winter headed toward spring. The AALS interviews had been over for some time. With candidates now making the rounds of campus visits, the offers were starting to trickle in. Everyone wanted the scoop, and Solum had always been the one to provide it.

I was, therefore, surprised when the posting soliciting the pertinent information from law schools disappeared from the top of Solum's blog about a week after it first appeared in early February, if I recall correctly. This curious irregularity straightaway begged the question of whether Solum had been recruited as a co-conspirator. The home page had already set a precedent, so it wasn't out of the question that my advisers would be harnessing an additional digital medium to generate further irregularities symbolically alluding to the unofficial reality, which would further embroil me in semantic and existential indeterminacy with a further challenge to my intellectual vanity. By further shifting the conspiracy's incentive structure in favor of interpretation 1, the additional evidence would augment my faith in that outcome while leaving me with less of an excuse for failing to unmask the conspiracy if the outcome were otherwise. The quid pro quo revolved around the availability of some opportunity at Stanford "at some point in the year" and the persistence required to traverse the "informal route." Given its temporal aspect, the Entry-Level Hiring Survey could be readily deployed to speak to these intimations and thereby become the perfect instrument for the art of making someone wait.

I was well aware that such speculations invited the verdict that I was losing more marbles, compulsively seizing upon chance features of my environs as evidence for an idée fixe. Solum taught at Illinois, not Stanford, so wasn't this a bridge too far? I thought not. The law school world is a small one, and Barbara was well connected, especially to people who, like Solum, shared her twin passions for legal theory and law faculty placement. She had referenced him in her recent email and could at any rate anticipate that I'd be plumbing the depths of the much-acclaimed hiring survey—known to all legal academic insiders—for any morsels of information, both as to the market generally and Stanford specifically. Would Stanford be making an entry-level hire, or wouldn't it—as Weisberg stated and Dick intimated? Barbara knew the nature of my perplexities and could have seized upon the survey as another venue for her meta-level machinations. The suggestion may spark incredulity, but she could have readily anticipated that precise reaction. The plausible deniability she was cultivating would incarcerate me in a simulacrum of madness by leading me step by step toward conclusions whose rationality could not be reckoned from the outside. Barbara would, once again, be operating one level up, and, once again, the challenge would be to operate two levels up.

At any rate there was no point speculating further at this early date. As with the home page, the question would be settled through a falsifiable prediction that no one who was not in my position would think to make or consider sensible. If Solum was either abandoning the survey that year or merely recommencing it at a later date, that alone would be of no moment. But I soothsaid that the survey's timing and content would be marked by noteworthy irregularities that would be intelligible by reference to the unofficial reality, just like the home page. "Every 'good' scientific theory is a prohibition: it forbids certain things to happen," and mine forbade the survey from playing out as it always had in years past. Time would tell.

The Key

The gaslighting continued apace when I stepped into my office at the law school sometime in mid-February to find a key resembling my own set squarely on my desk, right between my computer and the desk's front edge. Curious, I placed it in the lock and found that it was a second key to my office.

One might assume that a janitor had dropped or forgotten it. Presumably janitors are the only ones carrying around extra keys to other people's offices, since they're the only ones entrusted to enter them as part of their duties. Yet this etiology was only superficially plausible. What was the probability that the janitors used individual keys rather than a master key—whose loss they would have soon detected upon trying to enter the next office? Even if they employed individual keys, what was the probability that one had become detached from its keychain in order to land squarely in front of my chair, neatly perpendicular to the desk's edge, where I couldn't miss it—and that of all the keys that might have gotten accidentally decoupled in my office it just happened to be the one to my office? You don't need a PhD in statistical physics to appreciate that it's infinitesimal. The janitors in fact had no cause to venture that far into my office in the first place. Their only responsibility was emptying the trash bin adjacent the doorway, so there was no need even to set foot in the room. I had occupied numerous academic office spaces over the years and this was my first such experience.

For all these reasons I concluded that one of the conspirators or their minions had planted the key right where I was sure to see it, in another episode of the same palace intrigue. A second key to my office was another symbolic allusion to my highest hopes, a continued presence at the law school after the expiration of the fellowship in August, signifying a second chance, as it were. In an unexpected display of charity, the conspirators were evening the scales a bit by doling out an additional scrap of evidence probative of an underlying controversy, thereby placing another arrow in my quiver (the very argument I'm now making).

The ultimate meaning of their beau geste was, of course, unknown, as the key was permeated by the same ambiguities that defined the situation at large. Was it a token of good faith, dealt out as reassurance of their commitment to realizing interpretation 1? Or did it rather betoken their overweening conviction that the thick cordon of plausible deniability in which they had wrapped themselves would never be unraveled? In that case the gesture was intended to further submerge me in the morass of the unofficial morality until I passed the point of no return. It would then constitute yet another gambit to challenge and then deflate my intellectual vanity—which the elites were again humoring with "institutional support" for "the gap between the representation experienced and the true position occupied in a social field or space."

Like the home page, the key's status as evidence presupposed a background web of allusions, intimations, and ambiguations, knowledge of which could be readily disclaimed. The janitorial explanation was absurdly improbable on close consideration. But it comported with people's everyday, prereflective cognitive heuristics for navigating the surrounding world and so would strike most observers as the singularly obvious explanation for the key's anomalous presence, despite its unlikelihood. This bias had a philosophical explanation with which I'd been acquainted since my undergraduate days. In his landmark *Being and Time*, Heidegger observes:

> In our "description" of that environment which is closest to us—the work-world of the craftsman, for example,—the outcome was that along with the equipment to be found when one is at work [in Arbeit], those Others for whom the "work" [Werk] is destined are "encountered too." If this is ready-to-hand, then there lies in the kind of Being which belongs to it (that is, involvement) an essential assignment or reference to possible wearers, for instance, for whom it should be "cut to the figure." Similarly, when material is put to use, we encounter its producer or "supplier" as one who "serves" well or badly. When, for example, we walk along the edge of a field but "outside it," the field shows itself as belonging to such-and-such a person, and decently kept up by him; the book we have used was bought at So-and-so's shop and given by such-and-such a person, and so forth. The boat anchored at the shore is assigned in its Being-in-itself to an acquaintance who undertakes voyages with it; but even if it is a "boat which is strange to us," it still is indicative of Others. The Others who

> are thus "encountered" in a ready-to-hand, environmental context of equipment, are not somehow added on in thought to some Thing which is just present-at-hand; such "Things" are encountered from out of the world in which they are ready-to-hand for Others—a world which is always mine too in advance.[1]

Heidegger was here seeking to deflate the Cartesian prejudice according to which everyday consciousness is theoretical and proto-scientific. This characteristically modern conception of the mental holds that everyday consciousness is just a cruder, more error-prone, variant of the theoretical stance that science actualizes with greater rigor. As thinking beings, we confront a world comprised of discrete objects with both self-contained qualities and quantifiable relations. And it is the task of rational thought, our distinctively human capacity, to draw out what those are.

But Heidegger maintained that this rationalistic rendition of the mind as essentially theoretical is a distortion. Everyday consciousness encounters not a bare agglomeration of objects but a world of intertwined meanings wherein articles are grasped from a holistic sense of how things work, a prereflective, unarticulated "understanding of Being." This web of significances isn't an afterthought, the product of an independent cognitive act—"somehow added on in thought to some Thing which is just present-at-hand," as Heidegger puts it—but rather a feature of primordial human apperception. We do not infer an umbrella's purpose from a knowledge of its causal properties—its dimensions and water-resistant materials. That would be to apprehend it as "present-at-hand." Instead we happen upon its purpose primordially and without inference. Umbrellas are encountered as "designed to keep us dry," what Heidegger terms "ready-to-hand." Our experiential worlds are structured according to the concrete uses of things, not their deracinated scientific properties, and those uses in turn embody collective social understandings of how things and people work. The theoretical, scientific stance that the philosophical tradition casts as basic is in fact derivative, presupposing an artificial disengagement that, if reified, can obscure our everyday default condition as engaged agents navigating those social understandings.

This is high theory indeed, which Barbara cautioned against. But she and the rest understood its implications intuitively. The key wouldn't explode their plausible deniability because most people presented with such evidence would process it as ready-to-hand rather than present-at-hand. Just as an umbrella is primordially cogitated as "designed to keep us dry," so the second office key would be cogitated as "dropped or forgotten by janitor" should I attempt to adduce it in support of my allegations. Folks would reflexively trace its provenance to some causal chain that comported with their everyday, holistic grasp of the social world, giving short shrift to unique facts of the case inasmuch as they confounded that visceral sense of things. In contrast, my exit from the ambient culture in August had positioned me to process my environment as "present-at-hand." Having adopted a disengaged, scientific stance, I could subject the key's curious presence to a more exacting forensic analysis anchored in all the available data—rather than mere cultural common sense.

Whether I could persuade anyone else to forsake that common sense and accept that the key was one of the conspiracy's long tendrils was another matter, though. As with the home page, the facts pointed to human artifice rather than blind accident. Even die-hard skeptics should recognize that my reading of events is no more unlikely than the key's having landed on my desk by happenstance. But, alas, people's cultural cognition would instinctively elide the absurd improbability of the janitorial hypothesis, which is readily apparent upon careful reflection.

One of my critics ultimately conceded that human artifice had to have been at work but suggested that maybe someone was just snooping around my office and had left the key there to put me on edge. But I possessed no state secrets, and this was a scene out of some convoluted Hollywood thriller. Believing it would have required some actual paranoia. And yet this outlandish explanation had a modicum of cultural resonance, making it more palatable to this critic than my own more theoretically elegant account of all the available evidence. This was just a microcosm of my entire dilemma: a scientifically rigorous stance liberated from unthinking cultural reflexes would be slandered as unhinged conspiracism and paranoia—one more testament to the conspiracy's perverse ingenuity. Here as elsewhere this cabal had connived to generate conditions under which an epistemically virtuous man would find himself calumniated as a knave or madman, an outsider to the reality-based community, reduced to a kind of cognitive Job unrelentingly punished for his very probity. Barbara had remarked in September that one as reasonable as I couldn't be expected to wrap his mind around anything as unreasonable as law school hiring, and she was presently exploiting my cold logic to railroad me into a simulacrum of madness.

The Toledo Affair

The plot thickened when Dick reappeared on February 27 with the following email:

> Hi, Rony. This may be worth applying for. I've copied below the relevant parts of an e-mail that Toledo's dean (William Richman) sent to Larry Kramer.
>
> —Dick Craswell
>
> Very likely, we will need a visitor to teach two terms of civil procedure and some upper level courses for the 2010–2011 academic year, so I am writing to you to solicit your help in identifying prospects. Of course, we would be interested in a lateral who wanted to escape inclement weather to winter in Toledo.
>
> We also would be interested in hearing about (or from) persons interested in beginning law teaching. The position is a podium visit with no guarantee of a permanent tenure-track opportunity. That said, in the past we have made several tenure track offers to visitors

> who have performed well. Moreover, as you know, its easier to get a job elsewhere with a year of experience and a whole faculty full of folks willing to help.
>
> The University of Toledo College of Law traditionally has been a good place to break into law teaching. We devote a substantial amount of our resources to new faculty. Additionally we supply abundant help, support, coaching, encouragement, etc. to beginners. In this particular case, I am willing to share all my materials with a new colleague, notes, slides, sample exams etc.

As anyone can gather from a cursory glance at my CV, nothing there suggests an iota of interest in civil procedure.[ii] I did reap a Dean's Achievement Award in the subject for my first-year performance at Texas, but first-year classes are just a game in the end. In contrast, teaching and teaching well above all require a certain passion for the subject, or at least some minimal level of interest beyond sheer indifference, which is precisely what any sapient being would glean from my CV. Dick understood this perfectly well. And so, I called his attention to the obvious, with the usual understatement and the usual small talk:

> I'm not a hard core civ pro person, but I could certainly teach it for a year so long as Toledo isn't looking for someone more committed to the subject. I did most of my growing up 2 hours south of there, so the gig would bring me back full circle to my Ohio roots. Should I just email Dean Richman with a resume?
>
> Not much news on the fellowship/VAP [visiting assistant professorship] front so far. Penn let me know that they've decided

---

[ii] Civil procedure refers to the rules by which courts conduct civil cases. Whereas substantive law addresses issues such as a defendant's liability to a plaintiff, civil procedure addresses questions such as whether a plaintiff may bring her case in federal rather than state court or in one state rather than another, as well as whether the plaintiff can sue only on her own behalf or also on behalf of a class of similarly situated people.

> not to do any hiring for their VAP this year, but otherwise no word one way or the other.

Dick replied:

> I'd be surprised if being committed to civ pro were an absolute requirement for them, especially for this sort of 'podium' (i.e., teaching coverage) visit.
>
> I'd send him the same package you sent out last fall – that is, c.v., research agenda, and mss article or book chapter (whatever you've got currently that presents you in the best light).
>
> And since you've got those Ohio roots, it wouldn't hurt to mention them in your cover letter!
>
> — Dick

I contacted Dick on March 4, a few days later, for some logistical clarification:

> Hi Dick,
>
> The dean of Toledo is actually Douglas Ray, not William Richman. Richman is a civ pro professor and I assume the person whose courses need to be filled in. It's Richman I should contact, right? Thanks.
>
> Rony

He replied:

> Yes, that's right. I was wrong when I identified Richman as the dean, but Richman is the person you should write to. In fact, I've already written to him touting you as a possibility, so he's expecting to hear from you.
>
> Sorry about the mix-up.
>
> —Dick

Dick had apparently gone out of his way to goose Richman's interest. Seating himself beside me at the next luncheon, he was eager to verify that the materials were en route to Toledo. The naive onlooker would perceive only a beneficent placement adviser pulling every string to help a soon-to-be unemployed Stanfordian put bread on the table. But Dick's enthusiasm for this opening was highly peculiar and began to make sense only as a further evolution of the conspiracy's metalevel machinations.

Dick understood perfectly well that my chances of securing this post were negligible. Maybe having a serious interest in civil procedure wasn't an "absolute prerequisite," but it was very nearly that. Toledo may not be the most prestigious law school in the country, but the competition for entry into legal academia is stiff enough that Richman would face no difficulty identifying more suitable prospects. Plenty of practicing lawyers out there were eager to escape their spirit-sapping firm jobs, and their career paths had given them the incentive to recall something from their first-year civil procedure courses, as mine had not. It would be evident to Richman that I had no love for his bailiwick and was interested in the gig only for lack of better options.

Someone whose primary specialization was, say, administrative law might persuade Richman that he was also interested in civil procedure and would do a good job of teaching it. Administrative law and civil procedure (along with property and some other subjects) are your bread-and-butter, meat-and-potatoes kind of law, which is what law schools such as Toledo tend to focus on. In contrast, I had been pondering how alternative accounts of the relationship between modernity and premodernity shape our understanding of religious neutrality. How this would induce a civil procedure specialist to hand off his courses to me, Dick did not explain. Richman was looking for a stand-in who could do his courses full justice, and that meant at a minimum someone who shared his intellectual culture. It was self-evident that I didn't. From where he was sitting, I completely had my head in the clouds. He would be allergic to my research agenda, culturally oppressed by it, just as Barbara had foreseen months earlier. The only serious question was how many seconds it would take for my materials to land in the recycling bin.

Notwithstanding my stellar first-year civ pro performance, there was also a serious question about my bare-bones competence, especially as the responsibilities involved upper-level courses. Rehashing my first-year civ pro syllabus might not have been an overwhelming challenge. I probably still had my meticulously crafted course outline buried somewhere in my hard drive. But was Richman supposed to just gamble that I would master the intricacies of challenging subjects such as federal courts or conflicts of law in time for the fall term, despite my manifest apathy toward them? Not if his faculties were intact, which I presumed they were, so I couldn't very well see Dick urging him to so recklessly roll the dice.

Dick understood all this and understood that I understood it. After all, he was directing me to submit the same application materials I had distributed in the fall, deemed well-nigh career ending by Barbara, and now *after* the hiring season's outcome had confirmed that assessment. Dick could ignore the obvious because this flirtation with Toledo had nothing to do with landing me a job and everything to do with furthering the conspiracy's endgame. Dick had "all appearances on [his] side, those of learning and those of morality." But those appearances were just that and no more. Only the charade of the official reality compelled him to go through the motions of vigorously promoting my interests—just like Barbara with the recommendation. This was hollow virtue signaling intended for public consumption, should that day come. An academic insider could readily gather the obvious futility of this outreach to Toledo. But the nature of the farce wouldn't be apparent to the unschooled layman, who didn't operate one level up and would defer to the purported judgment of Stanford Law's placement adviser.

That judgment was in truth another manifestation of the academic habitus, serving to again broadcast the discreet polemics of academic hatred, that charge of extra violence that attaches to the methodical erasure of all external signs of violence. Barbara had once thought me easily competitive to teach at a top-fifteen or -twenty law school. Later that same morning Joe had put me on notice that I could forget about being hired outside the top fifty, as lesser schools would be intimidated. Instead, I was suited to a "top-flight" job, as he put it in an email earlier that summer. Yet I was now being touted for a temporary position with a substantial teaching load unrelated to my intellectual interests at a law school ranked well outside the top fifty. The point was to underscore just how far I had fallen, just how much my insolence and presumption had cost me. I had set myself above the intellectual magistrature of the sacred college of masters, and I was now going to be taken down a peg or two—and all behind a facade of good faith, normalcy, and altruism. The contrast between the promise held out by set 1 and the reality of this doomed application to Toledo was just another "splitting of the ego," as Bourdieu says, further "institutional support" for "the gap between the representation experienced and the true position occupied in a social field or space."

That institutional support operated by a familiar logic. Was I going to whine about being promoted at lowly Toledo rather than at Stanford or another more glittering institution? Just as my home page claims would trigger the "people who think websites are communicating coded messages to them = crazy," heuristic, so any questions about Toledo would trigger the heuristic of "vain academic upset about not getting recognition, seen it before." The conspirators were operating one level up because they understood how to produce a subtext any objection to which would be self-discrediting. The problem wasn't deficient recognition but my attempted self-consecration and the ensuing backlash from the academic habitus. But this true state of affairs couldn't be cognized from within that habitus, which bestows a benign veneer on the intellectualized and sublimated conservatism of the liberal elites; Dick's recent outreach was only the latest instance.

Vindication

All was quiet on the western front for the rest of March, which allowed me to begin putting my reflections on the year's events to paper, laying the intellectual foundations for this very work. Solum's Entry-Level Hiring Survey had been reinstituted online early in the month, and I awaited the outcome of my prediction that it would be marked by further irregularities. To my surprise my entry in the Law & Humanities workshop at Columbia in June had been among the 5 to 10 percent of papers selected, and Nomi Stolzenberg, a law professor at the University of Southern California and one of the workshop organizers, wrote to me that they were quite intrigued by mine.

Unfortunately, I couldn't attend. My mother, who resided permanently in Israel, had been sojourning in San Francisco for a couple of years, where my brother also lived. Since she would be repatriating to Israel soon, she had booked an Alaska cruise for the three of us as a kind of farewell adventure, and the dates conflicted with the workshop. Given her high hopes for this family voyage, I couldn't very well abscond and replied to Stolzenberg that family matters would keep me away. I might have anticipated this problem sooner, but the situation had left me unduly dour about the paper's prospects. At any rate this additional line on my CV wasn't going to save me at this late hour. Maybe I'd have left the conference with some contacts, but I was in no shape to give it my all. My cultural oppression at the hands of my alma mater had taken its toll, both mentally and physically. I was now being battered by the march of time, as my disempowerment grew more salient with each passing day. For each passing day was one less opportunity for the vindication of interpretation 1 and, hence, one more argument for the truth of interpretation 2—and all the ramifications thereof.

Even so, this symbolic victory validated my sense earlier in the fall that the intellectual core of the paper I then delivered to Barbara was incisive and original, despite that draft's surmountable shortcomings. Stolzenberg would write to me again in May:

> Hi Rony,
>
> I've been meaning to write to you for some time, but am only now just finding time as we finally reach the end of the semester. I just wanted to say how disappointed we all were that you weren't able to come to this year's conference. Everyone was sorry you couldn't come, but I am particularly so, as it seems that we have many common interests and a similar orientation to the topic of law and religion. I, too, have been working on religion and secularism, the older meanings of religion and secularism that you excavate are very similar to ideas that I have been working on. If you are interested in sharing work, please feel free to send me drafts any time, and I'd be happy to give you feedback – and likewise, if you have an interest, I'd be happy to share my work on these subjects with you as well.
>
> I hope our paths cross in the future.
>
> All the best,
>
> Nomi Stolzenberg

My research methodology stood vindicated. Following my intellectual gut heedless of the New Class's lumbering machinery of argumentation, I had let notes pile atop notes and headed into August 2009 without a polished job-talk paper. My acquaintance with the contributions of Establishment Clause experts was, moreover, skeletal. Against Barbara's advice, I hadn't mastered the case law and instead erected a mental labyrinth in which I would flail away for months. And yet this unruly path eventually yielded a paper that could win accolades from an entire committee of law and humanities mavens. I went rogue in the process, running roughshod over ambient mores. But such had been necessary to attain the August epiphany, which would enable new insights on religious neutrality and much else, including my most perilous and dystopian of predicaments. I replied to Stolzenberg that I'd be delighted to exchange work and would touch base again when I had a more advanced draft of the paper.

The McConnell Affair

Another symbolic victory arrived on Wednesday, April 28, when I received the following email with "olin fellowship application" in the subject line:

> Dear Rony,
>
> I don't think we have met (have we?) but I am on the Olin Fellowship selection committee, to which you have applied. Please swing by my office some time and introduce yourself, so that I can put a face with the name.
>
> —Regards,
>
> Michael McConnell
> Stanford Law School

Michael McConnell was a former federal appellate judge, a religious conservative, and an eminent scholar of law and religion, among other things. Upon leaving the bench he accepted an invitation to join the Stanford Law faculty, where he had already been visiting periodically. Larry once lionized him as "the leading authority on law and religion in the United States." While Larry was no neutral actor when it came to touting his own faculty, this encomium was more than plausible. McConnell hadn't yet alighted on the Stanford campus when everything went down in September. But Larry and

Barbara both had urged that I confer with him. With characteristic prescience Barbara anticipated that as a "smart non-secularist" McConnell would "appreciate the subtlety" of my argument, and something like that had now come to pass. McConnell was on record inveighing that modern liberalism "proclaims its neutrality toward competing ideas of virtue and the good life, but is committed in practice to the promotion of particular ideals and—even more—to the eradication of others."[2] So his research clearly dovetailed with mine.

Serendipitously, I was about to introduce myself to him at right around this time, just when he reached out to me in his capacity as Olin fellowship selection committee member. The Olin fellowship was among the law fellowships to which I'd applied earlier in the year after being apprised of the Gaither fellowship's supposed "strict two-year limit." The Olin was a one-year gig that paid slightly less than the Gaither but was otherwise similar. Sponsored by the right-of-center Federalist Society, it could be embedded at any interested law school. I had already begun to suspect that mine wasn't just another résumé in the stack before this email from McConnell, as the Federalist Society had contacted me a few weeks earlier to request an official copy of my Texas transcript (with some sense of urgency, it seemed). The application instructions hadn't insisted upon official transcripts, and they didn't request an official Stanford transcript, but my first-year Texas grades were stratospheric and unofficial Texas transcripts had a homemade look to them.

I wrote back to McConnell the next day, Thursday, April 29, to set up a meeting and avouch my interest in his own intellectual journey:

> Dear Michael,
>
> What a coincidence! We haven't met, but another coincidence is that I was hoping to chat at some point about your "God is Dead" article, some of whose formulations I employ in my work. So maybe I can introduce myself through that. Is sometime next week good, say Wednesday, or is earlier better? Thanks for your interest.

> Best,
>
> Rony

He wrote back the next day, Friday, that he would be around through Wednesday morning but that that day was the least scheduled. I replied that I couldn't make it that day because I lived in San Francisco and had other commitments. Could we meet next week instead? He replied:

> Next Wed I head to the airport immediately after my morning class. I have some time Mon and Tues, but not a lot. (BTW, let me stress that getting together is NOT a prerequisite to the fellowship; I just like to connect with the Stanfordians. So, you should not strain to make this work.)
>
> — Regards,
>
> Michael McConnell
> Stanford Law School

I replied by stressing that I was at any rate "hoping to discuss some of the interests (and suspicions) we share in common." The fellowship wasn't the only reason to meet. Would Monday or Tuesday work? We could always continue our conversation upon his return if he was short on time.

Dick had asked to be updated with any news from the fellowship search. So I relayed the glad tidings emanating from McConnell, writing that same day:

> Hi Dick,
>
> Just to update you on my fellowship search, it appears that the conservatives are taking an interest in me, as I thought they might. Michael McConnell is on the selection committee of the Olin/Searle fellowship to which I applied earlier in the year. I will be having a chat

> with him next week. The recipients will be announced in mid-May. I have as yet to hear from any liberals.
>
> Best,
>
> Rony

"I have as yet to hear from any liberals" was an allusion to the liberal conspiracy and the quid pro quo. Dick had hinted at an opportunity at Stanford "at some point in the year," and nothing had yet materialized. Dick didn't respond to this, and it was also crickets from McConnell.

So I emailed the latter again two weeks later, on May 11, assuming that he was back in town since classes were still in session (the law school had recently transitioned to the quarter system to fall in line with the rest of the university and promote interdisciplinarity, one of the major reforms Larry had shepherded). I wrote:

> Hi Michael,
>
> Are you back and, if so, around tomorrow? I could stop by and chat. If Thursday is better, that works for me as well.
>
> Best,
>
> Rony

Two days later he answered with a laconic, "Alas, I am away." Brevity is indeed a virtue. Still, I would have expected some acknowledgment of the general overture to meet, especially as I was reciprocating his own such overture of late April. McConnell chose otherwise, however, and I replied simply, "I understand." Only at this point did McConnell elect to correspond like a normal person, querying, "What is your schedule over the next two weeks?" I duly answered the next day, Friday, May 14, that I was flexible and could work around his schedule. I heard nothing for four days, until Tuesday, May 18, when he responded:

> I would still like to meet you. Your projects are of considerable interest to me. Are you planning to be on campus, maybe Thursday morning?
>
> — Regards,
>
> Michael McConnell
> Stanford Law School

I replied that Thursday morning worked and asked about a good time but received no answer. I decided to just swing by his office that morning anyway, rolling in around ten to find that he was nowhere in sight.

McConnell's dealings with me over these weeks had been most peculiar. Meetings can be tough to schedule and get beset by unforeseeable delays, and no one is perfect about returning emails. All the same, the general pattern here was strongly redolent of Josh's and Barbara's earlier policy of flattery-cum-avoidance. McConnell had initiated contact on April 28, and I responded by declaring my reliance on his research. It wasn't clear whether he'd settled on offering me the Olin fellowship when he first introduced himself, but he was seriously considering it, at the very least. He had announced himself in his capacity as a selection committee member, stressed that meeting wasn't a prerequisite for the fellowship, and later professed a "considerable interest" in my projects, which was unsurprising given the support they lent his own views. My religious neutrality paper had been well received by the Law & Humanities workshop, and it probably made an impression on McConnell as well.

Yet his correspondences became curiously irregular after I notified Dick of his outreach. Why hadn't I received further word about the fellowship? If someone else had ultimately been selected, McConnell might have composed a quick and dirty rejection note such as: "I was disappointed that we couldn't offer you the fellowship about which I contacted you. As you know, the process is highly competitive, and we can't hand one to every deserving applicant. However, I'm still intrigued by your project and would love to chat sometime." This would have been trite and slightly awkward inasmuch as he'd be acknowledging raising my hopes gratuitously, but it still would have been within the bounds of normal academic etiquette (and consistent with his own desire to "connect with the Stanfordians"). In contrast, to raise expectations gratuitously, dash them, fail to even acknowledge this, and then stand me up for a long-awaited rendezvous seemed to fall outside those bounds. And yet this reprised behavior patterns I had seen before.

As for Dick, his silence was equally odd. He had displayed great enthusiasm for the prospect of my teaching civil procedure at Toledo, going out of his way to tout me there despite my manifest unsuitability. One therefore might have expected him to be at least as energetic about the Olin fellowship, which was more prestigious, more useful, more appropriate to my interests, and more geographically convenient. I could remain in the Bay Area rather than pack my worldly belongings for a one-year stint in cold, aesthetically nondescript Toledo, which had seen better days in the heyday of the industrial revolution. Stanford would also have me for another year on the Federalist Society's dime. With Dick having gone to some lengths to sell me to a stranger at another law school across the country, one might think he'd do the same with a Stanford Law colleague up the stairs or down the hall, especially when this coworker had already cued his interest in me. But Dick gave no whispers of any such effort.

All this aberrant behavior was demystified by the unofficial reality, which provided it with the logical cogency in which it was superficially lacking. I would undertake further research on McConnell later in the summer, but the situation was clear in its outlines: Dick didn't respond that he would be touting me to McConnell because he had instead apprised McConnell of our shadowy counterworld—the tectonic shift of September 2009, the quid pro quo, my silent struggle against Stanford. The predictable effect was to obliterate whatever inclination McConnell had to hand me the Olin. McConnell was a conservative, but he couldn't have fathomed the political significance of my insurgency, which I myself was only beginning to register. Viewing my actions through a conventional lens, he was surely scandalized by what must have struck him as an egregious breach of academic collegiality devoid of higher redemptive meaning. Hence, his change of heart on the fellowship and general flightiness. Now caught up in a nameless drama, he was obliged to resort to the evasions and halfhearted overtures I have documented. I was radioactive and he wasn't about to give succor to so appalling a fellow. Because he was precluded from disclosing why, he had to maintain a charade of rhetorical continuity with his initial enthusiasm while ensuring that nothing came of it. This stratagem was readily ensconced in business as usual. Missing meetings or forgetting about emails are quotidian thought-heuristics that only fortified the plausible deniability. In contrast, the subtle irrationalities suffusing our correspondences became salient only if set against background facts that could be easily denied.

Should I have tried to circumvent Dick's influence and not alerted him to McConnell's outreach? While I might then have secured the Olin fellowship, it would have been a Pyrrhic victory. I was operating in a milieu "where everyone depends on everyone else, at once his competitor and client, his opponent and judge, for the determination of his own truth and value, that is, of his own symbolic life and death." Legal academia is a small world and word travels fast when it needs to. How helpful would McConnell have continued to be once brought into the loop about my crimes and misdemeanors? Things might have gotten interesting but probably not in a good way. What was another fellowship with me as a marked man? Given these realities, I resolved to stay focused on what was steadily becoming my long-term strategic vision, to vindicate my research agenda by exposing Stanford. As distant as that prospect seemed, it was my one avenue of control amid an ever-mounting sense of powerlessness—now corroborated by McConnell.

An Invitation to Observe

The McConnell Affair took a new turn later on the very day we were supposed to meet (May 20) after I opened the following email:

> Hello Rony:
>
> I am writing to invite you to participate as an observer at the Federalist Society's annual Academic Job Talk Workshop. The workshop will feature ten or so candidates on this year's academic job market rehearsing their job talks in front of a group of professor commenters, led by Professor [name redacted] of the University of [name redacted]. As you are contemplating the academic job market in the near future, this is a great opportunity to preview the process by watching other job talks and get useful advice as to your own strategy from our group of professors. It will take place Juen [*sic*] 24–26 at the Palmer House Hotel in Chicago; we will be covering transportation and lodging. I do hope you will be able to join us; please let me know at your earliest convenience!
>
> best,
>
> Erin
>
> Erin L. Sheley
> Deputy Director, Faculty Division
> The Federalist Society for Law and Public Policy

I had no connections with the Federalist Society apart from the fellowship application about which McConnell had first contacted me, so this invitation had to stem from that. What had begun as an overture to meet, accompanied by intimations of a career-salvaging fellowship, had deteriorated into elusiveness and flattery, which now had morphed into this invitation to spectate other job seekers in Chicago. As per the email, a conference participant was someone ready to hit the law faculty hiring market the upcoming fall. Participants had become experts in their subject, written polished job-talk papers, and were now heading to this workshop for a practice run. In contrast, observers were just contemplating hitting the market at some indeterminate future date and needed a preview of the whole thing. A subsequent email informed that the workshop's "faculty experts will want to talk to the observers about potential job talk topics for the future." An observer might be toying with some ideas but presumably lacked a mature intellectual agenda or serious work product.

The mystery, then, was why I had been invited to attend as an observer rather than as a participant, when I would not only be hitting the market that fall but had already done so the previous year. Sheley was strangely confident that she knew my status. But the Federalist Society should have gleaned from my Olin fellowship application that I was in the second year of a Stanford Law fellowship and from there deduced that I was readying to hit the market. My advisers' recommendation letters also should have disclosed this much. The faculty experts wanted to discuss "potential job talk topics for the future" with observers. But the Overview, which I had included with my application, advertised that I already had plenty such topics. Indeed, I had additionally submitted a sixty-five-page job-talk paper, the very paper that had elicited intimations of an Olin fellowship and McConnell's "considerable interest" (as well as Stolzenberg's considerable interest). The Federalist Society could also have learned from my résumé that I had a PhD, two academic publications (including a book), and years of college teaching experience. The cumulative effect of all this should have been to confirm my attendance as a participant. The Federalist Society's invitation, then, was one more curious irregularity added to the vast confluence of curious irregularities besetting me since September 2009.

The mystery dissolves within the *unofficial* reality. So seen, the purpose of this invitation was to help paper over the irregularities in McConnell's conduct by providing our correspondences with the rational denouement they otherwise lacked. It now turned out that McConnell had enough "considerable interest" to extend this invitation to observe through an intermediary but not quite enough to meet with me personally, let alone to offer the infinitely more valuable fellowship about which he had first contacted me. That didn't make a whole lot of sense, but it still made more sense than an abrupt cessation of emails right as we were supposed to get together, and so it shored up the conspiracy's plausible deniability against the additional exposure lately generated by the McConnell Affair.

At any rate I was more than happy to observe the workshop. It was a free trip to Chicago and a good way to occupy myself for a few of the dog days of summer (which can get pretty chilly in parts of San Francisco). It seemed like there would be much of interest to observe. An email from one of the workshop leaders forewarned attendees:

> What happens at the workshop should stay at the workshop. The critique we will give you is hard hitting and brutally honest, it is unlikely you will encounter any appointments committee half as critical as we are, but it is our job to prepare you for the encounters you will have on the market. As you will see some of my advice is not politically correct, but I urge you to understand that my role is to help you get a job in the world that exists, not to engage in a protest against it.

My anthropological curiosity was piqued, as here was an opportunity to study *Homo academicus* up close in his natural habitat. My intellectual focus had already been wandering from religion to the nature of my academic environs, and it would be fascinating to hear different perspectives on this dog-eat-dog world of legal academia. After all, this caveat identified the precise origins of my woes, my stubborn defiance of the world as it exists, which had come at the expense of finding a job within it. Could I not have simply produced a book review for Barbara or apprenticed myself to Jane Schacter or audited Polinsky's law and economics seminar? These things would have been a tad easier than scheming to subvert the intellectual magistrature of the sacred college of masters. The book review, the seminar, and the rest of it might have seemed like things of the distant past, but they lived on in a present that was forever hostage to its past.

The workshop agenda brought home the profound apartness that now held me aloof from my professional environs. The notice further advised:

> The critique will focus primarily on the style and structure of your talk, on the assumption that your subject area mentors have worked out substantive problems, but we will also question hard on substance in an effort to provide you the most life like mock talk experience. There will be people in the room you do not know, and they will question not only as themselves but as representatives of perspectives that I assign to them. Please come dressed as you plan to dress for your job talk. A few words of warning: cufflinks, particularly shiny ones should not be worn. All men's dress shirts should be a solid color and free of any shiny stripes or other embellishments. Ties should not be distracting. Women or others with long hair should practice in front of a mirror to see if they have any unnoticed motions like twirling hair or always pushing it away from their face that might distract an audience. In such instances, hair should be pulled back in a non-distracting way. Women who normally wear heels and walk well in them may wear them if they wish, but if you are not used to this don't try it as we will be working a great deal on body posture and breathing.

I understood perfectly well that women face special career challenges that men are privileged to not confront. But I was facing my own special challenges that any normal human being need not confront, and I would have been among the clear favorites in any oppression Olympics. Granted that mine was a first-world problem if ever there was one, but it was deeply undermining as these go. What was unnoticed hair twirling compared with the insidious regime of semantic and existential indeterminacy that now tyrannized me? What were the challenges of heels and bad posture compared with the splitting of my ego, that ever-widening gap "between the representation experienced and the true position occupied in a social field or space"? My true position was as an observer, a far cry from the high hopes that Joe, Barbara, and Larry had in times past announced for me. This was, moreover, a position I had to occupy in stultifying isolation, away from the sympathy of my fellow *Homo sapiens*. The conspiracy had in its poetic deviousness punished my foolhardy protest against the world handed down to me with the solitary confinement and unpersoning of the unofficial reality. Joe had once hailed me as the very opposite of Sarah Palin—was this what it meant to occupy that station? I believed so, because she was quite possibly the last person on Earth liable to work herself into my present straits.

CHAPTER 8

More Curious Irregularities

June–August 2010

Thinking Like a Lawyer

It was already early June and Larry Solum's 2010 Entry-Level Hiring Survey still hadn't been updated since its reinstatement in early March. Against all precedent, the very same "preliminary results" had remained on his website for the last few months. Entry-level hiring was over by now. Yet the survey, which had been extensively updated and finalized by this time in years past, did not reflect this. As I had predicted, it proved to be curiously irregular this time around, and the symbolism was patent. As seen through the lens of the unofficial reality, "preliminary results" meant "some schools might still be hiring," and that in turn meant "Stanford might still be needing you." The poetic imagination was staggering.

Those dismissing this exegesis as farfetched must still account for my predictive success here—no less astonishing than my divination of set 1's longevity. Skeptical readers are welcome to credit me with supernatural clairvoyance. I prefer an explanation that comports with natural causality as we have come to know it. However outlandish my hypothesis may seem, it had that virtue. I would await further developments in the survey before reaching any final conclusions, of course. As with everything else, the sincerity of the message was another matter.

I do not recall when, exactly, I made another observation, but here is as good a place as any to introduce it. Given Dick's intimations about some unanticipated opening to instruct constitutional law at the law school, I checked the upcoming year's course scheduling for any clues. Since Larry now and again taught the class, I examined his schedule and found that he was slated to teach three courses during the 2010–11 academic year. These would be Conflict of Laws in the fall and then two courses in winter, Constitutional Law and Think Like a Lawyer, an introduction to legal reasoning for nonlawyers, to be team-taught with Professor Mark Kelman.

I thought it unusual for a dean, with a busy schedule and unremitting responsibilities and stresses, to be encumbered with so heavy a teaching load. One course a year was the norm for a dean, so far as I knew. Two was more than enough. This anomaly called for an explanation. Was Stanford's staff somehow inadequate to its needs? Did Larry then volunteer to pick up the slack despite his packed schedule and far-ranging duties? Larry's excellence as a pedagogue was beyond question, and he undoubtedly possessed the stamina to teach three courses (or more) if need be. But why burden a busy dean with added teaching duties that others could be counted on to execute, if not quite as well, then at least well enough? They could always bring in a visitor from another law school who would be happy to boast of having sojourned at Stanford.

It wouldn't have been hard to devise some unusual yet plausible-sounding administrative explanation for this anomalous state of affairs. But this latest curious irregularity flowed readily from the unofficial reality. If three courses were an unusual and unfairly onerous teaching load for a busy dean, then perhaps that dean would have too much on his plate to follow through with it when the time came. Larry might teach Conflict of Laws in the fall, thereby fulfilling his usual teaching obligations, but come winter find himself deluged by unforeseen pressures and compelled to abandon his other courses. Kelman could assume full responsibility for Think Like a Lawyer. But what of Constitutional Law? Here was an unanticipated teaching need, and whoever was tasked with solving the problem might not have time to conduct a "full search" for a suitable substitute instructor—precisely as Dick had prophesied. And lo and behold, I would be available to fill in. That would be my new foothold at the law school, with this random good fortune serving as the cover of plausible deniability for interpretation 1 of the quid pro quo.

Perhaps it was all just coincidence. Admittedly this particular hypothesis had no testable consequences. But Larry did indeed seem to be thinking like a lawyer. The postmodern self-referentiality was clever indeed—one level up, at the least. The truth, of course, was that we had all been thinking like lawyers for too long already. Barbara was thinking like one when she crafted the knockout email, just as I was thinking like one when my reptilian fight-or-flight instincts kicked in and I returned fire with the works-in-progress email. We were surely thinking like lawyers the next day, after the incandescent fury of Bob Weisberg betrayed my advisers' true sentiments. The title of Larry's surprising third course appeared to allude to this basic continuity, the invisible thread that, having snaked itself through our relationship, now entwined our paths at one level up.

As with the rest, the sincerity of the message was another matter. The advertised teaching load might have been designed only to encourage certain inferences. But then it would at least be another arrow in my quiver. Like the home page, the office key, and the irregularities in the hiring survey, it would constitute another modicum of evidence for the existence of an underlying controversy that I might capitalize on to siphon off some of my alma mater's symbolic capital. Of course, exploiting that evidence would require authenticating it as such, which was entirely my burden per the terms of our agreement. Feeling secure in their plausible deniability, the conspirators understood that any argument I mustered would have to run up against some unusual yet plausible-sounding administrative explanation that better comported with our everyday grasp of the world—a familiar problem by now.

To Be Pathologized

Early June was also when I embarked on the much-ballyhooed Alaska cruise with my mother and brother. Maintaining good relations with Mom had become vital, as she was coming under the influence of my brother and others who imagined I was descending into some heretofore undocumented mental disorder.

Indeed, they had organized conference calls around my condition and run my interpretation of the home page past lawyer friends. As I would later learn, I had been caricatured as contending that set 1 constituted a legally cognizable offer. One needn't be an attorney, or even a high school graduate, to recognize the absurdity of the idea. Yet just such beliefs were now being imputed to me. The home page did facilitate a certain "meeting of minds," as they say in contracts. I was being asked to sit tight and not sue in exchange for either a job or evidence for the existence of an underlying controversy one interpretation of which might have moved Stanford to give me a job but ultimately wouldn't. Obviously, I would have been more pleased with the former. But fanciful or not, that preference wasn't equivalent to the ludicrous suggestion that a legally cognizable agreement had been formed. The conspirators' supreme creativity was now being misread as my lunacy. I had been pathologized, and so no one was much concerned with the pesky details of what exactly I believed and why.

As I was to learn on the cruise, these discourses had upset my mother, who now demanded an accounting of why I had thus far in life failed to secure permanent employment—first in philosophy, then at a law firm, and now at a law school. As to philosophy, I felt one exculpatory factor was that most humanities PhDs just don't find tenure-track jobs these days. Only rarely do philosophy departments advertise for experts on human nature, which isn't really considered a valid specialty, and my writings didn't get published until after I'd left philosophy. There was also luck, which, as Weber observed, plays an outsized role in academic hiring. As to getting no-offered by the law firm, I accepted the uncoerced testimony of a senior partner that they'd overhired summer associates and I had intimidated some of the younger attorneys intellectually. I subsequently managed to land another big law job within a few months despite my scarlet letter, so the episode was no great stain on my record.

But how to explain this latest debacle at Stanford? Was I going to tell my mom that I'd reaped the whirlwind after mounting an ideological insurrection against the New Class and its technocratic antipathy to the sovereign intellect and thought for thought's sake? Like most everyone in my San Francisco circle, she lacked the capacity for abstraction and integrative complexity required to comprehend the intricate chains of causation and webs of meaning that I have been charting. My rhetorical impotence only reinforced her emerging conviction that I had lost my wits and that this latest misadventure merely consummated a recurring logic of folly and ruin.

Did I ever pause to consider the possibility that my research agenda had jumped the shark? Could I not appreciate the utter strangeness of my hypothesis? The strangeness was undeniable. But the question to my mind was whether it was stranger than the only conceivable alternative. I thought not. Which of the following scenarios is more improbable?

Scenario 1—My sensory perceptions and inferences therefrom were largely sound, at least in their general outlines if not in all the details. I was indeed in the crosshairs of a liberal conspiracy bent on gaslighting me as payback for my own manipulations, which had been necessitated by my resistance to the academic habitus and the modern disciplinary society that helps sustain it.

Scenario 2—I was a stressed-out Stanford fellow who had taken leave of his senses and descended into delirium. Waking up one fine morning, I began to fancy myself a Spartacus of academia but really was only its Don Quixote, tilting at windmills in a delusional crusade against the sublimated and intellectualized conservatism of the liberal elites. Desperately trying to weave my sundry paranoid imaginings into a coherent narrative, I concluded that my employer's home page was communicating a coded message to me. Despite the collapse of my faculties, my febrile mind strived to cabin any motivated cognition by subjecting my conspiracy theory to the scientific method, whose results would be immune to my biases. Recalling Karl Popper from grad school, I predicted—against precedent and good sense—that images on my employer's home page would no longer rotate. This strange prophesy was strangely borne out. Against all odds, a long, convoluted chain of capricious deductions culminated in a falsifiable yet unfalsified prediction that no one not in my position would have thought to make or considered sensible. I then elected to challenge my overwrought conjectures anew by issuing another such prediction about the Entry-Level Hiring Survey and was uncannily vindicated yet again (more on this later in this chapter).

Both scenarios are weird and improbable, but since one must be true, the question is, which would be more extraordinary? I submit that this is the second scenario and that the first is therefore the better explanation for the strange course of my Stanford Law experience. The second scenario defies all explanation beyond chance and coincidence. The first dispenses with happenstance and is cogent as the outcome of my manifold affronts to the prevailing ideology. Odd though it was, the unofficial reality exhibited the structural logic of the academic habitus, encompassing all the telltale behaviors of *Homo academicus*. This I couldn't dismiss as chance and coincidence.

Skeptics may wave away my allegations as another instance of our species's age-old, all-too-human propensity to misattribute misfortune to hidden sources of purposive agency. Some have suggested that this penchant for seeing conscious intent behind meaningless environmental vagaries was a useful evolutionary adaptation in our ancestral environment, where it kept us on guard against potential predators, notwithstanding that it can fuel unhinged conspiracism under modern conditions.[1] However, any such evolutionary explanation wantonly mischaracterizes my thesis, which attributes the misfortune in question to the structural forces released when my deviance upset ambient cultural norms. Richard Hofstadter observes of the conspiracist mindset:

> Unlike the rest of us, the enemy is not caught in the toils of the vast mechanism of history, himself a victim of his past, his desires, his limitations. He is a free, active, demonic agent. He wills, indeed he manufactures, the mechanism of history himself, or deflects the normal course of history in an evil way. He makes crises, starts runs on the bank, causes depressions, manufactures disasters, and then enjoys the profits from the misery he has produced. The paranoid's interpretation of history is in this sense distinctly personal: decisive events are not taken as part of the stream of history, but as the consequences of someone's will.[2]

The theory of the unofficial reality does not qualify as paranoid conspiracism under this definition, for it is ultimately anchored in the nature of the academic habitus and the broader cultural currents that fuel it, as the discussion in chapter 6 makes clear. I have posited my gaslighting, and hence the purposive agency that was engineering it, as emanations of those structural forces, not as the products of any free-floating malevolence uprooted from the constraints of history. My advisers were unconscious conduits of the academic habitus, not disembodied agents of evil. "Paranoid conspiracism" is a tempting thought-heuristic by which to summarily dispose of my most peculiar claims. But like the other thought-heuristics I have already surveyed, it is undercut by the pesky factual details of my allegations. I leave to the reader to judge whether this is the fevered prose of a raving lunatic.

The Federalist Society Workshop

I would enter into further confrontations with *Homo academicus* beginning on June 24, when I took an early morning flight to Chicago to observe at the Federalist Society's Academic Job Talk Workshop. The special challenges facing right-of-center academics in liberal-dominated law schools would be a recurring topic of conversation. The society had scheduled a special panel discussion on the subject, but the lamentations would suffuse the entire schedule. One professor advised that, though a conservative, he was a registered Democrat because that was how to exert influence in Chicago politics. He also proclaimed that conservatives enjoy better relations with their children than do liberals. Interestingly, a fair number of the workshop organizers weren't conservatives at all but rather liberal Democrats sympathetic to their plight, like white freedom riders joining their black brethren in a struggle for equal dignity.

Much of the discussion focused on the dos and don'ts of the recruitment process and legal academia generally. Candidates dining out with campus interviewers should watch the price of their entrée. The lobster was verboten. Not only was it pricey, it was cumbersome to eat and could leave one looking undignified in what was, after all, just another interview. We should also be cautious with alcohol, both for its actual effects and the impression that imbibing it could leave.

Moving on to campus life, we were advised that fellows should limit themselves to raising one question every three faculty luncheons. Untenured faculty should limit themselves to every other luncheon. Only tenured faculty had license to speak up weekly. I hadn't received this memo until now, but it confirmed my cultural deviance anew. I hadn't raised my hand every single Wednesday but at least half the time, unwittingly arrogating the prerogatives of full-fledged faculty. I had also asked follow-up questions, thereby implying the inadequacy of the initial response, which couldn't have helped matters. The luncheon director once remarked on the thoughtfulness of my questions. But whatever points I'd scored through their quality had surely been forfeited by their inordinate quantity. The Wednesday luncheon was one of my few attempts to heed Joe's and Barbara's guidance, and I had bungled even that.

The importance of watching one's words was stressed repeatedly. A workshop organizer related that she had nearly lost out on a job after scorning the dog of Cass Sunstein, a famous legal scholar then at the University of Chicago. This bespoke an ingrained disdain for all canines, not a particularized antipathy for Sunstein's pooch specifically, she explained, but the distinction was initially lost on Sunstein, who had been wounded. They're on good terms now—I think—but perhaps not as good as they'd be if she loved dogs in general and Fido in particular. Some will fault Sunstein for overreacting. But there are a lot of dog lovers out there, me included, who would feel much the same way. Sunstein was, if anything, too forgiving in eventually letting it go.

I believe Kant condemned animal cruelty as a bellwether of cruelty to humans. And his general intuition that our regard for animals betrays something about our regard for members of our own species was confirmed by the intellectually gratuitous harshness with which this dog-despising organizer critiqued the moot job-talk/interview performances of some participants. The most egregious instance was her treatment of one who had coauthored some law and medicine articles with his father, a physician, when she belabored the supposed peculiarity of the collaboration with such sardonic interest that one could think something about it was scandalously inappropriate. Family members may not make ideal coauthors. But sometimes a cigar is just a cigar, as Freud reminded us, and that surely holds true of coauthored publications as well. Perhaps she was insinuating only a failure to launch. Either way, it struck me as subtle bullying masquerading as good-natured ribbing. Participants had been promised "hard hitting and brutally honest" critiques, but this was scarcely the kind of critique they could reasonably expect to face on the market, so I didn't accept that her motives were pristinely altruistic.

The primary task of observers was to watch and learn. But at one point we were invited to share any projects we were contemplating, and I elected to discuss my religious neutrality paper. Dick had remarked on the difficulty of encapsulating my thesis in a mere twenty minutes, and I now had only a fraction of that. I didn't make it for longer than thirty seconds before being barraged with questions and comments, my responses to which would be similarly interrupted by another such barrage. Some of the audience feedback was substantive, but at least half seemed directed against my very right to pursue the project. The woman behind me sniped that religious neutrality was an exhausted subject and listed three recent cases in rapid succession—as though expecting me to address them while knowing full well that I wouldn't be given the chance. Another attendee remarked that my project was more befitting someone like Bruce Ackerman, an eminent constitutional theorist at Yale. I'd in fact been imbibing Bruce Ackerman of late and found him interesting but didn't see why he was better suited to tackling the problem of conservative claims of cultural oppression. Nothing I'd read indicated he had any interest in the subject.

The academic habitus was reliably at work. Having arrived on the scene as an "observer," I remained "most lacking in symbolic capital," without the academic credibility required to undertake a project of such seeming breadth. Failing to display "a respect for distances, that is respect for the *order of succession*," the project stood suspect as an underhanded ploy to arrogate unmerited *celeritas*, just like the Overview nine months earlier. My detractor had invoked the august name of Bruce Ackerman as the symbolic embodiment of the *gravitas* that I lacked.

I might have tried to silence the howling mob by crowing that the project—140 pages now—had won accolades from Stolzenberg and the other Law & Humanities conference organizers. I might also have trotted out the "considerable interest" of Michael McConnell, their own patron saint. Did anyone *dare* question this judgment from "the leading authority on law and religion in the United States," who as such couldn't have been so easily impressed? I wouldn't abase myself to their level, however, and restricted myself to my intellectual subject matter despite all the ad hominems flying around the room. I managed reasonably well under the circumstances, I think. A participant later remarked to me that everyone had been "too quick to judge," which was at once true and false. They were indeed too quick to discount the merits of my research agenda. But they weren't too hasty in sizing up my reserves of symbolic capital, their snap judgment of which was perfectly accurate. At any rate I was attending the workshop to satisfy my anthropological curiosity, to monitor *Homo academicus* in his natural habitat. So I couldn't very well allow myself to take the natives' reactions personally.

I would continue my ethnographic fieldwork that evening when we headed off to Maggiano's for dinner, where some who had pilloried me that afternoon proved more receptive to the project, after the libations and casual atmosphere loosened their cultural conditioning. I eventually found myself seated by a professor who thought it fitting to occupy the table's attention with complaints about how Martha Nussbaum—a grandee of law and philosophy—had pilfered an idea for an article he had proposed they coauthor. He had suggested they collaborate to explore the pre-Socratics' affinities with postmodernism, and she just ran off and wrote up the paper all on her own. I listened attentively and tried to feel his pain. The truth, though, was that the universe was big enough for two more articles on the pre-Socratics and postmodernism. Nussbaum was guilty of petty larceny at worst, assuming his version of events was true. Nothing kept him from authoring another such article himself if he had something to say. Indeed, he could have penned a response to Nussbaum.

The proposal was, moreover, importunate and parasitic, given that Nussbaum surely had more to say when it came to ancient Greek philosophy. He was a nice guy, though—just not terribly self-aware on this front.

The next day was more of the same, with participants receiving more "hard hitting and brutally honest" criticism. Much of it was genuinely useful, but I continued to sense in the room a diffuse disgruntlement in search of some outlet. In his practice interview one participant ceaselessly referenced his PhD in economics in connection with his research, the institution where he earned it, and what it contributed to his candidacy. Everyone felt this was unduly repetitive, and one participant quietly groused that this individual was vainly aggrandizing himself at the expense of non-PhDs (the mere JDs). That his degree-granting institution wasn't particularly prestigious only added insult to injury, to her mind. In my view his locution was just maladroit. He invoked his PhD ad nauseam because those were his formative years, so he simply needed to vary his phrasing when stressing that point.

The Whole Trick of Pedagogical Reason

The workshop was eye-opening, and I departed Chicago with a better understanding of why McConnell's intimations of a fellowship had so quickly devolved into an invitation to observe. Yes, the Federalist Society had every indication that I should be attending as a participant. But there was a bigger picture that a careful thinker such as McConnell had surely pondered. Upon learning of my subversive activities, he wanted to help teach me an indelible lesson. I had declined to acquiesce to a milieu "where everyone depends on everyone else, at once his competitor and client, his opponent and judge, for the determination of his own truth and value, that is, of his own symbolic life and death." And McConnell was driving home that I, too, was reliant on others for that determination, the proof of which was my relegation to observer status, which events at the workshop then ratified. This wasn't without precedent. Set 1 had already reduced me to an observer in another way. I had sought to consecrate myself, and the recurring message was that such vainglory will incur the wrath of the powers that be.

As I've stressed, that wrath was always cloaked in plausible deniability, and the McConnell Affair had shed new light on its workings. *Conservative Claims of Cultural Oppression* observes, along with the sociologists Peter Berger and Thomas Luckmann, that "nihilation" grants institutions "a kind of negative legitimation." Whereas affirmative legitimation "maintains the reality of the socially constructed universe," nihilation "*denies* the reality of whatever phenomena or interpretations of phenomena do not fit into that universe," in an imperious ploy "to account for all deviant definitions of reality *in terms of* concepts belonging to one's own universe."[3] Accordingly,

> The threat to the social definition of reality is neutralized by assigning an inferior ontological status, and thereby a not-to-be-taken-seriously cognitive status, to all definitions existing outside the symbolic universe. The threat posed by these definitions is thus "conceptually liquidated." ...
>
> The deviant conception must ... be translated into concepts derived from one's own universe. In this manner, the negation of one's universe is subtly changed into an affirmation of it. The presupposition is always that the negator does not really know what he is saying. His statements become meaningful only as they are translated into more "correct" terms, that is, terms deriving from the universe he negates.[4]

If unmasking the conspiracy was going to be a daunting challenge, one reason was these strategies of nihilation and conceptual liquidation. Mine was a silent struggle against the intellectual magistrature of the sacred college of masters, against the prevailing ideology and its ascetic antipathy to the unregimented, self-directed mind as restive license and sterile self-indulgence. But Stanford's own maneuverings within that struggle were calibrated to generate rhetorical conditions under which it could be pegged as a struggle within the magistrature—as a bid for exogenous consecration rather than self-consecration. The Federalist Society workshop was merely the latest such maneuver. Any complaint that my attendance as an observer rather than a participant betrayed a conspiracy could be breezily dismissed with the familiar social heuristic: "Vain, entitled academic whining about not getting his due—we've seen it all before." The ideological nucleus of my insurrection, my gambit to subvert the jurisdiction of the magistrature, would thus stand nihilated, conceptually liquidated, ideologically translated into an affirmation of the academic habitus as immutable bedrock reality.

As I have discussed, the Toledo Affair proceeded in the same key. In both cases my ideological resistance to the habitus could be trivialized as mere disgruntlement, a pedestrian sour grapes grievance that only legitimized the dominant culture. The powers that be could thereby translate my deviant paradigm of intellectual life into the "more 'correct' terms" by means of which my stated position could be discounted as a post hoc rationalization for my career setbacks. This interpretation was belied by the fact that my anti-establishment impulses took root in my twenties, well before those setbacks. The setbacks contributed to my radicalization, but they were ultimately the effect, and not the cause, of my adversarial attitudes. Even so, the nihilation would strip my advocacy of whatever resonance it might otherwise enjoy. I had logic, narrative coherence, and above all predictive power on my side. But these would be unavailing in the face of my "not-to-be-taken-seriously cognitive status." The conspiracy's most ambitious foray on this front had been the home page, and everything from there on out was just a further elaboration on its devious logic, driving home the recurring message that "the negator does not really know what he is saying." The intellectual magistrature had "all appearances on its side, those of learning and those of morality." And the conspirators were persuaded that those appearances would prevail over reason and evidence—which, through their association with me, would also accrue a not-to-be-taken-seriously cognitive status.

A more advanced iteration of my job-talk paper was in good working order by early July, replete with new refinements and explorations. I wrote to Stolzenberg, who had proposed we exchange work, on July 13:

> Hi Nomi,
>
> I now have the first two chapters of my Establishment Clause book in pretty much their final form and would love to get some feedback from you. I read your piece on Mozert and agree that we are not only addressing many of the same issues but also approaching them from similar perspectives, both trying to articulate the paradoxically illiberal features of liberalism. As you put it in that piece, the question is how "neutral exposure" can be simultaneously thin and thick, both neutral as to ultimate values and at the same time the imposition of a particular way of life. The explanation, I'm arguing in the book, is that it can qualify as thin only from within the modern liberal identity, whose imposition will reasonably be resented by those not sharing it.
>
> I've printed up some copies for various interested parties and will send you one. Please email me anything you're working on and we can then chat sometime.
>
> Best,
>
> Rony

Stolzenberg's article examined certain Christian fundamentalists' legal challenges to "critical reading" curricula in public schools, which they claimed were infringing on their religious freedom. Neither rejecting nor endorsing religion, these courses merely exposed students to a range of viewpoints before leaving them free to make up their own minds. Hence, the neutral exposure. These fundamentalists dismissed such neutrality as fraudulent, however, because its cumulative effect was to inculcate an individualistic worldview hostile to the faith they would impart to their offspring. That's why neutral exposure can be "simultaneously thin and thick." It is thin inasmuch as no particular ideal of the good life is being formally espoused but thick inasmuch as the unspoken upshot of liberal neutrality is to cultivate an autonomous disposition, a culture-specific ideal of the good life that fundamentalists reject as sinful, making it less neutral than it seems.[5]

Joe's and Barbara's guidance was also both thin and thick. It was thin, that is, neutral, inasmuch as there was nothing inherently ideological about, say, penning a book review for Barbara's journal or auditing Polinsky's law and economics seminar. But it was thick in its cumulative cultural upshot, which was to reify a technocratic paradigm of intellectual life and correspondingly devalue the competing virtues exemplified by the wayward path of the fellowship—following your intellectual gut, thinking for yourself instead of for "the field," taking ideas to their logical conclusion, wherever that is. These virtues and the eccentricities they were bound to spawn in inimical cultural environs had facilitated both *Conservative Claims of Cultural Oppression* and my present plight, which had finally clarified the previously obscured marrow of my Janus-faced collegial relations. The second year of the fellowship only made explicit what had already been implicit in the first, releasing the latent centrifugal forces that would reveal the heretofore hidden thickness of my advisers' nostrums. To borrow from McConnell, Joe and Barbara "proclaim[ed] [their] neutrality toward competing ideas of virtue and the good life, but [were] committed in practice to the promotion of particular ideals and—even more—to the eradication of others."

Did my advisers' expectations truly pose an existential threat to my research agenda? Rawls defines liberal virtue as "reasonableness and a sense of fairness, a spirit of compromise and a readiness to meet others halfway."[6] Could I not have met them halfway? Would writing a book review or auditing a seminar have been all that time consuming? This objection misses something fundamental. Bourdieu highlights why liberal virtue is a Trojan horse for something murkier and more problematic:

> The whole trick of pedagogical reason lies precisely in the way it extorts the essential while seeming to demand the insignificant: in obtaining the respect for forms and forms of respect which constitute the most visible and at the same time the best-hidden (because most "natural") manifestations of submission to the established order, the incorporation of the arbitrary abolishes what Raymond Ruyer calls "lateral possibilities," that is, all the eccentricities and deviations which are the small changes of madness. The concessions of *politeness* always contain *political* concessions.[7]

This high theory was my dilemma in a nutshell. In expecting me to take their counsels and exhortations to heart, Joe and Barbara imagined they were demanding only "the concessions of *politeness*." They had taken me under their wings, enabling me to pursue my passion and sparing me the travails of sweatshop hours in a big law firm. In exchange they were hoping for a modicum of deference to their superior experience, wisdom, and expertise. And I had indeed withheld that modicum. But for cause, I submit, because tendering it would have involved a "*political* concession" to the cultural pathologies of liberalism and academia. Penning a book review or attending a seminar weren't necessarily all that laborious. But cumulatively such endeavors would have acculturated me to the New Class ethos and its "respect for forms," instilling me with the "expressive discipline" and scholarly *gravitas* that the still-subconscious telos of my research agenda called on me to subvert. The road not taken might have yielded a cleaner and timelier job-talk paper. But the truth of conservative claims of cultural oppression would then have adhered to me only, as Schopenhauer says, "as an artificial limb, a false tooth, a wax nose does," not as a natural appendage that could truly interface with the world. My strongest instincts wouldn't permit my research agenda to be thus defanged.

There was my dissimulation, yes. But there was also this "trick of pedagogical reason," in whose face my dissimulation was a survival mechanism necessitated by an asymmetrical power relationship. In pleading for the ostensibly insignificant, Joe and Barbara were laboring to extort the essential, to preempt the "eccentricities and deviations" and "small changes of madness" that would culminate in the August epiphany, my exit from the New Class culture, and the insights flowing therefrom. The difference between my personal skullduggery and my employer's broader cultural and institutional variant was akin to that between the individual tax cheat and a corporate lobby that pushes self-serving tax loopholes under the mantle of the public interest. Backed by power, Stanford's trick of pedagogical reason could just fade into the unnoticed, taken-for-granted background of things, where it registers as an innocuous request for the concessions of politeness. Because I was not so privileged, my own hustle was salient as such and could be readily pegged as the doings of a singular scoundrel.

Uncovering the heretofore hidden meaning of conservative claims of cultural oppression had to come at the expense of academic realpolitik because both the cultural oppression and the realpolitik emanated from the same source—the disciplines and repressions of the liberal culture as manifested in the sublimated and intellectualized conservatism of that culture's elites. This I had now tasked myself with unmasking, both theoretically and in praxis, and that mission had necessitated the eccentricities, deviations, and small changes of madness that defined the first year of the fellowship, culminated in the epiphany, and then precipitated the critical events of September 2009. Those events, not Legal Theory, were the true crucible of my research agenda. What preceded them was merely their prehistory, a protracted incubation that, easily destabilized by extraneous stimuli, would compel me to hibernate in obscurity for month after month. As I explained in chapter 2, my superficially shambolic and scattershot research methods were precisely what had been required to carve out the neural pathways by which to check out of the ambient culture. I couldn't approach that task as just one responsibility among others, to be put on hold as necessary in due consideration of other priorities. On the contrary, it demanded a certain illiberal ruthlessness that had to run roughshod over much else. My advisers hewed to prudence and moderation whereas I subscribed to the wisdom of excess. Between these there could be no compromise, so I would not be seduced by the siren song of liberal virtue, an ideological instrument of the dominant dispensation.

It had now been nearly a year since it all began and was therefore time to commence the job search anew. The paper had reached a new zenith, but my prospects were bleak as ever. This would be my second go at it, a scarlet letter in law school hiring. That the fellowship had lapsed without bearing fruit would also be a red flag. And little else mattered absent faculty support, as the McConnell Affair had amply demonstrated. I was now persona non grata at Stanford, it seemed. At best my recommenders would issue faint praise. At worst they would relate the events of September 2009 and all that ensued, which wouldn't endear me to most appointments committees. Still, I resolved to give it a go.

In connection with this, now seemed like a good time to touch base with McConnell and further test my suspicions. I emailed him on July 28:

> Hi Michael,
>
> I will soon be sending off my application materials for the AALS conference and was wondering whether I could include you among

> my references. I know we haven't even gotten around to chatting yet. But I thought that, as you read and approved of some of my work, you might serve as a reference at least as to that. Given my present research focus, liberal hypocrisy and the Establishment Clause, including you could be highly advantageous to me. All of my present recommenders are liberals. I now have a more advanced version of that work than the one I believe you may have read and would at any rate love to hear your reaction to it at some point.
>
> Best,
>
> Rony

I had designed this email to test whether McConnell had been conscripted into the conspiracy and was now in the fray. If McConnell couldn't meet to discuss the research in which he'd professed a "considerable interest"—because he was busy, out of town, or whatever—that could be chalked up to life as usual. But this wouldn't prevent him from serving as a reference. Doing so required no special effort on his part unless an appointments committee happened to contact him about me, which was also life as usual for professors. As I was careful to clarify, I wasn't asking him to speak to anything outside his ken. But his correspondences suggested a favorable view of my religious neutrality work, and he could at least convey that much—which was worth something coming from "the leading authority on law and religion in the United States," as Larry anointed him. It was also something to which he likely would agree under normal circumstances. He was a Stanford Law professor. I was a Stanford Law graduate and fellow. And professors usually are keen to promote their own grads and fellows.

Instead McConnell replied with a once-again laconic, "Will you be in Palo Alto in the last half of September?" and left it at that. I answered that I would be and would touch base with him again then. By making my future availability the issue, McConnell deflected my opening request about serving as a reference, which formed the more pressing heart of the message. Now aware of my trespasses, he couldn't back me in good conscience. But he couldn't flatly refuse this either, given the official farce that I remained in the law school's good graces. He had to maintain a modicum of rhetorical continuity with his earlier manifestation of interest in me because he couldn't broach that which would explain any discontinuity—the unofficial reality. So he threaded this needle by deflecting the request with vague intimations of some future meeting. This merely confirmed the unofficial reality—because it was that reality, and not the official one, that once again explained McConnell's behavioral irregularities.

The Entry-Level Hiring Survey Revisited

In the first week of August Larry Solum's Entry-Level Hiring Survey finally was taken down from the head of his blog and eventually archived alongside surveys of previous years. It was removed in its preliminary iteration, which hadn't been updated since early spring, if at all. The historical practice had been to publish new, more comprehensive, iterations of the survey as the results trickled in, with notes to keep everyone abreast of recent developments. In 2004, for example, update 33 apprised: "Yale leads with 20, Harvard has 18 and Stanford (10) is close behind. Chicago has 6. Berkeley has 5. Columbia, Michigan, Penn, Georgetown, and Virginia have 4 each. Howard and Texas are next with 3 each." Going beyond the call of duty, Solum also provided a pie chart to help readers visualize the relative positions of these and other schools. The 2006 survey had gone through eighteen iterations by May. The 2007 survey announced in April that Solum "hope[d] to begin preparing the full version of the report soon," asking readers to submit any additional information by May 1. But this year Solum had maintained what looked like the same "preliminary report" up till early August before finally retiring it, with his blog till then announcing, "Once again, it's time for the Entry-Level Hiring Survey," as though it hadn't been under way for about five months already. As one commentator on another law school blog would later observe, Solum's 2009 survey "was more complete than his 2010 version." What did it all mean?

Because the "preliminary report" was no longer up, it was no longer broadcasting the possibility of additional hires (and hence one at Stanford). On the other hand, the retired survey was ostensibly incomplete; there was no final version to announce that the hiring had concluded. This structured ambiguity reflected what would have been the unseemliness of retaining an announcement about the preliminary results of the 2009–10 faculty recruiting season now that the 2010–11 season was under way. The resulting compromise—archiving an incomplete, preliminary iteration of the survey—could be likened to the bifurcation of the home page into set 1 and set 2. Both were concessions to social normalcy and plausible deniability, which had to be weighed against my own need for evidence, as per the quid pro quo.

Skeptics will remonstrate that Solum might have just lost interest in the whole thing. Perhaps he was overwhelmed by more pressing obligations and repeatedly procrastinated on updating the survey before just throwing in the towel come August. That was unlikely for a number of reasons. In the first place it bears emphasis that any such loss of interest was something I had divined before the fact. I hadn't predicted the curious irregularities in all their details, admittedly, but to have foreseen them at all was already no mean feat. Those irregularities may not have been direct evidence of the quid pro quo. But they were direct evidence of my predictive prowess, which cried for an explanation. Such prowess transposed to the New York Stock Exchange would make me a rich man in short order.

Second, it didn't make sense for Solum to have just lost interest or become overwhelmed by other duties. That hadn't occurred in years past. And he had begun relying on SurveyMonkey the previous year, which presumably was labor saving. Solum had solicited survey responses on the understanding that he would compile them into a completed survey tabulating, ranking, and studying the comparative placement prowess of the country's top law schools. Nothing in the record suggested that he would casually tune out his reciprocal obligations to the respondents and others craving the survey results. So some sufficiently weighty countervailing rationale had to be at work—especially when SurveyMonkey now automated the process. The survey had been domiciled at the head of the blog, not behind some inconspicuous link, an indication of its importance for the legal academic community.

Nor did the record suggest that Solum was somehow undisciplined. He was also in the practice of posting abstracts of academic papers recently uploaded to SSRN, often grading these as "recommended" or "highly recommended" for his readers. So he took his blog seriously and had more than enough energy to run SurveyMonkey and compile the final iteration of the survey, which couldn't have been more taxing than the paper evaluations. Even if he had been genuinely deluged by other obligations, he would have been foolish to call it quits on the survey merely to review a few more papers than he'd otherwise have time for. The paper reviews generated symbolic capital by cultivating his consecratory authority. But the survey was a lot more sensational, and it, too, was a font of symbolic capital. From a cost-benefit perspective, the optimal course would have been to evaluate a few fewer papers, which would have gone unnoticed, and complete the survey—rather than leaving the hungry masses hanging high and dry. Although consistent with everyday thought-heuristics, the procrastination thesis also fails to explain why the initiatory "Once again, it's time for the Entry-Level Hiring Survey" remained up through the entire survey period. That curious irregularity would have taken seconds to remove and only drew attention to the ostensible dereliction. So, clearly, something unusual must have overridden both Solum's narrow self-interest and his routine sense of ethical obligation.

I submit that his real interests and obligations were ideological. Solum taught at Illinois rather than Stanford. But the intellectual magistrature of the sacred college of masters has universal jurisdiction.

So he would have been as scandalized by my deviance as was Barbara and could have identified with her retributive impulses, her clandestine quest for a double revenge. He, too, was versed in the art of making someone wait. So why not help out a colleague by generating further intimations that there was hope for me? The stronger the total force of these intimations, the more dogged I would be by semantic and existential indeterminacy, and the less tempting would be the legal route. Yes, he would disappoint the folks awaiting the frisson of the final tally, but he'd be taking a stand in defense of something he believed in by assisting in my ongoing gaslighting, this purification ritual to reassert the academic habitus against a reviled agitator and designated Other. There would also be the satisfaction of being "in on a special project" that was at once easier and less prosaic than running a computerized survey. Oh, to savor the sweet taste of plausible deniability! His contribution wouldn't earn official recognition. But word would spread in the relevant circles, where he'd be a hero.

All this may be a little too much mind reading for some readers' tastes. But Dick had taken note of this penchant back in September 2009, and it was facilitated by my attunement to the higher truth of conservative claims of cultural oppression, the decolonization of the mind that had exposed the hidden machinations of the elite culture, including those in my midst. Certainly, the anomalies in the survey admit of other explanations. I do not pretend that my exegesis carries the weight of a written confession. But that exegesis does not stand alone, for it sprung from a theory that had yielded *two* falsifiable yet unfalsified predictions that no one not in my position would have thought to make or considered sensible, one about the survey itself and the other about the ostensibly unrelated home page. The theory was also highly congruous with the host of other curious irregularities I've documented and will continue to document. Again, I remind readers to assess the evidence cumulatively against the total background I am presenting—like scientists rather than climate change deniers.

CHAPTER 9

The End of an Era

September 2010–January 2011

The Law-School View of What "Prejudices" Must Be Stamped Out

My pickings on the market were slim, as expected. The conservative bastion of Pepperdine University Law School did evince some interest, with an inquiry about my ability to support the school's Christian mission. That didn't necessarily mean accepting Jesus Christ as my lord and savior. Still, there were serious questions about my suitability. So, on September 19, I wrote to Dick for some wisdom and insight:

> Hi Dick,
>
> The conservatives are once again taking an interest in me. Pepperdine recently emailed me with a request for additional information, part of which concerns the nature of my religious identifications and my ability to support the university's Christian mission. I usually conceive of myself as an atheist but am thinking it might be safer to package myself as an agnostic, given that mission, and given that I cannot in fact deny God's existence with mathematical certainty. Would this be

> mere puffery of the sort that is only to be expected of job seekers, or would I be crossing the line into misrepresentation?
>
> On a different note, the fellows are permitting me to meet with them during this hiring season, as I am an emeritus of the group, and I will be giving a moot job-talk on October 4. I thought I would provide you with a copy of the paper here in advance, in case you have spare time and inclination, as there has been progress since the version you read.
>
> Best,
>
> Rony

Some problems are destined to repeat themselves again and again. Whether I was engaging in "mere puffery of the sort that is only to be expected of job seekers" or rather "crossing the line into misrepresentation" was precisely the question looming large in my advisers' minds a year before. I hadn't misrepresented myself in the crudest, most transparently unethical, sense of fabricating works in progress out of whole cloth in a calculated ploy to sell a bill of goods. On the other hand, the cumulative message broadcast by my application materials had to appear grossly inconsistent with my anemic output that year if viewed through the lens of the elite culture.

Whether I had crossed the line into misrepresentation ultimately turned on whether those materials and the path leading to their production signified what I presumed they did, my exit from that culture and accession to the standpoint of conservative claims of cultural oppression. My advisers discounted this putative achievement as a hollow conceit, mere *celeritas*, and trivialized my research agenda accordingly. I, on the other hand, looked upon their very reactions as part and parcel of that agenda's three-dimensional unfolding into the nature of my predicament as an academic job seeker. That unfolding was the higher truth that redeemed my half-truths, that which would actualize the potential that my advisers had once upon a time divined in my project.

These conflicting narratives made it impossible to ascertain the bottom-line duplicity of my application materials in real time, as this judgment turned on whether my philosophical jiujitsu would be vindicated by the future course of events. That is, it turned on moral luck, as I suggested to Barbara in November. As Joe and Barbara's Gauguin, I had early on abandoned them for a Tahiti of the mind, absconding from their rightful claims on me while "putting a great deal on a possibility which has not unequivocally declared itself," as Bernard Williams says (see chapter 1). This was the possibility that Barbara's academic realpolitik would in some fashion or other become co-opted by my own research agenda, by the higher, heretofore hidden, truth of conservative claims of cultural oppression, which had percolated within the tacit dimension during the first year of the fellowship before growing articulate and self-conscious with the epiphany. Could the starry-eyed dreamer somehow prevail over the no-nonsense realist, or would my research agenda be snuffed out before it could truly draw breath?

Should I prove unequal to my task, my defiance would stand discredited as obtuse arrogance, vain self-delusion, and an insolent betrayal of trust after September 2009. I would then amount to a grifter and miscreant—like Dostoevsky's Raskolnikov torn apart by the pangs of conscience but with no one to whom to confess. I had axed the old pawnbroker when I fired off the works-in-progress email that decisively legalized my collegial relations, and nothing but self-recrimination would come of it if I failed to imbue this arguably impetuous deed with the higher redemptive meaning I believed it could support. Such a feat wouldn't extinguish Joe's and Barbara's legitimate grievances against me. But, like Gauguin, I could then look upon those grievances as part of a larger multifaceted story of supramoral significance and not the whole story. With this supersession of morality by art, I would emerge as a miscreant with a mission, a miscreant with something interesting to say. Whatever the bellyaching, there would be the fact that I had to break some eggs to make an omelet. The true meaning of my undertakings, and hence the validity of my far-flung presumptions, was being governed by moral luck, the one power in the universe capable of redeeming my waywardness. And it was increasingly apparent that my own moral luck would have to come at the expense of Barbara's. Despite her expertise in the subject, she had forgotten about this wild card when she breezily concluded that the sum of my transgressions to date was dispositive of the moral equation—which could swing in my favor in the fullness of time.

For the moment, though, more immediate matters beckoned. Dick was apparently amenable to the kind of puffery I was now proposing, writing back:

> Interesting!
>
> I'm not the best person to try to judge how the folks at Pepperdine will interpret such an answer. As far as I'm concerned, though, describing yourself as an agnostic sounds entirely permissible (i.e., either label is technically correct, as long as one doesn't have to specify which side bears the burden of proof).
>
> I guess the only thing I might worry about is if you've ever described yourself publicly as an atheist (where "publicly", these days, includes things like blog posts). If so, and if people at Pepperdine found out, they might then object to your having "passed yourself off" as an agnostic.
>
> Does this help?
>
> —Dick

This, too, harkened to a recurring problem. Having alluded to the origins of our present discord in my initial question, I now alluded to the risks it portended:

> That is useful. I've never blogged, or even commented on a blog, but have repeatedly entertained the idea that I might one day become a blogger, and this electronic age is rife with opportunities for

generating unintended consequences. I think I'll say that I'm "strictly speaking" an agnostic, and thereby provide myself with an escape hatch should the worst case scenario you envisage materialize.

That "this electronic age is rife with opportunities for generating unintended consequences" was the risk the conspirators had myopically minimized when they resolved to deploy set 1 and hide the quid pro quo in plain sight. Ten months had now elapsed since my "informal networking" chat with Dick, and it was increasingly apparent that I would be left with no recourse but to leverage the home page to spawn the "unintended consequences" that the conspiracy had so smugly discounted. Stanford had deposited its symbolic capital as surety for the quid pro quo, and I would be within my rights to avail myself of it if they forced my hand. This latest message to Dick was a reminder to that effect.

If the conspiracy rested easy that any such gambit would come apart at the seams, one important reason was the logical circularity of the enterprise. Set 1 was evidence for the events of September 2009, but its status as evidence in turn presupposed those events. The conspirators were persuaded that I would never happen upon a mechanism that could bootstrap each half of the equation onto the other in order to realize the probative value of set 1. I had such a means at my disposal, however—conservative claims of cultural oppression—into which my own oppression could be readily shoehorned, giving it the human cogency and logical form withheld by dominant cultural narratives. My advisers had always been intrigued by those claims, but as elites they could never be captivated by my faith in their higher truth, and I could one day utilize that truth to problematize the home page and unravel the conspiracy.

As I first explained in chapter 3, I had eschewed Say's law—"the more people are saying, the more there is to be said"—in favor of the tacit dimension and the antithetical principle that the less people are saying, the more there is to be said. That principle was anathema to *Homo academicus*, a naturally loquacious species and platinum card–carrying member of the chattering class. But it was axiomatic to my research agenda and was now being tested in my response to this latest career challenge. Rather little was said *during* the fellowship. Indeed, my collegial interactions were so meager that I've handily managed to document most all of them here. Pursuant to Say's law, the conspirators supposed this paucity meant there would be little to say *about* the fellowship, because the dots were too few and far between to be meaningfully connected. This was their fundamental miscalculation. Blinded by their technocratic prejudices, they couldn't fathom that my ostensible solipsism cocooned something universal, that I was the antithesis to their thesis, the clash of which would articulate the hidden cultural contradictions of our milieu. Whereas I was enthralled by a philosophical odyssey, they saw only a vexatious imbroglio. So they couldn't discern the bottomless layers of rich human meaning that dwelled quietly beneath and between the sparse tangible data points, waiting to be uncovered and woven into a subaltern countercultural discourse that would disrupt their categories and neutralize their Ring of Gyges. That discourse would run against the grain of elite opinion without settling the truth of my allegations. But it could raise troubling questions by foregrounding human motives that liberal rationalism must disingenuously deny or paper over.

My research agenda had always been galvanized by the gnawing sense that liberalism is an ethos and not just a family of policy prescriptions stemming from certain philosophical abstractions. This means the elites may be driven by structural forces that operate below the threshold of consciousness and outrun individual intention, which will then be freighted with a subterranean cultural meaning that the elites in their rationalism cannot perceive. This philosophical blind spot had now been exemplified by my advisers' stealth and subterfuge. Stuck in their New Class bubble, they conceived of the unofficial reality as simple pest control, a philosophically inert expedient for managing a rogue fellow now off the reservation. Accordingly, they were insensible to how their policy of allusion, intimation, and ambiguation betrayed their broader ethos, the academic habitus—a deep reservoir of cultural meanings and philosophical perplexities that I could leverage to deconstruct my academic unemployment and render our byzantine power struggle intelligible to third-party nonbelligerents. I would simply apply the tools of critical theory to my own sui generis cause, thus making it less sui generis.

The affinities between conservative claims of cultural oppression and my own beef with the elites can be gleaned from the late Justice Antonin Scalia's blistering dissent in *Romer v. Evans*. There the Supreme Court held unconstitutional Colorado's "Amendment 2," which would have given Coloradans free rein to discriminate against gays in employment and housing by barring municipal ordinances forbidding this. Justice Scalia notoriously admonished the court:

> When the Court takes sides in the culture wars, it tends to be with the knights rather than the villeins—and more specifically with the Templars, reflecting the views and values of the lawyer class from which the Court's Members are drawn. How that class feels about homosexuality will be evident to anyone who wishes to interview job applicants at virtually any of the Nation's law schools. The interviewer may refuse to offer a job because the applicant is a Republican; because he is an adulterer; because he went to the wrong prep school or belongs to the wrong country club; because he eats snails; because he is a womanizer; because she wears real-animal fur; or even because he hates the Chicago Cubs. But if the interviewer should wish not to be an associate or partner of an applicant because he disapproves of the applicant's homosexuality, then he will have violated the pledge which the Association of American Law Schools requires all its member-schools to exact from job interviewers: "assurance of the employer's willingness" to hire homosexuals. ... This law-school view of what "prejudices" must be stamped out may be contrasted with the more plebeian attitudes that apparently

> still prevail in the United States Congress, which has been unresponsive to repeated attempts to extend to homosexuals the protections of federal civil rights laws.[1]

The suggestion is that while the liberal elites—"Templars"—purport to stand for equality, they perpetuate inequality inasmuch as they are privileged to shield their own prejudices from the scrutiny they regularly mete out to conservative ordinary Americans, or "villeins." Templars routinely base their own hiring decisions on "irrational" criteria that are not germane to job performance narrowly construed but still foster workplace environments that are in keeping with their particular cultural sensibilities.[2] But this is a privilege that the crusader-priests of liberalism deny their social inferiors, whose prejudices they target daily for legal intervention and cultural stigmatization. Seen in this light, the "equal protection" question posed by *Romer* wasn't whether gays were to enjoy equality with heterosexuals in the face of Coloradans' traditionalist prejudices but whether these particular prejudices should enjoy equality with those indulged by the liberal elites, who are privileged to freely associate with whom they please, ungoverned by exogenous regulation.

The elites believe themselves above prejudice, but their selective attention to certain prejudices to the arbitrary neglect of others is itself a prejudice, a parochial cultural preference dissembling as tolerance pure and simple. Hence, Scalia's lament that the court had "mistaken a Kulturkampf for a fit of spite" in tracing Amendment 2's motivations to bare animus against homosexuals.[3] He was in agreement with Roger Scruton that what the elites cast as a clash "between dark intolerance and enlightened reason" is really "nothing more than a clash of prejudices"; the difference is that "one side frankly admits that the feelings it brings into this dispute are moral, [whereas] the other hides its bigotry behind a mask of reason, serenely expecting to carry the day."[4]

Liberals will decry Scalia's rebuke as another conservative false equivalency that trivializes grievous harms. The suggestion is that it's arbitrary to discount discrimination based on snail consumption or hatred of the Chicago Cubs as a strictly personal misfortune while highlighting that based on sexual orientation as a pressing social ill calling for legal and political solutions, as these prejudices are all equally irrational from a certain perspective. But while a handful of law students may now and then falter in interviews owing to their preferences in food or baseball, such occasional bad luck isn't commensurate with the systemic discrimination faced by gays and lesbians. Whatever uncomfortable moments these students' tastes and preferences may at times create are trivial compared with the visceral animus that sexual minorities may confront routinely. What Scalia acerbically waves away as a parochial "law-school view of what 'prejudices' must be stamped out" is a response to that asymmetry, which exists objectively in the world and not as a cultural artifice of Templar sensibilities.

Scalia is more than a little obtuse in papering this over. Even so, his argument trades on a higher truth that is better illustrated by my own employment challenges. Anecdotes abound of academics who did everything right yet found their careers in freefall because of departmental rivals or vindictive advisers driven by politics of one kind or another to run roughshod over merit. As should be clear, I do not contend that my own fall from grace belongs in this familiar category. There is no question that I faltered by the meritocratic metrics of my milieu and that I never really had the makings of an elite, despite the superficially promising signs. I do argue, however, that those meritocratic metrics do not meet the high bar of social justice—which conservatives recognize is highly elastic (or "indeterminate," as Barbara put it).

When conservatives deny the persistence of widespread racism and attribute racial disparities in wealth and social status to dysfunctional family structures, criminality, or disdain for education, the left-liberal rejoinder is that these self-defeating behavior patterns, to the extent they are truly widespread, are themselves attributable to various forms of racism, including a "white culture" that stacks the deck against minorities by conditioning upward mobility on assimilation to culturally alien norms.[5] In this vein I'm claiming that the deck was always stacked against me by an academic ethos that celebrates certain intellectual virtues to the unjustified detriment of others, in the interests of those privileged by this historically contingent cultural dispensation. Notwithstanding Dick's willingness to chalk up my stillborn candidacy to bad luck, meritocracy is no illusion, but it fulfills a culturally thicker social function than is acknowledged by the "law-school view of what 'prejudices' must be stamped out."

As Jacoby observes, "Universities encourage a definite intellectual form." The naturally obeisant thrive, provided the other desiderata of academic flourishing—smarts, work ethic, and luck—are in place. Those who, whether owing to genetics or environment, lack such good breeding and cannot develop the requisite *gravitas* will be denied entry to the country club, regardless of the other desiderata. I managed to get one foot and only one foot in the door of the country club because my advisers saw enough of those other desiderata in me that they allowed themselves to just wish away my essential deviance. As revealed by the futility of their repeated exhortations, my recalcitrance proved to be an "immutable characteristic" that couldn't be helped any more than can sexual orientation. As a minority of one, I was differently oriented toward the life of the mind, eschewing inherited consecratory authority in favor of self-consecration and thinking for the field in favor of thinking for oneself. I could no more internalize the New Class ethos of expressive discipline than a naturally effeminate gay man could be expected to start vocalizing like John Wayne.[6]

The conspirators processed the fruits of this deviance as a bid for unearned *celeritas*. But I've been arguing that this technocratic lens, through which the autonomous, unprofessionalized mind appears unserious and rudderless, is bigotry hiding "behind a mask of reason, serenely expecting to carry the day"—the secularized asceticism of the liberal elites culturally exalted as hard-won circumspection and discipline. These ostensible virtues are an identitarian "instrument of the transformation of individual and collective limits into the choice of scientific virtuousness," as Bourdieu says. Yet such distortions are broadly immune to the scrutiny and intervention of cultural outsiders, and this good fortune—this good moral luck—is what props up the Templars' claims to superior virtue. They can be boundlessly tolerant, indeed embracing, as to race, sex, sexual orientation, gender identity, and all the rest so long as the magistrature's consecratory authority isn't challenged. For their celebration of diversity does not reach neurodiversity, and modernity's discontents will always remain unwelcome as threats to the rationalization of intellectual life, impediments to the "progress" of which I proved incapable. Social justice as conceived by the liberal elites costs them nothing, making it an easy virtue. In contrast, my own more expansive vision of social justice—the affirmative action represented by interpretation 1—*would* have cost something, requiring a self-reflexivity to which Templars are unaccustomed.

I emerged from September 2009 as a troublesome interloper at the law school, and my gambit to muscle my way into continued employment there may have been presumptuous. But so, too, is compelling conservative Christian schools to hire gay and lesbian teachers, which more than a few law professors would unreservedly support. Both forms of forced association are culturally oppressive because both proceed on the premise that a taken-for-granted hero-system is a mere prejudice to be cabined by enlightened principles. Beholden to the "law-school view of what 'prejudices' must be stamped out," my advisers didn't credit me with any such principles. So they had to discount my deviance as the primrose path of *celeritas*, and for the same reason homosexuality gets denigrated as nihilistic and degenerate. That deviance was just as offensive to the social identity of *Homo academicus* as was homosexuality to that of the conservative evangelicals backing Amendment 2. Unlike unlettered villeins, however, *Homo academici* are Templars given free rein to serenely indulge their prejudices behind a mask of reason.

Hence, the conspirators' complacent conviction that my gaslighting was a strictly personal ordeal that could never speak to anything larger. They had the privilege of drawing the boundary between public and private in keeping with their own privileged identities. That demarcation was socially constructed, however, and so might one day be unsettled. As Harvey Mansfield observes:

> We must not look at public and private statically as a distinction that never changes; we must remember that the public emerges from private, latent interests or opinions that find expression. The public, the political, needs to be asserted; what is public now was once asserted, what will be public in the future will be asserted against what is public now.[7]

Feminism and its politicization of the personal are a case in point. And so, too, was my own resistance to oppression, which could be asserted as public and political through a countercultural narrative that articulated the universal interests latent in my ostensible solipsism, problematizing the "law-school view of what 'prejudices' must be stamped out" by disclosing the dark underside of the elites' enlightened cosmopolitanism as it plays out in a fallen world. Templar prejudices are exponentially subtler than racism or homophobia, so they usually pass under the radar. Even so, their workings could be smoked out through a suitably sophisticated hermeneutics of suspicion, which the conspirators were now forcing me to propound.

Mine was an extreme case of academic crash-and-burn, to be sure, but extreme cases are sometimes needed to illustrate general truths that otherwise get papered over. The general truth in question is liberal privilege, Templar privilege, which my yearlong gaslighting distilled with microscopic clarity. The conspirators rested easy in their plausible deniability because they correctly gauged that I couldn't indict them without also indicting myself. Since my allegations made sense only by reference to my own derelictions, I would have to fall on my sword just to begin making my case. And yet the conspirators failed to appreciate that both indictments cohered at one level up as elements of a wider, suprapersonal indictment of Templar privilege—the root cause of my derelictions and, hence, their grievances. Joe had been struck by my ability to entertain opposing viewpoints, and it would be by weaponizing that charity and fair-mindedness that I would neutralize my colleagues' Templar privilege.

As Barbara was apprised, I had adopted an "objective attitude" in the wake of September 2009. And that attitude disclosed that, as with the marginalized minorities chastised by conservative moralists, my ostensibly dysfunctional behavior was a symptom of inequitable social conditions. These had bred Templar cultural hegemony, which rewards its adherents while debilitating its discontents. Liam Gillespie delineates the nature of this domination:

> The *habitus* therefore not only confers unfair levels of socio-cultural privilege upon certain individuals (through the bestowal of cultural capital), it also invisibilises this privilege. As a result, the struggle to change the socio-cultural conditions of the *habitus* is inherently difficult. This is because dominant subjects are able to exercise their dominance *merely by conforming to the status quo and by "being themselves,"* while those who are dominated must effect a rupture of the *habitus* from within the *habitus* itself. Put differently, within the *habitus*, the dominance of dominant subjects appears "objective." The dominant can just "be," while the dominated must first "clear the way" *before* they can "be."[8]

This was my oppression in a nutshell. I was being punished for my derelictions, but those could not be helped if I was to "effect a rupture of the *habitus* from within the *habitus* itself" and thereby "clear the way" for my research agenda to come to its own. I was a rebel without a cause because only the success of my rebellion could reveal my cause, which the cultural and linguistic hegemony of the chattering class had initially obscured from view, leading to my seemingly shambolic research methods. Seen through this broader cosmopolitan lens, my idiosyncrasies harbored human universals, bearing the seeds of a challenge to the prevailing vision. Eschewing the trappings of deracinated New Class professionalism, I wasn't content to just pass about sealed containers of condensed thought that would never unfold into worldly plenitude. But mustering the conditions under which such became possible had to bring me into conflict with the dominant culture, engendering all the havoc recounted in these pages.

This silent backstory was why that havoc harbored a philosophical meaning that, while invisible to the "law-school view of what 'prejudices' must be stamped out," could be mined to properly theorize my gaslighting. Because the deeds of all concerned were ultimately attributable to the structural inequality I've detailed, I could expose those deeds by exposing the inequality. My class-based analysis would unmask the regime of scholarly supremacy that had shackled me from the start, of which the unofficial reality was just a rarefied expression. The conspirators had arrogantly discounted the risks of their enterprise because, eyeing our palace intrigue through a narrowly legal lens, they were blind to how my own more interdisciplinary approach could make the personal political by subsuming their academic realpolitik within my protean research agenda. Unbeknown to them, their very hostility to that agenda as it matured during the fellowship had fueled its three-dimensional unfurling into worldly plentitude. Thus would the very project they'd by then written off completely enable me to unmask the systemic oppression that had stymied my career aspirations for these many years, before culminating in my final downfall. Being culturally insensible to this eventuality, they fancied that I'd become unglued when I'd in fact become *unleashed*—untethered from their contingent socially constructed reality, yes, but not from reality as such. I grasped that distinction whilst they elided it, and this blind spot was why the home page was "rife with opportunities for generating unintended consequences," why the epicenter of my abject subjugation by the law school might one day serve as the springboard for a future resurgence.

The Law School That Dared Not Speak Its Name

As things stood, though, I was just a former fellow laid low by the might of Stanford. Given the ongoing fiction that my fellowship hadn't been extended owing only to some fixed administrative regulation, I remained active in the fellows group. I had been going through the motions of normalcy for some time already and saw no reason to drop the pantomime just yet. Exploiting this facade, I determined to further test my surmise that McConnell was in the fray. He had asked in July about my availability in late September, so I now wrote him again:

> Hi Michael,
>
> I don't know whether you're around these days. But as I mentioned, I'm eager to discuss the problem of religious neutrality with you, and to hear your thoughts on what I've been writing. I'm actually doing a moot job-talk on October 4 at 2:00. Would you be available to attend?
>
> Best,
>
> Rony

With characteristic breviloquence McConnell responded, "I can try. Do you need a definite answer?" to which I replied, "No need for a definite answer, but I've attached the paper in case you're able. Otherwise, I'm sure we'll chat at some later point." As I had predicted, McConnell said the minimum required to maintain some semblance of rhetorical continuity with his initial expression of interest in my doings. In July he had seized on the suggestion that we meet to dodge the more immediate question about serving as a reference. Now he seized on the moot job talk to deflect this renewed invitation to get together, issued as follow-up to his original dodge. McConnell had no intention of attending the talk, but the farce of the official reality compelled him to feign uncertainty.

The talk went as well as I could have hoped. A group of fellows, along with professors Mark Kelman and Jane Schacter, were in attendance. I presented my paper for twenty minutes and then turned to questions and comments. Apologizing for being a "wet blanket," Kelman assessed that while the paper itself was "clear and nuanced," the presentation fell flat. That was fair enough. One reason was what Dick characterized as the "rich and complex" nature of my intellectual agenda, which wasn't readily summarized. The other was that I was just going through the motions at this point. Battered by time and running on fumes, I was painfully cognizant of a fate taken hostage to forces that could not be so much as confronted.

The question-and-answer period went smoothly, though. True to form, Jane Schacter, a gay rights activist, asked how my argument bore on same-sex marriage. The question was probably invited by my term of art, "cosmological orientation," which was a play on sexual orientation and encapsulated my thesis that liberals and conservatives are divided not only by different ideas but by different forms of consciousness. After the exercise wound down, Schacter raised what she called an important question about the nature of my own cosmological orientation. I didn't have a ready answer, but the inquiry confirmed that I was indeed an alien presence at Stanford.

Exiting the room, Kelman threw me a wink and a nod—the universal symbol of plausible deniability—thereby confirming that he, too, was in the loop, as I'd already suspected. He was in set 1, in cahoots with Larry in Think Like a Lawyer, a good pal of Joe and Barbara's, and above all another Jew in a largely Jewish conspiracy.[i] His dog whistling to the unofficial reality was plain as day. I barely knew Kelman, so there were no other unspoken understandings between us to which the gesture could conceivably have referred. Naturally, he supposed that I would only discredit myself as psychotic if I ever

---

[i] See chapter 6 of my work in progress, "The Critical Theory of Academia," at ronyguldmann.com, for an exploration of my saga's Jewish dimensions.

trotted it out as evidence of his complicity. Indeed, this epistemic oppression was part and parcel of what he intended the gesture to convey (and celebrate). It was just a microcosm of my entire dilemma, as he also understood. Like all the rest, Kelman was operating one level up and couldn't fathom that I might rise to the occasion, learn to operate *two* levels up, and somehow win this protracted game of four-dimensional chess. This failure of imagination was not without precedent. Dominant classes have from time immemorial given short shrift to the resilience and resourcefulness of the downtrodden and marginalized, never having themselves confronted conditions that could spur these qualities by sheer force of necessity.

Sam Bray—one of two Olin fellows who had arrived that fall as acolytes of McConnell—later emailed me: "Good job today—you've got a great project and now it's just about showing it in the best possible light. Your answers to questions were superb, and that's the hardest thing about the whole process." If only he were right—if only the questions really were the hardest part. They were not in my case, as my adroit repartee could not rescue me from the regime of semantic and existential indeterminacy under which I continued to languish. Now that a year had elapsed, that indeterminacy was eating away at my foundations, as my highest hopes crumbled before grim realities confirmed by the march of time.

Notwithstanding my imminent demise, on October 20, just a week before the recruitment conference in Washington, Northwestern Law School invited me to interview. One of the interviewers had been among the faculty experts at the Federalist Society workshop. I had humored his grievance against Martha Nussbaum at Maggiano's, and that had evidently paid off. I booked a flight to Washington, where I would once more be trudging through the halls of the Marriot Wardman Park Hotel for the sake of a single interview, forced to relive the nightmare of 2009 amid throngs of eager beavers full of high hopes. In the meantime I arranged to meet with Dick before my departure. The announced purpose of this conferral was to prepare for the interview, but my true design was to exploit the occasion to solicit a long overdue update on my situation.

To this end, I asked Dick when he thought I could expect to hear back from Northwestern, using knowing undertones to cue that I was invoking "Northwestern" as a stand-in for Stanford. Catching my drift, Dick raised his fingers to form air quotes and, with equally knowing undertones, answered, "At Stanford, we call people in December. You'll have an offer by the end of the year"—closing the air quotes right at "Stanford." The law school that dared not speak its name had finally done so. Officially, Dick was citing Stanford as a familiar example that might shed light on Northwestern's practices. But unofficially he had invoked it in connection with the quid pro quo. Hence, Dick's air quotes, by which he signaled that he was suspending the ostensible semantic context of the official reality. So understood, his advertence to Stanford was *not* to Stanford qua useful reference point but to Stanford qua former employer and conceivable future one.

Dick's utterances were nonsensical within the official reality for four reasons. First, because the AALS interviews would be taking place in late October, it was most implausible that Northwestern, Stanford, or any other law school would wait until December before calling prospects back. Hiring committees liked to touch base with promising candidates soon after the conference, generally within the week. Second, Dick's talk of an offer was premature. I hadn't even completed a preliminary interview at the conference, let alone been invited for a follow-up campus visit, and offers can flow only after these visits. It made no sense for Dick to be getting ahead of himself in this manner. I had solicited an educated guess as to when I might "hear back" from Northwestern, not when they might extend an offer. So his talk of an offer wasn't prompted by the official text of my query. Third, Dick conveyed certainty rather than possibility when announcing that "you'll have an offer by the end of the year." Given that he was in no position to guarantee an offer from Northwestern, or even a campus visit, "you could get an offer" would have been more sensible.

Finally, Dick's time frame—"before the end of the year"—was either wildly implausible if *year* meant the calendar year or stating the obvious if it meant the academic year. Was I going to get a call-back from Northwestern in December, make my way to Chicago for campus interviews that very month, and then secure an offer before Christmas? Law school hiring doesn't work that way. Schools invite multiple candidates back to campus, and elite ones such as Northwestern usually take their time before making offers. Indeed, I recall Bob Weisberg's divulging to us fellows that elite law schools are herdlike and will wait to verify that candidates are attracting interest elsewhere before extending offers. So an offer from Northwestern before January was well-nigh inconceivable. Did Dick then mean that the offer would come before the end of the *academic* year, before May or June? But when else would it come? Any such prediction would have been gratuitous, and Dick wasn't given to gratuitous utterances, as I've stressed.

Dick's linguistic contortions were fully intelligible, however, in the framework of the unofficial reality, in whose long shadow our conversation was transpiring. Dick conveyed certainty rather than possibility in reflection of the quid pro quo agreement, my end of which had been kept. His talk of a call in December and an offer by year's end made sense in the context of our "informal networking" consultation the previous December, when he suggested that some law school might at some point be needing someone to fill in constitutional law on short notice. Since the course was taught in January at Stanford Law, December was the latest such a contingency could arise. Here as elsewhere, only in connection with the unofficial reality did Dick's pronouncements make any sense whatsoever. The sincerity of those pronouncements was another matter, especially at this late hour. But these logical lapses were at the very least another arrow in my quiver, further evidence for the existence of an underlying controversy that I might one day exploit to extract a fresh infusion of symbolic capital from my alma mater.

Delta lost my luggage somewhere between San Francisco and D.C., so I arrived at the interview in shorts and unshaven, which befitted one "most lacking in symbolic capital." My interviewer assured me that my dishevelment was excusable under the circumstances, which was a rational response. But we wouldn't have to show up at interviews in suits in the first place if people were rational animals, so his promised forbearance rang hollow. The conversation went smoothly but not spectacularly, as I was now enervated by all that had come to pass. As in my moot job talk, I was running on fumes and just going through the motions. He asked how many other interviews I had on my plate and I answered truthfully, that he was it. That couldn't have helped, unless he was so self-assured as to attribute this state of affairs to his superior wisdom and judgment. That seemed unlikely. He was the one complaining about Martha Nussbaum, after all. At any rate I heard no more from Northwestern.

The Preamble

It had been clear for some time which way the winds were blowing and that I was indeed staring into the abyss. Pursuant to interpretation 2, I would be reaping not a job but only some modicum of evidence for the existence of an underlying controversy, one interpretation of which might have yielded a job in some parallel universe but could not in the one at hand. This conclusion was completely irresistible once December rolled around. Because constitutional law was taught in January, there was now barely time for an emergency to somehow crop up.

December did offer one consolation, though, when Stolzenberg emailed me on December 29 to say that reading my religious neutrality paper had been one of the pleasures of her winter break. On a critical note she did have a few quibbles with my failure to cite certain luminaries, admonishing me to "give credit where credit is due." I had never read, and therefore hadn't relied upon, their work, so I didn't see what I owed them. But, as Gouldner says, the "New Class is a cultural bourgeoisie who appropriates privately the advantages of a historically and collectively produced cultural capital" (see chapter 3). The paper had improved markedly since September 2009, but my respect for academia's bourgeois values evidently had not.

These admonitions aside, Stolzenberg had read the paper with "enormous interest and profit." Sizing it up as "really deep, subtle, complex, exciting stuff," she assayed that I was making "genuinely novel and important contributions—no mean feat."[ii] Grandiloquent and half-baked though the Overview may have been, this was where the bloviation had finally led. As academic insiders know, genuinely novel and important contributions are the exception rather than the rule even among seasoned scholars, who enjoy the luxury of laboring under conditions less trying than my own—blessedly unencumbered by the albatross of the unofficial reality and hence the soul-hollowing malaise that was and remains a constant source of distraction.

Stolzenberg was just echoing Barbara's gushing praise for a much rougher version of the paper as "subtle, iconoclastic in the best way, and really, really interesting," questionably dispensed more than a year earlier. But the accolades wouldn't save me now any more than they did then, and in the end they only aggravated the fissure between the "representation experienced" and my "true position occupied in a social field or space." The decisive confirmation of that position arrived a few days later in January, once school was back in session. As during the previous winter break of December 2009, set 1 was replaced by holiday greetings only to be restored with the start of winter quarter in January. But there was one curious difference now in January 2011. A ninth slide featuring the Preamble to the United

---

[ii] This paper now forms chapter 9 of *Conservative Claims of Cultural Oppression* (pp. 538–622), available at ronyguldmann.com, as noted in the preface.

States Constitution had been inserted into set 1 (exhibit E in appendix 1), where it would remain for a fortnight before being discarded, returning set 1 to its original eight slides.

Ever since my December 2009 "informal networking" chat with Dick, the looming question had been whether the home page was symbolically alluding to an actual job teaching constitutional law or had merely been structured to elicit the logical inference thereof. The truth itself was now being symbolically alluded to, in the first change to the home page (besides the holiday greetings) in approximately fourteen months. At just that point in the year when interpretation 1, had it been accurate, would have yielded an actual constitutional law course to teach, I was instead receiving symbolic confirmation of interpretation 2, through a mere allusion to constitutional law.

I knew the Preamble was dear to Larry's heart. The cover of his magisterial *The People Themselves* featured a fragment of it. Its opening words, "We the People," resonated with his popular constitutionalism, calling for the revival of democratized constitutional interpretation against the newfangled usurpations of a lawyerly elite uncritically accepting of judicial supremacy.[9] In its present deployment, however, the Preamble was making known certain lawyerly elites' equally complacent conviction that the skeletons now in their closets would never be brought to light, which they broadcast by doling out this final and definitive confirmation of their yearlong conspiracy to reduce me to a conspiracy theorist, going out of their way to put to rest any lingering doubts in my own mind. It was one final allusion to what would never be and was never going to be. While I would have preferred a different outcome, the conspirators had certainly held up their end of the bargain with this pièce de résistance. I could scarcely complain of being shortchanged of evidence for an underlying controversy, as the Preamble offered a panoramic view of its entirety.

Had a computer glitch pulled the Preamble out of the ether in order to expand set 1, and had another glitch then disappeared it two weeks later? If so, the home page had been surprisingly free of such glitches during the preceding fourteen months. The transient appearance of this venerable national symbol belied the shibboleth that the state of the home page was a matter of indifference to the powers that be. Skeptics and detractors would insist that I alone cared about it. But, clearly, someone other than me had cared about it enough to will that set 1 be augmented with the Preamble for two weeks and only two weeks in January 2011, even as they had allowed the configuration to remain undisturbed throughout the preceding fourteen months. Generally insouciant webmasters do not find themselves overtaken by such abrupt, ephemeral, and downright bizarre urges in the ordinary course of business, which was why I was left to conclude that the Preamble's insertion was rather more calculated.

Maybe the Preamble wasn't quite the proverbial smoking gun. But it was damn well close, clear and convincing evidence that my alma mater was now in the business of devouring its own. No reasonable person standing in my position could think to belittle its probative value. The Preamble wasn't, strictly speaking, scientific evidence for my hypothesis, granted. I hadn't ahead of time issued a falsifiable prediction such as: "If there is a liberal conspiracy at Stanford, then the Preamble to the U.S. Constitution will feature within set 1 come January 2011; if there isn't, then it won't." Still, it would be a peculiar coincidence indeed for a wholly capricious chain of overwrought deductions regarding the subterranean significance of set 1 to now be confronted with an event so temporally and symbolically consonant with that posited significance. Peculiar though the unofficial reality may have been, such a coincidence would be more peculiar still.

Readers will judge whether this gauging of peculiarity is just confirmation bias. But one needn't strain logic to appreciate the uncanny congruity I've underscored—which may be described as poetic. The alternative to my exegesis is a sequence of events in which the functionary routinely responsible for curating the home page loses all interest in rotating the images for more than a year, except for swapping the holiday greetings in and out; rekindles just enough interest in January 2011 to decide willy-nilly that set 1 just wasn't complete without the Preamble (incongruously, the only nonhuman element therein); changes his mind two weeks later and removes the Preamble; and once again loses all interest in the home page so as to leave set 1 intact for another four months (after which a new format would be instated). I submit that this etiology is more doubtful than my own more theoretically robust hypothesis, according to which the éminence grise behind the home page was "thinking like a lawyer," operating one level up with all the signature deftness of a Stanford lawyer, no less. This scenario, wherein the Preamble's ephemeral appearance in January 2011 reverberated the Pandora's Box opened in September 2009, may be sui generis and improbable. But so, too, is the alternative delineated above. Show me another law school where that kind of thing happens.

To wave away the Preamble as a nothingburger is to betray a reflexive resistance to any cultural narrative or conception of human nature that would lend my argument proper resonance. That resonance is, in fact, supplied by conservative claims of cultural oppression, for they alone explain how this treasured symbol of transparency and accountability could have been commandeered as an instrument of gaslighting, in a celebration of absolute power and plausible deniability, at one of the nation's preeminent citadels of liberalism. The conspirators' great achievement was to have generated a truth calculated to be just as self-evident to my own inner lights as it was invisible to the eye of public reason. Drunk on their unchecked authority, they had led me all the way to liberalism's toxic core, memorializing this journey with a decisive acknowledgment of the star chamber before which I had always stood. How could I complain? Was this heart of darkness not what I'd been chasing all along?

CHAPTER 10

The Winter Counteroffensive

January–February 2011

The Dilemma

Instating the Preamble on the law school website was a coup de grâce and kiss-off, a digitized smirk of impish delight at my final, unceremonious defenestration from Stanford. The noose around my neck had been tightening by the day, and here was the final tug. Clearly I had been mistaken for some neophyte who was out of his depth and overplaying his hand, and some form of reprisal was in order. But what? The legal route had always been there. It wouldn't advance my professional fortunes, but nor would it destroy them, as they were already in tatters. The statute of limitations on defamation in California had already run, however, and that was only the most prosaic of the many obstacles I would doubtless confront.

Was I really going to expose machinations of such guile before a randomly selected jury? Lacking firsthand acquaintance with the academic habitus, this jury would never fathom how the cumulative cultural meaning of my machinations could have inspired Barbara in her own. Nor could it be given to understand that it was in my nature to pursue this game to the nth degree and that Barbara in her sublime vengefulness was cognizant of the severe emotional distress being inflicted on an eggshell plaintiff. Could this jury be made to appreciate the poetic resonance of the Preamble's evanescent appearance or the legal academic community's heavy emotional investment in the high-stakes survey? Could it wrap its mind around the distinction between opportunistic verifications and Popper's "risky predictions"? Would I have to retrieve my graduate school notes and give a lecture on Popper? Would I invite Bourdieu (if alive) as an expert witness to attest that it is indeed one of the "classic procedures of university polemics" to "designate opponents only by allusions, insinuations, or undertones understood solely by those initiated in the code"? Outsiders to academia would never get why my promotion at Toledo was a farce. People would roll their eyes at my exegeses of Dick's linguistic contortions, breezily dismiss these as trifling, and conclude that I was reading tea leaves. My invisible persecution was a hypertrophying of *Homo academicus*'s instinctual gaslighting tendencies. But those unacquainted with these tendencies might never be brought to recognize my persecution as but an extreme manifestation of an endemic phenomenon.

The appearance of the Preamble was compelling evidence that I had been gaslighted. While this curious irregularity hadn't been the subject of a falsifiable yet unfalsified prediction, it was exceedingly consonant with a theory that had yielded two such predictions, one about the home page itself and the other about the ostensibly unrelated survey. Attributing the Preamble to happenstance requires a leap of faith greater than any I've taken in these pages. And yet it could be recognized as another of the conspiracy's long tendrils only if considered in the context of the cumulative evidence, as the consummation of an ever-thickening plotline with myriad subtleties. How many people would have the patience for that? They were infinitely more likely to just elide this wider background and glibly dismiss the Preamble with the tired refrain that its ephemeral appearance admitted of other explanations—just as climate change deniers dismiss the evidence for climate change.

Because the likelihood of empaneling a jury that operated one level up was infinitesimal, this avenue would only discredit me. The masses would misread the conspiracy's ingenuity as my lunacy and dismiss me as a crackpot. The profound, mind-boggling, and awe-inspiring perversity that first announced itself with the Preamble appeared once again in the course of these reflections, as it hit me that one of the nation's greatest law schools had gone out of its way to construct a case against itself that it knew could never be prosecuted within a flawed judicial system. My claims were plainly more suited to an interdisciplinary graduate seminar than to a courtroom, where I could only beclown myself. The elites' ability to beguile ordinary Americans is not to be underestimated, as conservative culture warriors tirelessly remind us.

A contractual complaint based on the preemptive quashing of my fellowship renewal petition stood on firmer legal footing than an action for slander (which might not have occurred in the technical legal sense). I recalled from my employment law class that California courts sometimes find that the terms of employee handbooks have been impliedly incorporated into employment contracts. Was the website posting making known the fellowship's flexible duration analogous to an employee handbook? If so, had that flexibility been implied in my contract, generating a right to a good faith review of my renewal request? The case was without precedent, but the argument wasn't frivolous. The fellowship wasn't just another exchange of services for remuneration. On the contrary, I provided no services of any sort, the role having been defined by the specific objective of placement in a tenure-track job, which can be frustrated by all manner of vicissitudes. My contract didn't guarantee an extension. Stanford would have been within its rights to spurn the petition on substantive grounds upon a good faith review. But that wasn't the same thing as invoking a provably nonexistent "strict two-year limit."

There *were,* in fact, ample grounds for denying my petition—the delays, the misleadingly optimistic forecasts of impending progress, and all the breaches of academic etiquette. But the imperative to cordon off the official and unofficial realities meant that my sundry derelictions had never been officially documented as performance problems. The only documented performance assessment was Barbara's fulsome praise for my job-talk paper as "great work" and her disingenuous prediction that it would sustain my candidacy. Scathing as it was, the knockout email addressed only the marketability of my CV without savaging my overall performance—and this after Dick had signed off on that CV with "This looks MUCH better. Good job." In line with her policy of flattery-cum-avoidance, Barbara would later volunteer to recommend me to other law schools, ostensibly an acknowledgment of my worthiness, so the official reality simply gave her no grounds for refusing to so much as consider my petition to stay on at Stanford for another year. The rending apart of the two realities had made all the evidence against me inadmissible. Given how the conspiracy had exploited that rupture in its own favor, I had no qualms about now doing the same. *Actually* suing anyone for anything was far from my mind in the immediate aftermath of September 2009. But the proposition was less repugnant now, in the wake of all that had transpired since. Gaslighting was a lawful activity last I checked, but it gave me a casus belli unavailable earlier. I was now fully radicalized and Stanford had thrown down the gauntlet. We were locked in a zero-sum game that I would not permit myself to lose.

Still, a contractual lawsuit also held little appeal. Whatever its legal merits, it would involve innumerable practical difficulties and introduce further entropy into an already weltering existence. Remaining in San Francisco to prosecute a lawsuit, or for any reason really, was becoming increasingly untenable as my pathologizing by friends and family reached fever pitch. They had staged a surprise "intervention" during which they alleged that I was hallucinating and hearing voices in consequence of neurological degeneration. Having ambushed me at what was supposed to be a casual Sunday brunch, the interveners insisted that bifurcating the home page system into set 1 and set 2 was technologically impossible and that my rendition thereof was therefore delusional. That was provably false, but these San Francisco liberals would resort to whatever lies and half-truths served their purposes. I had recently been cited for an expired vehicle registration sticker, and this was cast as a case of wanton lawlessness—"police troubles," as someone put it. The slightest missteps—from this minor civil infraction to tripping over myself at a party after a beer too many—were read as further symptoms of the syndrome. I defended myself with reason and argument. But the interveners dismissed these as intellectualization and lawyering, without elucidating how such characterizations harmonized with my alleged neurological degeneration. My natural frustration with the cynicism was in turn dismissed as irritability. Unlike my own, theirs was *not* a falsifiable theory. On the contrary, it was more gaslighting by yet another Bay Area cabal, which was now a way of life for me.

Setting aside the practical and emotional challenges of a lawsuit, this was never what the conspiracy was truly about. It couldn't have flowered as it had absent its legal dimension, which was what first instigated all the allusion, intimation, and ambiguation. But it rapidly outgrew its seamy origins, with its legal dimension having spawned, and then become eclipsed by, something bigger, the real-world instantiation of my research agenda. My secret trial and invisible persecution had finally clarified that agenda's inner essence and telos, transforming the nebulous intimations of the tacit dimension into concrete digital reality as I was vaulted into headlong confrontation with the prevailing ideology. Thus did I come to share in the fate of conservative culture warriors, when I found myself stripped of my symbolic capital and flung to the bottom of the elites' cognitive hierarchy, left bereft of epistemic authority.

With my research agenda and personal tribulations now melded as two facets of a single enterprise, I would have to expose Stanford through the medium of my research agenda, not in a courtroom but on paper, where the odyssey began. I was after Stanford's symbolic capital, not its lucre. I wanted to speak truth to power and record a cultural moment, vindicate a thesis and discredit Say's law—not redress pecuniary injury—so the accusatory instrument would have to be academic. My own hands were hardly unsullied, so I couldn't sanctimoniously deplore my gaslighting as an unpardonable injustice. There was in fact an argument that I had it coming, some of which I have outlined for the reader. But there was another side of the story, too, and that it might never get aired would be an unpardonable injustice. This airbrushing from history of the unofficial reality was precisely the outcome willed by the star chamber of Stanford, and it would have to be averted by any means necessary. My advisers had excised their pound of flesh. With their claims now satisfied, I would advance my counterclaims and rescue my Stanford legacy from the memory hole in which they would inter it.

An Insurgency Begins

To this end I would need to stir the hornets' nest and develop a contemporaneous record of my beliefs—begun a year earlier with the works-in-progress email. That record might not satisfy die-hard skeptics, but it could put to rest any suggestion that I had simply confabulated the unofficial reality out of whole cloth years after the fact. So on February 13, 2011, I emailed Larry Solum, with "Release of 2010 Entry-Level Hiring Report" in the subject line:

> Dear Professor Solum,
>
> I am a former Stanford Law fellow who is (at least theoretically) still on the academic job market and am, for this reason, writing to urge you to release the 2010 Entry-Level Hiring Report on Legal Theory Blog, as the latest available results are from 2009. This would be of considerable assistance to me, since I'm seeking a better understanding of the trends as I undertake my future career decisions. As the preliminary

> results were available until August before being removed, I can reasonably infer that at least part of your work is already cut out for you.
>
> I hope this isn't importunate or otherwise inappropriate. Everyone is obviously grateful for your services on this front in the past (and other fronts too), and I certainly wouldn't be pestering you if I thought I was speaking for myself alone. But my operating assumption is that making the 2010 Report available even now would serve to augment the utility of what I am also assuming will be the 2011 Report, as well as cast a new light on the 2009 Report. For there are many people beyond just myself who are interested in studying the trends. The Report has, moreover, often served as a useful starting point for the reflections and ruminations of other scholars, from which we've all likewise benefitted.
>
> I don't actually know whether you're a utilitarian, so I may be presuming too much. But releasing the Report would admit of both act- and rule-utilitarian justifications, in case you are. It also admits of deontological defenses, in case you're not, as this would be to fulfill a promise impliedly extended to those who went out of their way to provide you with the information that you elicited. And if you're an ethical egoist or nihilist, then why the hell not just release the data, as you've at any rate been disposed to do so before?
>
> Best Regards,
>
> Rony Guldmann
> James C. Gaither Fellow (retired)
> Stanford Law School

Solum didn't respond and I wasn't expecting him to. But here was a way to lay out the facts and highlight why the fate of the survey that year lacked any self-evident rationale. He had seen fit to bring it to completion in years past as a service to the law school community, and that had generated ethical obligations from which he'd apparently absconded. Solum was philosophically inclined, and these weren't difficult points.

More critical was the matter of the home page and set 1, whose anomalous longevity I needed to document. I produced a short brief titled "Rational Critique of the Stanford Law Homepage Oligopoly" (exhibit F in appendix 1). Holding myself out as a concerned alumnus, I emailed it to Stanford's information technology director on February 14, copying Larry and two associate deans:

> Dear Mr. Watson,
>
> I am writing as a concerned alumnus and former Stanford Law fellow in order to express my reservations about a change of policy in the management of our law school homepage, a problem which I dub the "Stanford Law Homepage Oligopoly." Everything is explained in the attached document.
>
> If this should be directed at someone else, please feel free to forward it to the appropriate party. I've also copied Dean Kramer along with Associate Deans Showalter and Johnson in case the matter is of any interest to them, as it may fall within the purview of their proper concerns and responsibilities.
>
> Best Regards,
> Rony Guldmann
> James C. Gaither Fellow (retired)
> Stanford Law School
> Class of 2008

I wasn't going to detail my thoughts about the quid pro quo publicly at this early date, given the obvious rhetorical liabilities of doing so. But the Rational Critique set out all the predicate facts—the bifurcation of the system, the contents of set 1 and set 2, the cessation of rotations about fifteen months earlier, and the ephemeral appearance of the Preamble during the first half of January 2011. It also critiqued the ostensible irrationality of the status quo and offered some suggestions for improvement. The featured professors shouldn't be enjoying an oligopoly over the home page, I admonished. Amazing though they were, the publicity should be spread equitably across the law school's entire pantheon of distinguished scholars.

Sabrina Johnson, the law school's associate dean for communications and external relations, responded the next day:

> Dear Mr. Guldmann—
>
> Thank you for your email and suggestions for improving our website homepage. We will certainly take them under consideration as we move forward.
>
> Best,
>
> Sabrina

This response confirmed my account of the now-operative home page policy. Sabrina would have had no reason to thank me for my recommendations and commit to taking them under advisement had they rested on a false premise. Her reply furthermore betrayed that the oligopoly was a matter of conscious design, not mere neglect. Notably, she did not say something to the effect of: "Oops. Guess we dropped the ball on that! Thanks for letting us know. We'll fix immediately." Nor did she tender some sensible rationale for the policy that had somehow escaped me.

Sabrina's response might be discounted as bland corporatespeak, which it was. But that choice of parlance didn't dictate the logical content of the response. She might instead have answered: "We appreciate your concern with this issue. We will certainly turn our attention to it as soon as possible." That would have been the ultimate in bland corporatespeak, saying absolutely nothing. Yet she went beyond this when she promised to take my criticisms under advisement, thus acknowledging their pertinence. Sure, the promise may have been hollow, but the rules of bland corporatespeak would not have prevented her from telling me it was a glitch had it in fact been a glitch. That would have been the easiest way to dismiss me, and the purpose of bland corporatespeak is to make nonissues out of issues, not vice versa. In any case, there were plenty of other reasons to conclude that the home page hadn't simply slipped from everyone's mind, such as the undeniable internal coherence of set 2, the winter holiday removals of set 1, the evanescent appearance of the Preamble, the regular updating of home page text, and, of course, common sense. As I've stressed, academic departments just tuning out the existence of their websites for more than a year is not a regular feature of the world as we know it.

The Rational Critique censured the home page oligopoly as inconsistent with Stanford's long-standing commitment to diversity. Set 1, I observed, was marked by "an overrepresentation of Jews, an underrepresentation of women, and *no representation whatsoever* of any non-white minorities."[i] It, therefore, "promotes *exactly* the stereotypes which any self-respecting law school should be fighting to erode or eliminate." I seized on Sabrina's response as an opportunity to reiterate these misgivings, writing back:

> Dear Sabrina,
>
> Thank you for turning your attention to the matter. I would just like to add by way of elaboration that whatever one thinks of my other arguments, I believe my concerns about diversity will be especially weighty over the next few months, as Stanford competes with its rivals to attract top minority students.
>
> No doubt, they will be turning to the homepage to do their research. And while one would hope that its substantive contents will be the dispositive factor, they will, just like everyone else, be influenced by their fair share of irrational, perhaps unconscious associations. Regrettable though it is, appearances do matter. That's why law schools devote such care and attention (and funds) to other arguable superficialities, like brochures and such. And a homepage is indeed a

[i] Jayashri Srikantiah certainly doesn't sound like the name of a white woman. But I knew her only by her image and must have mistaken her for a southern European.

> brochure among other things, which is why I believe it should receive the kind of thoughtful care that brochures and the like receive as a matter of course—at least absent some particularly strong and unusual reason to do otherwise.
>
> This wouldn't even have to entail the toppling of the oligopoly if the objections are strong, as it could be temporarily dislodged and then restored later in the spring. Or it could be merely augmented, if the objections are even stronger, which would dilute, but not destroy, its prominence.
>
> Best,
>
> Rony

My claims invited reflexive incredulity because they concerned something that seems trivial in the ordinary course of life. But as I stressed in an earlier chapter, well-managed organizations pay heed to a host of ostensible trifles, especially in order to advertise their diversity. Like most universities, Stanford placed a premium on recruiting black professors, who could then serve as role models for historically marginalized black students. So why not take credit for this? The unofficial reality unravels the mystery. The protracted want of black professors on the home page evinced not neglect or racism but the presence of a sufficiently weighty countervailing factor, my persecution by a star chamber. If black faces were excluded from set 1 to facilitate its overrepresentation of Jews, that was because so many Jews were implicated in the conspiracy.

Random Noise

I also needed to document the McConnell Affair, so I decided to once more apply for the Olin fellowship. I had no prayer of actually landing it, now that McConnell had been turned against me, but here was an opportunity to look into some of the irregularities I've detailed. I began on February 11 by emailing Barbara, Dick, and Josh to request that they resend the letters of recommendation they'd drafted the previous year. They responded with predictable solicitude. Josh once again elected to flatter me, requesting my latest CV and paper drafts because he "would like to have them on file." This served no real purpose. Everyone knew I was finished, indeed a marked man, but it helped augment the conspiracy's plausible deniability and highlight my perennial powerlessness before it. The situation had begotten endless openings for passive-aggressive histrionics, and Josh's newly rekindled interest in me and my academic corpus was just the latest of these—just the latest "institutional support" for "the gap between the representation experienced and the true position occupied in a social field or space."

I then wrote to the Federalist Society under the pretense that I was trying to figure out what I'd done wrong the previous year in order to avoid the same pitfalls this time around. Why had McConnell's intimations of a fellowship deteriorated into an invitation to spectate a workshop? I provided the Federalist Society with a full transcript of our early correspondences, titled "Professor McConnell in His Own Words," which then led to some email exchanges with the Federalist Society's Lee Otis on February 16. He was in Hawaii on a working vacation but graciously took the time to address my perplexities, explaining that while I was right to infer that my application had received a "serious look," he couldn't broach the selection committee's deliberations. The process was highly competitive and the committee had to make some tough calls. I responded in pertinent part:

> I want to make myself perfectly clear lest there be any misunderstanding: I certainly wouldn't be wasting your time with any complaints about merely having come close but not close enough, since that is the fate of many an applicant. Nor am I asking anyone to give an account of their subjective judgments.

> My concern is rather the confluence of curious irregularities which I described in my email to Barrett [the fellowship's administrator], the most glaring of which is the contradiction between my status as someone who came close enough to actually be CONTACTED by Professor McConnell (that's not your run-of-the-mill "serious look" applicant) and my other status as one who later became classified as an observer, as I explained in that email. I received not only a "serious look," as you put it, but also a series of emails.

Otis answered that I "might find that generally Professor McConnell is interested in knowing people who are of potential interest and are at Stanford." I rejoined that McConnell's general friendliness and sociability were hardly in doubt but that those attributes had not been displayed in my particular case, as shown by our correspondences' anticlimactic denouement.

As to my observer status, Otis advised that "we tended to assume that people applying for fellowships were not actually going on the market so our default was to invite applicants we were interested in as observers." "Participants," he went on, "were generally people who were finishing fellowships or VAPs [visiting assistant professorships]." But finishing a fellowship, I retorted, was precisely my status, which the Federalist Society had surely gleaned from my CV, especially if I had received a "serious look." By its own criterion I should have been brought in as a participant. Otis advised that inviting applicants as observers was their default. But why did they require a default when they were in possession of the information that obviated the need for one? Only a small handful of observers had attended the workshop, so it wasn't as though an entire stack of abortive fellowship applications had been summarily redesignated as an observer stack without attention to individual dossiers. Of the two Olin fellows who arrived at Stanford that fall, one had attended the workshop as an observer and the other as a participant. So Otis's default setting hadn't been operative in their case. Nor, I suspected, had it been in mine.

Given that about eight months had now elapsed since the workshop, the casual onlooker might conclude that I was just pettifogging about being denied some trifle of status or prestige. Nothing could be further from the truth. The point, rather, was that the conspiracy had from the outset nestled its stealth and subterfuge in phenomena that seemed readily attributable either to the normal randomness or irrationality of human affairs (like set 1 or the Preamble) or to automatic institutional processes impervious to human intervention (like the fellowship's "strict two-year limit"). I would need to explode this deceptive veneer, because what had been passing for normal human randomness or reflexive administrative practice were the well-documented signature behaviors of *Homo academicus*. There was conscious calculation behind my observer status, a reckoning that originated in sins against the magistrature that would then spur the academic habitus to reassert itself in a purification ritual dedicated to my subordination. Whether Otis knew it or not, his contradictions were traceable to this foundational project, which my insolent pettifoggery was merely serving to ventilate.

Curious to hear Dick's reaction, I had emailed him earlier that day with a copy of my inquiry to the Federalist Society, asking him "whether there's anything in your own (vaster) experience that might shed some light on this, if light indeed needs to be shed." Dick's response was threefold. First, if the question was "whether I know why they did the various things they did, the answer is that I don't." Dick didn't "have any contacts in the Federalist Society" and didn't "usually go to their gatherings," so he was "not the best person to ask." Whatever happened last year was "pure speculation on my part." Second, there is a lot of "random noise in most hiring processes," so it's "often a mistake to impute too much rationality to the process." And, finally, if my question was whether complaining was helpful, the answer was "of course not." Irrespective of the justice of my cause, those on the receiving end of such complaints don't like having to explain themselves and will react defensively, if at all. Dick had "never known even a single instance where any good ever came from asking the person in charge of a hiring process some version of the 'why didn't you hire me?' question (or any of the related questions like, 'why did your process treat me this way?')."

Dick was of course correct that this airing of grievances wasn't going to get me anywhere. That was never the point, though. That this second go at the Olin was moribund was a foregone conclusion. Its only purpose was to histrionically harvest evidence of the unofficial reality—like all my communications around this time. Dick's reaction to my inquest was useful in that regard. I had adverted to his vaster experience ostensibly to solicit a general professional analysis of the situation, not to imply specific, firsthand knowledge of the relevant events. That Dick would suggest that I was implying such knowledge suggested he had reason to think that I had reason to imply it. Such a reason indeed existed, as we both knew.

After all, I had emailed Dick about McConnell's budding interest in offering me the Olin, as Dick had held himself out as my advocate and asked to be kept abreast of my fellowship search, going out of his way to promote me at Toledo. So, one would have expected him to do the same with McConnell, as I have discussed. This undeniable fact lay at the core of the mystery, and Dick's recitals were calibrated to skirt it. Dick had no contacts in the Federalist Society and didn't usually go to their gatherings. But did he have contacts at the University of Toledo Law School? Did he usually go to their gatherings? Probably not. But that hadn't kept him from touting me to Professor Richman. What mattered weren't Dick's contacts with the Federalist Society but his contacts with McConnell, who was just up the stairs or down the hall. Dick's professions of ignorance and detachment were legerdemain to misdirect from this glaring inconsistency. The official reality gave rise to the expectation that he would do what he could to fortify McConnell's interest in me. That Dick had to skirt this fact with red herrings about his nonattendance at Federalist Society events therefore confirmed the unofficial one—corroborating my surmise that McConnell had been apprised of it and then acted on this knowledge. And so, I rejoined in pertinent part:

> Thanks for your feedback. I certainly agree with most of what you say as a general matter, but it's not relevant to the case at hand. The difference is that I'm NOT asking anyone to account for their subjective judgments ("why didn't you hire me?"). I'm asking them to account for concrete FACTS and concrete BEHAVIORS which are not obviously attributable to the normal randomness of things.

The intellectual magistrature of the sacred college of masters was hiding behind what superficially appeared as random noise. But I had encountered enough such noise at Stanford to see past those appearances. It is "often a mistake to impute too much rationality to the process." But often is not always, and the conspirators were relying on precisely this platitude to camouflage their machinations. It was a talking point in the service of plausible deniability. Dick's admonitions once more betrayed a regime of conceptual liquidation and nihilation, there to safeguard institutional legitimacy by reducing its opposition to its own terms of discourse. Most academics imagine they deserve more recognition than they get, and Dick was reducing my inquest to this clichéd grievance, casting it as immature frustration with the normal vicissitudes of human affairs in order to saddle me with a "not-to-be-taken-seriously cognitive status"—business as usual now.

Hence, the indispensability of conservative claims of cultural oppression to my dawning crusade. They would offer a vantage point whence to overcome my subaltern status by tracing all the random noise at Stanford to the liberal elites' covert illiberalism, the unofficial social hierarchy subjugating their cultural adversaries. Only in this way would I overcome my own such subjugation, which Dick was now reinforcing. He was operating one level up. But my research agenda would enable me to operate at a higher level still.

The Implied Covenant of Good Faith and Fair Dealing

Turning my agitation back to the conspiracy's epicenter, Stanford itself, I emailed the law school's human resources director on February 17 with the following inquiry, titled "employment complaint/request for official legal position," and copied the university's ombudsman, David Rasch:

> Dear Director Trimble,
>
> I am an SLS alumnus and was the James C. Gaither Fellow here at the law school from September 2008 to August 2010, and am writing to file an employment complaint in connection with the preemption of my application to extend that fellowship beyond that two-year period.
>
> That request was lodged with one Professor Barbara Fried in November 2009 and then denied three weeks later on the grounds that the Gaither fellowship has a "strict" two-year limit (and after what I was told would be a consultation with Dean Kramer). There was therefore no individualized review of the merits of any kind. Quite the contrary, I was simply denied standing to produce an application or put forth any arguments on my own behalf.
>
> But Professor Fried's assertion (sent by email) stands in DIRECT CONTRADICTION to the following two official SLS publications:
>
> http://www.law.stanford.edu/school/giving/gaither/
>
> http://www.law.stanford.edu/experience/scholarlylife/fellowships/gaither/
>
> One of these actually quotes Professor Fried, and both state unambiguously that while Gaither fellowships will typically span two years, the duration can also be longer or shorter in reflection of individual circumstances.
>
> I'm no expert and the facts of the case are undoubtedly without precedent. But my semester's study of employment law right here

> at Stanford and intuitive legal sense tell me that these statements may very well have been implied into my contract, much like rights enumerated in an employee manual, thereby entitling me to the individualized review of the merits which I was denied.
>
> This conclusion seems to me strengthened by what any insider understands is the inherent nature and purpose of law school fellowships. Far from constituting just another form of temporary remuneration, they are rather intended to promote the specific end of long-term academic employment, and frequently involve the foregoing of other, more lucrative and less risky, career routes (as was the case with me). This, I suspect, may also elevate the preemption I've described into a violation of the implied covenant of good faith and fair dealing.
>
> I have yet to seriously research or ponder all of this, though, and am therefore requesting the law school's official legal position on such a matter, so that I may reflect upon it as I formulate my own.
>
> Sincerely,
>
> Rony Guldmann
>
> 02/17/11

It would be a little while before I received a response. In the meantime I reached out to Dick to see if I could provoke a reaction to my email to Trimble:

> Hi Dick,
>
> I just wanted to let you know that your pessimism about the Federalist Society's reaction to my inquiry may have been exaggerated, as they've been quite forthcoming, permitting me to clarify a number of points.
>
> You may recall that you recommended when we met in late October that I focus a little less exclusively on constitutional law and expand my research and teaching interests to, say, contracts. That was great advice, and very prescient, because I've forgotten all about

constitutional law and am now really into contracts—and may move on to other things yet!

You and Barbara both have my permission to use the complaint I filed with human resources as an exam hypo or small group activity topic the next time you teach contracts to the 1Ls—unless you consider it another inappropriate "why didn't you hire me?" inquiry, of course.

Is there any way I can leverage that achievement in the hiring process to offset the mistaken impression that I'm too much about philosophy and not enough about law?

Best,

Rony

No response was forthcoming. What could he say? Was he going to insist that, yes, my employment complaint was just another "why didn't you hire me?" grievance, another sign of immature frustration before the "random noise" of academic hiring and life generally? Did I "impute too much rationality to the process" in expecting that the stated grounds of Barbara's fateful decision be consistent with the law school's own public disclosures? These questions answer themselves, illustrating that nothing is easier than chalking things up to random noise. What might strike the casual observer as random noise was guided by a consistent logic, however, the logic of the unofficial reality and *Homo academicus*, which illuminated both my fellowship enigmas as nothing else could. What was the probability that a single law school fellow would encounter two such enigmas in the span of just six months and that both would be random noise rather than the modus operandi of the academic habitus? It was surely higher than the probability that the key and Preamble were meaningless accidents. It was also higher than the probability that paranoid ideation could have yielded my two falsifiable yet unfalsified predictions. But, still, it was quite low.

About a week earlier I had petitioned Dick for leave to attend the Wednesday faculty luncheon notwithstanding that I was no longer on payroll. The law school was already subsidizing my email account at $16 a month until May, and I didn't want to be importunate. But there had always been enough food to go around and my questions were once hailed as thought-provoking. Dick had directed that I address my petition to Larry, to whom I then wrote on Friday, February 18:

> Hi Larry,
>
> Dick thought you might be the one to ask, so I'm writing to request a preliminary injunction to attend the Wednesday faculty lunch while your lawyers evaluate my arguments, unless they're so facially implausible as to not warrant that.
>
> Best,
>
> Rony

Larry responded by requesting my phone number and we spoke soon thereafter. He began by inquiring whether I was still in the area. The answer should have been perfectly obvious, as it beggared belief that I'd be flying in weekly to the Bay Area from another part of the country just to attend the luncheon, enriching though it had always been. The familiar policy of feigned ignorance and detachment was reliably in play.

Larry next proceeded to interrogate my decision to legalize matters. The truth, as he well knew, was that our relations had been legalized for a while now. That legalization had erupted more than a year earlier—first in Barbara's knockout email, then in my works-in-progress email, and finally in the biblical fury of Bob Weisberg and in the home page. Nothing had been said of it. But that silence was itself part and parcel of the legal logic at play. If Larry could now feign bewilderment that I had taken the drastic step of lodging a complaint with human resources, that was because the bilateral legalization inhered in the shadow world of the unofficial reality, which had been sequestered from the official one. Larry was now exploiting this cleavage for rhetorical advantage. By attributing the legalization to me alone, he was angling to paint me as uniquely impetuous and intemperate when, in truth, there had been plenty of hubris on all sides. Yet this rejoinder was precluded to me. The only thing that might have upended Larry's rhetorical advantage—the unofficial reality—couldn't be broached. Accordingly, I chose to remain uninteresting and blandly extemporized that I'd legalized things because Barbara's representations were made in bad faith, leaving it at that.

The tables were turned, however, when the conversation turned to the substantive controversy, the fellowship, whereupon the sequestration worked to Larry's rhetorical disadvantage. Again and again, he reiterated their expectation that the fellowship would last two years. Again and again, I responded that the existence of this general forecast wasn't in dispute. It was clearly noted in the postings, but so, too, was the proviso that the fellowship could span longer under some circumstances. The issue wasn't my right to a renewal but my right to a good faith review of my request for one. The due process denied was procedural, not substantive. My objection wasn't to Larry's judgment on the merits but to his failure to ever issue one—which was sensible within the unofficial reality but arbitrary and capricious within the official one. As I wrote to him in a follow-up email later that day:

> You stressed your general expectation that the Gaither fellowship would span only two years. This is nothing that I've ever denied, because I acknowledged it in my letter to Director Trimble—just as I stressed the equally unambiguous general expectation that the duration would also be flexible. So all you're doing with that argument, if it even deserves to be called that, is arbitrarily emphasizing one side of the coin to the exclusion of the other.
>
> And while neither of us is a contracts expert, you don't need to be one to understand that the meaning of a contract isn't reducible to

> one party's general expectations. That doesn't dispose of the issue, of course, but it's the first step to doing so and one that I'm not sure you've taken.

Elaborating on my employment complaint, I drew a comparison with my stint at Fordham University back in the day. That fellowship was also expected to last two years. But it had been announced as a teaching postdoc. Fordham's practice was to rotate newly minted PhDs in and out to instruct the philosophy component of the core curriculum (Fordham is run by good Jesuits). They just liked bringing in new faces. That being the understanding, I would never have thought to whine about not being considered for a third year. The Gaither served a different purpose, however, as detailed in the employment complaint, which gave rise to a different set of reasonable expectations.

As to the broader policy question, I further opined:

> To examine it all on the policy level, was it even minimally rational of you to make a specific decision like the one at issue on the basis of general expectations begat years earlier without even pausing to consider whether there might be any countervailing considerations at work in the case at hand? Is that how most of your decisions are undertaken?
>
> I'm sorry, but that's not a very utility-maximizing way of going about most things, especially with what was an INVESTMENT of the law school's assets. Would you automatically sell your stock in a company solely because you had anticipated that you would then be doing so a couple years back? And if you don't hold yourself to those kinds of "strict" two-year limits in your personal capacity, why would you do so in your capacity as Dean?

In truth Larry had ample reason to conclude that this particular investment of law school resources had gone south. While defensible philosophically, the path of the fellowship was patently not what Barbara had in mind when she boasted that the Gaither fellowship would "provide an opportunity for some of our most promising graduates to develop as scholars and teachers." I had surely developed during these two years, as a conspiracy theorist, a critical theorist of academia, and perhaps as a sleuth and lawyer—but not as a scholar or teacher. Given that the road taken stood as a direct repudiation of the values animating Barbara's announced aspirations for the fellowship, she would have faced no difficulty defending her decision. Contrary to my polemical employment complaint, it was in fact I who was in breach of the implied covenant of good faith and fair dealing. I had my reasons, as expounded throughout this memoir, but those reasons didn't erase facts on the ground.

Larry's rhetorical dilemma was that those facts had been hived off from the official reality and impounded in the unofficial one, encrypted in the home page oligopoly and the web of allusion, intimation, and ambiguation that surrounded it. Just as I was rhetorically hamstrung from citing the conspiracy's failure to make good on its intimations of continued employment as the reason for the controversy's legalization, so he was rhetorically hamstrung from citing my waywardness as his reason for not extending the fellowship. After all, Barbara had lauded my paper as "great work" and predicted it would get me through the hiring season successfully. This ended in disaster, but Barbara then spun my joblessness not as the fruit of my own derelictions but as some great mystery to be collectively pondered, suggesting that I maybe "triangulate" my impressions with those of other observers. When I did that, Dick chalked up the situation to chance alone, which was not illuminating. They couldn't cite the real factors because these were too entangled with the events of September 2009, the untouchable third rail of my collegial relations. So Larry had no choice but to deflect the official gravamen of my complaint with spurious arguments. He was in the right substantively, but I was in the right procedurally. Because my grievance was ostensibly procedural, the rhetorical upper hand was mine.

Toward the close of the conversation, Larry asked whether my employment complaint bore any relationship to my concerns about the home page and offered to explain it. No doubt, he could have concocted some superficially plausible administrative explanation, but I wasn't going to get drawn into so rhetorically prejudicial a conversation here. I replied that I would be declining to discuss the broader context of the employment complaint at this time. The real question, though, was why Larry would raise the possibility of some connection between the two issues. Sure, both originated with the same troublemaker during the same week. But neither referenced the other, and there was no apparent logical basis for positing a relationship. What did my call for professorial equity on the home page have to do with the fellowship? Only in the context of the unofficial reality could a nexus be drawn: the employment complaint was the outcome of how the quid pro quo proposed by set 1 had played out.

Larry's very curiosity regarding a link thus suggested he knew what it consisted in. I also wrote him in follow-up:

> You also asked me whether there was any connection between the employment complaint and the other one about the homepage oligopoly. As I explained, I have my reasons for declining to address the broader context of the former at this point in time. But since you did not elect to similarly restrict yourself, I can ask you (and without any hypocrisy) why you thought there might be a connection, or why you thought that I thought there might be one—though you too can decline to answer that question.

Decline he did, and for the same reason I did, because anything else would have been to broach the unofficial reality, to address that system of allusion, intimation, and ambiguation that could itself only be alluded to and intimated at but never acknowledged. Larry would have liked to provoke, and then discredit, an acknowledgment from me. But our mutual complicity in the affair meant that I could readily turn the provocation back on him—and elicit the same unresponsiveness. Larry prevailed rhetorically on the legalization question whereas I prevailed rhetorically on the fellowship renewal question, while the matter of the home page was a draw. That was precisely what could be expected to follow from the unofficial reality—just like McConnell's elusiveness, Dick's linguistic contortions, and Barbara's flattery.

Having discussed everything else, we turned to the conversation's ostensible raison d'être, my petition to attend the Wednesday faculty luncheons. Larry apologized that he couldn't oblige me here, as the luncheon had become overcrowded of late. Such was the surreality of the situation. I had insinuated the threat of a lawsuit and the reason I couldn't attend the luncheon was overcrowding. Here, as elsewhere, academic etiquette had to be observed.

Continuing Legal Education

My employment complaint seemed on solid ground legally (within the official reality), but I hadn't scoured the case law or consulted expert opinion, so I determined to further agitate by emailing my former employment law professor, Alison Morantz, for her thoughts. My message noted that there was no particular reason she should recall me, though I'd been an active class participant despite my unexceptional performance on the final. I now needed some "continuing legal education." Could she tender an opinion, of a strictly academic nature, regarding the merits of my employment complaint? It described a very general fact pattern that could be readily decoupled from its Stanford setting, I assured, so she wouldn't be involving herself in the dispute per se. Indeed, it would suffice if she just pointed me to the relevant case law. As a law professor, she had an interest in the equitable administration of justice, which her assistance would be promoting. I obviously didn't possess Stanford's resources, so this would help even the scales.

I dispatched a similar plea to my former evidence professor, Miguel Mendez, who was in semiretirement at another law school. Impeaching witness credibility was a much-beloved topic in the course, and he would grow giddy whenever the discussion turned to it. So I asked him about the impeachment value of Barbara's prevarication regarding the fellowship's "strict two-year limit." I also asked whether Larry's involvement in the matter could serve to impeach his credibility. *Falsus in uno, falsus in omnibus.* As with the email to Morantz, I assured that his assistance wouldn't involve him in the case per se and would advance the equitable administration of justice.

My third email of this nature was to Professor Deborah Rhode, who had taught me Gender, Law, and Public Policy in autumn 2006 and then Legal Ethics in autumn 2007. Rhode had grown annoyed with me in the former when my term paper failed to cite enough of her feminist friends. Obviously, being cited in a student paper doesn't confer any cred, but my apparent disinterest in their contributions was a breach of decorum, an affront to the intellectual magistrature. I had sown the seeds of my present tribulations early.

Legal Ethics, the following year, was also fraught. Rhode had divided us into study groups, each member of which was supposed to write a short essay weekly, circulate it to their cohorts for feedback, and then revise accordingly. At a certain point late in the term, Rhode finally got wind that many of us weren't writing and circulating our papers in a timely fashion. They were to be turned in all together at the end of the term, so the procrastination seemed like a victimless crime or venial sin at worst. But Rhode was of another mind and reserved some class time for a rather moralistic sermon chastising our dishonesty, when she urged the guilty to come clean to her with individual confessions during office hours. She wasn't on to our true identities, but she hoped we would heed this appeal to conscience and seek absolution.

Taking this to heart, I came forth to out myself as among the delinquents. I pleaded extenuating circumstances, as I'd been busy job hunting as a third-year law student, and then related the debacle at the law firm that summer. Would this, I ventured to ask, be a good final essay topic? Rhode was sympathetic. Finding work as a no-offered third-year was a genuine challenge, she acknowledged. At the same time she was irked by the suggestion that I could have been cast aside as "too smart" to work at the firm and gently chided that I best not take this explanation at face value. I, in turn, was piqued at her incredulity. My telling of events wasn't some self-aggrandizing narrative but verbiage emanating directly from a senior partner's mouth, after his unprompted confession that the stated basis for my no-offer was a smoke screen for undisclosed considerations. He and my associate mentor had then volunteered to defy firm policy by serving as references, which they wouldn't have done to rescue someone who had underperformed or whom they had cause to dislike. At any rate Rhode was more impressed with my newfound rectitude than with my smarts, as not every sinner had repented, and I ended up doing respectably in the course.

So I now asked her to size up my employment complaint as a matter of legal ethics. Putting all technical contractual questions aside, did Larry and Barbara have a professional responsibility as lawyers to disclose the fellowship's flexible duration and review my request in good faith? Again, I stressed that the question was logically severable from its Stanford origins. Ever the assiduous student, I was trying to apply what I'd taken away from her class.

Neither Rhode nor Morantz answered my request for "continuing legal education." But Mendez later wrote back:

> Hi Rony:
>
> I don't think that I can provide you with the advice you need. Because I am still affiliated with Stanford as an emeritus and occasional lecturer, responding to your request would place me in a conflict of interest.

I had hoped to head off this response with my stock assurance that the legal issues could be decoupled from their empirical setting. But Mendez was evidently unpersuaded, and I wrote back, "I fully understand. Thank you for responding, though." Maybe Mendez's reply made sense. Maybe it made so much sense as to go without saying, which would explain why Rhode and Morantz said nothing at all. Even so, I would have hoped for a modicum of self-reflexivity here. Law professors stand for truth and justice, not narrow institutional interests, I'd been taught. Yet these professors had now declined to operate one level up, as was consistent with my general research findings.

An Intent to Annoy or Harass

I had copied David Rasch, the university's ombudsman, on the employment complaint and on February 28 followed up on it by sending his office a "Call for an Official Inquest into the Possible Imbecility of Kramer, et. al." The title of the document was explained as an ironic reference to Joe's multilayered remark in December 2008 that I'd dismissed my colleagues as imbeciles. The substance of the document addressed all the contradictions I've detailed—between Barbara's knockout email and her praise for my job-talk paper the following week, or between Dick's boundless enthusiasm for Toledo and his apparent indifference to the manifestly more suitable, realistic, and advantageous Olin fellowship. Barbara had written off my application materials as well-nigh career ending. Yet Dick later urged that I recycle the same documents in my subsequent fellowship search and with Toledo—and after Barbara's low opinion of them had been vindicated by events. The faculty's signals to me were downright chaotic, I complained. These and other contradictions dissolved inside the unofficial reality but remained imponderable mysteries inside the official one, which was what my call for an inquest was designed to highlight.

Ignoring the conclusions of my own research, I had Pollyannaishly credited my Stanford colleagues with a richer sense of irony than they in fact possessed. Taking my epistle literally, Rasch clarified that his office did not conduct inquests and offered only neutral mediation. That I had indeed misjudged my alma mater's capacity for irony was further confirmed shortly thereafter with the following rebuke from Stanford's Office of the General Counsel:

> Dear Mr. Guldmann
>
> Dean Kramer forwarded me your February 17, 2011 "Employment Complaint/Request for Official Legal Position" regarding your employment as a Gaither Fellow by the Stanford Law School from September 2008 through August 2010. The terms of your employment were governed by the August 26, 2008 offer letter. That letter provided that the appointment was for a two-year fixed term beginning on September 1, 2008. The letter makes no reference to the possibility of renewal or extension. During your fellowship, you requested that an extension to your fellowship be considered. It was and the request for an extension was declined. No further express or implied contract was formed between the parties beyond the initial agreement governing your two-year appointment. There will be no further internal review of your "employment complaint."
>
> The tone and language used in your recent flurry of email communications with representatives of Stanford Law School and others at Stanford have caused disruption and concern and are not acceptable. You are expected to cease engaging in these communications, whether by email, telephone or any other manner. Any further communications from you of this nature will be presumed to be undertaken by you with an intent to annoy or harass the recipient. If your communications continue, the University will take further appropriate action.
>
> Melissa Burke
> Office of the General Counsel

Clearly, I had ruffled some feathers. But in threatening "appropriate action," Burke was implying that I'd committed, or was on the verge of committing, some legally cognizable transgression. What was this, precisely? Her vague and impressionistic rendition of my activities—a "recent flurry of email communications," unacceptable "tone and language"—was not illuminating. If she was threatening to release the hounds with "appropriate action," then it behooved her to specify what that would involve and what exactly could trigger it. What rate of email communication would *not* constitute a flurry? And how was my tone being gauged, given that the tone of written communication is usually subject to interpretation? Burke needed to unpack all this. I replied:

> Dear Ms. Burke,
>
> Please let me assure you that I am very far from trying to harass anyone with whom I've been in communication. The attached document is intended to assuage your worries on that front and perhaps clarify any misunderstandings which may have arisen.
>
> Sincerely,
>
> Rony Guldmann

Taking her to task for what struck me as baseless accusations, the attached letter raised all the issues she had cavalierly elided. The "Call for an Inquest Concerning the Possible Imbecility of Kramer, et. al." was, I clarified, a farcical illumination of a serious issue, as its contents confirmed. As to harassment, had I been stalking anyone or hounding people who asked not to be contacted? Had my fusillade of emails been directed at any single individual who appeared uninterested in hearing from me? Far from it, each recipient was sent a single email, unless they replied. Was my email to Professor Mendez harassment? If so, why did he respond in so friendly a fashion? Turning to the core of the controversy, I further remonstrated:

> You stated in your opinion that my request for a fellowship extension had been "considered" before it was "declined." But can you please clarify the senses of "considered" and "declined" which you are intending here? Given that the grounds for denial were the fellowship's "strict" two-year limit, there is a fairly obvious sense in which that request was NOT considered, since the purpose of "strict" two-year limits is by definition to preempt the consideration of such requests. So I'm discerning a logical quagmire in your argument which likewise ought to be "considered." Similarly, "declined" connotes discretion—e.g., I can only decline someone's offer if I am in a position to also accept it—but that is likewise facially incompatible with the actual grounds proffered and documented in email.

Was there or wasn't there a "strict two-year limit" on the fellowship? If there was, how could my request have been considered? If there wasn't, then hadn't Barbara prevaricated, as my employment complaint alleged in so many words? My request for renewal had certainly been noted, for it had been received, and maybe Burke was employing "considered" liberally to mean "noted." But the two weren't the same in my book, and I would have appreciated some semantic precision from a Stanford University attorney.

To be fair, she was only doing her job and couldn't choose her facts. My request had in fact been "considered" but only at one level up, in light of realities of which she had no cognizance. These explained the contradiction between Barbara's averment that, "alas," my request couldn't be considered owing to a "strict two-year limit" and Stanford's own public disclosures, a contradiction that had now transmogrified into this latest contradiction between Barbara's original representation and this new revelation that the request had been considered after all. Burke's gaslighting was just the tail end of a vast regime of institutional gaslighting in which she'd been unwittingly caught up.

Unsurprisingly, she balked at my call for clarification, replying: "Thank you for your response. As I indicated, there will be no further University review of your employment complaint. I will not be responding to the other content of your email." I wrote back and admonished:

> Dear Ms. Burke,
>
> You're obviously entitled not to respond any further. But I do want to make my position clear just so there is no misunderstanding as regards to it in the future.
>
> 1. You've leveled extremely VAGUE and AMORPHOUS accusations of harassment and other reproachable acts against me, which is why I can't discern what specifically these are referring to. One of my email communications, for example, was to Dean Kramer, who responded to it with a phone call. So that OBVIOUSLY wasn't harassment. The simple fact is that you've provided me with no means for distinguishing something like this from whatever it is which you deem objectionable.
> 2. You've furthermore THREATENED me with "appropriate action" without specifying what that would consist in or explaining the precise grounds for undertaking it. I, by contrast, have endeavored to explain myself with the utmost precision at every turn and have threatened nothing.
> 3. I then wrote to you for the purpose of clarifying all the resultant confusion and you declined to do so. That's your right, indisputably, but if anyone is being "harassed" here, I believe that is ME.
>
> Sincerely,
>
> Rony Guldmann

Burke's charges of harassment were just another ploy to saddle me with a "not-to-be-taken-seriously cognitive status." None would pay the least attention to my allegations if first persuaded that my email to Morantz about California employment law was somehow akin to an ominous midnight phone call from a creepy stranger with a deep, rasping voice. Burke was insinuating as much by her word choices and subsequent disengagement, including her warning that I "cease engaging in these communications, whether by email, telephone or any other manner." I hadn't engaged in any communication other than by email (besides Larry's call to me). So there was no sense in invoking the peril that I might communicate by telephone or some "other manner" except to insinuate that I might be capable of more nefarious undertakings.

As I have explained, conceptual liquidation or nihilation affirms the institution's legitimacy by reducing its opposition to its own terms of discourse. And such was in play when Burke responded to my suggestion that she "consider" her position's logical infirmities with "there will be no further University review of your employment complaint." As I would later demur in a final email, I hadn't appealed for any further review. Far from badgering her to reconsider her position, I had merely asked that she clarify it in light of the contradiction I had exposed. In spinning my request as she did, Burke was contriving to translate a negative critique of her logical lapses into an affirmative acknowledgment of her decision-making authority, with my alleged pestering redounding to my "not-to-be-taken-seriously cognitive status."

My calculated, farseeing gambits to harvest evidence of the unofficial reality were now being cast as a paroxysm of wanton trolling. Such is the nature of power, which entrenches conditions under which the oppressed and marginalized are railroaded into discrediting behaviors, so that their very resistance to the dominant order ends up legitimizing it. As Foucault says (see chapter 1), "Each society has its regime of truth, its 'general politics' of truth," discourses that it "accepts and makes function as true." All the nihilation and conceptual liquidation had turned my deviance into just such a discourse. Even so, Burke had "mistaken a Kulturkampf for a fit of spite," to borrow from Justice Scalia, just like my advisers and the elites generally. Her threats, accusations, and deflections were further proof of my alma mater's devotion to appearance over truth and expediency over reason. As such, they were another piece of a puzzle whose assemblage would disclose the higher truth of conservative claims of cultural oppression.

At any rate I wasn't going to continue down this road. My academic prospects were long dead. No one was in a mood to reconsider whether my renewal request had ever been considered, let alone to consider whether any want of consideration should itself now be reconsidered. I had collected some useful material during these weeks, including Burke's recent casuistry, but my guerrilla tactics could carry me only so far. With the balance of power decidedly against me for the time being, I was in no position to fend off the wrath of Stanford. Renewed action would have to await more propitious conditions, when the Count of Monte Cristo would resurface from his long-forgotten banishment into obscurity to hunt down his ancient persecutors. I was playing a long game, and revenge is a dish best served cold. From the beginning, I had styled myself the prophet of conservative claims of cultural oppression, allowing this obsession to run roughshod over all else. So it was fitting that I now accept my exile to the wilderness, where I might truly come to my own. There was but one path forward if the phoenix was ever to rise from its ashes: I would snatch victory from the jaws of defeat by theorizing my gaslighting as the concrete empirical vindication of my prematurely written-off research agenda. Such was the shape that my "intent to annoy or harass" would now be forced to assume.

CHAPTER 11

Meditations on an Aftermath

A Radiance That Streams Inextinguishably from the Gateway of the Law

My fellowship experience had been utterly Kafkaesque, with my alma mater serving as judge, jury, and executioner for a crime whose nature could not be disclosed to me. Just as my professional path had recapitulated *The Trial*, so my personal life had recapitulated *The Metamorphosis*. With friends and family having pathologized my beliefs, I had by now become an insect in their eyes—unaware, uncontrollable, and needing containment. Given Kafka's centrality to my new life circumstances, I retrieved his famous parable *Before the Law* one day in the winter of 2011 as I was readying to decamp for Israel, where I would spend the next few years. This parable had always spoken to me in a special way that I could never quite articulate. I now perceived that it uncannily encapsulated the whole inner telos of my convulsive Stanford Law experience. The parable reads:

BEFORE THE LAW stands a doorkeeper. To this doorkeeper there comes a man from the country and prays for admittance to the Law. But the doorkeeper says that he cannot grant admittance at the moment. The man thinks it over and then asks if he will be allowed in later. "It is possible," says the doorkeeper, "but not at the moment." Since the gate stands open, as usual, and the doorkeeper steps to one side, the man stoops to peer through the gateway into the interior. Observing that, the doorkeeper laughs and says: "If you are so drawn to it, just try to go in despite my veto. But take note: I am powerful. And I am only the least of the doorkeepers. From hall to hall there is one doorkeeper after another, each more powerful than the last. The third doorkeeper is already so terrible that even I cannot bear to look at him."

These are difficulties the man from the country has not expected; the Law, he thinks, should surely be accessible at all times and to everyone, but as he now takes a closer look at the doorkeeper in his fur coat, with his big sharp nose and long, thin, black Tartar beard, he decides that it is better to wait until he gets permission to enter. The doorkeeper gives him a stool and lets him sit down at one side of the door. There he sits for days and years. He makes many attempts to be admitted, and wearies the doorkeeper by his importunity. The doorkeeper frequently has little interviews with him, asking him questions about his home and many other things, but the questions are put indifferently, as great lords put them, and always finish with the statement that he cannot be let in yet.

The man, who has furnished himself with many things for his journey, sacrifices all he has, however valuable, to bribe the doorkeeper. The doorkeeper accepts everything, but always with the remark: "I am only taking it to keep you from thinking you have omitted anything." During these many years the man fixes his attention almost continuously on the doorkeeper. He forgets the other doorkeepers, and this first one seems to him the sole obstacle preventing access to the Law. He curses his bad luck, in his early years boldly and loudly; later, as he grows old, he only grumbles to himself. He becomes childish, and since in his yearslong contemplation of the doorkeeper he has come to know even the fleas in his fur collar, he begs the fleas as well to help him and to change the doorkeeper's mind. At length his eyesight begins to fail, and he does not know whether the world is really darker or whether his eyes are only deceiving him. Yet in his darkness he is now aware of a radiance that streams inextinguishably from the gateway of the Law. Now he has not very long to live.

Before he dies, all his experiences in these long years gather themselves in his head to one point, a question he has not yet asked the doorkeeper. He waves him nearer, since he can no longer raise his stiffening body. The doorkeeper has to bend low toward him, for the difference in height between them has altered much to the man's disadvantage. "What do you want to know now?" asks the doorkeeper, "you are insatiable." "Everyone strives to reach the Law," says the man, "so how does it happen that for all these many years no one but myself has ever begged for admittance?" The doorkeeper recognizes that the man has reached his end, and to let his failing senses catch the words roars in his ear: "No one else could ever be admitted here, since this gate was made only for you. I am now going to shut it."[1]

The subject line for Larry's wake-up email of August 24, 2009, had read, "what's the story?" Was this not the answer to his question, a story that he himself would have a hand in narrating? The legal dimension of events had been the story's indispensable conceptual scaffolding, its proximate cause and logical precondition. But here was its true inner marrow, the unconscious mythic archetype that our mutual policy of allusion, intimation, and ambiguation had, unbeknown to us, loosed upon the world.

From 2005 onward, I had been striving to "reach the Law." Upon a successful transfer application, I arrived at Stanford Law School in the fall of 2006 as a "man from the country," the Texas Hill Country, to be exact. Pining to enter the gates of legal academia while clinging to my headstrong ways, I was strangely persuaded that "the Law … should surely be accessible at all times and to everyone." Yet this was not to be, and, as in the parable, I would soon encounter unexpected difficulties. Entry to the Law was forbidden me when Barbara quashed my fellowship renewal request on the basis of a procedural falsehood. Thus did she proclaim that the Law was not accessible at all times and to everyone. In promulgating set 1, she announced that I would instead have to wait for it.

I waited and waited, hoping against hope that the doorkeepers would make good on their intimations and allow me entry to the Law, at whose gate I sat patiently day after day until an entire year had elapsed. But I was to reap not entry to the Law but only "a radiance that streams inextinguishably from the gateway of the Law." What was the Stanford Law home page other than a gateway of the Law? What was that gateway's radiance other than the logical inference of law school employment—entry to the Law—that set 1 and its anomalous longevity had been calibrated to invite? That radiance streamed onto my laptop from the Stanford server, becoming inextinguishable upon the abrupt cessation of the customary professorial rotations more than a year earlier. This gate, moreover, had been *made only for me*, because the vicissitudes of September 2009 were why it was configured as it was. The brief appearance of the Preamble in January was merely the decisive confirmation of that customization.

As in Kafka's parable, my insatiable hankering to reach the Law would incrementally reduce me to abject dependence and servility. With my entire existence transfixed on the inscrutable black hole of the conspirators' true designs, the rest of the world would recede from view as I "fixe[d] [my] attention almost continuously on the doorkeeper," insatiably parsing the linguistic and behavioral minutiae by means of which the conspirators alluded, intimated, and ambiguated. Like Kafka's traveler, I wearied the doorkeeper with my importunity, petitioning Dick for admittance in "little interviews." And every time, his curious contortions of language, logic, and good sense were varied ways of replying "it is possible ... but not at the moment." I might stumble upon a fortuitous offer "at some point in the year" but not now. The Olin fellowship was another gateway of the Law, and entry was denied there, too, when McConnell's more robust overtures were replaced by an invitation to spectate a workshop. And what was my plebian status there as an observer other than a measure designed to alter the distance in height between myself and the doorkeepers very much to my disadvantage, just as in the parable?

Thus was my haplessness broadcast to me again and again from every quarter. From hall to hall at Stanford stood one doorkeeper after another—Joe, Barbara, Larry, Dick, McConnell—each more powerful than the last. Then there was the most frightful one of all, one too terrible to behold: Burke with her talk of harassment and appropriate action. I had sought to consecrate myself, and my advisers punished this restive vainglory by asserting themselves as sentinels standing guard at the gateway of the Law. That gate was made for me alone, yet I would be refused entry. Indeed, it had been fabricated for no other purpose than to deny me entry, through the art of making someone wait. The plausible deniability in which my advisers had ensconced themselves would, moreover, enable them to feign a haughty indifference toward me, just like Kafka's doorkeeper, even as they had gone out of their way to perform their yearlong morality play. In that show of persistence that Barbara had said would be required to traverse the "informal route," I strove to reach the Law. But rather than reaching it, I found myself awed by a radiance that streamed inextinguishably from its gateway. Was this how it was all to end? Had I now grown irreversibly childish, left with nothing but to curse my bad luck—an exhausted, broken man sapped of will and direction? As announced by the Preamble's interim appearance in January, the gateway of the Law was now shut.

Only at this moment could I truly register the profound deviousness of the conspiracy, which surely rivaled my own. Its plausible deniability wasn't just a defensive stratagem but an attack on the foundations of my identity that aimed to hobble my very capacity for autonomous self-determination. The sociologists Berger and Luckmann lay bare the nature of the assault:

> The individual cripple or bastard has virtually no subjective defense against the stigmatic identity assigned to him. He is what he is supposed to be, to himself as to his significant others and to the community as a whole. To be sure, he may react to this fate with resentment or rage, but it is *qua* inferior being that he is resentful or enraged. His resentment and rage may even serve as decisive ratifications of his socially defined identity as an inferior being, since his betters, by definition, are above these brutish emotions. He is imprisoned in the objective reality of his society, although that reality is subjectively present to him in an alienated and truncated manner. Such an individual will be unsuccessfully socialized, that is, there will be a high degree of asymmetry between the socially defined reality in which he is *de facto* caught, as in the alien world, and his own subjective reality, which reflects that world only very poorly. The asymmetry will, however, have no cumulative structural consequences because it lacks a social base within which it could crystallize into a counter-world, with its own institutionalized cluster of counter-identities. The unsuccessfully socialized individual himself is socially predefined as a profiled type—the cripple, the bastard, the idiot, and so on. Consequently, whatever contrary self-identifications may at times arise in his own consciousness lack any plausibility structure that would transform them into something more than ephemeral fantasies.[2]

This was my position in the winter of 2011, as I found myself saddled with the socially predefined profile of a failed academic aspirant. Most Stanford Law fellows secure tenure-track employment sooner or later, becoming elites somewhere or other, but occasionally someone falls through the cracks, and that turned out to be me. Such was the "stigmatic identity" I'd been fearing since September 2009, and its haunting specter had now fully materialized before me.

This fall from grace was far from the whole story, of course, or the reader wouldn't have made it this far. And this fact—the sundering of the two realities—could not but yield what Berger and Luckmann would call a "high degree of asymmetry" between my subjective reality and the socially defined reality, between the singularity of what had truly transpired at Stanford and the banality of how it appeared. Outwardly, in terms of the official reality, the fellowship had been a costly misadventure—the squandering of a priceless opportunity, the derailment of a career, and a lost two years. But at its hidden interior had lain the three-dimensional realization of my research agenda, the story of the term paper that came to life, transcending the rationalization of intellectual life toward a posttechnocratic vision of the scholar's vocation. While I proved to be an ineffectual job hunter, I had undertaken a silent struggle against the intellectual magistrature of the sacred college of masters, exposing the academic habitus in an existential rebellion against the prevailing ideology. My research agenda had thereby been reborn, not in the idle chatter of the academic conference or faculty luncheon but in the fire of my secret trial and invisible persecution, with the higher truth of conservative claims of cultural oppression now adhering to me not as an artificial limb, a false tooth, or a wax nose does, but like a natural limb seamlessly interfacing with the world. To borrow from Stolzenberg, this was "really deep, subtle, complex, exciting stuff." Far from just falling through the cracks of academia, I had beheld a radiance that streams inextinguishably from the gateway of the Law, a feat never before executed by any law school fellow anywhere (including Yale).

My graceless entry into the 2009 hiring season notwithstanding, this was nothing to sneeze at.

My dilemma was that I had no "social base" where this achievement could "crystallize into a counter-world, with its own institutionalized cluster of counter-identities." With the conspiracy enshrouded in plausible deniability, I couldn't rally support for my cause from denizens of the consensus social reality, the official reality. Instead, that cause would define my subjective reality alone and be dismissed as fantasy, delusion, and disturbance—a mere phantom of the imagination that would consume me while yielding "no cumulative structural consequences." This was precisely the condition to which the conspiracy had connived to abase me. The bluster and grandiloquence of my application materials had given profound offense, and my advisers then harnessed the application process itself to deflate my presumptions.

To be sure, my performance on the market was the outcome of a complex host of factors, responsibility for which could not fairly be laid at their feet. As I discussed in chapter 1, the roots of our strife lay in certain structural features of Western modernity itself, which it goes without saying cannot be ascribed to individual design.[ii] The issue, however, wasn't responsibility but *ultimate truth*: that events at Stanford had been exponentially more remarkable than was captured by my new social profile as an abortive academic candidate. The conspirators had sought to rob me of precisely this truth while concomitantly imprisoning me within it. In winter 2011 it looked like they had succeeded. The home page was a high-tech lynching if ever there was one, to borrow a term of art from Justice Clarence Thomas, the assassination not of character but of identity itself.

This comeuppance was the logical consummation of the ideological and temperamental divide that had compromised my collegial relations from their inception. I had always been a black sheep, an

ii See my work in progress, "The Critical Theory of Academia," at ronyguldmann.com, for a further elaboration of this thesis.

irritant to the guardians of normalcy, and so had to be treated as such by the powers that be once they realized I couldn't be reformed. Berger and Luckmann observe:

> The intellectual is thus, by definition, a marginal type. … His social marginality expresses his lack of theoretical integration within the universe of his society. He appears as the counter-expert in the business of defining reality. Like the "official" expert, he has a design for society at large. But while the former's design is in tune with the institutional programs, serving as their theoretical legitimation, the intellectual's exists in an intellectual vacuum, socially objectivated at best in a subsociety of fellow-intellectuals. …
>
> Just as the withdrawing intellectual needs others to assist him in maintaining his deviant definitions of reality as reality, so the revolutionary intellectual needs others to confirm *his* deviant conceptions. This requirement is much more basic than the obvious fact that no conspiracy can succeed without organization. The revolutionary intellectual must have others who maintain for him the *reality* (that is, the subjective plausibility in his own consciousness) of the revolutionary ideology.[3]

My "theoretical integration" with the wider society, and especially my academic environs, had always been tenuous, and this had troubled Joe from the outset. He and the rest were "official experts" well integrated with prevailing institutional programs—Stanford Law professors, intellectual magistrates of the sacred college, good liberals. Comfortably ensconced in the might and glory of Stanford, they validated the system as the system validated them. I, in contrast, was a contrarian by nature, a "marginal type" out of step with the times and instinctively adversarial to the dominant culture. Even so, I happened to strike the right chords with these official experts, touching something in them that transcended their prescribed identities as serious scholars.

To their credit, they got intrigued, which was how I won their accolades and the fellowship. Yet mere intrigue could not align our basic interests, which were locked in conflict despite the transitory seduction.

From grad school onward, I had played the counterexpert scheming to redefine social reality against the New Class and its official experts. My Stanford adventure was simply the logical fruition of this congenital recalcitrance, the true inner wellspring of the conflict. Joe, Larry, and Barbara had hoped against hope that I could be reformed into an official expert. But my strongest instincts wouldn't be contained. And this incorrigibility was why mine became a disembodied fellowship, as I once announced before Barbara, why I hibernated as a "withdrawing intellectual" during the first year of the fellowship before becoming radicalized as a revolutionary one during the second. With the ensuing crackdown by the powers that be, I would defend the subversive counterideology of autonomous self-consecration against the ancien régime of inherited consecratory authority, upholding ideas against contributions, thinking for yourself against thinking for the field, and the liberty of the tacit dimension against the tyranny of Say's law.

The conspirators chastened this insurgency by meting out poetic justice, taking my insurrection to its logical conclusion until my estrangement from the consensus social reality had passed the point of no return. They went out of their way to dish out further evidence of the unofficial reality—not only the home page but also the key, the survey, and so on—to draw me ever further into its shadowy depths. Each piece of evidence was yet another challenge to my intellectual vanity and hubris, which grew accordingly until I became unpersoned, immersed in and defined by a world that couldn't be validated from without. They knew my inferences were eminently rational when set against their total factual backdrop. The epistemic force of my falsifiable yet unfalsified predictions could not have been lost on them. But they equally understood that the truth was too peculiar and improbable to be readily integrated into any recognized cultural script. My gaslighting had been facilitated by understandings that seemed too nuanced, localized, and downright idiosyncratic to enjoy widespread social resonance. Happy fellows are all alike; every unhappy fellow is unhappy in his own way, to paraphrase Tolstoy. The iron cage of the unofficial reality lacked Berger and Luckmann's "plausibility structure," and this void threatened the plausibility of my very self—now relegated from the public world of human action to the private one of the mind's eye.

The conspiracy expected that this incarceration would be my undoing, that I would live out the rest of my days flailing away in a quixotic quest to vindicate the truth of the unofficial reality and therefore of my own being. The more mightily I would struggle, the more bitter would be the ignominy of defeat. Wrapped in a cocoon of bitterness and resentment, I would be plunged into a self-perpetuating downward spiral through which the truth itself would consume me. I might rage at the truth's suppression, but it would only be "*qua* inferior being"—as a failed academic job seeker—that I'd be doing so. I had played the counterexpert, and this regime of enforced solipsism aimed to ensure that I'd live out my days atomized and deracinated, languishing in silence and voicelessness, a spent force hermetically confined to the counterworld we had collaborated to build. I could bang against the walls of this prison all I pleased, but I'd only be hurting myself. In this way would my emotions become brutish, as Berger and Luckmann say, and thus self-discrediting. I would no longer be operating one level up because that lofty ambition will have flung me one level *down*. The appearance of the Preamble in January was an invitation to walk down this path of total erasure.

Conservative Claims of Cultural Oppression Revisited

I saw the trap laid. But I could not shirk the challenge. It was either slay my dragons or be devoured by them. There was no third way.

With my very powers of agency hanging in the balance, my emerging revanchism was a therapeutic necessity, not self-indulgence. That revanchism went to the very heart of conservative claims of cultural oppression, to which my own fate was now firmly wedded. From the outset I had sought to penetrate the meaning of those claims on the visceral level that grips their defenders. A merely academic study wouldn't do because I needed to undergo some variant of the conservative ordeal, relinquishing my liberal privilege so as to fall under the heel of the liberal jackboot. The fellowship accomplished nothing short of this. I, too, was now culturally oppressed by liberalism, cast to the margins by the "law-school view of what 'prejudices' must be stamped out," as Scalia put it, and my new calling was to expose this unnoticed state of affairs.

My trials along the way could have been predicted, as they flowed logically from my thesis. More than once I would encounter skeptics who, unable to impeach the linear logic of my arguments, still couldn't bring themselves to picture my advisers going out of their way to gaslight me in the manner alleged. This struck these skeptics as just too unbecoming the supreme dignity of a Stanford Law professor. Inserting the Preamble into set 1 didn't seem all that time consuming. Neither did placing a second office key on my desk neatly perpendicular to its edge. Even so, these naysayers would demur that my advisers must have had better things to think about. How important could I have been to warrant such attention? Surely their minds were occupied with classes, conferences, and so forth—not with plots to further beleaguer me with semantic and existential indeterminacy. My deviance may have offended their sensibilities, but could it really have whipped up so zealous a reaction?

Yet these skeptics would have had no difficulty picturing conservatives going out of their way to persecute sinners against conservative cultural sensibilities—that is, gays, the transgendered, single mothers, and other perceived outliers. As with liberals generally, the skeptics' operative assumption was that conservatives are animated by powerful identitarian, and hence potentially authoritarian, psychic compulsions that do not similarly afflict liberals—who uphold only rational, secular goods validated by hard-nosed audits of tangible human welfare. Hence, the skeptics' inability to envision my advisers' targeting me as alleged, which derived from their broader inability to think of liberals as *driven by identity*, by a socially constructed hero-system delivering Ernest Becker's "feeling of primary value, of cosmic specialness, of ultimate usefulness to creation, of unshakable meaning."[4] The received wisdom tells us that whereas conservatives are captive to identity, liberals enjoy a higher consciousness (or "wokeness") that transcends all hero-systems. That rancorous conservatives direct subterranean dog whistles against their enemies goes without saying, but the well-lettered freethinkers of Stanford could never sink to this level. Learned liberals living by the light of reason would never gaslight when they are, like Carl Becker's Enlightenment philosophers, "emancipated ones, looking out upon a universe seemingly brand new because so freshly flooded with light, a universe in which everything worth attending to is visible, and everything visible is seen to be unblurred and wonderfully simple after all, and evidently intelligible to the human mind."[5]

My research agenda had always had these prejudices in its crosshairs, from its inception in Legal Theory. As Jonah Goldberg says, liberals' denial of ideology makes it "impossible to argue with their most basic ideas and exceedingly difficult to expose the totalitarian temptations residing in their hearts." This broad cultural immunity had now given the conspiracy its plausible deniability vis-à-vis yours truly, immunizing it from fact, logic, and "risky predictions." The conspirators' motives were intelligible only inasmuch as I presented an ideological challenge to the prevailing vision. But how could I conceivably have done so when the liberal elites stand above ideology, as the received wisdom tells us? My secret trial and invisible persecution had refuted that wisdom, however, betraying the totalitarian temptations that, until my arrival on the scene, had remained comfortably nestled in quotidian academic realpolitik. Such was my colleagues' liberal privilege, which my research agenda would eventually ventilate and remove.

Liberalism markets itself as what naturally remains upon lopping off the blinkered horizons of a benighted premodern past, of which conservatives are the enigmatic contemporary residue. But being viscerally incredulous of liberalism's self-congratulatory Enlightenment narratives, conservative culture warriors see liberalism as more parochial and historically contingent than its defenders can acknowledge. Although liberalism's publicized agenda upholds the fulfillment of ordinary human desire shorn of illusory metaphysical commitments, conservatives suspect that liberals are covertly animated by a spiritual ideal, a secularized religiosity, a set of disciplines and repressions upholding a parochial hero-system. The elites' cognitive hierarchy between the enlightened and the benighted is merely a secularized narrative of salvation and sin, a hero-system masquerading as the transcendence of all hero-systems.

Hero-systems are socially cultivated webs of meaning production that symbolically exalt their adherents above the merely physical, contingent, and animal. As outgrowths of hero-systems, liberalism and conservatism share the essential conservatism of all such systems, of all identity preservation. But because they are sublimated and intellectualized, the hero-systems of the liberal elite are more readily camouflaged in the secular and pragmatic, allowing their true animating impulses to pass under the radar. Their primary outlets lie in various professional enclaves that serve to privatize the elites' own rarefied brand of conservatism—dedicated to the conservation of their own symbolic capital. Christopher Lasch observes:

> The culture wars that have convulsed America since the sixties are best understood as a form of class warfare, in which an enlightened elite (as it thinks of itself) seeks not so much to impose its values on the majority (a majority perceived as incorrigibly racist, sexist, provincial, and xenophobic), much less

> to persuade the majority by means of rational public debate, as to create parallel or "alternative" institutions in which it will no longer be necessary to confront the unenlightened at all.[6]

The "parallel or 'alternative'" hero-systems of the liberal elites are comparatively self-contained, governed by internal norms that benighted outsiders are ill-credentialed to impugn. Because they are cruder and more exposed to public view, the more pedestrian hero-systems of conservatives are vulnerable to forms of scrutiny to which their privileged counterparts on the Left are generally impervious. Perforce, all such systems spawn a distinctive panoply of authoritarian and hierarchical impulses. But those of conservatives are more easily recognized as such, giving the liberal elites an unearned reputation for superior moral courage. That courage will typically falter in spheres that implicate the elites' own identities, where their ideological opponents will be "conceptually liquidated" with an efficiency that conservative culture warriors cannot muster. The Federalist Society workshop was intended "to help you get a job in the world that exists, not to engage in a protest against it." But outside academia, people do protest the existing world and occasionally manage to change something in it, fomenting far greater "disruption and concern" than I managed to stir up at the law school. The elites can simply brush aside the protests with a shrug or strongly worded email. Conservative claims of cultural oppression are a reaction to this liberal privilege and the plausible deniability that enables it.

Discerning as always, Barbara had challenged me to explain why those claims weren't just vapid ad hominems against the unremarkable human peccadillos of liberals. The explanation lies in the foregoing inequalities, against which the ad hominems are ultimately directed. Those inequalities are always being driven home to conservatives beneath the genteel surface of liberal argument, irrespective of the ostensible issue. As Gouldner observes of the New Class and its culture of critical discourse (CCD):

> CCD treats the relationship between those who speak it, and others about whom they speak, as a relationship between judges and judged. It implies that the established social hierarchy is only a semblance and the deeper, more important distinction is between those who speak and understand truly and those who do not. To participate in the culture of critical discourse, then, is to be emancipated at once from lowness in the conventional social hierarchy, and is thus a subversion of that hierarchy. To participate in the culture of critical discourse, then, is a political act.[7]

The liberal elites may not agitate to shame and stigmatize the transgendered or unwed mothers. But they still feel themselves emancipated from a certain kind of lowness, as Gouldner puts it, which they announce by their unwavering exasperation with an atavistic conservatism that refuses to die. Liberals' "conservaphobia" is the corollary of a hero-system predicated on a cognitive as opposed to religious, ethnic, or economic hierarchy. Whatever the ostensible issue, the elites are dramatizing "a relationship between judges and judged" in a bid to operate one level up. This superciliousness is couched in a utilitarian facade, as a pristinely rational response to the documented perniciousness of a fossilized traditionalism. But conservatives are well attuned to the performative dimension of liberal discourse and the subterranean identitarian satisfactions it affords its participants—at conservatives' unacknowledged expense.

Conservatives feel culturally oppressed because the liberal elites' dominion over the means of cultural reproduction positions them to entrench this New Class hierarchy "between those who speak and understand truly and those who do not" and then dismiss conservative resistance to that hierarchy as mindless reaction, reptilian fear and aggression to be exposed, chastened, and subdued by more sophisticated souls. Having anointed themselves the guardians of reason and enlightenment, the liberal elites guard this lofty perch with a regime of microaggressions calculated to browbeat and silence resisters. So conservatives naturally feel worked over and gaslighted, weighed down with a "not-to-be-taken-seriously cognitive status." Protest though they may, they will find their grievances classed as symptoms of inner conflicts that exasperated liberals alone can diagnose.

The fellowship was my firsthand encounter with this dark underside of liberalism. The conspiracy was properly classed as a liberal conspiracy because its motivations arose from the same disciplinary impulses that also animate a gamut of politically liberal attitudes, which demand the inhibition of a whole suite of default human impulses that now offend against enlightened sensibilities.[8] The elites' moral crusades may succeed in uprooting certain bona fide prejudices. But they uproot much else in the process and are ultimately galvanized by something more basic and all-encompassing than moral opposition to bigotry: a fundamental drive to reform the unruly masses into rational, productive citizens immune to flights of moral, religious, or intellectual fancy. As Charles Taylor observes, for modern elites the lower orders are "not [to be] left as they are, but badgered, bullied, pushed, preached at, drilled, and organized to abandon their lax and disorganized folkways and conform to one or another feature of civil behavior." To this end, these elites will "apply a single model or schema to everything and everybody" in an effort to "eliminate anomalies, exceptions, marginal populations, and all kinds of non-conformists."[9]

These ordering impulses are best known to us in the context of "political correctness," but they are equally at play in the rationalization of intellectual life, which is animated by a kindred moralism that likewise targets certain "lax and disorganized folkways." My advisers had been targeting my own such folkways from the outset of the fellowship. Barbara's technocratic intellectual vision—her "exaltation of academic 'reliability'" as Bourdieu says—was merely a local iteration of the secularized asceticism that has shaped the modern liberal identity historically, a rarefied variant of the cognitive hierarchy that oppresses conservatives the world over. Hers was a religious drive to uphold the magistrature, accompanied by a primordial hostility to self-consecration as a cardinal sin against order and decency. These are *human* impulses, not uniquely conservative ones, which the liberal elites can only pretend to rise above. The elites have "all appearances on [their] side, those of learning and those of morality." But they, too, partake of the crooked timber of humanity, and those appearances merely perpetuate a more sophisticated variant of "traditional values," accompanied by a more sophisticated variant of anti-intellectualism. The ostensibly discredited moralism of old has simply abandoned its traditionalist garb in favor of state-of-the-art disciplinary power, where it hides behind a secular veneer.

The New Class affects devotion to autonomous reflection as a superlative value. Yet my own reflections proved too unruly for its taste, which called for the *obsequium* and *gravitas* in which I was irreparably deficient. These ideals are identified with intellectual seriousness pure and simple, which only accredited professionals are competent to define. I pierced this veil of illusion, however, when I determined to consecrate myself. Having transgressed against the privatized conservatism of the liberal elites, I was persecuted accordingly, reduced to the fate of conservatives when I, too, was relegated to a "not-to-be-taken-seriously cognitive status." Beholden to their own traditionalism, the conspirators *had* to process threatening emancipatory ideals as nihilistic agitation, challenges to civilization and good order as such. Hence their overconfidence, a concomitant of their inability to entertain a more capacious interpretation of my insurgency—one operating a level up.

Their plausible deniability was just a localized microcosm of the plausible deniability enjoyed by the elites generally, which I'd been laboring to erode since the heady days of Legal Theory. That's what the fellowship had finally enabled. The conspirators' ideological wrath demonstrated that liberals can indeed be driven by "vague premonitions or erosion or unraveling" to persecute offenders against order and decency (see chapter 1). What might be papered over as mere offense to sensibility was, in fact, an attack on my advisers' hero-system, which they would defend as vigorously as do conservatives' celebrated "ordinary Americans." If the liberal elites usually appear more tolerant, that is only because they usually have no reason to be anything else. With their enclaves insulated from exogenous ideological intervention, they exercise untrammeled control over their cultural environs and therefore need not act on their hero-systems in overt ways that would betray them as such. But this composure is subsidized, not earned, enabled by liberal privilege, not liberal virtue. The elites can be liberal on sundry social issues, castigating the hidebound horizons of others, because they are never required to extend their live-and-let-live attitudes into the specific milieus where their own identities operate. That's the answer to Barbara's question, raised the day she first floated the fellowship, of whether liberals are truly more tolerant or merely appear as such. As it happened, it would require all that followed, and her own indispensable contributions to this, to give her her answer—which I would have to learn firsthand to learn at all.

Conservative claims of cultural oppression are a subterranean protest against the liberal elites' good moral luck. I became my advisers' bad moral luck when my self-consecratory research agenda upset the cultural self-governance they took for granted. For this I would never be forgiven. My arguable cause of action for slander rested on a single uncertain inference that skeptics will dismiss as without great significance. But because it was symbolically entwined with my self-consecratory ambitions, that single inference stood as a rebuke to the order of things, highlighting the cultural contingency of, and thus exposing a vulnerability in, the dominant hero-system. In steadfastly resisting the academic habitus, I compelled my advisers to reaffirm their hero-system through a purification ritual against a dehumanized Other whose protracted agony would reconsecrate profaned ground. This slow-motion auto-da-fé laid bare the higher, heretofore hidden, truth of conservative claims of cultural oppression, absent which the conspiracy's motives must remain opaque. The unwashed masses could be counted on to remain reliably incredulous of my oppression because they wouldn't grasp that my arguable cause of action bore a symbolic meaning capable of inspiring such retribution from the elites—what I've been trying to explain here.

As per Berger and Luckmann, the "threat to the social definition of reality is neutralized by assigning [it] an inferior ontological status." And that was what the conspiracy had all along connived to foist upon me. Having been ejected from the New Class and reduced to a conspiracy theorist in the wake of September 2009, I was no longer among those "who speak and understand truly" and instead stood muzzled by the unofficial reality, at the receiving end of "a relationship between judges and judged." Although subtler than the cultural enforcement actions of conservatives, this persecution was unusually overt by the standards of *Homo academicus*, requiring measures to which he is most unaccustomed. And this exposed what routinely lies concealed, because my insurgency would unmask liberalism's covertly illiberal performative dimension. My colleagues' campaign to reduce me to a conspiracy theorist was the Platonic embodiment of that subterranean layer of social meaning, laying bare identitarian compulsions that could no longer hide behind a veneer of academic realpolitik.

The elites may operate one level up. But as Nietzsche observes, "almost everything we call 'higher culture' is based on the spiritualization of *cruelty*, on its becoming more profound," and that profundity had now been encapsulated in my Stanford Law saga.[10] The spiritualized cruelty that befell me was human through and through. The liberal elites are simply privileged to indulge in sublimated iterations of human nature's default impulses even as they exhort their social inferiors to rise above those impulses' cruder variants toward a higher humanity.

Detractors will say I should be grateful for having been admitted to Stanford and receiving the fellowship rather than presume to lecture the law school professoriate. Perhaps, but I note that conservative culture warriors feel much the same way about immigrants of color so ungrateful as to issue left-wing criticisms of American society—a sentiment that professoriate will roundly condemn as xenophobic. My unorthodox research methods were necessary to remove the elites' moral luck and bring this hypocrisy to light. That is why I disseminate these meditations with a clear conscience. The liberals of Stanford are merely getting a taste of their own medicine, exposed in just the way they would expose the Sarah Palins of the world—shown up as not her opposites, to borrow from Joe.

He and Barbara were distressed by my ongoing inability to formulate any semblance of a clear thesis when we conferred in December 2008. But the thesis in question was being lived in the turn taken by our relationship that late autumn morning, silently germinating behind the mask of my navel-gazing. The navel-gazing would eventually metastasize into something more problematic still, and that now allows me to formulate the once-elusive thesis: What conservative claimants of cultural oppression were to my colleagues, so my colleagues were to me, just as I was to them what they were to the claimants. I wound up standing in the same relationship to the traditional values of academia as liberal academics do to those of conservative ordinary Americans. By taking the ethos of liberalism to its logical conclusion, I inflicted on the elites what was just the mirror image of the cultural oppression they relentlessly mete out to the ordinary American.

"Professionalism silently installs the New Class as the paradigm of virtuous and legitimate authority," notes Gouldner. But the unprofessional path of the fellowship had uncovered contingent power relations where the elites would see virtuous authority and deterministic social structures where they would see individual agency and desert. As Gouldner also observes:

> The culture of critical discourse must put its hands around its own throat, and see how long it can squeeze. CCD always moves on to auto-critique, *and* to the critique of *that* auto-critique. There is an unending regress in it, a potential revolution in permanence;

> it embodies that unceasing restlessness and "lawlessness" that the ancient Greeks first called anomos and that Hegel had called the "bad infinity."[11]

For all my railing against the New Class, the irony should not be lost that, although I emerged as a class traitor, this treachery was itself a manifestation of that stratum's innermost tendencies, the New Class turned on itself. As my alma mater's self-generated and self-propelled auto-critic, I have put my hands around its throat, squeezing for hundreds of pages now, all to reveal the sectarian where the elites parade the universal. I am Stanford's *anomos*, its lawbreaker.

This was the interpretation of the underlying controversy that I strangely fancied should have moved Stanford to give me a job. Exasperated by my ongoing failure to turn my desultory philosophical musings into something concrete, Joe had beseeched me to explain their relationship to the law and my colleagues' work. And this would be accomplished through the subsequent legalization of our relations, which would fuse the law, my colleagues, and my research into an indissoluble whole. High theory is risky, but my invisible persecution by the forces of liberalism and academia would concretize my thesis as was not yet possible during my days of innocence as a bright-eyed third-year law student. I would discover the missing concreteness in a radiance that streams inextinguishably from the gateway of the Law, which my advisers would bestow upon me. I ignored their sundry nostrums, but the ensuing acrimony would prime them for the higher task of my gaslighting, the true crucible of my research agenda.

The Ancient Claims of Philosophy

My research concluded that the antipathy between liberal elites and conservative culture warriors is at base an updated iteration of the older antagonism between moderns and premoderns, a metaphysical conflict between reflexivity and embodiment. I could now appreciate that my own personal Kulturkampf with the elites constituted such a clash as well, because my research methods embodied aspirations that the modern disciplinary society must excommunicate and calumniate. My (arguable) empirical slander by my colleagues had its beginnings in this broader cultural slander, which was as much of a but-for cause as any of my acts or omissions. William Barrett observes:

> As a human being, functioning professionally within the Academy, the philosopher can hardly be expected to escape his own professional deformation, especially since it has become a law of modern society that man is assimilated more and more completely to his social function. And it is just here that a troublesome and profound ambiguity resides for the philosopher today. The profession of philosophy did not always have the narrow and specialized meaning it now has. In ancient Greece it had the very opposite; instead of a specialized theoretical discipline, philosophy was a concrete way of life, a total vision of man and the cosmos in the light of which the individual's whole life was lived. These earliest philosophers among the Greeks were seers, poets, almost shamans—as well as the first thinkers. Mythological and intuitive elements permeate their thinking even where we see the first historical efforts toward conceptualization; they traffic with the old gods even while in the process of coining a new significance for them. ... Even in Plato, where thought has already become more differentiated and specialized and where the main lines of philosophy as a theoretical discipline are being laid down, the *motive* of philosophy is very different from the cool pursuit of the savant engaged in research. ...
>
> The ancient claims of philosophy are somewhat embarrassing to the contemporary philosopher, who has to justify his existence within the sober community of professional savants and scientists. The modern university is as much an expression of the specialization of the age as is the modern factory. Moreover, the philosopher knows

> that everything we prize about our modern knowledge, each thing in it that represents an immense stride in certainty and power over what the past called its knowledge, is the result of specialization. Modern science was made possible by the social organization of knowledge. The philosopher today is therefore pressed, and simply by reason of his objective social role in the community, into an imitation of the scientists: he too seeks to perfect the weapons of his knowledge through specialization. Hence, the extraordinary preoccupation with technique among modern philosophers, with logical and linguistic analysis, syntax and semantics; and in general with the refining away of all content for the sake of formal subtlety.[12]

Here were the roots of both my long-standing alienation from academia and my more recent strife with Stanford. Beneath my advisers' hodgepodge of counsels lay the overarching demand that I justify my existence (and paycheck) within "the sober community of professional savants and scientists," as Barrett says. Joe and Barbara were admonishing me to accept my "objective social role" in that community in an "imitation of the scientists." Hence, Barbara's advice to break the project up into articles and post them on SSRN, where the results could be reviewed by her vaunted experts in the field. Hence, too, her suggestion to drop by the Stanford Humanities Workshop, where the latest advances in behavioral research would be announced, along with pressing new questions to which the scholarly community would now have to turn its collective attention. Steeped in her technocratic paradigm, Barbara saw the intellectual as a specialist occupying a distinct place along a vast assembly line of knowledge, stolidly contributing her bit to an ever-improving finished product—the "state of the field"— while sealing herself off from everything within and without that would distract from this lumbering machinery of argumentation. Barbara was asking me to assume my rightful place along this assembly line. Her designs were publication, citation, and distinction, which she wished upon me as well.

My advisers had my best interests at heart as viewed through these technocratic blinders. But, like the philosophers of old, I approached philosophy as a concrete way of life to be pursued away from the hustle and bustle of marketplaces and production lines. That which my advisers upheld as professional seriousness I eschewed as the cultural pathologies of the modern order—most fully embodied in that order's vanguards, the liberal elites. Breaking ranks with these elites, I placed less stock in the promise of cumulative knowledge and instead trusted the sovereign mind's ability to harvest knowledge from life itself, unaided by the overbearing mediation of experts, who are to contemporary intellectual life what medieval Catholicism was to pre-Reformation Latin Christendom. I agreed with Lasch that "in their drive to insulate themselves against risk and contingency—against the unpredictable hazards that afflict human life—the thinking classes have seceded not just from the common world around them but from reality itself."[13] So I forsook that insulation in pursuit of the risk and contingency absent which certain deeper truths cannot be accessed, going rogue in order to preserve the conditions under which this might become possible. If notes piled atop of notes, if hours turned into days, days into months, and months finally into an entire year as I rolled into the 2009 hiring season without a serviceable job-talk paper, that was in order to pursue conservative claims of cultural oppression as a way of being that had to be lived in some fashion before it could reveal itself theoretically. Accordingly, I declined to sacrifice the human substance of my subject matter to airs of specialized competence and professional seriousness.

This project then culminated in the August epiphany, which exhumed and resurrected the mythological and intuitive elements of the mind exiled by academic professionalism and respectability. In entering upon the standpoint of conservative claims of cultural oppression, I recovered an earlier, premodern layer of the human reality. Contrary to certain parochial interpretations, my rational faculties remained intact. But they now operated in healthy dialogue with that atavistic dimension, anchoring my research agenda in something primordial that simultaneously spurred and resisted theorization.

The Overview announced that tension and synthesis, to Barbara's profound distress and embarrassment. The epiphany had returned me to an intellectual state of nature. Now an Aristotelian god content to think only of his own thoughts, I had followed my muse in blithe disregard for the earthly institutions that were subsidizing it, materially breaching the social contract of academia. This elemental insouciance communicated to appointments committees that one of the law school's fellows was immaturely basking in *celeritas* and could not be relied upon to assume his objective social role in a community of sober-minded savants. That's why I had to be "knocked out," as Barbara so eloquently put it. Yet her interpretations would prove self-refuting, neutralized by my legal and philosophical jiujitsu when her evil eye for my application materials only accelerated the logic that had led to their production, liberating my research agenda from the paper to which it was first confined so that it could unfurl three-dimensionally into worldly plenitude. Having spilled over into the very nature of my predicament as an academic job seeker, the problem of conservative claims of cultural oppression could finally emerge as a concrete way of life, just as philosophy had been for the philosophers of old.

The ancient claims of philosophy could not but leave me floundering for a long while. The culture I inhabited was millennia removed from the primeval waters in which those claims had first germinated. The present was alien while the past was inaccessible, and so no future could be envisioned. My research couldn't traffic in the mythological when the culture in which I dwelled had lost its mythological moorings in an ancient past. Perhaps a reactionary at heart, I stood athwart my times, but in the name of what, exactly, I couldn't quite say. My advisers' unwitting assistance would enable me to one day conquer these formidable obstacles, however. For my invisible persecution at their hands would bestow the missing mythology, a new attunement to the primordial wellsprings of human reflection in "a total vision of man and the cosmos." The radiance that streamed inextinguishably from the gateway of the Law was that vision. Unbeknown to my oppressors, the siren song of the home page was a modern-day portal to those primordial wellsprings that could once more nourish the ancient claims of philosophy.

That portal was first unlocked by the August epiphany, when the order of nature would wreak havoc with the carefully wrought yet always precarious designs of arrogant mortals. Josh was curious about whether I had turned religious, which I hadn't in any traditional theistic sense. But the epiphany was my break with key axioms of the modern, secular order, including the rationalization of intellectual life, which had now yielded to an alternative paradigm of the thinker's vocation. The epiphany alone couldn't supply the conceptual apparatus whereby to translate that break into rational discourse, however. A more theorized understanding of my circumstances would have to await my secret trial and invisible persecution, whose tribulations gradually yielded such enlightenment.

This coming to consciousness recapitulated the archetypal formulation of the philosopher's vocation, Plato's *Allegory of the Cave*, which, like much else, now spoke to me in a new way. Plato's mouthpiece, Socrates, asks his interlocutors to

> imagine human beings living in an underground cavelike dwelling, with an entrance a long way up, which is both open to the light and as wide as the cave itself. They've been there since childhood, fixed in the same place, with their necks and legs fettered, able to see only in front of them, because their bonds prevent them from turning their necks around. Light is provided by a fire burning far above and behind them. Also behind them, but on higher ground, there is a path stretching between them and the fire. Imagine that along this path a low wall has been built, like the screen in front of puppeteers above which they show their puppets ...

> Then also imagine that there are people along the wall, carrying all kinds of artifacts that project above it—statues of people and other animals, made out of stone, wood, and every material.[14]

These miscellaneous artifacts cast their shadow on the cave wall, which is all the prisoners can witness. Because they've been chained in place their whole lives, they cannot "see anything of themselves and one another besides the shadows that the fire casts in front of them." Unable to turn around to trace the genesis of these shadows to the machinations of the puppeteers and the fire above them, the prisoners "believe that truth is nothing other than the shadows of those artifacts." Habituated to these shadows alone, any among them who was "freed and suddenly compelled to stand up, turn his head, and look up toward the light" would be "pained and dazzled" and strongly tempted to return to the shadows, which would be more apprehensible than this mysterious light they had never glimpsed before. Anyone who resisted the pull to turn away and instead clambered toward the light would find himself dumbfounded and disoriented upon returning to the realm of shadows, which he could no longer call home. The disorientation would only discredit him in the eyes of his fellow cave dwellers. Mistaking their dusky shadow world for the measure of truth, they would chafe at this awkward traveler's strange conviction that their world was but a dim reflection of a higher reality, judging that his "eyesight [was] ruined and that it isn't worthwhile even to try to travel upward."[15]

Yet the philosopher's vocation is to brave these tribulations and steadfastly ascend the cavernous path from darkness to light. Socrates explains why:

> The visible realm should be likened to the prison dwelling, and the light of the fire inside it to the power of the sun. And if you interpret the upward journey and the study of things above as the upward journey of the soul to the intelligible realm, you'll grasp what I hope to convey, since that is what you wanted to hear

> about. Whether it's true or not, only the god knows. But this is how I see it: In the knowable realm, the form of the good is the last thing to be seen, and it is reached only with difficulty. Once one has seen it, however, one must conclude that it is the cause of all that is correct and beautiful in anything, that it produces both light and its source in the visible realm, and that in the intelligible realm it controls and provides truth and understanding, so that anyone who is to act sensibly in private or public must see it.[16]

This now described my mission. The many would predictably chafe at my seemingly convoluted allegations as simple delirium. But as Socrates well knew, the hoi polloi can always be relied upon to so slander the philosophical enterprise. Other Stanford affiliates happening upon set 1 were just imprisoned cave dwellers, after all, gazing upon the purely "visible realm" of the home page as ultimate reality and unabridged truth, mistaking its procession of images—Kramer and Bankman, Sullivan and Kelman, Spaulding and Spaulding—for a brute self-explanatory given. That was their habit and prejudice, so they could be counted on to scorn and ridicule any who dared suggest that they'd been beguiled by degraded visual manifestations of a higher truth that cannot be accessed visually. That was precisely my contention: the truth in question was the unofficial reality and its vindication of my research agenda. Set 1 was no random aggregation of web images but the digitized shadow of that truth—the fire illuminating my entire fellowship experience. Conservative claims of cultural oppression were an "intelligible realm" because they were what imbued set 1 with an intelligibility that wasn't otherwise apparent, revealing just why this visible realm was configured as it was.

If the truth of those claims was Socrates's fire, then my advisers had been serving as the puppeteers by whose machinations that truth was murkily communicated to me. Their puppetry enjoyed a plausible deniability that would be exceedingly difficult to explode. But this daunting challenge stood at the heart of the philosophical enterprise.

The intelligible realm will always enjoy plausible deniability before those imprisoned in the realm of shadows, which I would now have to transcend. Only by exposing this cabal of puppet masters could I make "the upward journey of the soul to the intelligible realm" and recover my shattered self. Whatever the risks and hardships, I would have to climb up behind, and thus outflank, those who presumed they had outflanked me.

I had impudently discounted my advisers' counsels because these partook of the realm of shadows that I was clumsily clambering to escape. Hence, Joe's distress at the state of my collegial relations, which was a harbinger of the philosophical enterprise those relations would one day foist upon me. That enterprise would be most unwelcome not only to my colleagues but to all imprisoned cave dwellers, my skeptics and detractors, who upon hearing my recondite allegations would respond with instant scorn and derision, gauging that my "eyesight [was] ruined and that it isn't worthwhile even to try to travel upward." But these slings and arrows were inherent to my chosen vocation, and I'd be shirking the task at hand if I allowed myself to be deterred by the haters. After all, this was the task for whose sake I had sacrificed a career and much else; it was the higher redemptive meaning of my fall from grace, and it had slipped entirely under my advisers' radars.

Joe chided me for dismissing my colleagues as imbeciles when he should have known that my attitude here was rather more nuanced. Allan Bloom writes in *The Closing of the American Mind*:

> Enlightenment begins from the tension between what men are compelled to believe by city and religion, on the one hand, and the quest for scientific truth on the other. To think and speak doubts about, let alone to propose substitutes for, the fundamental opinions was forbidden by every regime previously known to man. Doing so was thought to be, in fact was, disloyal and impious.

> Of course, the men of the Enlightenment were not the first to recognize this tension. It had existed and been known to exist since science emerged in Greece sometime between the eighth and sixth centuries B.C. Enlightenment thinkers were aware that there had been surpassingly great philosophers, mathematicians, astronomers and political scientists from that time on, who had suffered persecutions and been compelled to live on the fringes of society. The innovation of the Enlightenment was the attempt to reduce that tension and to alter the philosopher's relation to civil society. The learned society and the university, the publicly respected and supported communities of scientists—setting their own rules, pursuing knowledge according to the inner dictates of science as opposed to civil or ecclesiastical authority, communicating freely among themselves—are the visible signs of that innovation. The earlier thinkers accepted the tension and lived accordingly. Their knowledge was essentially for themselves, and they had a private life very different from their public life. They were themselves concerned with getting from the darkness to the light. Enlightenment was a daring attempt to shine that light on all men, partly for the sake of all men, partly for the sake of the progress of science.[17]

Seen from one level up, my wayward path at Stanford was my break with this Enlightenment project and its rosy promise of a new modus vivendi between intellectual and society—a rift that was predictably pathologized by that project's institutional champions. The distance holding me aloof from my colleagues sprang from my visceral sense that the historical tension between civil society and the pursuit of truth couldn't be so readily smoothed over. If I harbored certain reservations about them, these were in reaction to their Pollyannaish faith that this circle could be squared, that the quest to get from darkness to light could be domesticated, institutionalized, and routinized at no cost. Incredulous of this vaunted rapprochement, my more atavistic sensibilities looked askance at the prevailing order, commanding an "intent to annoy or harass," as Burke would say. The intellectuals of the pre-Enlightenment lived this basic antagonism and suffered persecutions for it, just as I had. In contrast, the liberal elites of the current year cultivate Jacoby's "proper deference" and "pleasant demeanor" as superlative virtues while arrogating the mantles of Socrates and Galileo as reservoirs of cultural capital and tokens of class distinction.

Conservative culture warriors smell this hypocrisy instinctively, and I was drawn into their orbit because I did as well. We made for strange bedfellows, as I had no truck with their policy agendas. But they were enemies of academia, and the enemy of my enemy was my friend. Moreover, their cultural grievances served to channel my own counter-Enlightenment impulses. Their perennial orneriness and recalcitrance resonated with me as echoes of the agonism and contrarianism that had been exiled from the learned community of the Wednesday faculty luncheon. With their atavism reinforcing me in my own, I would appropriate their claims of cultural oppression as mediums through which to access the ancient claims of philosophy. Both sets of claims labor under the same oppression, the disciplines and repressions of liberalism and their overly civilized outgrowths in the New Class and its culture of critical discourse, from which I, too, had suffered. The Enlightenment project begins by liberating from the tyranny of popular anti-intellectualism. But it ends by substituting a new tyranny within intellectualism, the tyranny of academic realpolitik, which wields the cudgel of professional seriousness against whatever might be germinating inside the tacit dimension.

As Mansfield observes, meritocrats define virtue "in conventional ways so that it can be recognized and scored by those in authority," expecting that "their merit should be recognized and promoted through an educational system that does the manly job of self-assertion for them by giving them honors they do not have to claim or fight for."[18] My troubles at Stanford stemmed from my resistance to this intellectual pacification and the mystique of credentialism for the liberal mind, where meritocracy holds sway as reason itself. Dick had explained back in late August 2009 that schools would be asking, "What is this guy's future research going to look like?" But that was precisely the question I could not answer. The aloofness that disconcerted Joe from the beginning was intrinsic to a research agenda whose virtues couldn't be "recognized and scored by those in authority." Targeting as it did the silent performative dimension of liberalism and the subterranean cultural oppression this represents for conservatives, my research agenda itself had to become subterranean in a repudiation of Say's law. Because it was inarticulable in advance of its three-dimensional unfurling into worldly plenitude, that agenda was inherently recalcitrant to the meritocratic evaluation decreed by liberal rationalism. The metric of success would have to be disclosed by success itself. And that in turn would have to be delivered not by professional merit but by moral luck, which would retroactively determine whether my uprising was indeed a Kulturkampf and not a mere fit of spite.

That meant I would now be forced to fall back on my comparatively uncredentialed wits as my sole bulwark of defense against the leviathan of Stanford's sedimented meritocratic might, in whose long shadow the ancient claims of philosophy stand deprecated as the primrose path of *celeritas*, burdened like me with a "not-to-be-taken-seriously cognitive status." Fortunately, though, those unsung wits had been tutored by conservative claims of cultural oppression, and this would allow me to relativize the meritocratic might to a socially constructed hero-system and the distortions inherent thereto. Those distortions had been articulated in a radiance that streams inextinguishably from the gateway of the Law, a digitized symbol of meritocratic tyranny that I would unmeritocratically wield in defense of my unaccredited dissidence.

In fairness to Joe, though, in December 2008 I had yet to traverse the path that would bring me to these realizations, so a misunderstanding was all but inevitable. I was ahead of myself from the start and inveterately presumed more than I could truly deliver at the time, always banking on moral luck to someday close the gap. Though I had dismissed Josh's insinuation that I didn't know what philosophy *is* as an irritable overreaction to the project's intrinsic challenges, I could see in retrospect that it harbored a profound truth. Nietzsche observes:

> What a philosopher is, that is hard to learn because it cannot be taught: one must "know" it, from experience—or one should have the pride *not* to know it. But nowadays all the world talks of things of which it *cannot* have any experience, and this is most true, and in the worst way, concerning philosophers and philosophical states: exceedingly few know them, may know them, and all popular opinions about them are false.[19]

This isn't changed by an advanced degree, peer-reviewed publications, or any other marker of academic distinction. Much as I resisted the rationalization of intellectual life, I had yet to find a viable alternative to it when I chatted with Josh in May 2009. I was only going through the motions of being a philosopher without having undergone the crucial experiences that truly make for one. So he was in a way right to call out my presumption and ignorance.

This problem had now been remedied, however. My invisible persecution was the rite of passage I needed, for it was also an invisible pedagogy and my true training ground as a thinker, vaulting me into a state that no individual can will and no degree can confer. The radiance that streamed inextinguishably from the gateway of the Law was conceived as the instrument of my abject subjugation and gaslighting. But it had steadily and unostentatiously transfigured into the light guiding my ascent to the intelligible realm, bestowing a framework of meaning through which I could at last express myself. That wasn't yet doable in December 2008 when I met with Joe and Barbara, whose subsequent plotting would compel the articulacy I could not achieve unassisted. Irony of ironies that their very bid to reduce me to voicelessness should have led me to my voice, unlocking the potential they had always discerned but also misread. That misreading was why they could believe they had given me nothing even as they had given me everything. And so I felt reassured that I remained their student on some primordial level, even amid this most frightful and tragic of experiences. Barbara had carried out her sublime vengeance. But this Cassandra was a complex creature of paradoxes and contradictions, and I could now recognize that what had first announced itself as the dark night of her vengefulness was equally the shining light of her wisdom.

No doubt, Templars will dismiss all these apologetics with sighs of exasperated impatience, wearily rejoining that, be this as it may, academia has certain known rules of the road that I freely admit having flouted and that all these airy ruminations do not affect this bottom line. Indeed, they do not, or the reader wouldn't be reading any of this. And yet not everyone is in the enviable position of making such love-it-or-leave-it arguments, as attitudes that Templars are culturally licensed to exalt as professional seriousness will elsewhere stand reviled as blinkered provincialism. Templars' sighs of impatience are privileged as villeins' are not—and as mine are not. Templars may further argue that their lumbering machinery of argumentation is all that stands between us and chaos, as illustrated by the dystopian consequences of my own anarchic path. Maybe, maybe not. But I again note the essential conservatism of the elites' refrains—a page out of Edmund Burke and another illustration of my thesis.

A Hard, Unwanted, Inescapable Task

Looking back at the whole sweep of the fellowship, I could see that it was always destined to fail in conventional terms. Its outcome was foreordained by recurring dynamics that had always permeated my collegial relations, whatever the ostensible issue, here encapsulated by Nietzsche's Zarathustra:

> A truth that penetrates only sensitive ears he calls a lie and a thing of nothing. Truly, he believes only in gods who make a great noise in the world!
>
> The market-place is full of solemn buffoons—and the people boast of their great men! These are their heroes of the hour.
>
> But the hour presses them: so they press you. And from you too they require a Yes or a No. And woe to you if you want to set your chair between For and Against.
>
> Do not be jealous, lover of truth, because of these inflexible and oppressive men. Truth has never yet clung to the arm of an inflexible man.
>
> Return to your security because of these abrupt men: only in the market-place is one assailed with Yes? or No?
>
> The experience of all deep wells is slow: they must wait long until they know what has fallen into their depths.
>
> All great things occur away from glory and the market-place: the inventors of new values have always lived away from glory and the market-place.
>
> Flee, my friend, into your solitude: I see you stung by poisonous flies. Flee to where the raw, rough breeze blows.
>
> Flee into your solitude! You have lived too near the small and the pitiable men. Flee from their hidden vengeance! Toward you they are nothing but vengeance.[20]

These were the reasons why mine was destined to become a "disembodied fellowship." My manifold deceptions were ultimately survival mechanisms in the face of being routinely "assailed with Yes? or No?" from every which way. Joe was demanding a Yes or a No the day Barbara popped the idea of a fellowship. Notwithstanding my performance in Legal Theory, he and Larry were at a loss about where, exactly, the project was heading, so I needed to wrap it up with a definitive position, preferably an exoneration of liberalism. Barbara then pressed for a Yes or a No in December 2008, when she counseled against the futility of writing on and on without a clear thesis. She pressed again a few months later in February 2009, when she urged me to expedite a short project summary for the scrutiny of her Georgetown colleague. My advisers assailed me so because they hoped to one day herald me as one of their great men of the marketplace. I was to be a rising young scholar making "a great noise in the world," perhaps with a big splash on the Entry-Level Hiring Survey that would redound to the might and glory of Stanford. Hence, Barbara's warning that, with law and philosophy a rarefied and nonessential niche subject, committees would seek assurances that they were hiring "the best" law and philosophy candidate, to which end it behooved me to circulate a paper draft sooner rather than later. As the hour pressed her, so she pressed me, just as envisioned by Nietzsche.

But pressed I would not be. Defying the tyranny of meritocracy, I would not be one of their great men, a mere "hero of the hour," and as a lover of truth placed myself "between For and Against," knowing it would be long before Yes and No questions could even be formulated. As Joe had been the first to appreciate, conservative claims of cultural oppression sprang from a "deep well" whose bottom had yet to be plumbed. The true inner meaning of my submersion in the tacit dimension had yet to grow self-conscious and articulate. In the meantime it could only vex and eventually enrage, as my advisers swiftly lost patience for what struck them as meandering confusion and navel-gazing. Having risen to eminence as leading authorities in their fields, they were perforce creatures of glory and the marketplace and expected the productivity, predictability, and publicity that I silently disdained as hindrances to my own murkier path. Joe was cued into this muted contempt in accusing me of dismissing my colleagues' intelligence. That was a misreading, as I have explained. But by their actions, those colleagues did betray themselves as "solemn buffoons" in the specifically Nietzschean sense, inflexible ones who treat the "experience of all deep wells" as a conceit. They discounted the Overview as the ultimate conceit and responded with a hidden vengeance, just as Nietzsche prophesied, gaslighting me into a vortex of semantic and existential indeterminacy until I found myself banished to the solitary confinement of the unofficial reality.

The events of September 2009 might at superficial glance seem like a cavalcade of improbable accidents. But I believe the ostensible vicissitudes played out a certain necessity that was fated to express itself somehow irrespective of happenstance and contingency, impelled by a demiurge that had always been implicit in my research agenda but that I could recognize only retrospectively. Nietzsche observes:

> More and more it seems to me that the philosopher, being *of necessity* a man of tomorrow and the day after tomorrow, has always found himself, and had to find himself, in contradiction to his today: his enemy was ever the ideal of today. So far all these extraordinary furtherers of man whom one calls philosophers, though they themselves have rarely felt like friends of wisdom but rather like disagreeable fools and dangerous question marks, have found their task, their hard, unwanted, inescapable task, but eventually also the greatness of their task, in being the bad conscience of their time.
>
> By applying the knife vivisectionally to the chest of the very *virtues of their time*, they betrayed what was their own secret: to know of a new greatness of man, of a new untrodden way to his enhancement. Every time they exposed how much hypocrisy, comfortableness, letting oneself go and letting oneself drop, how many lies lay hidden under the best honoured type of their contemporary morality, how much virtue was *outlived*. Every time they said: "We must get there, that way, where you today are least at home."
>
> Facing a world of "modern ideas" that would banish everybody into a corner and a "specialty," a philosopher—if today there could be philosophers—would be compelled to find the greatness of man, the concept of "greatness," precisely

> in his range of multiplicity, in his wholeness and manifoldness. He would even determine value and rank in accordance with how much and how many things one could bear and take upon himself, how far one could extend his responsibility.[21]

As Burke conveyed in no uncertain terms, the Stanford Law community had come to view me as a disagreeable fool, and her threats of appropriate action revealed that I was furthermore suspect as a dangerous question mark. Yet this is the fate of all philosophers, if Nietzsche is to be believed. I could scarcely feel like a friend of wisdom with my readings of the home page, the second office key, the survey, and so forth. I had always found myself in contradiction to my today, and the shadow world of the unofficial reality merely consummated that alienation.

Dick had advised me to take interviewers "where they're at" during our first tête-à-tête in September 2009. But that was out of the question when my research agenda dictated: "We must get there, that way, where you today are least at home." Following in the footsteps of the philosophers of old, I had made an enemy of the ideal of today—the rationalization of intellectual life, the intellectual magistrature of the sacred college of masters, the cultural pathologies of liberalism as manifested in the "law-school view of what 'prejudices' must be stamped out." Everything else emanated from this fundamentally adversarial disposition, which now revealed itself to my Augustinian introspection. I had issued misleadingly optimistic assurances of impending progress, tirelessly deluding myself that I was on the cusp of that crucial breakthrough. But all the detours and delays, I now grasped, were only to be expected of a "man of tomorrow and the day after tomorrow," which the fellowship was not designed to accommodate. The root of my failure on the market was my untimeliness. The ostensible causes—like the belatedness of my paper and CV—were merely symptoms of an underlying lag between my times and the principle upon whose altar I had now sacrificed myself—autonomous self-consecration.

I never pined for this martyrdom and would have been satisfied with a job just about anywhere. Stanford—the law school that operates one level up—would have been just icing on the cake. As Joe was fond of saying, all that matters is getting a job somewhere, not where it is, because it's smooth sailing from there on out. But that charmed life was not what fate held in store for me. Much as I had yearned for the holy grail of a tenure-track job over the years, the hard truth was that no law school or other faculty of whatever prestige could have been expected to endure one such as myself in its ranks, any more than a Southern Baptist church could be expected to tolerate the presence of a polyamorous transgendered lesbian preaching liberation theology. It scarcely mattered in the long run and big picture that my 2009 application materials weren't timely circulated. What I stood for was anathema to the dominant order, so I was bound to be anathematized in some fashion or other, and it was in retrospect no great shock that my bid to join the smart set should have been rebuffed. I might have become an elite in a radically transformed culture that had overthrown New Class hegemony, but this was not to be in the world at hand.

Notwithstanding the authenticity of the works in progress, there *was* an underlying fraud. My advisers were within their rights to feel misled and betrayed because I had never truly been a "rising young scholar." That was just a socially respectable disguise, provisional camouflage under whose surface something darker was gestating perfidiously, something too primitive and barbarous to ever be welcomed by the highly civilized mandarins of the Wednesday faculty luncheon. Bob Weisberg's incandescent rage that Wednesday afternoon in September 2009 was the direct physiological expression of this bitter pill, which that day's fallout would teach me to swallow.

My savage, atavistic nature lay well veiled from me right up till then, when I was at last revealed to myself as a Manchurian candidate. With this self-awakening I was left to accrue symbolic capital through unilateral conquest rather than voluntary exchange between productive, rationally self-interested agents committed to equal respect and reciprocity. This illiberal campaign of spoils and plunder meant the "hard, unwanted, inescapable task" of "applying the knife" of conservative claims of cultural oppression "vivisectionally" to the virtues of my time, of exposing "how much hypocrisy, comfortableness, letting oneself go and letting oneself drop, how many lies lay hidden under the best honoured type" of my "contemporary morality."

And who were my elite colleagues if not the superlative embodiments of that type? The hypocrisy, lies, and "letting oneself drop" had been plentiful at Stanford. Why did Barbara reverse course after the knockout email and laud my efforts as "great work," proclaiming against her own better judgment that I was now a marketable candidate? Why did Dick accede to Barbara's grim assessment of my application materials, only to later recommend that I recycle them in my fellowship search? And why did McConnell intimate at a fellowship, announce an interest in meeting, and then aver a "considerable interest" in my research, only to turn elusive and decline to avouch that interest to other parties? These contradictions were ultimately the contradictions of the prevailing ideology, which it had now fallen upon me to expose. My colleagues basked in their technocratic bubble as a great cultural milestone. But beneath their "modern ideas" was a milieu "where everyone depends on everyone else, at once his competitor and client, his opponent and judge, for the determination of his own truth and value, that is, of his own symbolic life and death." This was the dark underside of the liberal virtues celebrated in my midst, which my silent struggle against Stanford had now revealed to me alongside my true métier as a muckraker of elite decadence.

The conspiracy was overly sanguine in its brinkmanship because it egregiously misread my motivations, reducing them to careerism and ego. These played their part, certainly, as I have acknowledged throughout. Indeed, such motives remain operative as I write. But they were never the whole story, the rest of which is once again laid bare by Bourdieu:

> A greater understanding of the mechanisms which govern the intellectual world should not ... have the effect of "releasing the individual from the embarrassing burden of moral responsibility." ... On the contrary, it should teach him to place his responsibilities where his liberties are really situated and resolutely to refuse the infinitesimal acts of cowardice and laxness which leave the power of social necessity intact, to fight in himself and others the opportunist indifference or conformist ennui which allows the social milieu to impose the slippery slope of resigned compliance and submissive complicity.[22]

Receiving the James C. Gaither Fellowship was a great honor, and I in turn honored that high station in assuming these responsibilities—that is, in my own way, in the only way I could. Contrary to certain academic shibboleths, these duties could not be postponed till after I secured tenure somewhere. With all the slings and arrows it drew upon me, Bourdieu's advice proved rather less practical than Joe's and Barbara's. And yet my ostensible self-sabotage and self-immolation were precisely how I exercised my "right to define [my] own concept of existence, of meaning, of the universe, and of the mystery of human life"—which good liberals should not begrudge me, even in their own backyards.[iii] Begrudged I was, though, and this was, as I've stressed, owing to the sublimated and intellectualized conservatism of the liberal elites. As seen through their blinders, I had metastasized into a cancerous cell within the law school community, with my ego abruptly multiplying to the detriment of the host organism. But viewed through a more progressive lens, the tribulations of September 2009 were the compulsory birth pangs of a novel experiment whose promise could not yet be fathomed. As Barbara divined minutes before floating the fellowship, conservative claims of cultural

---

[iii] Planned Parenthood v. Casey, 505 U.S. 833, 843 (1992).

oppression suggest "there is something indeterminate to liberalism." What followed would confirm just that, when the path of the fellowship would compel me to deploy the ideals of liberalism along the previously invisible vector of the academic habitus.

The indeterminacy of liberalism had germinated within me during the first year of the fellowship before becoming embodied in the home page during the second. And it had now yielded a great task and destiny to replace the shattered dreams of youth. In the spirit of Stanford and Silicon Valley I would blaze a new trail of creative destruction. The conspirators had sat in judgment of me. But I, too, was sitting in judgment of them. There was my secret trial, but there was also theirs, prosecuted from within my own star chamber according to my own jurisprudence. From these proceedings I would promulgate the critical theory of academia, with Stanford, my great white whale, serving as exhibit A. My insurgency had already overthrown the yoke of *gravitas* and penetrated the outer, ideological perimeter of the liberal conspiracy. It was now time to commence the assault against its inner, institutional defenses and maybe help foment academia's belated entry into the Axial Age.

In shining a light on my invisible persecution, I would mount what Foucault calls "an insurrection of subjugated knowledges." "Located low down on the hierarchy, beneath the required level of cognition or scientificity," such knowledge originates in a "memory of hostile encounters" and "owes its force only to the harshness with which it is opposed by everything surrounding it."[23] High theory, indeed, but also the brass tacks of my fellowship experience. The unofficial reality was that memory of hostile encounters, a memory that lay epistemically subjugated by the conspiracy's plausible deniability and the discursive violence latent therein. But I would learn to surmount these daunting obstacles. Although low on the Templar hierarchy, my subjugated knowledge could be raised to "the required level of cognition" once articulated as the real-world incarnation of my research agenda. I had bitten the dust on the job market. But my academic unemployment was a social construction, as much the outcome of my environs as of my conduct therein, and could accordingly be *de*constructed, shown up in all its cultural contingency.

Forsaking the Federalist Society's advice I would lodge my protest against the existing world and deal a stinging defeat to academic realpolitik, in what would be the first shot of a new round of the culture wars. Other law school fellows had taken their stands against racism, sexism, homophobia, cruel and unusual punishment, and sundry violations of international law. But not content with such easy pickings, I instead took aim at the "law-school view of what 'prejudices' must be stamped out," and that original fastidiousness was what had brought me to my present struggles against the New Class, our now ascendant cultural bourgeoisie. This is an enlightened, cognitive elite, unquestionably. But it remains only a "flawed universal class," as Gouldner observes, and events at Stanford betrayed that the cognoscenti, too, are subject to their own blindness and hubris.[24] The conspirators were our best and brightest, the smartest guys in the room. Yet their collective brilliance ended up by reinforcing their collective prejudices and, with these, their hubris, which my muse now called upon me to ventilate. Yale had *God and Man at Yale* while Harvard had *Harvard Hates America*, and my own alma mater was long overdue for its own moment in the spotlight—at one level up from the rest, naturally.

Now clear-sighted as to the nature of my jihad, I could see in hindsight that what Barbara had diagnosed as my proclivity to "make specimens" of people was perhaps more worrisome than I could then appreciate. But that penchant had always lain latent in my research agenda, spurring me on inexorably according to an invisible logic, and I would hold Stanford to account by dint of it. As a further irony, this endgame would fulfill Barbara's prescription, issued alongside her diagnosis, that I acknowledge our collective absurdity, that "we're all absurd," for that was now amply corroborated by events at Stanford. Reflecting on Barbara's prophetic prescience alongside my own premonition all through the summer of 2008 that I'd be engrossed in the project full time by the upcoming fall, I couldn't help but wonder whether we were all vessels for forces larger than ourselves, wooly-minded though that sounds, with these signs from a wise providence auguring a distant yet destined day of reckoning when balance would be restored to the universe. As the reader can gather, my sources of solace in these darkest of hours were very limited. I'd been left with nothing in life but to ponder my own gaslighting.

The American Scholar

And yet it was in the midst of these ruminations that the project now before the reader first crystalized in my mind's eye. I would bring *Conservative Claims of Cultural Oppression* to completion and, with this achieved, harness those claims to exhume what had truly been afoot at Stanford beneath the shallow surface of the leafy Palo Alto calm. I might become a laughingstock in elite quarters, among the haters and bien-pensants of the liberal establishment, who would say I had fallen down a right-wing rabbit hole, becoming consumed by a burning hatred of modernity, intellectuals, and expertise. Right-thinking citizens of all stripes would wave away my subterranean saga as a tempest in a teapot. But others in the course of human events had suffered worse for their convictions, and the grievance culture provided new ideological resources that would enable me to couch my deviance in the lingua franca of victimhood as I brought forth my own claims of cultural oppression. I obviously couldn't hack it as a company man, and it was time to strike out with my own brand. I would just have to suck it up, embrace my newfound vocation as a conspiracy theorist, and learn to wear my tinfoil hat with pride. It was publish or perish, and the Great Deed beckoned.

This would be no walk in the park, not only as an intellectual challenge but as a personal one, too, given my new stigmatic identity and life circumstances. The gateway of the Law was now shuttered. And my convoluted professional journey meant there was no going back to philosophy, either. The academic ship had sailed. While I would eventually emerge as a practicing attorney, finding suitable private-sector employment would prove challenging. The legal job market had tanked by 2011, and my puzzling résumé would raise many eyebrows. How to explain the convoluted course of my Stanford Law experience? If I couldn't even properly summarize my religious neutrality paper in a twenty-minute talk, there was no hope of doing the fellowship justice in a law firm interview, where I'd have less time than that. Here, too, I would be "most lacking in symbolic capital." Aside from my law degree and the corresponding student debt, I was back at square one, right where I had stood nearly six years earlier when I U-Hauled it out of Brooklyn for Texas, hoping to survive the New York City traffic unscathed to reach the relative safety of New Jersey. So much for upward mobility. This denouement wasn't what I was expecting the morning I sat down to take the LSAT at New York University after a fitful night of tossing and turning. But "the life of the law has not been logic; it has been experience," said Oliver Wendell Holmes, and I had at least lived that life.[25]

While I would chance upon some souls during my subsequent wanderings who could fathom the pathos of my plight, it would remain opaque to many others, including family, for whom the whole epoch was a blank screen upon which they could project most anything. The cleft between official and unofficial realities didn't heal when I fled the Bay Area but would continue to haunt me in all my days to come, keeping me perennially alienated from the official one. The radiance that streamed inextinguishably from the gateway of the Law had seared itself indelibly into my being and would irradiate all I touched, turning everything around me into another reminder of the ongoing dissonance between my public identity and my private one, between my life as it was and my life as the Fates had intended it to be. I was now in my wilderness years. Neither Templar nor villein, I would live adrift in the shadows as a forlorn exile, clinging to the one slender reed by which my moral luck hung as I wondered daily whether I was equal to my task. There were no support groups out there for survivors of my sui generis trauma. I had only the consolations of philosophy.

But character is destiny, and I could hold no grievance against a logic that, while unchosen, emanated directly from my own being. Back in grad school, I had anticipated that my first, ultimately abortive, dissertation topic would draw on Ralph Waldo Emerson's "The American Scholar," his iconic 1837 oration to the Harvard chapter of Phi Beta Kappa. Looking back on the twists and turns of my equally abortive quest for an academic career, I could see that Emerson had put his finger on the precise nature of my deviance, the problematic aloofness that had disconcerted Joe from the outset:

> Flamsteed and Herschel, in their glazed observatories, may catalogue the stars with the praise of all men, and the results being splendid and useful, honor is sure. But he, in his private observatory, cataloging obscure and nebulous stars of the human mind, which as yet no man has thought of as such—watching days and months sometimes for a few facts; correcting still his old records; must relinquish display and immediate fame. In the long period of his preparation he must betray often an ignorance and shiftlessness in popular arts, incurring the disdain of the able who shoulder him aside. Long must he stammer in his speech; often forgo the living for the dead. Worse yet, he must accept—how often!—poverty and solitude. For the ease and pleasure of treading the old road, accepting the fashions, the education, the religion of society, he takes the cross of making his own, and of course, the self-accusation, the faint heart, the frequent uncertainty and loss of time, which are the nettles and tangling vines in the way of the self-relying and self-directed; and the state of virtual hostility in which he seems to stand to society, and especially to educated society.[26]

Watching days and months for a few facts as I catalogued "obscure and nebulous stars of the human mind" while "correcting still [my] old records" (revising) was precisely how I had occupied myself during the fellowship. My advisers in their pragmatism would have had me pursue "display and immediate fame"—dispatching ingratiating emails to luncheon speakers, networking at the Humanities Center, and so forth. But I instead remained transfixed by that obscure and nebulous star of the human mind whence conservative claims of cultural oppression emanate, "stammer[ing] in [my] speech" with my repeated failure to put forth a clear thesis. As Emerson foresaw, this jagged path would go hand in hand with "an ignorance and shiftlessness in popular arts"—currying favor with academic gatekeepers, producing a marketable CV, academic hiring generally. And as the fellowship's dispiriting denouement confirmed, that ignorance and shiftlessness had indeed incurred me "the disdain of the able"—Joe, Larry, Dick, Barbara, and others—who had readily "shoulder[ed] [me] aside" through the solitude of the unofficial reality, a source of considerable self-accusation, uncertainty, and lost time, as detailed in these pages. Added to all this were a state of more than merely virtual hostility with "educated society"—the cognitive elites of Stanford, as attested to by Burke—and the penury ensuing from the decision she defended.

Going from one of Stanford Law School's most promising graduates and academic aspirants to a mere conspiracy theorist is indeed a long way to fall. And maybe I was just another casualty of the culture wars who was ranting ad nauseam against the elites—as Thomas Frank would argue, nursing vapid cultural grievances as a balm for essentially financial frustrations. The reader will judge. But I quietly retained a Whiggish faith that this downfall would one day be redeemed by the very principles that had first precipitated it. These, too, are captured by Emerson, whose words remain true to this day:

> The scholar is that man who must take up into himself all the ability of the time, all the contributions of the past, all the hopes of the future. He must be a university of knowledges. If there be one lesson more than another, which should pierce his ear, it is, The world is nothing, the man is all; in yourself is the law of all nature, and you know not yet how a globule of sap ascends; in yourself slumbers the whole of Reason; it is for you to know all, it is for you to dare all. ... This confidence in the unsearched might of man belongs, by all motives, by all prophecy, by all preparation, to the American Scholar. We have listened too long to the courtly muses of Europe. The spirit of the American freeman is already suspected to be timid, imitative, tame. Public and private avarice make the air we breathe thick and fat. The scholar is decent, indolent, complaisant. See already the tragic consequence. The mind of this country, taught to aim at low objects, eats upon itself. There is no work for any but the decorous and the complaisant. Young men of the fairest promise, who begin life upon our shores, inflated by the mountain winds, shined upon by all the stars of God, find the earth below not in unison with these, but are hindered from action by the disgust which the principles on which business is managed inspire, and turn drudges, or die of disgust, some of them suicides. What is the remedy? They did not yet see, and thousands of young men as hopeful now crowding to the barriers for the career, do not yet see, that, if the single man plant himself indomitably on his instincts, and there abide, the huge world will come round to him. Patience—patience; with the shades of all the good and great for company; and for solace, the perspective of your own infinite life; and for work, the study and the communication of principles, the making those instincts prevalent, the conversion of the world.[27]

Thus would I learn to own my nothingness, so that a phoenix might one day rise from the ashes of the James C. Gaither Fellowship.

With all my bridges burned, I would never become an elite—whether at Stanford, Toledo, or anywhere else. But I wasn't down for the count. I could still soldier on, ride the storm, and one day resurface as a transcendentalist hero in lone rebellion against a soul-crushing machine—which thankfully involved no application process.

I am Emerson's prophesied single man, and Stanford was the site of his most unforeseen, uncomprehended, and unwelcome emergence. I could not deliver the courtly musings celebrated there. For I labored under a more rugged, more all-American, ideal that was bound to grate against elite sensibilities. The overarching message recurrently transmitted by my manifold derelictions—"The world is nothing, the man is all"—could not but rankle my more cosmopolitan colleagues, for whom such yeoman self-reliance was the simple-minded delusion of the now-obsolete "American freeman," a stubbornly atavistic refusal of a rapidly changing and interconnected world in which all rational beings must take their place. My colleagues' guiding light wasn't the distinctive vocation of the American Scholar but the universal canons of technocratic productivity, managerial competence, and meritocratic excellence, shared by enlightened elites the world over. I stubbornly rejected these fruits of modern progress and was punished accordingly. Yet the trials and tribulations that ensued would not break me. Having planted myself indomitably on the instincts that had first yielded my Legal Theory term paper, I abided there patiently until a "huge world" did finally come around to me, the unofficial reality and all the wisdom it begat. This huge world, this obtrusion of the eternal upon the quotidian, has now been documented. I would never rise to the top of any field, as my advisers had once hoped, for I had instead *become* the field, and all thanks to their classes. *That* is my gratitude.

Emerson's "remedy" is not for the faint of heart. The fellowship left some permanent scars. But there is no art without suffering, and the vitality of youth wasn't truly crushed. Indeed, it was already reconstituting itself at one level up, replenished by the inextinguishable fire of conservative claims of cultural oppression—now weaponized for a single purpose. Sobered but not chastened, I would "strive to reach the Law" as indefatigably as ever, knowing that it is darkest before the dawn. The elites' conspiracy to reduce me to a conspiracy theorist had succeeded, but I would emerge from the ordeal as a conspiracy theorist of a different order. I had felt the wrath of Stanford, and now Stanford would feel mine. Here was the entire outline of my academic bildungsroman. All that remained was to fill in the details, which I have now done, and I hope I have left the reader with something "fantastic—subtle, iconoclastic in the best way, and really, really interesting."

APPENDIX 1

EXHIBIT A: CV

Rony Guldmann, J.D., Ph.D.

James C. Gaither Fellow, Stanford Law School
599 Nathan Abbott Way, Stanford, CA 94305
guldmann@stanford.edu; [phone number redacted]

Education

Stanford Law School, Stanford, CA

- J.D., May 2008
- Haifa Summer Law Institute, Haifa, Israel (July-August 2006)
- University of Texas (First Year of Law School (2005-2006))
- Texas GPA: 4.14; Stanford GPA: 3.68

Indiana University, Bloomington, IN

- Ph.D. in Philosophy, August 2002
- Dissertation: "Two Orientations Toward Human Nature"
- Minor in Intellectual History

University of Michigan, Ann Arbor, MI

- B.A. in Philosophy, May 1995
- Senior Honors Thesis: "Heidegger, Time, and Freedom"
- Hebrew University of Jerusalem, Jerusalem, Israel (Junior-Year Abroad, 1993-1994)

Fellowships & Awards

- James C. Gaither Fellowship (Stanford Law School, 2008-2010)
- Dean's Achievement Award in Civil Procedure (UT Law, Spring 2006)
- Dean's Achievement Award in Constitutional Law (UT Law, Fall 2005)
- Dean's Scholarship (UT Law, Fall 2005)

- Philosophy Department Award For Academic Excellence (Indiana University, 1999)
- Nelson Summer Fellowship (Indiana University, 1999)
- Open Fellowship (Indiana University, 1996)
- High Honors for Philosophy Senior Thesis (University of Michigan, 1995)
- Class Honors (University of Michigan, Fall 1993, Spring 1995)
- Sophomore Honors Award (University of Michigan, 1993)

Publications

- Two Orientations Toward Human Nature, Aldershot, UK: Ashgate Publishing Limited, 2007. (reviewed in *The Review of Metaphysics*, June 2008)
- Determinism and Forbearance, 32 Social Theory and Practice 97-135 (January 2006)

Teaching

- Most Interested: Constitutional Law, Torts, Criminal Law, Law & Culture, Philosophy & Law, Employment & Discrimination Law, Critical Theory
- Also Interested: Contracts, Evidence—open to others

University Teaching Experience

Fordham University, Bronx, NY *Teaching Fellow*
Sept 2003-May 2005
Designed and Instructed:

- Philosophy of Human Nature: Plato's *Republic*, Augustine's *On Free Choice of the Will*, Descartes' *Meditations*, Rousseau's *Emile*.
- Philosophical Ethics: Aristotle's Nichomachean Ethics, Kant's Groundwork, Mill's Utilitarianism, Nietzsche's On the Genealogy of Morals.

Iona College, New Rochelle, NY *Adjunct Professor*
Sept 2002-May 2003
Designed and Instructed:

- Moral Philosophy (same as introduction to ethics below)
- Human Nature: Augustine, Hobbes, Robert Wright (*The Moral Animal*), Nietzsche, Marx, Freud, Dewey, William James, Ernest Becker.

Hofstra University, Hempstead, NY *Adjunct Assistant Professor*
Sept 2001-June 2003
Designed and Instructed:

- Introduction to Ethics: Mill (*Utilitarianism*), Kant (*Groundwork* and *Truthfulness*), Nietzsche (*Genealogy*), subjectivism, relativism, psychological and ethical egoism (Francis Hutcheson, John Dewey, Joseph Butler, Ayn Rand), Sissela Bok (*Lying*), & selected articles.
- Introduction to Philosophy: Philosophy of Religion (David Hume, Richard Swinburne, William James), Moral Luck (Thomas Nagel), Personal Identity (Anthony Quinton, Bernard Williams).
- Contemporary Ethical Dilemmas: Abortion, euthanasia, affirmative action, sex equality: sexual harassment, sexual violence (Catherine MacKinnon vs. Camille Paglia), paternalism and drugs, freedom of speech/pornography, justice and economic equality (Rawls, Nozick, Singer, Walzer).
- Environmental Ethics: Cultural roots of environmental problems, economic thinking, animal rights, anthropocentrism, ecofeminism, world hunger, obligations to future generations.

Indiana University, Bloomington, IN *Associate Instructor*
Sept 1997-May 2000
Designed and Instructed:

- Human Nature: Hobbes (*Leviathan* & *Man and Citizen*), La Rochefoucauld (*Maxims*), Rousseau (*Origin of Inequality*), Thoreau (*Walden*), Schopenhauer (Selected Essays), Nietzsche (*Genealogy*), Ernest Becker (*Birth and Death of Meaning, Denial of Death, Everyman as Pervert*).
- Freedom and Equality: Rousseau (*Origin of Inequality*), Marx (*Manuscripts*), Ernest Becker (*Escape from Evil*), Ortega y Gasset (*Revolt*

of the Masses), Nietzsche (*Genealogy*), Mill (*On Liberty*), Sartre ("Bad Faith" – from *Being and Nothingness*), Fromm (*Escape from Freedom*), Bergmann (*On Being Free*).

Instructor for Philosophy of Work distance learning course (Marx, Weber, Terkel, Veblen)

Graded and conducted discussion sections for:

- Two Ways To Wisdom (comparative survey of ancient Chinese and ancient Greek philosophy): Greek Thought: Presocratics, *Republic, Phaedo, Euthyphro, Apology, Nichomachean Ethics*, Epictetus' *Handbook*. Chinese Thought: Confucianism, Daosim, Mohism, and Legalism).
- Meaning of Life (Existentialism): Kierkegaard (*Fear and Trembling*) and Sartre (*Nausea, Existentialism is a Humanism, Bad Faith*).
- Dark Side of Rationality (logic and its relation to actual thinking)
- Introduction to Ethics (on the ethical significance of evolutionary psychology): Survey Textbook, *The Second Sex, The Moral Animal.*

Other Work Experience

[Big Law Firm, LLP, Silicon Valley, CA] *Summer Associate*
May 2007-Aug 2007

- Helped employers defend against employee lawsuits
- Helped employees sue employers

Educational Testing Service, Ewing, NJ *Online GRE Scorer*
Sept 2002–Sept 2004

- Graded arguments and essays in written section of Graduate Record Examination

Long Island Business Institute, Flushing, NY *Instructor*
April 2001-July 2002

- Taught Business English/English as a Second Language to Asian immigrants

Princeton Review, Ann Arbor, MI and Bloomington, IN *Instructor*
Sept 1995-Dec 1997

- Conducted SAT/GRE classes and tutorials

Inter-Cooperative Council, Ann Arbor, MI *Recruiting Coordinator*
Dec 1995-May 1996

- Implemented successful recruitment campaign to increase membership in university housing cooperatives

Greenpeace Action, Ann Arbor, MI *Canvasser*
Aug 1995-Dec 1995

- Engaged in door-to-door and street solicitation, consistently exceeding quota

Journal Service

- Referee for International Philosophical Quarterly
- Referee for Philosophy of Science

Foreign Languages

- Fluent spoken French; proficient written French
- Fluent spoken Hebrew

References

Joseph Bankman, Ralph M. Parsons Professor of Law and Business, Stanford Law School

- [email and phone number redacted]

Joshua Cohen, Professor of Political Science, Philosophy, and Law, Stanford Law School

- [email and phone number redacted]

Barbara Fried, William W. and Gertrude H. Saunders Professor of Law, Stanford Law School

- [email and phone number redacted]

Larry Kramer, Richard E. Lang Professor of Law and Dean, Stanford Law School

- [email and phone number redacted]

Synopses of Works in Progress

Books

- *Conservative Claims of Cultural Oppression: Conservatism as a Liberation Movement*, investigates cultural conservatism's predilection for incorporating the relativistic intellectual temper of the left into its critiques of the left. Where the multicultural left critiques the hegemonic cultural aspirations of the white Eurocentric male, conservative claimants of cultural oppression critique those of an arrogant class of liberal elites, which exploits the legal system in order to foist its parochial moral and cultural predilections upon recalcitrant ordinary Americans—a sentiment that has been repeatedly invoked by the likes of Justice Antonin Scalia and Robert Bork. If *Lochner* era jurisprudence reflected the interests of the traditional capitalist class, so expansive interpretations of the First and Fourteenth amendments now reflect those of the new verbal class. *Conservative Claims of Cultural Oppression* asks whether these much-advertised feelings of cultural oppression are delusional, the thesis set forth by Thomas Frank in *What's the Matter with Kansas?*, or whether there is in fact a sense in which expansive interpretations of some constitutional freedoms can be culturally oppressive to those who do not embrace them.
- *Beyond the Jurisprudence of American Exceptionalism: On the Impossibility of the Establishment Clause* argues that the ideal of state neutrality between religious belief and disbelief is best understood a social fiction, perhaps a Noble Lie. It is a fiction that expresses, not any grand ideals of impartiality or equal respect, but the outcome of a potentially one-sided

cultural compromise. It also reflects the fact that the deep structure of Establishment Clause doctrine is ultimately *theological*, because secular modernity arises out of religious dispositions that become concealed but do not disappear. What many commentators have lamented as the embarrassing incoherence or inconsistency of this doctrine arises out of the fact that it is impossible to craft a conception of neutrality, non-exclusion, or non-coercion without lending surreptitious expression to the very self-understandings with respect to which judicial impartiality is being expected.

Articles

- *True Merit as a Noble Lie: Anti-Discrimination Law as the Construction of Human Dignity* takes issue with the tendency to dismiss "true merit" as an empty abstraction to the extent it has not been operationalized economistically—that is, in terms of factors extrinsic to any such disembodied virtue. True merit, I argue, must *appear* arbitrary only to the extent an economistic framework is first *presupposed*, which it need not. This ideal, fictional though it may be, represents a secularized, democratized, an naturalized variant of the predestined salvation that Weber associated with the Protestant work ethic, and should therefore be evaluated not only economistically but culturally as well.
- *The Culture of Deconstruction: Multiculturalism as Spiritual Revenge* offers a Nietzschean analysis of multiculturalism in general and, specifically, of the anti-discrimination claims that emanate out of what Richard Ford calls racial culture. I argue that its own self-interpretation notwithstanding, multiculturalism—or at least important aspects thereof—is to be understood as a secularized iteration of traditional Judeo-Christian values and that these values are potentially nihilistic, implicating as they do a disposition to *revaluate values*. This, unfortunately, will sometime entail a surrendering of efforts to implement change empirically in order to more thoroughly implement it symbolically or ideationally. And this may be the ultimate, albeit surreptitious objective of many culturally-based anti-discrimination claims, which should render them suspect before the law.

- *Radical Feminism and Moralism* is a Hegelian and Sartrean critique of the brand of feminism embodied in the work of Catherine MacKinnon and the similarly-minded. I argue that the freedom which radical feminism would uphold is as such an abstraction whose concrete meaning is always indeterminate, a function of the broader cultural, and perhaps individual, understandings in which it is embedded. In advancing this abstraction, radical feminism concomitantly advances a culturally parochial conception of selfhood, a Protestant or Kantian understanding of the will, in the process discrediting as sexism other such conceptions that need not be thus interpreted—and that *are* thus interpreted only in expression of the culturally parochial understandings of agency that radical feminism privileges.

EXHIBIT B: THE OVERVIEW

Overview of Publications and Works in Progress

Publications

- ***Two Orientations Toward Human Nature* (Ashgate: Aldershot), 2007**

Our culture entertains a schizophrenic attitude toward human nature. On the one hand, egoism is very commonly held to be our most powerful drive. It also plays a crucial cultural role, explaining capitalism's appeal and providing a foundation for our individualism. Those uncomfortable with this "tough-minded" starting point usually dispute only the ubiquity of egoism, rather than challenging the conceptual framework.

By contrast, much of the continental intellectual tradition makes curiously little use of egoism as a *concept*. Instead of conceptualizing human action in terms of egoism and altruism, this second orientation toward human nature speaks of wholeness and alienation, authenticity and inauthenticity, self-transparency and self-deception. Our default setting is not self-interest, but aversion to reflection on our lives and the structure of our societies, uncritical acceptance of local mores, and a tendency toward social conformity.

These incommensurable conceptual schemes lead to radically different portraits of modern life. Whereas the tough-minded often employ Darwinian metaphors to make sense of the free-market, the second orientation characterizes pecuniary ambition as a contemptible quest for "bourgeois respectability" or, more contemporarily, the mark of a hapless "cog in a machine." Where the first orientation observes self-centeredness, the second discerns depersonalization at the hands of mass culture. While individualism is axiomatic to the first orientation, it is, for the second, a rare achievement of exceptional persons, an ideal that has only half-succeeded even in societies that advertise a commitment to it. The contrast between being "out for number one" and Thoreau's remark on the mass of men's "lives of quiet desperation" aptly conveys the magnitude of the chasm. And yet we selectively take up both orientations on different occasions without being disturbed by their *prima facie* incompatibility.

I argue that orthodox approaches to the study of human nature, which attempt to locate it somewhere along a continuum between egoism and altruism, are sterile and misleading. The philosophically interesting question lies not *within* the egoism-altruism continuum, but *between* it and the continuum's belonging to the second orientation. Which of these most revealingly conceptualizes human nature? Is their incompatibility illusory? If so, how are we to reconcile the radically diverging portraits of modern life in which they culminate? If they are mutually exclusive, why do both resonate with us on select occasions? Investigations of human nature commonly attempt to distinguish the respective influences of biology and socialization. But before asking *why* we are as we presently are, we should focus on the deceptively modest question of *what* we presently are, not on our behaviors' *origin* but their *meaning*. The first, or tough-minded, orientation is a seriously flawed framework for addressing human nature because it is mostly concerned with the degree to which individuals can rein in their egoism. While egoism is undoubtedly a fact of human life, casting it as an ultimate motivation produces a misleading picture of agency. The tough-minded ignore the connection between action and our self-understanding by casting the former as an *instrument* employed by the self to extract advantages. I dispute this model and argue that action is better understood as an effort to express and corroborate one's self-understanding by responding to a life-world constituted by meanings that pre-exist self-interested deliberations. These meanings reflect an understanding of what is *intrinsically* worthwhile – rather than merely personally advantageous. This understanding is culturally induced. Debates on the degree to which we can or ought to renounce our personal interests distract us from addressing why we experience anything as being in our interests and from discerning culture's role in determining this.

I claim that most thinkers of the second orientation rely on something like the second model of action and that it allows them to address social and existential problems that cannot even be raised within the tough-minded framework. The latter is ill-suited to tackle the problem of alienation because it ignores that human motivation, however egoistic, presupposes conviction in the significance of one's goals and that this conviction may be unsuccessfully inculcated by modern culture. Moreover, egoism offers no account of the impersonality noted by the second orientation, a phenomenon that would be explained by our being born into – and failing to scrutinize – a pre-existing worldview. Conformity to the latter is conducive to equanimity but may hamper individual self-realization, a concept likewise given short-shrift by the tough-minded. Individuality is a rare achievement because it is difficult to do without the sense of personal validation that accompanies uncritically accepting a socially corroborated view of life's meaning. The egoism that is the tough-minded's starting point is only the byproduct of the rigidity created by this uncritical acceptance.

- **"Determinism and Forbearance," in *Social Theory and Practice*, January 2006**

Determinism and Forbearance is a response to what I consider to be the inadequacies of Peter Strawson's *Freedom and Resentment*. Strawson's account of normal human relationships is, I argue, underdescriptive on multiple fronts, one of which is its failure to adequately appreciate the extent to which our attitudes toward moral responsibility can be influenced, or at least troubled, by scientific developments suggesting a deterministic picture of human behavior, such as insights about the influence of DNA or early childhood upbringing. I put forward a framework for understanding the significance of such discoveries, arguing that while we cannot help but be influenced by them in certain contexts, our estimates of others' level of moral responsibility is ultimately a function of our *idealizations* of their agency, idealizations that must rest on faith rather than scientific evidence alone.

Books in Progress

- ***Conservative Claims of Cultural Oppression: Conservatism as a Liberation Movement***

> The Court has mistaken a Kulturkampf for a fit of spite. The constitutional amendment before us here is not the manifestation of a "'bare ... desire to harm'" homosexuals, ... but is rather a modest

attempt by seemingly tolerant Coloradans to preserve traditional sexual mores against the efforts of a politically powerful minority to revise those mores through use of the laws.

Justice Antonin Scalia, dissenting in *Romer v. Evans*

They had borne your Cross, they had borne decades in the hungry and barren wilderness, living on roots and locusts—and of course, it goes without saying that you may point with pride to those children of freedom, of a love that is free, of the free and magnificent sacrifice they have made in your name. Remember, however, that there were only a few thousand of them, and those were gods—but what about the rest? And in what way are the other human beings to blame for not having been able to bear the same things as the mighty? In what way is the weak soul to blame for not having the strength to accommodate such terrible gifts? And indeed, did you really only come to the chosen ones and for the chosen ones? But if that is so, then there is a mystery there and it is not for us to comprehend it. And if there is a mystery, then we are within our rights to propagate that mystery, which they must obey blindly, even in opposition to their consciences. And that was what we did. We corrected your great deed and founded it upon *miracle*, *mystery* and *authority*. And people were glad that they had once been brought together into a flock and that at last from their hearts had been removed such a terrible gift, which had brought them such torment. Were we right, to teach and act thus, would you say? Did we not love mankind, when we so humbly admitted his helplessness, lightening his burden with love and allowing his feeble nature even sin, but with our permission? Why have you come to get in our way now?

Dostoevsky's *Grand Inquisitor*,
rebuking Jesus for a surprise return to earth

"For over two hundred years," laments Roger Kimball, "the Left has had an effective but unearned monopoly on the rhetoric of virtue." What is clear is that conservatives will no longer acquiesce in this state of affairs, which is being increasingly resisted through *conservative claims of cultural oppression*. What is the meaning of this phenomenon? These claims can mutate endlessly and assume an astonishing variety of forms. But they are united in representing a hermeneutics of suspicion, the upshot of which is always that the left is secretly guilty of the very same vices for which it condemns religious traditionalists and other conservatives.

Justice Scalia has claimed cultural oppression prolifically, suggesting, for example, that the gay rights movement constitutes an attempt to impose the cultural predilections of a coterie of arrogant elites upon less eloquent but more wholesome ordinary Americans. These ordinary Americans, so go conservative claims of cultural oppression, are struggling to preserve their native culture from the exogenous influence of aloof rationalists contemptuous of their indigenous ways and incredulous of their ancient and ineffable wisdom. In a similar spirit, Robert Bork has argued that 1st Amendment claims in defense of unregulated pornography are expedients whereby entertainment elites disempower local communities by peddling their decadent wares. There are also more even-tempered ways of contributing to this discourse. In his comprehensive anthropological treatise on the "bobos"—the bourgeois bohemians—David Brooks describes "socially approved act of antistatus deviance," through which to mock "your own success in a manner that simultaneously displays your accomplishments and your ironic distance from them." Where is this more or less rarefied resentment coming from?

Secular liberalism is, in the eyes of these claimants of cultural oppression, the imposition of a parochial worldview under the banner of endlessly manipulable abstractions like autonomy, equality, diversity, and neutrality, the systematic inculcation of a false consciousness trained to mistake the parochial for the universal. Secular liberals may inveigh against the oppressiveness and hypocrisy of cultural conservatives, but then they should be prepared to have their own oppressiveness and hypocrisy unmasked as well. There can be no doubt: Conservatism has come to understand itself as a *liberation movement*. These claims of cultural oppression advance a politics of recognition demanding that religious and cultural conservatives be understood on their own terms, rather than dismissed as hateful, benighted, or misologistic—that is, dismissed as "clinging to guns and religion," or as driven by a "bare … desire to harm" homosexuals.

Of course, not all those who claim cultural oppression do so on their own behalf. Thus, Camille Paglia condemned the media's treatment of Sarah Palin, arguing that

> One of the most idiotic allegations batting around out there among urban media insiders is that Palin is "dumb." Are they kidding? What level of stupidity is now par for the course in those musty circles? (The value of Ivy League degrees, like sub-prime mortgages, has certainly been plummeting. As a Yale Ph.D., I have a perfect right to my scorn.) People who can't see how smart Palin is are trapped in their own narrow parochialism -- the tedious, hackneyed forms of their upper-middle-class syntax and vocabulary.

Blessed are the poor in spirit. If conservatism is coming to understand itself as a liberation movement, then Sarah Palin is its messiah figure, a leader who will not bow to cultural oppression no matter how far the screws are tightened. She may be driven off the political stage temporarily, but not without the hint of a second coming.

The traditional conservative understands himself to be harmed by liberalism in the same way liberals are harmed by liberalism—that is, in the same way that everyone is harmed by misbegotten principles and policies. But the conservative claimant of cultural oppression carries a more individuated grievance against liberalism, believing himself in possession of special standing to complain of uniquely suffered harms. The claimant understands himself to be oppressed, not primarily by discrete policies, by the underlying moral, cultural, or spiritual decadence of which these policies are symptomatic—a decadence with which liberals identify, and so from which they do not suffer.

The grievance is not simply that liberalism impedes the implementation of conservative ideas, but that it impedes, or seeks to impede, conservatives in their *authenticity* as conservatives. Anxiety about this threat to conservative authenticity is evoked by Lino Graglia, who laments that, being themselves products of the elite culture, the Justices of the Supreme Court are acutely self-conscious of their standing in the eyes of academic scholars, who are to the Justices what "the New York Times' drama critic is to a playwright." Much as *Lochner* era jurisprudence reflected the interests of the then-dominant capitalist class, so our contemporary jurisprudence reflects those of the now-dominant verbal class. Far from being purely personal, the judiciary's policy preferences reflect the heteronomous surrender of their own consciences before a quasi-hegemonic liberal dispensation. It is now the duty of the conservative, not the liberal elites, to lift veils of illusion and speak truth to power, for it is not the conservatives who have the power.

Wittingly or not, conservatism has been absorbing the intellectual temper and conceptual apparatus of the left into itself, effecting a dislocation in ideological space. What might have been dismissed as mere ad hominem rhetoric, mere self-indulgent distraction from the "real issues," can then be interpreted as a *critical theory of the right.* The traditional conservative seeks to *criticize* liberal principles and policies. The conservative claimant of cultural oppression, on the other hand, is more concerned to *expose* these principles and policies as epiphenomenal upon liberals' parochial cultural predilections. Liberalism, argues Bork, is not a "stable agenda" but "a movement away from, an impulse" that must "continually reinvent itself." Liberalism is therefore less a set of principles than a way of being, a style of thought and feeling that conceals itself in principles. Being but a post-hoc rationalization for something more primordial, liberalism can never be appeased and must only be resisted. What appear as crude ad hominem attacks, then, can be better understood as attempts to deconstruct the ideological superstructure of liberalism by exposing the lifestyle choice from which it draws its resonance.

But what is the meaning of this critical theory—or rather, what meaning would it have if its expounders were to satisfactorily articulate it? We can *recognize* these conservative claims of cultural oppression without difficulty. But we have as yet to *understand* them. Can these attempts at deconstruction be themselves deconstructed—outflanked perhaps?

The conventional wisdom, set forth by Thomas Frank in *What's the matter with Kansas?*, holds that these claims are manufactured by cynical politicians eager to extract political advantage from economically driven resentments at the same time as they distract from the objective origins of these resentments.

But this diagnosis, I argue, reflects a certain understanding of human nature that arose during the Enlightenment and has been internalized into the self-understanding of secular liberals, an understanding wherein symbolic self-affirmation is cast as a secondary pastime of *homo economicus* focused on the rational pursuit of taste-satisfaction, and who therefore becomes irrational to the extent he assigns such affirmation a higher priority. But the Continental intellectual tradition is on one level defined by its dispute with this economistic rendering of human agency, which pervades the Anglo-American intellectual scene. This was the subject of my *Two Orientations Toward Human Nature.*

This tradition thereby offers us a very different vantage point on these claims as they operate in both the law and culture, revealing the profound stakes represented by this constant struggle to expose ideologically inspired baselines for gauging the existence of ideological neutrality. It suggests that Frank is only partially correct and that Paglia's argument, as usual, contains one important grain of truth, not that Palin is smart in the absolute sense Paglia envisions, or represents herself as envisioning, but that the culture of secular liberalism seeks to ethnocentrically impose the empirico-deductive rationality indigenous to it upon a very different culture—the culture of claiming cultural oppression.

Stephen Colbert has argued that "reality has a liberal bias." Certainly, this may be said of reality as conceptualized and experienced *naturalistically*. Liberals will not recognize the Kulturkampf that is discerned by Justice Scalia, and instead insist on conceptualizing the stakes naturalistically—for example, as concerning the perpetuation of "homophobia" rather than the preservation of "traditional mores"—some fit of spite or other. What they overlook, however, is that the very ability to thus conceive of the stakes is facilitated by a particular cultural identity, a naturalistic cultural identity that will quite naturally provoke the ire of those who do not participate in this "lifestyle." This lifestyle goes unrecognized by virtue of what Charles Taylor describes as the strong tendency of modern culture to "'naturalize' the features of the modern liberal identity," rather than seeing it as "one, historically constructed understanding of human agency among others."

Liberalism upholds the naturalistic or theoretical stance against stances of symbolic self-affirmation. But the naturalistic or theoretical stance *is itself* a stance of symbolic self-affirmation. After all, the motivation for writing *What's the Matter with Kansas?* could hardly have been entirely pecuniary. The "ideal of the modern free subject, capable of objectifying the world, and reasoning about it in a detached, instrumental way" is, Taylor writes, a novel variant of a "very old aspiration to spiritual freedom" with Greek and Christian roots, an aspiration whose "motive force…is closely akin to the traditional drive to spiritual purity."

This is the disposition identified by David Brooks, the disposition to be fully in the world but not quite fully of it. It is also the great unabsolved hypocrisy of the liberal elites, a hypocrisy that conservative claimants of cultural oppression can bewail but never fully understand—which is a source of cultural oppression in its own right. For human consciousness is created out of cultural meanings sustained by a social reality that can, depending on its shape, be genuinely oppressive to certain consciousnesses, depending on their shape. It is precisely such a consciousness that is being articulated through conservative claims of cultural oppression. If these claims can seem unintelligible, this is because the claimants are like Kafka's K, a *seemingly* tolerant man who wakes up to find himself hounded by the Court for a crime the nature of which he cannot be given to understand—a most *un*-American form of prosecution.

Like the Grand Inquisitor's flock, these claimants want liberation from their own oppressed consciousnesses—consciousnesses oppressed by the possibility of what others recognize as freedom. For the claimants, the question is not whether others have a right to be free, but whether *they* have an *obligation* to be free. They will not be *forced* to be free, as Rousseau would require. As punishment for this refusal, they have been branded as haters, homophobes, and so forth. And indeed, the branding has been unfair. All these are only *symptoms.* Scientifically speaking, which is how secular liberals *purport* to be speaking, this refusal is in fact an *incapacity*—or disability, depending on one's perspective. The elitist hypocrisy never ends.

Conservative claims of cultural oppression will seem cynical, or even unintelligible, only when interpreted in a *fundamentalist* fashion—that is, as a set of empirical claims. But conservative claims of cultural oppression are not ultimately empirical, and sophisticated theologians will always seek out a deeper *moral* truth. Martha Nussbaum asks that we not hide from our humanity. But this is no great feat if that "humanity" happens to coincide with one's identity. What about the rest, though? The Grand Inquisitor has been struggling against such elitist hypocrisy for millennia, and he is not prepared to give up the fight. He can, however, be *monitored.*

- ***Beyond the Jurisprudence of American Exceptionalism: On the Impossibility of the Establishment Clause***

It is a well known lament of conservatives that the intellectual classes have, through the courts alongside other means, instituted a regime, perhaps a religion, of secularism or secular humanism, the advancement of which is predicated upon the disparagement of traditional religion and its devotees. These are *conservative claims of cultural oppression*. While some liberals would agree that the courts have at times been insufficiently sensitive to the nature and needs of religion, the liberal instinct is to dismiss as extravagant these more robust claims to the effect that the public schools have been infiltrated by an evangelizing, quasi-conspiratorial secular humanism, or that the Establishment Clause has become a tool of oppression operating surreptitiously in the service of this and other plots.

To these claims, secular liberals respond that, assuming some sense can be given to the notion of a secular religiosity, this is a label best reserved for countries like Turkey or France, which have sometimes directly suppressed certain forms of religious self-expression, like the wearing of headscarves. But since such policies and the attitudes underlying them would never be tolerated in the United States, warnings about the encroachment of an ideological secularism are dismissed as merely another iteration of conservatism's politically expedient false populism.

This diagnosis, I argue, is mistaken. Close scrutiny of the conceptual architecture of some important Establishment Clause rulings suggests a pattern of discrimination that is pervasive and systematic. Conservative claimants of cultural oppression are being discriminated against *on the basis of their premodern sensibility*. The operation of this largely unconscious form of religious discrimination has thus far been obscured because the riddle of the Establishment Clause is ordinarily framed in terms of a question about the respective prerogatives of the religious and the secular. But this debate conceals the existence another one going on underneath, unacknowledged and unnoticed, a debate about the respective prerogatives, not of the secular and the religious, but of the modern and premodern understandings of *the relationship between the secular and the religious*, a divergence of understanding that is itself of religious origin and significance. It is this competition between opposed *cosmological orientations*—between alternative forms of religious *consciousnesses*—that drives what many commentators have lamented as the embarrassing line-drawing problems and logical inconsistencies plaguing Establishment Clause doctrine.

Secular liberals can maintain their incredulity toward these grievances only because their own self-understandings are implicated in what Charles Taylor calls "subtraction stories." These are

> stories of modernity in general, and secularity in particular, which explain them by human beings having lost, or sloughed off, or liberated themselves from certain earlier, confining horizons, or illusions, or limitations of knowledge. What emerges from this process—modernity or secularity—is to be understood in terms of underlying features of human nature which were there all along, but had been impeded by what is now set aside.

These grievances become more credible, and the constitutional stakes more complicated, once subtraction stories are themselves sloughed off as illusions and limitations of knowledge, once it is understood that the secular consciousness arose as a permutation of a religious one and carries its origins forth with it. The premodern and modern sensibilities then become constitutionally commensurable, as the modern sensibility which has been privileged must be understood as representing, not any culturally neutral enlightenment, but the perhaps accidental outgrowth of the premodern sensibility. Even the "non-belief" with respect to which the Supreme Court purports to be neutral is a phenomenon that is partly defined by that that which it negates, as Hegel understood it must. And the "hostility" toward religion that the Court conservatives have time and again lamented must be understood as a constitutive element of the modern identity, not individual caprice, an element that itself arises out of a religious tradition and carries a religious meaning. "Secularization" is always the secularization *of* something that is not itself secular.

The riddle of the Establishment Clause cannot be unraveled so long as this Clause is interpreted according to a jurisprudence of *analytical understanding*—that is, according to the back-and-forth of arguments and counter-arguments between putatively autonomous minds. This is simply to acquiesce in the presumptions of Enlightenment atomism. But the interpretation of the Establishment Clause is a social and historical, not individual project. By contrast, the jurisprudence of *dialectical Reason* seeks to understand, not only individual positions, but the historically generated forms of consciousness that make those individual positions possible, intelligible, and even persuasive. It seeks knowledge of the *Whole*, as Hegel says—and the Whole did not begin in 1787, or even 1776 or 1620. The jurisprudence of dialectical Reason is not a jurisprudence of American exceptionalism—it is a jurisprudence of *mutation*, not subtraction.

Nor is it a jurisprudence of politeness, as has been thought to befit the subject of religion. The Supreme Court's articulation of such concepts as "neutrality" and exclusion from "the political community" discriminates on the basis of cosmological orientation, an immutable characteristic. Placing the state's imprimatur of approval upon the modern sensibility, these articulations will have a negative disparate impact upon conservative claimants of cultural oppression and other Americans with premodern sensibilities, producing a legal and cultural narrative in which the modern self-understanding is celebrated to the detriment of the premodern one, leaving premoderns feeling like outsiders to the political community, as Justice O'Connor would have had to put it. In this work, I will

1. expose the existence and workings of this form of religious discrimination,
2. demonstrate that the stridency of unrelentingly expansive interpretations of the Establishment Clause is best understood as a sublimated and secularized Puritanism,
3. demonstrate that exaggerated anxiety about theocratic encroachment threatens to culminate in self-fulfilling prophesies, contributing to a self-reinforcing cultural and doctrinal neurosis, and

4. demonstrate that the our self-understanding is always implicated in the interpretation of the Establishment Clause and that this practice is an inherently theological enterprise which always risks devolving into idolatry.

From these showings, it follows

1. that Americans with premodern sensibilities have been the victims of religious discrimination,
2. that this discrimination has been inflicted by the courts, which have been violating the Establishment Clause in the very process of interpreting it, and
3. accordingly, that the Supreme Court should enter an injunction restraining itself and all other courts from any further interpretation of this Clause until such time as a remedy can be devised.

Articles in Progress

- ***The Culture of Deconstruction: Multiculturalism as Spiritual Revenge***

Abdul JanMohamed writes that "[g]enuine and thorough comprehension of Otherness is possible only if the self can somehow negate or at least severely bracket the values, assumptions, and ideology of his culture … " This "entails in practice the virtually impossible task of negating one's very being." JanMohamed thereby expresses a powerful current of thought and feeling within the multicultural left, the sense that racism and ethnic hostility are not mere individual prejudices to be overcome through individual morality, but ingrained expressions of culture and the subjectivities shaped by it—and therefore things to be overcome culturally.

For practical purposes, this means the culture and subjectivity of the dominant white dispensation. In the sphere of anti-discrimination law, some have understood this to justify establishing legal protections against various forms of cultural discrimination, in the workplace and the classroom. On this view, racism and ethnic hostility ultimately emerge out of a certain ethnocentrism that refuses to recognize minority groups on their own terms, which means to value their characteristics as they value them. Thus, Barbara

Flagg argues that "[b]ecause whites do not conceive of themselves as a distinctive racial group, their 'consciousness' of whiteness is predominantly unconsciousness of whiteness." For this reason, "white people frequently interpret norms adopted by a dominant white culture as racially neutral, and so fail to recognize the ways in which those norms may be in fact covertly race-specific." In a similar vein, Gary Peller describes how black nationalists objected to the presumptuousness with which white America mistook its parochial ideals for a "realm of universal, culturally-neutral social practices." Attempts to introduce notions of cultural discrimination into anti-discrimination law might then be understood as part and parcel of a more general cultural project of moral-spiritual self-purification—which JanMohamed acknowledges is destined to remain a merely regulative ideal.

Others, however, have greater faith in the realization of this ideal. This optimism was eloquently articulated by the Reverend Jeremiah Wright at his address to the NAACP of Michigan. Given in the midst of the political fiasco that Wright had created for his former parishioner, the talk was themed "different is not deficient." Relying on the research of Janice Hale, the author of *Learning While Black*, Wright argued that African-Americans and other minority groups had been victimized by arbitrary norms and meaningless labels functioning to stigmatize the merely different as deficient. Thus, Africans, who have a right-brain subject-oriented learning style are not fairly judged according to the standards that would be appropriate to the left-brain object-oriented learning style of Europeans. Whereas the latter is logical and analytical, the former is creative and intuitive. African-American students who would be judged deficient by the European standard must instead be respected as simply different, a difference that is evidenced, Wright observed, by their unsurpassed ability to memorize hip-hop lyrics. Wright warned that there remain haters in the world incapable of getting their heads around the simple proposition that different does not mean deficient. Nevertheless, he urged, we can seek to change how we see both others and ourselves, in order to promote the universal equality to which the African-American Church has always been committed.

But what is the *meaning* of this universal equality, this ideal of moral-spiritual self-purification? And is it in fact what it pretends to be? Might we not instead say, with Nietzsche "Bad air! Bad air! This workshop where *ideals are manufactured*—it seems to me it stinks of so many lies"? This ideal stems, Wright has often emphasized, from the liberationist theology of his church's prophetic tradition, which his critics do not care to understand before proceeding with their criticisms. Wright's admonition is fair enough. So what is the nature of the tradition which has been so misunderstood? Nietzsche observes,

> The slave revolt in morality begins when *ressentiment* itself becomes creative and gives birth to values; the *ressentiment* of natures that are denied the true reaction, that of deeds, and compensate themselves with an imaginary revenge. While every noble morality develops from a triumphant affirmation of itself, slave morality from the outset says No to what is "outside," what is "different," what is not "itself"; and *this* No is its creative deed.

Invented by the Jews in ancient times, the slave revolt in morality constitutes a *revaluation of values*, an effort to overcome the status quo symbolically rather than physically, by imposing a new interpretation on the values of the dominant class—by representing what the latter called "good" as instead "evil," and thereby representing oneself as "good," when one would otherwise be "bad"—that is, inferior to the good: "It was the Jews who, with awe-inspiring consistency, dared to invert the aristocratic value-equation (good = noble = powerful = beautiful = happy = beloved of God) and to hang on to this inversion with their teeth, the teeth of the most abysmal hatred (the hatred of impotence), saying "the wretched alone are the good; the poor, lowly, impotent, lowly are the good..." The Jews did not retain a monopoly on this inversion, however, as this technology was left freely available in the public domain:

> Did Israel not attain the ultimate goal of its sublime vengefulness precisely through the bypath of this "Redeemer," this ostensible opponent and disintegrator of Israel? Was it not part of the secret black art of truly *grand* politics of revenge, of a farseeing, subterranean, slowly advancing, and premeditated revenge, that Israel must itself deny the real instrument of its revenge before all

> the world as a mortal enemy and nail it to the cross, so that "all the world," namely all the opponents of Israel, could unhesitatingly swallow just this bait? And could spiritual subtlety imagine any *more dangerous* bait than this? Anything equal to the enticing, intoxicating, overwhelming, and undermining power of that symbol of the "holy cross," that ghastly paradox of "God on the cross," that mystery of an unimaginable cruelty and self-crucifixion of God *for the salvation of man*? ...Israel, with its vengefulness and revaluation of all values, has triumphed again and again over all other ideals, over all *nobler* ideals.—

Whatever the particular shape it assumes, the slave revolt in morality seeks to discredit the existing scale of values as false or parochial, and so to discredit those values' prideful adherents as the slaves of their own arrogant illusions.

Is it not now multiculturalism, or at least many of the impulses behind it, that today carries forth the mantle of the great slave revolt?—in a more therapeutic and more democratic fashion, to be sure, as befits the age. Is multiculturalism not in the least engaged in what Nietzsche called a *spiritual revenge*? Discrete claims of cultural discrimination in the workplace and elsewhere are perhaps the symbolic mediums through which to effect a revaluation of "white bourgeois values"—which may mean, *American* values—to assail its cultural presumptions by symbolically highlighting their relativity and contingency—that is, revealing these presumptions *as* presumptions.

It does not matter whether one calls these presumptions idolatry or false consciousness. All deconstructionists—whether secular or religious, liberal or conservative, black or white, straight or gay—are in the business of upholding traditional Judeo-Christian values. For they are all playing the same wicked game—a game that will always be played so long as America is to remain a salad bowl rather than a melting pot. For every salad bowl must give rise to a *culture of deconstruction*. The only question is who will play that game the *best*. Clearly, this will always be those who are prepared to deconstruct the culture of deconstruction itself—and, with it, *themselves*.

In the case of multiculturalism, the game is not merely to promote racial and ethnic equality "with all deliberate speed" but to, simultaneously and contradictorily, instantiate that equality *now*, by revaluating the values on whose basis that equality could be disputed, by attaching a new valence to old stereotypes and thereby inverting the established hierarchy of good and evil—at least with respect to learning styles and working styles. Are these indigenous cultures of racial and ethnic minorities always in fact indigenous, or might many of them constitute constructions erected for the purpose of *denying recognition* to the dominant white culture, with its pretensions to normative universality?

Richard Ford and other commentators have observed that racial and ethnic minorities will often have internalized negative stereotypes of themselves, and that this may find expression in their legal claims. It should be added, however, that some will have internalized these stereotypes more *creatively* than others—that is, for a purpose of reinterpreting those stereotypes and thereby placing a question mark besides the normative frameworks from which those stereotypes originally issued, the "secret black art of truly *grand* politics of revenge."

However, it does not follow from the fact that one plays this game *well* that it is always *worth* playing. What worked for Israel at one time will not necessarily work for all peoples under all circumstances. So much is confirmed by the "results" of Hale's research. The slave revolt in morality was never designed as an all-purpose instrument. Even Israel itself has disposed of it.

Certainly, the Reverend Wright is to be admired for his charisma and conviction. It is the priest, Nietzsche remarks, that represents the "*essentially dangerous* form of human existence," the soil out of which "man first became an interesting animal," out of which "the human soul in a higher sense" did "acquire *depth* and become *evil*"—the "two basic respects in which man has hitherto been superior to other beasts!" Yet it is precisely for this reason that one must ask whether what is good for the priest is also good for the flock. The priest has always had a vested interest in discrediting the "European" learning style. "The truths of religion are never so well understood as by those who have lost the power of reason," said Voltaire. One must ask whether the enterprise being urged by Wright and Hale, herself a priest's daughter, in fact empowers those who are being asked to carry it forth, or whether the time for fiery prophets is past, prophets who, in privileging morality over reality, tilt at windmills, disempowering their flock while empowering their right-brain subject-oriented enemies—at which point Wright and Hale will be ready with more advice.

And *why* is this advice being offered? Naturally, it is offered out of *ressentiment* toward the "powerful physicality,... flourishing, abundant, even overflowing health" of the knightly-aristocratic class—toward the man who "shakes off with a *single* shrug many vermin that eat deeply into others." It is offered out of *ressentiment* toward the priest's *former* parishioner. Why, according to Wright, had he been renounced by that parishioner? The latter was a mere politician, a man of the world, who would say what he had to say, and therefore lacked the holiness of the man of the cloth, who would always remain true to himself and his God. There is a reason why Moses could not be permitted to enter the Promised Land, his services rendered notwithstanding—no agreements were made on this front. Wright offers his revaluation of all values as compensation for past oppression. But we also know from Nietzsche that that which does not kill us makes us stronger. The affirmative action that Wright would bestow upon disadvantaged minorities is therefore already *inside* them, and there is no need for Wright to bestow it.

But then the fiasco was more than a fiasco. It was, as Hegel would say, the *cunning of Reason*. For the real is always the rational, when properly comprehended. The only question remaining is whether Reason will also make an appearance within the culture of multiculturalism and its forays into the law.

- ***Radical Feminism and Moralism***

Catherine MacKinnon says that obscenity is "a moral idea; an idea of judgments about good and bad." By contrast, pornography "is a political practice, a practice of power and powerlessness. Obscenity is ideational and abstract; pornography is concrete and substantive." But whether this is the case will depend upon one's conception of human nature. This neat demarcation between moralism and substantive power relationships becomes questionable if humans are ideational beings and if the concrete is always grasped through the abstract—that is, if we abandon a naïve empiricism. In that case, we would have to ask whether the concepts invoked by radical feminists in discussions of sexual harassment and pornography—such as denigration and objectification on the one side and equal respect on the other—admit of a culturally neutral construal, or whether they will always be giving expression to culturally parochial ideals of selfhood, and in the process rejecting other such ideals that are in themselves neither sexist nor anti-sexist, neither feminist nor anti-feminist.

Hegel's critique of an abstract, culturally-neutral Kantian autonomy raises the possibility that strands of radical feminism are, notwithstanding their own self-interpretations, deeply *conservative*, the unacknowledged secularizations of original sin, original sin re-described and reinterpreted, surreptitiously embedded in what understands itself as an empirically-minded liberation movement. Indeed, the fact that the tough-minded character of radical feminism is repeatedly emphasized may be *prima facie* evidence that it is not in fact so tough-minded.

Many radical feminist analyses, I argue, are corrupted by their incorporation of Christian, specifically Protestant, understandings of the will, understandings which falsely moralize human drives that need not be interpreted as carrying any intrinsic moral valence. These analyses could proceed more perspicaciously were they to recognize that feminism is never "unmodified," because the concrete meaning of its ideals will always grow out of the cultural dispensation in which any feminism will embed itself—there is always freedom of choice here. Woman, like man, is *condemned* to be free, to update Sartre's dictum.

- ***True Merit as a Noble Lie: Employment Law as the Construction of Human Dignity***

True merit has been coming under assault. Robert Post has argued that a "sociological" conception of antidiscrimination law—according to which the law aims to rectify certain particularly egregious social practices—should replace the now dominant conception, which, in aspiring to instantiate an abstract ideal of genuine merit, perpetuates the fiction that there are no trade-offs to be had between this ideal and the imperatives of instrumental rationality. The latter inevitably requires us to define desert in terms extrinsic to this disembodied virtue that the law purports to be safeguarding.

In a similar vein, Mark Kelman and Gillian Lester have objected that the multicultural left manipulates anti-discrimination law, disguising what should be conceptualized as redistributive justice claims as anti-discrimination claims. Thus, advocates for the disabled will defend their demands for accommodations in the name of the individual's "potential," but "[p]otential is nothing more than realized output given certain inputs, just as productivity is net, not gross, productivity." The concept of "potential" is, on this view, no more than an arbitrary abstraction which has been lifted out of the chain of economic relations—and therefore the costs of accommodating a disabled employee—within which it could carry a non-arbitrary meaning.

But this, I argue, follows only on a reductionistic and economistic construal of this concept. "True merit," or whatever it is called, is indeed a social fiction, but is also an essential source of dignity in a democratic society, and so one which the law has understandably sought to uphold where it could. This ideal, I argue, may be best understood as a secularized, democratized, and naturalized variant of the notion of predestined salvation, which Weber associated with the Protestant Work Ethic. Secularizing this ideal, anti-discrimination law helps safeguard social identities from submersion in the external contingencies that would otherwise threaten them. Capitalism cannot assure that individuals are always positioned to take what they need, but its social legitimacy depends on upholding the other half of Marx's motto, by assuring individuals opportunities to give what they can, even if that sometimes means defining essential job tasks in a way that dictates what others may legitimately want of them.

Anti-discrimination law will indeed define essential job tasks in ways that are arguably artificial and arbitrary. However, these inconsistencies reflect not simply the gaming of the system, but the fact that the law can only selectively uphold the ideal of genuine merit, since the cultural meanings implicated in the particular case must be such as to render the Noble Lie believable. True merit is indeed fictional, but not any more fictional than the self to which it is imputed.

- ***Intellectual Honesty: An Ethnocentric Ideal?***

Asking what conquered the Christian God, Nietzsche answers that it was "Christian morality itself, the concept of truthfulness taken more and more strictly, the confessional subtlety of the Christian conscience translated and sublimated into the scientific conscience, into intellectual cleanliness at any price." Would the truth of this claim undermine the grounds for upholding intellectual honesty as a universal ideal? Can we meaningfully speak of non-Western cultures, or even certain Western subcultures, as possessing their own standards of rationality, or does this proposition simply contradict the very core of what rationality means?

I seek to answer these questions by examining the responses of Peter Winch and Charles Taylor to Evans-Pritchard's rendition of the Azande tribe's witchcraft-centered belief-system, in his famous *Witchcraft, Oracles, and Magic among the Azande.* While seemingly logical in certain contexts, the Azande also tolerate self-evident contradictions among some of their beliefs. Is this tolerance irrational, or is it appropriate to a different form of life with an indigenous standard of rationality? I attempt to chart a middle ground between these positions, arguing that while we cannot simply regard our ideal of rationality as but one among many, this ideal may be expanded as we attain a broader conception of essential human potentialities. However, our paramount commitment to the ideal of intellectual honesty fundamentally limits our sympathy for the practices of peoples like the Azande, whose willingness to sacrifice intellectual honesty for emotional equanimity must strike those not so willing as religiously offensive.

- ***Between Cynicism and Idealism: Nietzsche and the Slandering of Human Nature***

In this paper, I seek to reconcile what appear like two conflicting strands of Nietzsche's moral psychology. Much of it seems in agreement with psychological egoists like Hobbes and La Rochefoucauld. But at other times Nietzsche suggests that human agents are motivated by values, not calculating self-interest. Moreover, Nietzsche makes it clear that his idealized free-spirit will inculcate others with life-enhancing lives, possibly sacrificing himself in the process. I argue that the mature Nietzsche is ultimately not a psychological egoist. Rather than arguing for the ineluctability of egoism, Nietzsche traces the concept of egoism to slave morality in order to identify the psychological context within which it became a useful tool for conceptualizing human motivation. Far from defending psychological egoism, Nietzsche wishes to demonstrate why this theory is appealing to a certain kind of person.

EXHIBIT C: SET 1

Slide 1

© 2011Stanford University http://www.stanford.edu   Mostly Cloudy, 53 ° F.

Dean Larry Kramer lecturing; close-up of Dean Larry Kramer lecturing

Slide 2

© 2011Stanford University http://www.stanford.edu   Mostly Cloudy, 53 ° F.

Professor Joe Bankman chatting with a student; random students in class

Slide 3

© 2011Stanford University http://www.stanford.edu   Mostly Cloudy, 52 ° F.

Random students in class; Professor Mark Kelman lecturing

Slide 4

© 2011Stanford University http://www.stanford.edu

Mostly Cloudy, 53 ° F.

Professor Jayashri Srikantiah counseling students;
former dean Kathleen Sullivan lecturing

Slide 5

© 2011Stanford University http://www.stanford.edu

Mostly Cloudy, 52 ° F.

Professor Norman Spaulding chatting with students; different angle of Professor Norman Spaulding chatting with the same students

Slide 6

© 2011Stanford University http://www.stanford.edu

Mostly Cloudy, 52 ° F.

Professor Norman Spaulding lecturing; random students in class

Slide 7

© 2011Stanford University http://www.stanford.edu

Mostly Cloudy, 52 ° F

Random students chatting

Slide 8

© 2011Stanford University http://www.stanford.edu

Mostly Cloudy, 53 ° F

Random students in the library

EXHIBIT D: SET 2

Slide 1

 Fair, 59 ° F.

Dean Larry Kramer lecturing

Slide 2

 Fair, 57 ° F.

Former dean Kathleen Sullivan lecturing

Slide 3

 Fair, 57 ° F.

Deceased chief justice of the U.S. Supreme Court William Rehnquist, an alumnus of Stanford Law

Slide 4

 Fair, 59 ° F.

Random students chatting outside the law school

Slide 5

© 2011Stanford University http://www.stanford.edu Fair, 57 ° F.

Cyclists riding by the law school

Slide 6

© 2011Stanford University http://www.stanford.edu Fair, 57 ° F.

Random students in the library

Slide 7

Fair, 57 ° F.

A stack of law books

Slide 8

Fair, 57 ° F.

Random students chatting

EXHIBIT E: THE PREAMBLE

 Mostly Cloudy, 52 ° F.

EXHIBIT F: RATIONAL CRITIQUE OF STANFORD LAW HOME PAGE OLIGOPOLY

RATIONAL CRITIQUE OF STANFORD LAW HOME PAGE OLIGOPOLY

(distributed 02/14/11)

By Rony Guldmann
James C. Gaither Fellow (retired)
Alumnus, Class of 2008
Stanford Law School

1. Introduction

I am writing as an alumnus of Stanford Law School and a former Stanford Law fellow to convey my reservations about what I've noticed has been a change of policy in the management of the law school's homepage, which as you know broadcasts our spirit and ideals, not only to students, staff, faculty, and alumni, but to the entire world as well. If I remember correctly, the policy up until some fifteen or sixteen months ago was to rotate the picture sets of professors, students, etc. with some degree of frequency, so that the public might be introduced to the entire range of our distinguished and emerging scholars.

Two noteworthy changes appear to have transpired since that time. Firstly, the rotations have ceased, in consequence of which we're seeing the very same professors today as we were over a year ago. Secondly, the system appears to have been bifurcated, so that which picture set comes up will depend on which computer you happen to be using.

2. Facts on the Ground

The situation as it now stands appears to be as follows:

a. **Set 1**: Most non-Stanford connections so far as I can tell present us with:

i. Dean Larry Kramer
ii. Erstwhile Dean Kathleen Sullivan
iii. Joe Bankman
iv. Mark Kelman
v. Norman Spaulding
vi. Norman Spaulding
vii. Random students and a plausible candidate for a career counselor

b. **Set 2**: All Stanford connections and some non-Stanford connections present us with:

i. Dean Larry Kramer
ii. Erstwhile Dean Kathleen Sullivan
iii. Deceased Chief Justice and SLS graduate William Rehnquist
iv. A different set of random students and an indisputable monument

3. The Complaint

I certainly don't want to blow any of this out of proportion, as it's entirely conceivable that these changes of official policy admit of rationales of which I couldn't possibly be aware. Nevertheless, I thought it appropriate to bring the matter to your attention and to provide you with my own perspective as an alumnus who has many fond memories of many great professors—who I believe are entitled to more airtime than the present policy permits, with the aforementioned faculty enjoying what strikes me as an unprecedented oligopoly on the homepage and on the attendant publicity. This is not, so far as I know, the practice of any other top law school in the country (though I haven't studied it scientifically). Nor have I discerned any analogous mutations in the customs of my other alma maters, the University of Michigan and Indiana University.

a. **Set 1**

As to Set 1, let me stress that Larry Kramer and Joe Bankman are without a doubt among my very favorite professors, just as the writings of Kathleen Sullivan and Mark Kelman have inspired some of my own academic research. Nor are Norman Spaulding's scholarly contributions to be disputed, though I'm less well acquainted with them. Nevertheless,

I believe that all this is outweighed by the importance of communicating the *full* spectrum of Stanford's many accomplished scholars—and therefore scholarly innovations and teaching excellences—to the general public. That kind of comprehensiveness and ecumenicism is the hallmark of a great law school, and is something that could be advertised more effectively than the present policy permits.

There is concededly an argument to be made for keeping Dean Kramer in perpetual view, given his present role, just as there is one for maintaining Kathleen Sullivan's perennial presence, given her former role. But it's not obvious what distinguishes Joe Bankman, Mark Kelman, and Norman Spaulding from any number of other outstanding faculty, who deserve their fair share of the limelight too. Nor is it obvious why Norman Spaulding should be entitled to twice the coverage as anyone else. He's as good as they get, to be sure, which is why I'm not defaming him when I say that he's not *twice* as good as they get—the message that I feel is being communicated at present. Set 1 is moreover at odds with the law school's longstanding commitment to faculty diversity (and by extension student diversity via role modeling), marked as it is by an overrepresentation of Jews, an underrepresentation of women, and *no representation whatsoever* of any non-white minorities. It therefore promotes *exactly* the stereotypes which any self-respecting law school should be fighting to erode or eliminate.

b. **Set 2**

I do, however, support the change in policy toward the internal Stanford connections, given

i. that our own students already understand everything I've been saying,
ii. that showcasing our very greatest may help remind them of the heights to which they too should aspire, and
iii. that the pattern possesses an aesthetic and conceptual coherence (all black and white; heads of SLS, head of SCOTUS) which Set 1 lacks—at least as far as the reasonable observer can tell.

4. The Preamble

I also support what was an ephemeral change of policy transpiring during the first half of January 2011, when the sets described above were supplemented by the Preamble to the Constitution, which likewise communicates the right message to both our students and the world, because

a. it is our highest law,
b. Stanford's constitutional scholars—like Larry Kramer, Kathleen Sullivan, and Michael McConnell to name a few—are among the very best there are, and
c. Constitutional Law is my favorite subject (just kidding).

5. A Worthy Aspiration

I would also suggest that the new bifurcation be effectuated with greater precision, so as to eliminate any discrepancies between different non-Stanford connections (if that's technologically feasible and cost-effective), as these variations appear lacking in any rational basis.

6. Summary of Recommendations

In summation, my recommendations are:

a. Perfect bifurcation if possible.
b. Maintain status quo on all internal Stanford connections (Set 2).
c. Reinstate rotations on non-Stanford connections (Set 1), at least with respect to the slots presently occupied by Bankman, Kelman, and Spaulding, if not also those held by Kramer and Sullivan.
    i. Rotating four of the faculty slots would permit each member of the SLS faculty approximately 20 days of coverage a year.
    ii. Rotating all six would permit approximately 29.
        1. These numbers make stark the extent to which the status quo deviates from any reasonable standard of ideal competition.
d. Prohibit any professor (not just Spaulding) from occupying more than one slot at a time in any rotated set (at least absent special cause).

e. Institute diversity best practices on all non-Stanford connections.
f. Reinstate the Preamble uninterruptedly on all connections.

7. Conclusion

Thank you for your time and patience. I recognize that it is unusual for an alumnus to concern himself with an ostensibly routine matter of daily institutional administration. But the routine matter in question implicates broader concerns that are within the legitimate purview of any vigilant alumnus, as I've maintained from the outset. On the other hand, let me also reiterate that I trust any decision you render will be sensible, as I'm operating with just common sense and nothing more. Please feel free to contact me at guldmann@stanford.edu if I can provide any needed clarification or elaboration on what I would defend as

a. a more rational policy than exists at present (given the generally agreed upon purposes of law school homepages),
b. a more egalitarian arrangement that will more effectively serve the best interests of the law school as a whole, not merely those of select constituencies thereof, and
c. a pragmatic reconciliation of conflicting values that promises to combine the best of both the old and new paradigms.

No doubt, there are those who would dismiss all these worries as a needless distraction from more important things. But my own opinion is that anything which is worth doing is also worth doing right, and therefore also worth thinking through—and the solution in this case is just as costless as the problem may appear to be trivial. And speaking of costs, I will now conclude my musings by just noting that I do *not* favor the imposition of any penalties on the former oligopolists, as it's better to just break up the trust and move on, whatever the *mens rea* may have been.

APPENDIX 2

Memorandum of Law Concerning the Memoirist's Claims

Introduction

"Whether a statement is reasonably susceptible of an interpretation which implies a provably false assertion of fact—the dispositive question in a defamation action—is a question of law for the court." *Isuzu Motors Ltd. v. Consumers Union of United States, Inc.*, 12 F. Supp. 2d 1035, 1045 (C.D. Cal. 1998) (internal quotes and citations omitted). Accordingly, any claims of defamation against Rony Guldmann ("the Memoirist") arising from statements in *The Star Chamber of Stanford* ("the Memoir") would have to be dismissed for failure to state a claim, as his potentially controversial statements are all protected opinions, not actionable assertions of fact. More precisely, they consist in either (1) subjective impressions not susceptible to factual adjudication or (2) reasoned conjectures for which he does not claim to have conclusive proof. Both such statements are protected speech under the First Amendment. Given the Memoirist's consistently precise and circumspect language, no reasonable reader could be led to overlook his statements' subjective dimensions, which he takes pains to highlight.

Even if the Memoirist's claims could be read as statements of fact—and they cannot—they still would not carry a defamatory meaning given that his characterizations of any Would-Be Plaintiffs are largely favorable or neutral. Insofar as they are critical, they form part of the Memoir's broad cultural criticisms, which are not actionable. *See Weinstein v. Bullick*, 827 F. Supp. 1193, 1196 (E.D. Pa. 1993) ("The threshold question in a defamation action is whether the publication is capable of defamatory meaning. Whether a broadcast can be understood as defamatory is for the court to decide.").

Even if Would-Be Plaintiffs could plausibly allege that the Memoir contains provably false statements of fact that lend themselves to a defamatory interpretation—and they cannot—they still could not allege that this interpretation has been adopted on a widespread basis that could have resulted in tangible injury. Further, Would-Be Plaintiffs cannot prove, or even plausibly allege, that the Memoirist reached his conclusions either maliciously or negligently, which they must to recover damages.

Finally, because any defamation claims against the Memoirist would be transparently frivolous, they would amount to strategic litigation instigated solely to harass and stifle him in the exercise of his First Amendment rights. Accordingly, they would be subject to an anti-SLAPP (Strategic Lawsuit Against Public Participation) motion (jurisdiction permitting). For similar reasons, filing attorneys and their clients could be subject to Rule 11 sanctions (or analogous state law sanctions) should they fail to investigate the publication as a whole—including its intellectual dimensions, which shape the total context of any challenged statements, informing their meaning for the reasonable reader.

Argument

I. The Memoirist's Claims Are Nonactionable Opinion

The Memoirist's claims constitute nonactionable statements of opinion because he is fully transparent to his readers, at every turn making them aware of the degree of subjective certitude he asserts and his reasons for asserting it. There is no insinuation or innuendo. The Memoirist both introduces his claims as a theory and then unpacks them through a personal narrative that displays their subjective dimensions to the reasonable reader. He does not merely designate his statements as opinions but *shows* this by laying bare the train of thought that led him to form those opinions. *See Aviation Charter, Inc. v. Aviation Research Grp./US*, 416 F.3d 864, 870 (8th Cir. 2005) ("although ARGUS's comparison relies in part on objectively verifiable data, the interpretation of those data was ultimately a subjective assessment, not an objectively verifiable fact. ARGUS's *description of its process illustrates the subjective component of its assessment*") (emphasis added). From start to finish the Memoirist meticulously details the precise circumstances that gave rise to his beliefs. By providing a step-by-step chronicle of how specific empirical perceptions combined with his larger philosophical worldview to lead him to his conclusions, he leaves readers free to make of these what they will. *See* Restatement (Second) of Torts § 566 cmt. c (Am. Law Inst. 1977) ("A simple expression of opinion based on disclosed or assumed nondefamatory facts is not itself sufficient for an action of defamation, no matter how unjustified and unreasonable the opinion may be or how derogatory it is."); *Mathias v. Carpenter*, 402 Pa. Super. 358, 364–65 (Pa. Super. Ct. 1991) ("[A]ll the facts upon which the author based his opinion were disclosed. ... The reasonable reader, having access to the facts on which the comparison was based, could decide for himself or herself whether the facts supported the writer's comparison.").

The Memoirist cannot be accused of employing subjective language as cover for the insinuation of undisclosed facts. Given that his opinions invite incredulity on their face, his efforts to sway readers to them compel him to fully disclose his grounds for holding them. He can have no incentive to disguise undisclosed facts as opinions when it is impossible even to understand the nature of his opinions without a robust articulation of their full factual background. *See Biro v. Condé Nast*, 883 F. Supp. 2d 441, 461 (S.D.N.Y. 2012) ("[A] statement of opinion that is based on undisclosed facts is potentially actionable because it carries with it an implicit statement of those facts. On the other hand, a proffered hypothesis that is offered after a full recitation of the facts on which it is based is readily understood by the audience as conjecture.") (internal quotes and citation omitted); *Nicosia v. De Rooy*, 72 F. Supp. 2d 1093, 1105 (N.D. Cal. 1999) ("Nicosia argues that De Rooy's accusations of dishonesty imply assertions of fact which were never disclosed. The record, however, is replete with examples where De Rooy identifies specific representations by Nicosia and then reveals her basis for believing that such representations are inaccurate or false.").

A. Provably False Statements About Verifiable Facts May Still Constitute Nonactionable Opinion

Even if Would-Be Plaintiffs could plausibly allege that the challenged statements are provably false, such statements still constitute nonactionable opinion when the speaker discloses the limits of his or her substantiation, which the Memoirist does consistently. *See Ayyadurai v. Floor 64, Inc.*, 270 F. Supp. 3d 343, 360 (D. Mass. 2017) ("even a provably false statement is not actionable if it is plain that the speaker is expressing a subjective view, an interpretation, a theory, or surmise, rather than claiming to be in possession of objectively verifiable facts") (internal quotes and citation omitted); *Potomac Valve & Fitting, Inc. v. Crawford Fitting Co.*, 829 F.2d 1280, 1288 (4th Cir. 1987) ("[W]e reject the suggestion, advanced by the plaintiffs in this case, that any 'question of fact' which can be decided by a jury can be actionable as defamation. ... We hold that a verifiable statement ... nevertheless qualifies as an 'opinion' *if it is clear ... that a reasonable reader or listener would recognize its weakly substantiated or subjective character*—and discount it accordingly.") (emphasis added); *Chapin v. Knight-Ridder, Inc.*, 993 F.2d 1087, 1093 (4th Cir. 1993) ("even [a] statement capable of being proved false would be understood as author's opinion where it was a conclusory punch line following fully-disclosed facts") (citing *Potomac Valve*, 829 F.2d at 1289–90); *Phantom Touring, Inc. v. Affiliated Publ'ns*, 953 F.2d 724, 729 (1st Cir. 1992) ("Whether or not the allegation of intentional deception meets the 'provable as true or false' criterion, however, we think the context of each article rendered the language not reasonably interpreted as stating 'actual facts' about appellant's honesty. The sum effect of the format, tone and entire content of the articles is to make it unmistakably clear that Kelly was expressing a point of view only. As such, the challenged language is immune from liability.").

The Memoirist makes clear to reasonable readers which facts he asserts as provable (e.g., the email record), which facts he claims to know from direct experience but cannot prove (e.g., oral communications that left no record), and which facts he asserts solely on the basis of inference and conjecture (e.g., his having been gaslighted). Because readers are given to understand the epistemic status of each proffered fact, the Memoirist's claims are protected First Amendment speech, whether capable of being proved false or not. The challenged statements may *concern* facts that are in principle verifiable under certain conditions. But reasonable readers would not take the Memoirist to be "in possession" of those facts, because it is abundantly clear that he arrived at them through inference rather than immediate knowledge. *Ayyadurai*, 270 F. Supp. 3d at 360. The facts, if true, would constitute an objective feature of the physical universe that is theoretically verifiable. But the Memoirist lets it be known that they are unverifiable from his own finite standpoint, which is based on reasoned conjectures drawn from the limited information available to him. Reasonable readers could not be led to think that he has any proof for his conjectures beyond the evidence he lays out for their consideration. *See Haynes v. Alfred A. Knopf, Inc.*, 8 F.3d 1222, 1227 (7th Cir. 1993) ("Luther drank heavily; the proposition that a man's heavy drinking can, and that Luther's heavy drinking did, damage a fetus is represented in the book merely as Ruby's conjecture. A reasonable reader *would not suppose that she had proof*") (emphasis added).

Furthermore, while the Memoirist's conjectures regarding events in the world may be verifiable or falsifiable under some unlikely set of conditions, they remain nonactionable insofar as they stem from his inferences regarding the motives of various actors, statements about which are per se nonactionable. *See id.* ("[A]nyone is entitled to speculate on a person's motives from the known facts of his behavior."). If the Memoirist is entitled to speculate on other actors' motives, then he is also entitled to speculate on actions that he believes arose from those motives—so long as he discloses what he understands the relationship between the motive and the action to be, which he does consistently.

B. The Memoirist's Statements Are Protected Opinion Even If Their Disclosed Factual Underpinnings Are Contestable

Would-Be Plaintiffs may rejoin that even if statements capable of being proved false can qualify as opinions, the Memoirist's opinions are actionable insofar as the postulated facts underpinning them are false. However, this is merely to say that Would-Be Plaintiffs recollect certain conversations and encounters differently than does the Memoirist. A memoir is definitionally about distant memories, and reasonable readers understand that these are fallible, can conflict, and must often be taken on faith. The Memoirist expressly defines his opinions' factual underpinnings as "the facts as recollected from direct sensory experience" or as the "sensory data" (see introduction), thereby alerting readers to those underpinnings' subjective dimension. *See Information Control Corp. v. Genesis One Computer Corp.*, 611 F.2d 781, 784 (9th Cir. 1980) (a statement phrased in language of apparency "is less likely to be understood as a statement of fact rather than as a statement of opinion"); *Gregory v. McDonnell Douglas Corp.*, 17 Cal. 3d 596, 603 (1976) (a letter "cautiously phrased in terms of apparency" did not imply factual assertions).

Even if Would-Be Plaintiffs could plausibly dispute the truth of the Memoirist's recollections, they cannot dispute that these are in fact his recollections, which is how he introduces his opinions' factual predicates to readers. *See Partington v. Bugliosi*, 56 F.3d 1147, 1156–57 (9th Cir. 1995) ("we join with the other courts of appeals in concluding that when an author outlines the *facts available to him*, thus making it clear that the challenged statements represent his own interpretation of those facts and leaving the reader free to draw his own conclusions, those statements are generally protected by the First Amendment") (emphasis added).

The Memoirist furthermore puts readers on notice that his telling of events will likely be contested and that he cannot corroborate every recounted experience upon which his conjectures are premised. Because they arose in real-time interaction, rather than digitally, some of the proffered facts simply left no record of any kind. Readers are expressly charged with judging the Memoirist's credibility regarding these (see introduction), which they can do from their overall impression of his motives, tone, and reasoning, deciding for themselves whether the recounted experiences ring true with their larger worldviews and life experiences. *See Ollman v. Evans*, 750 F.2d 970, 983 (D.C. Cir. 1984) ("[We] cannot forget that the public has an interest in receiving information on issues of public importance even if the trustworthiness of the information is not absolutely certain. The First Amendment is served not only by articles and columns that purport to be definitive but by those articles that, more modestly, raise questions and prompt investigation or debate.").

The Memoirist would be misleading readers were he to foster the sense that his opinions' declared factual underpinnings should go unquestioned. But he expressly alerts, and then repeatedly reminds, readers that those underpinnings are open to dispute. Indeed, the predicate facts' disputability is itself among the major threads of the storyline—for example, the "plausible deniability" of the conspiracy—so it cannot be lost on reasonable readers. The Memoir's recurring nomenclature—such as the distinction between the official and unofficial realities and between "interpretation 1" and "interpretation 2" of the latter—repeatedly foregrounds that both the facts and their interpretation are up for debate and that the Memoirist is merely staking out his own position within that debate. *See Partington*, 56 F.3d at 1154 (when "an author writing about a controversial occurrence fairly describes the general events involved and offers his personal perspective about some of its ambiguities and *disputed facts*, his statements should generally be protected by the First Amendment") (emphasis added).

Accordingly, that an opinion's disclosed factual underpinnings are contestable does not ipso facto transmogrify that opinion into an actionable statement of fact. Allegations of falsity arising from conflicting memories of private encounters long past do not truly raise questions of verifiable fact. Absent secret recordings, it will typically be impossible to adjudicate such disagreements. Moreover, every opinion presupposes a gamut of disclosed or assumed facts some portion of which will be contestable. The principle that statements of conjecture remain nonactionable only inasmuch as all their factual predicates are incontrovertible would swallow the rule that conjecture is protected speech and perversely incentivize speakers to *limit* the disclosure of what they sincerely believe are the facts. The more they disclosed, the greater would be a plaintiff's opportunity to contest some detail of the total factual background being presented and then argue that the terminus of the speaker's deductions no longer qualifies as protected opinion.

The issue on a motion to dismiss is not whether some subset of an opinion's declared or implied factual underpinnings are contestable but whether those underpinnings are presented in a way that allows the audience to independently assess them. "[A]n opinion which is unfounded reveals its lack of merit when the opinion-holder discloses the factual basis for the idea; readers are free to accept or reject the author's opinion based on their *own independent evaluation of the facts.*" *Standing Comm. on Discipline of the United States Dist. Court v. Yagman*, 55 F.3d 1430, 1439 (9th Cir. 1995) (emphasis added) (internal quotes and citation omitted). Reasonable readers evaluate not only conclusions drawn from facts but also the postulated facts themselves. So long as the speaker truthfully reports the basis of his representations—for example, recollection versus email record versus public statement—he enables readers to independently evaluate their likely veracity. Statements based on contestable, allegedly false, facts are actionable when those facts are not disclosed, not when they are disclosed as contestable and then, in fact, contested. *See Redco Corp. v. CBS, Inc.*, 758 F.2d 970, 972 (3rd Cir. 1985) ("[I]f an opinion is stated in a manner that implies that it draws upon unstated facts for its basis, the listener is unable to make an evaluation of the soundness of the opinion. *In such circumstances*, if the underlying facts are false, the Constitution does not protect the opinion.") (emphasis added).

"A statement of opinion based on fully disclosed facts can be punished only if the stated facts are themselves false *and* demeaning." *Standing Comm. on Discipline*, 55 F.3d at 1439 (emphasis added). Even if Would-Be Plaintiffs could plausibly allege that the Memoirist's disclosed facts are false, they cannot allege that they are demeaning, as they are generally favorable or neutral and typically concern what seem like quotidian academic encounters. Opinions based on disclosed facts that are *both* false and demeaning can be defamatory because such facts can prejudice readers against the plaintiff, militating against a dispassionate evaluation of the opinion. In contrast, postulated facts that are contestable and allegedly false but not demeaning have no such effect and instead leave readers free to reach their own conclusions about both the facts and the inferences the speaker draws from them. *See also Cochran v. NYP Holdings, Inc.*, 58 F. Supp. 2d 1113, 1122 (C.D. Cal. 1998), *aff'd and adopted*, 210 F.3d 1036 (9th Cir. 2000) ("The facts underlying the subject of the alleged defamatory statement are disclosed in the [segment] and are not themselves alleged to be defamatory."); *Dodds v. American Broadcasting Co.*, 145 F.3d 1053, 1067 (9th Cir. 1998) ("an opinion based on an implication arising from disclosed facts is not actionable when the disclosed facts themselves are not actionable").

It is true that "[e]ven if the speaker states the facts upon which he bases his opinion, if those facts are either incorrect or incomplete, or if his assessment of them is erroneous, the statement *may* still imply a false assertion of fact." *Milkovich v. Lorain Journal Co.*, 497 U.S. 1, 18–19 (1990) (emphasis added). However, whether allegedly false predicate facts actually transmute the opinion premised on them into an allegedly false statement of fact in any given instance depends on the logical relationship between the predicate facts and the opinion. In some cases the truth of the opinion follows almost ineluctably from the truth of its predicate facts—for example, "Jones entered his neighbor's house when no one was home and walked out with a television. In my opinion, Jones is a thief." Here, the "opinion" is more or less a restatement of the facts and there is only the question of whether Jones truly acted as alleged. In such circumstances disclosed facts function no differently than implied undisclosed ones and offer no First Amendment protection apart from their truth. Their disclosure does not, standing alone, immunize the speaker from liability and warrant dismissal of the complaint.

But, in the instant case, the Memoirist's theorized gaslighting at Stanford Law School would remain a bona fide conjecture even if readers were to somehow disregard his disclaimers (and good sense) and treat the gaslighting's declared factual underpinnings as incontrovertible. Those underpinnings contribute to the plausibility of the Memoirist's conclusions, but their factual truth would not make his conclusions any less conjectural (as it would in the foregoing example). That is what disclosing the assumed facts discloses to the reasonable reader. A jury that adjudicated the Memoirist's recollection of some conversation as false might then be less inclined to believe conjectures that are based in part on that recollection, but this jury would be gauging the plausibility of his conjectures, not the truth of any factual assertions. *See ZL Techs., Inc. v. Gartner, Inc.*, 709 F. Supp. 2d 789, 798 (N.D. Cal. 2010) ("Most opinions are based at least in part on facts. That Gartner considered facts in forming its opinions does not mean that the opinions are objectively verifiable.").

While various contestable details of the total factual background may help explain how the Memoirist arrived at his conclusions, they do not explain why he retained them. As detailed from chapter 5 onward, he retained them because they enabled falsifiable yet unfalsified predictions that no one not in his position would have thought to make or considered sensible. Those predictions are, therefore, the core factual predicates of the Memoirist's conclusions, and he fully discloses them to readers. Because the predictions formed part of the Memoirist's inner mental life, Would-Be Plaintiffs have no basis for impugning his reports of them. And because he furthermore adduces his predictions as a reason to trust the recollected perceptions underlying the hypothesis that the predictions tested (see chapter 8), the accuracy of his recollections is itself the thesis of an argument rather than an assertion of incontrovertible fact. The Memoirist argues that paranoid ideation could not have yielded his falsifiable yet unfalsified predictions and that the recollected facts that had enabled those predictions can therefore be trusted. If reasonable readers agree, that is because they have been persuaded by this argument, not because the Memoirist has somehow coaxed them to treat his distant memories as an infallible record of indisputable facts.

C. Subjective Character of the Memoir's Claims Is Reinforced by Its Overall Tone and Structure

The foregoing points are supported by the Memoir's overall tone and structure. Already on the back cover, the Memoirist announces himself as a conspiracy theorist, thus putting readers on notice that they would be within their rights to approach his claims with skepticism. Given that secret trials and invisible persecutions are by nature unverifiable, the Memoir's subtitle conveys the same. As a psychological claim, the Memoirist's alleged gaslighting by representatives of Stanford Law School is inherently conjectural, so reasonable readers cannot conclude that he arrived at this allegation other than through conjecture. The Memoir cannot be read as anything other than an extended statement of opinion when its entire purpose is to chronicle how the Memoirist formed, and why he retained, certain opinions in the face of an uncertain and ambiguous situation. He has simply drawn out a sequence of inferences from his own sensory experiences, recorded that mental process on paper, and shared the results with interested others. If these activities are not protected by the First Amendment, then nothing is.

Not every sentence in the Memoir is prefaced with "I think" or some other acknowledgment of subjectivity. But the reasonable reader understands that so prefacing every statement would make for stilted prose, and the subjectivity is conveyed by the total context of any challenged statements, which communicates that the Memoir is a personal and political manifesto that does not purport to be an exercise in objective reportage. *See Ramsey v. Glassie Pewett Dudley Beebe & Shanks*, 1988 U.S. App. LEXIS 20347, at *3 (4th Cir. Aug. 18, 1988) ("we conclude that Bremer's remark was a non-actionable statement of opinion even if he did not preface it with 'I suppose'"); *Ollman*, 750 F.2d at 983 ("Some types of writing by custom or convention signal to readers that what is being read is likely to be opinion, not fact.").

Concededly, "there is authority against giving weight to cautionary or interrogatory language," as "it would be destructive of the law of libel if a writer could escape liability for accusations of crime simply by using, explicitly or implicitly, the words 'I think.'" *Id.* (quoting *Cianci v. New Times Pub. Co.*, 639 F.2d 54, 64 (2nd Cir. 1980)). But while cautionary and interrogatory language can sometimes be deployed cosmetically without affecting the statement's purport, that is patently not so with the Memoir, which acknowledges subjectivity in order to spur readers to reflection, not as window dressing.

Not only does the Memoirist "leav[e] the reader free to draw his own conclusions," he actively encourages this, routinely articulating likely objections to his viewpoint and then explaining why he is not persuaded by them. *Partington*, 56 F.3d at 1156–57. Allowing that his interpretations may be reasonably disputed, he argues only that they are more defensible than the alternatives, which he contends are less cogent than they appear at first blush. *See Phantom Touring*, 953 F.2d at 730 ("Of greatest importance … is the breadth of Kelly's articles, which not only discussed all the facts underlying his views but also gave information from which readers might draw contrary conclusions. In effect, the articles offered a self-contained give-and-take, a kind of verbal debate … Because all sides of the issue, as well as the rationale for Kelly's view, were exposed, the assertion of deceit reasonably could be understood only as Kelly's personal conclusion about the information presented, not as a statement of fact.").

D. The Memoir Promotes Core First Amendment Values

In challenging readers to critically reflect upon his claims, the Memoirist turns their attention to a panoply of social and cultural issues, especially in connection with the intellectual world (as shown by the bibliography). Indeed, he routinely interrupts the narrative in order to spell out how his larger philosophical worldview informs his interpretations of specific events. Two chapters are devoted solely to this purpose. In addition, readers interested in a further elaboration of the ideas guiding the Memoirist's inferences are invited to access drafts of the 97,000-word *Critical Theory of Academia* and the 296,000-word *Conservative Claims of Cultural Oppression* from his website.

Because it is impossible to evaluate his claims without simultaneously reflecting upon certain ideas, the Memoirist vigorously promotes core First Amendment values. The free circulation of ideas is a core First Amendment concern, and that provides any challenged statements with an additional layer of protection. *See Hustler Magazine v. Falwell*, 485 U.S. 46, 50–51 (1988) ("At the heart of the First Amendment is the recognition of the fundamental importance of the free flow of ideas and opinions on matters of public interest and concern. … We have therefore been particularly vigilant to ensure that individual expressions of ideas remain free from governmentally imposed sanctions."); *Bose Corp. v. Consumers Union*, 466 U.S. 485, 503–4 (1984) ("The First Amendment presupposes that the freedom to speak one's mind is not only an aspect of individual liberty – and thus a good unto itself – but also is essential to the common quest for truth and the vitality of society as a whole."); *Abrams v. United States*, 250 U.S. 616, 630 (1919) ("when men have realized that time has upset many fighting faiths, they may come to believe even more than they believe the very foundations of their own conduct that the ultimate good desired is better reached by free trade in ideas—that the best test of truth is the power of the thought to get itself accepted in the competition of the market") (Holmes, J., dissenting).

E. The Memoir's Cover, Spine, and Back Cover Blurb Do Not Imply Verifiable Facts

The Memoir's cover, spine, and back cover blurb are also not actionable, even when considered apart from the text inside. The title and subtitle do not imply defamatory facts because they do not imply facts of any kind. Seeing as the historical Court of Star Chamber sat in England and was abolished by Parliament in 1641, reasonable readers will conclude that the Memoirist is employing the term *star chamber* in a figurative sense, not that Stanford University convenes a literal star chamber court, whatever that would mean. The same is true of the subtitle. Given that universities lack the legal, political, or military power to initiate secret trials, it is again plain that the Memoirist is introducing metaphors that will be developed by the narrative and then reflected upon by readers—not implying undisclosed facts. The physical impossibility of a literal invisible persecution makes it doubly clear that the subtitle is not susceptible to a literal interpretation. So, too, does the Memoir's fantastical cover art, whose surreality will inform readers' understanding of the title and subtitle. *See Duboff v. Playboy Enters. Int'l, Inc.*, 2007 U.S. Dist. LEXIS 50717, at *23–24 (D. Or. June 26, 2007) ("the statements are 'no more than rhetorical hyperbole,' 'parody,' or 'loose' or 'figurative' speech, which is not actionable.") (quoting *Milkovich*, 497 U.S. at 16–17); *Standing Comm. on Discipline*, 55 F.3d at 1438 ("Even statements that at first blush appear to be factual are protected by the First Amendment if they cannot reasonably be interpreted as stating actual facts about their target. ... Thus, statements of 'rhetorical hyperbole' aren't sanctionable, nor are statements that use language in a 'loose, figurative sense.'") (citation omitted); *Ollman*, 750 F.2d at 982 ("An article or column, however, plainly does not have to include a complete set of facts to make it clear that a statement is being used in a metaphorical, exaggerated or even fantastic sense.").

The title and subtitle function to spur curiosity, not to imply facts, and they can spur curiosity precisely because they do not imply facts. Reasonable readers glimpsing the title or subtitle alone could form no opinion regarding their truth, as they would not even understand what they would be opining about. The title and subtitle, like the cover art, might convey the general idea that something problematic transpired at Stanford, but they cannot "produce a specific image of depraved conduct," as is required to allege defamation. *Cianci*, 639 F.2d at 64.

Likewise with the blurb on the back cover, which describes the Memoirist's experiences and not the actions of Would-Be Plaintiffs, who are identified only in the text, where statements concerning them will be understood as opinion, as discussed. Taken in isolation, statements in the blurb are too obscure to gain the assent of a reasonable reader, who will not know quite what to make of them. Like the title, subtitle, and cover art, their impact is purely emotive. The "gaslighting" alleged in those statements is an inherently imprecise term that, admitting of a panoply of clinical, political, and other meanings, does not allow for factual adjudication. *See Buckley v. Littell*, 539 F.2d 882, 893 (2nd Cir. 1976) ("the use of 'fascist,' 'fellow traveler' and 'radical right' as political labels … cannot be regarded as having been proved to be statements of fact, among other reasons, because of the tremendous imprecision of the meaning and usage of these terms in the realm of political debate"). Gaslighting is, furthermore, a psychological concept designating certain subjective motivations, comment upon which is ipso facto not actionable, as already noted. *See Nicosia*, 72 F. Supp. 2d at 1106 ("Manipulation … refers to subjective motivations and personality traits, which are not provable as true or false").

II. The Memoir's Claims Are Not Defamatory Even If Misread as Statements of Fact

Statements in the Memoir do not allow for a defamatory interpretation even when misread as assertions of ascertained fact rather than reasoned conjectures. In California "[l]ibel is a false and unprivileged publication by writing, printing, picture, effigy, or other fixed representation to the eye, which exposes any person to hatred, contempt, ridicule, or obloquy, or which causes him to be shunned or avoided, or which has a tendency to injure him in his occupation." Cal Civ. Code § 45. The Memoir cannot provoke such reactions because it does not expressly or impliedly impute to any actor any characteristics that would elicit hatred, contempt, or the like from a reasonable reader.

A. The Memoir Does Not Speak to Individual Moral Attributes

A "defamatory statement is one that impeaches an individual's honesty, integrity, virtue, or reputation." *Peterson v. XPO Logistics, Inc.*, 2017 U.S. Dist. LEXIS 182789, at *10 (D. Utah Nov. 2, 2017) (internal quotes and citation omitted). The Memoir's claims cannot be defamatory by this definition, as they do not even broach the issue of any actor's honesty, integrity, or virtue (or imply that any reputations are undeserved). They avoid this because they avoid the distortions here described by the sociologist Pierre Bourdieu, whose methodology informs the Memoir's theoretical framework:

> [T]hose who frequent the borderland between scholarly and ordinary knowledge—essayists, journalists, academic journalists, and journalistic academics—have a vital stake in blurring the frontier and denying or eliminating what separates scientific analysis from partial objectification, imputing to single individuals, or to a lobby, effects which in fact implicate the whole structure of the field.

Pierre Bourdieu, *Homo Academicus*, trans. Peter Collier (Stanford, CA: Stanford University Press, 1988), 4.

Would-Be Plaintiffs cannot plausibly allege a defamatory communication because the Memoirist's research methodology eschews the temptations of "academic journalism" and articulates "the whole structure of the field" of his academic experience, examining the conduct of individual actors only in the context of the larger structural forces that are the real subject of the book.

The Memoirist clarifies from the outset that he is scrutinizing the "cultural pathologies of liberalism and academia," not the enduring moral attributes of the narrative's antagonists, a topic that lies outside the scope of the Memoir. He elucidates those antagonists' surmised actions by reference to cultural context and social causality—for example, the "academic habitus" as elaborated in chapter 6—not in connection with "character," about which no position is taken and no negative inferences may be drawn. Reasonable readers will, therefore, understand those actions as a sui generis response to sui generis contingencies generated by the Memoirist's own behaviors in a specific cultural setting, not as manifestations of enduring personality traits that can be expected to recur in heterogeneous settings that do not implicate the cultural forces being examined. No reasonable reader could be induced to shun or avoid Would-Be Plaintiffs because no reasonable reader could be led to think that their conjectured conduct offers any meaningful information about their likely behavior under routine conditions (even if misread as an ascertained fact).

The introduction announces the Memoirist's intent to inflict reputational injury on certain cultural *values*, not on characters—since only the former play into his analyses—and the rest of the book proceeds accordingly. *See Avins v. White*, 627 F.2d 637, 643 (3rd Cir. 1980) ("The use of words like 'academic ennui' or lack of 'intellectual spark' connote to us no more than a subjective opinion of the educational atmosphere pervading DLS. As such, they more closely approximate a critic's review of an institution rather than a particular individual and are not factual statements disguised in opinion form."). Would-Be Plaintiffs may argue that an attack on their values is implicitly an attack on them. But the First Amendment dictates that any reputational injury to Would-Be Plaintiffs flowing from a loss of esteem for their values is nonactionable. *See W. Va. State Bd. of Educ. v. Barnette*, 319 U.S. 624, 642 (1943) ("If there is any fixed star in our constitutional constellation, it is that no official, high or petty, can prescribe what shall be orthodox in politics, nationalism, religion, or other matters of opinion or force citizens to confess by word or act their faith therein.").

B. The Memoir Contains No Suggestion of Criminal, Unprofessional, or Unethical Conduct

Nowhere does the Memoir suggest as either fact or opinion that any party was engaged in criminal conduct. Although the Memoir employs expressions like "conspiracy" and "quid pro quo" that may appear borrowed from criminal law, both the context and explicit disclaimers clarify that these terms are being employed in a loose, figurative sense that does not connote criminal activity. *See Greenbelt Coop. Pub. Ass'n v. Bresler*, 398 U.S. 6, 14 (1970) ("It is simply impossible to believe that a reader who reached the word 'blackmail' in either article would not have understood exactly what was meant: it was Bresler's public and wholly legal negotiating proposals that were being criticized. No reader could have thought that either the speakers at the meetings or the newspaper articles reporting their words were charging Bresler with the commission of a criminal offense."). The Memoirist also employs such language to describe his own conduct—referring, e.g., to his "crimes and misdemeanors" (chapter 7)—but reasonable readers would not understand him as confessing to a literal crime, and they would interpret similar statements about Would-Be Plaintiffs in the same way, as rhetorical flourishes.

Nor does the Memoir state or imply that Would-Be Plaintiffs at any point discounted the interests of their employer. On the contrary, the Memoirist attributes their surmised conduct to loyalty to institutional values, not narrow self-interest. There is no suggestion that Would-Be Plaintiffs are anything but professional in the normal execution of their duties and overall affairs. The Memoir critiques Would-Be Plaintiffs philosophically *for their professionalism*, so it cannot be plausibly characterized as imputing to them some deficit of professionalism. The Memoirist also does not suggest that Would-Be Plaintiffs' personal moralities are in the least deviant. Again on the contrary, the Memoirist routinely acknowledges that *he*, and no other party, is deviant, the moral outsider, which reasonable readers can at any rate gather. He is, therefore, in no position to assail Would-Be Plaintiffs' standing within their respective communities and cannot draw communal opprobrium upon anyone other than himself. *See* Robert C. Post, *The Social Foundations of Defamation Law: Reputation and the Constitution*, 74 Calif. L. Rev. 691, 711 (1986) ("The dignity that defamation law protects is thus the respect (and self-respect) that arises from full membership in society. … Persons who are socially acceptable will be included within the forms of respect that constitute social dignity; persons who are stigmatized as deviants will be excluded.").

In the small handful of cases where the Memoirist attributes knowingly false statements to Would-Be Plaintiffs, it is clear that those statements are traceable to the unique pressures of the situation at hand and not to some general penchant for dishonesty. There likely is nobody in the world who has never once prevaricated in unusual circumstances, so the Memoirists highly nuanced allegations cannot foment hatred or contempt in the reasonable reader, who will not hold Would-Be Plaintiffs to an unreasonable standard.

While the Memoirist's alleged gaslighting may be unorthodox, he does not cast it as in any way depraved and instead highlights what he considers to be its virtues, underscoring its indispensability to the success of his research agenda. He presents this gaslighting as problematic inasmuch as it foregrounds the philosophical and cultural questions the book is tackling, but the accompanying criticisms fall well short of what is required to support an allegation of defamation, even to the extent that they do imply facts. *Defamatory* cannot mean any characterization that is to some slight degree critical or unflattering—whether proffered as fact or opinion. *See Peterson*, 2017 U.S. Dist. LEXIS 182789, at *10 (D. Utah Nov. 2, 2017) ("An embarrassing, even though false, statement that does not damage one's reputation is not actionable as libel or slander.") (internal quotes and citation omitted).

C. The Tone, Nuances, and Total Context of Any Challenged Statements Preclude a Defamatory Interpretation

Reasonable readers will be attuned to the Memoirist's absurdist tone and to the nuanced moral valences he assigns to various actors and their deeds, including his own. Accordingly, they will not adopt *unnuanced* reactions like hatred, contempt, or ridicule, which the text actively discourages. Far from shepherding readers toward any one-sided moral judgments that could catalyze a defamatory interpretation, the Memoirist consistently challenges his audience's moral certitudes by highlighting the moral ambiguities implicated in his own account of events.

While the Memoirist dispenses gentle mockery of his subjects, this is amply interspersed with self-deprecating humor. Together, these communicate to reasonable readers that the commentary is proceeding in a spirit of levity, which likewise frustrates any defamatory inferences. *See Price v. Viking Penguin, Inc.*, 676 F. Supp. 1501, 1502 (D. Minn. 1988) ("[T]he 'literary context' factor ... requires consideration of the category of publication, its style of writing and intended audience. The statement is to be regarded *as part of a whole*, including *tone* and the use of cautionary language.") (emphases added); *Hoffman v. Wash. Post Co.*, 433 F. Supp. 600, 602 n.1 (D.D.C. 1977) ("the challenged publication must be *read as a whole*. Its content must be considered in its entirety and weighed in connection with its structure, nuances, implications and connotations") (emphasis added).

Would-Be Plaintiffs may not attribute a defamatory meaning to the Memoirist's allegations by decoupling them from the broader context in which he situates them, where he presents Would-Be Plaintiffs' alleged conduct as a *reaction* to his own heterodox behaviors. Rather, Would-Be

Plaintiffs must plausibly allege that the Memoirist's claims would incite hatred, contempt, and so forth against them even if read in proper context, which they cannot do. *See Celle v. Filipino Reporter Enters.*, 209 F.3d 163, 177 (2nd Cir. 2000) ("Challenged statements are not to be read in isolation, but must be perused as the average reader would against the whole *apparent scope and intent* of the writing.") (internal quotes and citation omitted) (emphasis added); *Farah v. Esquire Magazine*, 407 U.S. App. D.C. 208, 215 (2013) ("[T]he First Amendment demands that the court assess the disputed statements in their proper context. ... *Context is critical* because it is in part the *settings* of the speech in question that makes their ... nature apparent, and which helps determine the way in which the intended audience will receive them.") (internal quotes and citations omitted) (first emphasis added).

To withstand a motion to dismiss, Would-Be Plaintiffs must plausibly allege that a reasonable reader who had been swayed to the Memoir's empirical claims would discount the ironic undertones and nuanced moral valences that accompany them and then adopt moral judgments so facile as to spur hatred, contempt, and kindred reactions. They must plausibly allege that a reasonable reader would accede to the factual complexity presented in the Memoir while ignoring the moral complexity that the narrative attaches to the factual complexity. In other words, they must allege that a reasonable reader would be more partial to the Memoirist's cause than the Memoirist himself is. That is conceivable, but Would-Be Plaintiffs must "nudge their claims across the line from conceivable to plausible," a burden they cannot meet even if the challenged statements are assumed to be declarations of ascertained fact. *Bell Atlantic Corp. v. Twombly*, 550 U.S. 544, 570 (2007).

III. This Memorandum of Law Resolves Any Textual Ambiguities in the Memoirist's Favor

To the extent the text contains arguable ambiguities regarding any of the foregoing matters, these are resolved in the Memoirist's favor by this Memorandum's very inclusion in the Memoir. Because "the challenged publication must be read as a whole," this Memorandum (to which the copyright page, table of contents, and introduction all refer the reader) forms part of the total setting of any challenged statements. *Hoffman*, 433 F. Supp. at 602 n.1. Having read it, the reasonable reader will glean the Memoirist's intent to adhere to applicable laws, as evidenced by his efforts to ensure this, and resolve any textual ambiguities consistently with that intent, interpreting them as statements of opinion rather than fact and as cultural criticisms rather than moral ones. Accordingly, the Memoirist's interpretation of any challenged statements will also be that of reasonable readers.

IV. Even If the Memoirist's Claims Admit of a Defamatory Meaning, Would-Be Plaintiffs Cannot Plausibly Allege Tangible Reputational Injury

Even if Would-Be Plaintiffs could allege that the challenged statements are theoretically defamatory on some recondite interpretation—and they cannot—they still could not allege that they have suffered a tangible injury as a result of those statements. "Defamatory language not libelous on its face is not actionable unless the plaintiff alleges and proves that he has suffered special damage as a proximate result thereof." Cal. Civ. Code § 45a. Given that the Memoirist's statements are not libelous on their face, as shown in this Memorandum, Would-Be Plaintiffs must demonstrate that his statements have caused them financial harm or some other tangible loss. Would-Be Plaintiffs cannot allege this, however, as there exists no community wherein his statements could have such an effect.

Would-Be Plaintiffs' reputational interests consist in "the opinion which others in the community may have, or tend to have, of [them]." W. Page Keeton et al., *Prosser and Keeton on the Law of Torts* § 111 (5th ed. 1984). Thus, "harm to reputation is socially constructed: it is defined more by its effect on the 'others' who make up the plaintiff's 'community' than by its effect on the individual plaintiff. In determining whether a statement is defamatory, therefore, the decision-maker (in most cases, the judge) must first select the community in whose esteem the plaintiff has been diminished. The choice of community is thus a crucial factor in assessing defamation liability." Lyrissa Lidsky, *Defamation, Reputation, and the Myth of the Community*, 71 Wash. L. Rev. 1, 6–7 (1996). There are three relevant communities for a law faculty plaintiff:

> [I]t is amongst these very limited spheres, these relatively small segments of society that individuals tend to value reputation. Hence, very few individuals can lay claim to a truly national reputation. A law professor, for example, will value her reputation within her own law school community, consisting of her students and colleagues. She will also value her reputation within the national legal academic community. Aside from these small communities, unless she is particularly well-known, she will probably value her reputation only amongst her assorted family members and friends.
>
> This presents something of a dilemma for her, however, because each of these groups may have different norms of behavior that it seeks to uphold, different roles it expects her to play. Her reputation among her colleagues might not be harmed by an allegation that she is a lesbian; whereas, depending on her family's values, this allegation might seriously diminish her in their regard. On the other hand, an allegation of plagiarism is the kiss of death in the academic community, but may be relatively inconsequential outside of it.

Id. at 42

Would-be Plaintiffs' communities are thus (1) assorted friends and family; (2) the legal academic community (both local and countrywide); and, possibly, (3) the nationwide community (i.e., the public at large). Would-Be Plaintiffs cannot plausibly allege more than de minimus reputational injury in any of these settings, however. A defamatory statement "induces an evil opinion of one in the minds of right-thinking persons." *Kimmerle v. New York Evening Journal*, 262 N.Y. 99, 186 N.E. 217, 218 (N.Y. 1933). Because no "right-thinking" member of any of the foregoing three communities could be influenced by the Memoir to form an evil opinion of Would-Be Plaintiffs, they cannot allege actual losses ensuing from the challenged statements (as opposed to mere chagrin).

Most obviously, right-thinking friends and family members would be profoundly unaffected by the facially outlandish ruminations of an eccentric former student in a self-published book about events long past in which they had no involvement. These ruminations cannot inflict reputational injury within the legal academic community, either. The Memoirist critiques his theorized gaslighting by representatives of Stanford Law School as an *expression* of that community's values—for example, the "law-school view of what 'prejudices' must be stamped out," as explained in chapter 9—not as a deviation from those values. The natural tendency of any right-thinking member of the legal academic community will, therefore, be to reject the Memoirist's critique and identify with its targets, who are also right thinking. The Memoirist repeatedly stresses that his criticisms of Would-Be Plaintiffs are concomitantly criticisms of their wider community, so his statements cannot somehow turn that community against them. Right-thinking members of the legal academic community will either disbelieve the Memoir's allegations or believe them and approve of the conduct alleged. Neither possibility will ensue in reputational injury to Would-Be Plaintiffs.

Likewise with law students. Would-Be Plaintiffs cannot show that right-thinking Stanford Law students have identified with the highly idiosyncratic views of an obscure 2008 graduate and self-avowed conspiracy theorist rather than deferring to known and trusted teachers at a preeminent institution. Whatever legitimacy the Memoirist may enjoy by virtue of having graduated from Stanford will be dwarfed by the legitimacy that attaches to *being* Stanford. Those thinking otherwise would have to be rare exceptions, deviant and not right thinking, making any conceivable reputational injury de minimus. The Memoirist's statements may well spur the legal academic community (and perhaps other right-thinking communities) to form an evil opinion of *him*, exposing him to "hatred, contempt, ridicule, or obloquy," Cal Civ. Code § 45, but it is not "plausible on its face" that his statements could so impact any other party. *Twombly*, 550 U.S. at 548.

Even if Would-Be Plaintiffs purport to be "particularly well-known" such as to enjoy a national reputation beyond the legal academic community that is vulnerable to injury, they cannot plausibly identify a single normative reaction to the Memoir's claims within a nationwide community of the public at large. "Today, American culture is seemingly so diverse that it may be rare to find many individual values, past perhaps those which govern and restrict the basest and most hideous wrongs, which would permeate equally throughout communities. Communities are not standardized, are not shaped equally, and do not hold the same values from which a 'benchmark for determining what statements are defamatory' can be drawn." Daniel Lewis, *LMAO; That Guy is Such a @*%#!: Redefining Defamation Law's Stagnant Community Standard in a Rapidly Changing World*, 8 Fla. A&M U. L. Rev. 111, 120 (2012) (quoting Lidsky, *supra* at 7–8).

Given this fragmentation of value systems in a deeply divided America, any challenged statements will elicit a complex panoply of nuanced reactions as well as profound ambivalence and outright incredulity. The Memoirist's claims are deeply entwined with his reading of America's culture wars—within which he situates his own struggle against Stanford—so readers' reactions to any challenged statements will be just as varied as their larger worldviews. For "[t]o assume a common culture or normative consensus in American society, as in most modern societies, is to ignore the deep and divisive role of class, ethnic, religious, status, and regional culture conflicts which often produce widely opposing definitions of goodness, truth, and moral virtue." Joseph R. Gusfield, *On Legislating Morals: The Symbolic Process of Designating Deviance*, 56 Cal. L. Rev. 54, 55 (1968).

It is true that "certain norms continue to command widespread consensus," as "[t]he vast majority of Americans would condemn child molestation, cold-blooded murder, or treachery to friends, family or country." Lidsky, *supra* at 42. However, the Memoirist's allegations of gaslighting are far too rarefied to be credibly analogized to any widely recognized form of malfeasance. While gaslighting in general may carry negative connotations, the casualness with which accusations of it are often lobbed in political discourse and interpersonal conflicts suggests that it does not rise to a particularly high level of nefariousness in the minds of reasonable readers. Even if there were a right-thinking consensus as to gaslighting in the abstract, Would-Be Plaintiffs would have to demonstrate that one exists as to the particular form of gaslighting described in the Memoir, which they cannot do given the sui generis nature of the Memoirist's claims.

Thus, Would-Be Plaintiffs would have no factual basis for alleging the existence of a discernibly right-minded (or "reasonable") reaction to the Memoirist's allegations within society at large that is so unequivocally negative as to amount to "hatred, contempt, ridicule, or obloquy." Cal Civ. Code § 45. Absent a randomized study by qualified experts, any such allegation would be a "'naked assertion[]' devoid of 'further factual enhancement,'" and "unadorned, the defendant-unlawfully-harmed-me accusation[s]" will not pass muster. *Ashcroft v. Iqbal*, 556 U.S. 662, 678 (2009) (quoting *Twombly*, 550 U.S. at 557). Even if Would-Be Plaintiffs could identify some small subculture among the country's 330 million inhabitants that has been influenced by the challenged statements to form an evil opinion of them, they cannot demonstrate that their reputational interests have been concretely affected by that subculture, which would doubtless consist of a highly dispersed group of largely powerless individuals (perhaps disgruntled graduate students). The mere knowledge that there may be certain unidentified persons out there who silently condemn Would-Be Plaintiffs is not a legally cognizable injury and cannot even support Article III standing.

V. Would-Be Plaintiffs Cannot Prove the Requisite Scienter

Even if Would-Be Plaintiffs could plausibly allege that the Memoirist's statements have caused them actual reputational injury—and they cannot—in order to recover damages they must also show that the Memoirist was *aware* that his statements carried the potential to so harm them. This they also cannot do, as he has explained his reasonable belief that his statements do not harbor a defamatory meaning—even if mischaracterized as assertions of ascertained fact. *See Masson v. New Yorker Magazine*, 832 F. Supp. 1350, 1363 (N.D. Cal. 1993) ("the Court believes that awareness of defamatory meaning is properly an element of a defamation claim, particularly so in the case at hand in which the defamation is somewhat ambiguous and indirect.").

Furthermore, Would-Be Plaintiffs who purport to have suffered nationwide reputational injury within the community of the public at large also purport to be public figures and must accordingly prove actual malice to recover damages. *See Gertz v. Robert Welch*, 418 U.S. 323, 342 (1974) ("Those who, by reason of the notoriety of their achievements or the vigor and success with which they seek the public's attention, are properly classed as public figures … may recover for injury to reputation only on clear and convincing proof that the defamatory falsehood was made with knowledge of its falsity or with reckless disregard for the truth."). Should the Would-Be Plaintiff be Stanford University itself, it, too, must prove actual malice, as it is unquestionably a public figure. "[I]f the purpose of the public figure-private person dichotomy is to protect the privacy of individuals who do not seek publicity or engage in activities that place them in the public eye, there seems no reason to classify a large corporation as a private person." *Brown & Williamson Tobacco Corp. v. Jacobson*, 713 F.2d 262, 273 (7th Cir. 1983). This holds doubly true of preeminent universities, which seek the public eye for the express purpose of cultivating their reputations and not to merely sell consumer goods.

Public figure Would-Be Plaintiffs cannot prove actual malice, however, because the Memoirist evinces consistent concern for the truth of his claims, and it is psychologically implausible that he could have written the Memoir without believing them. People who machinate to harm others' reputations by confecting straight-out lies do not typically go to such lengths to spin facially outlandish narratives and then couch those narratives in complex academic arguments.

Even as private persons, Would-Be Plaintiffs cannot recover damages. "[T]he Supreme Court held that, when the substance of the defamatory statement makes substantial injury to the reputation apparent, the state is free to allow recovery of compensatory damages by a private individual for injury to his reputation caused by a defendant's negligence in publishing false and defamatory statements about him." *Lawlor v. Gallagher Presidents' Report, Inc.*, 394 F. Supp. 721, 732 (S.D.N.Y. 1975). In the instant case, however, reputational injury is logically preclusive of negligence. To allege reputational injury is also to allege that the challenged statements will be believed, but no reader could believe them without first evaluating the Memoirist's arguments for them. If readers are thereby persuaded, then his claims are plausible and he could not have been negligent in formulating them, even if they happen to be false. His negligence is thus inversely correlated to Would-Be Plaintiffs' reputational injury—a function of his claims' essentially conjectural character, as discussed earlier.

Would-Be Plaintiffs cannot prove negligence also because the Memoirist's inferences are premised on the theory of conservative claims of cultural oppression, as discussed throughout the Memoir.

Given that "[u]nder the First Amendment there is no such thing as a false idea," that theory cannot be adjudicated as false. *Gertz*, 418 U.S. at 339. And if it cannot be adjudicated as false, then inferences premised on it cannot be adjudicated as negligent, as that would be to fault the Memoirist for relying on ideas that he is constitutionally entitled to hold as true. Moreover, many of these ideas are drawn from Pierre Bourdieu's *Homo Academicus*, published by Stanford University Press, which the Memoirist uses to illuminate his own conditions at Stanford. So, even if ideas were actionable and universities were private figures, Stanford could not credibly argue that the Memoirist was negligent in relying on ideas that it saw fit to publish.

A finding of negligence is also ruled out by the Memoirist's documented efforts to avert error. On June 6, 2012, the Memoirist sent an email to the four advisers named in the Memoir's acknowledgments, where he announced his intent to write the Memoir, attached an early version of it, and offered to take any feedback under advisement. No response was received. The Memoirist also emailed Stanford University's ombudsman, David Rasch, that day, again attaching this early version and soliciting feedback. No response was received. "No reasonable trier of fact could find" that the Memoirist was negligent when he has gone out of his way to avert error in this manner. *Something Old, Something New, Inc. v. QVC, Inc.*, 1999 US Dist. LEXIS 18878, at *4 (S.D.N.Y. Dec. 7, 1999).

VI. Because the Memoirist's Statements Address Matters of Public Concern, the Action May Be Subject to an Anti-SLAPP Motion

"The purpose of the anti-SLAPP statute is to allow early dismissal of meritless first amendment cases aimed at chilling expression through costly, time-consuming litigation. … The anti-SLAPP statute specifies that it should be construed broadly, and … applies to any conduct in furtherance of the exercise of the constitutional right of petition or the constitutional right of free speech in connection with a public issue or an issue of public interest." *Verizon Del., Inc. v. Covad Communs. Co.*, 377 F.3d 1081, 1090–91 (9th Cir. 2004) (internal quotes and citations omitted). "[T]he issue need not be 'significant' to be protected by the anti-SLAPP statute—it is enough that it is one in which the public takes an interest." *Cross v. Cooper*, 197 Cal. App. 4th 357, 372 (2011). "[T]he matter must be of interest to a substantial number of people and not merely a small, specific audience." *Dawe v. Corr. USA*, 2009 U.S. Dist. LEXIS 45205, at *40–41 (E.D. Cal. May 20, 2009) (internal quotes and citations omitted). However, "[s]tatements made only to a limited, but definable portion of the public … are protectable if they occur in the context of an ongoing controversy, dispute or discussion, such that it warrants protection by a statute that embodies the public policy of encouraging participation in matters of public significance." *Trindade v. Reach Media Grp., LLC*, 2013 U.S. Dist. LEXIS 107707, at *31–32 (N.D. Cal. July 31, 2013) (internal quotes and citations omitted).

The Memoirist's statements are issued in connection with the public interest because they address matters in which the public has a demonstrable interest. Publications scrutinizing various facets of academia have been a staple of the nation's political and cultural debates for decades. These include Roger Kimball's *Tenured Radicals*, Dinesh D'Souza's *Illiberal Education*, and Allan Bloom's *The Closing of the American Mind*, to name only a few prominent examples. The Memoir sits comfortably within this tradition. Like the Memoir, books of this genre have occasionally centered on the writer's personal experiences at an elite, liberal-dominated institution, which may get named in the title—for example, William F. Buckley's *God and Man at Yale* or John Leboutillier's *Harvard Hates America*. The Memoir's sales cannot be ascertained as of this writing. But even if the book speaks to only "a limited, but definable portion of the public" (e.g., the Stanford community), the state of higher education constitutes "an ongoing controversy, dispute or discussion" for the general public, regardless of the size of the Memoir's readership. *Id.*

"[T]he focus of the speaker's conduct" in an anti-SLAPP motion "should be the public interest rather than a mere effort to gather ammunition for another round of private controversy." *Dawe v. Corr. USA*, 2009 U.S. Dist. LEXIS 45205, at *41 (E.D. Cal. May 20, 2009). The Memoirist does not attempt to gather any such ammunition, however, as there exists no private controversy between him and Stanford University or any of its affiliates, past or present. The Memoirist has not communicated with them in a decade and asks nothing of them. Any and all claims against them are purely philosophical.

One court held that statements relating to the self-governance of a gated community of three thousand residents implicated the public interest. *See Damon v. Ocean Hills Journalism Club,* 85 Cal. App. 4th 468, 479 (2000). If statements on matters impacting three thousand people at most can speak to the public interest, then so, too, do those in the Memoir, which takes up perennial philosophical questions. The Memoir critiques Stanford University as the embodiment of a particular cultural value system, and this has broadly public implications. While memoirs are inherently personal, the Memoir's personal dimension is inseparable from its intellectual one. By examining his ostensibly personal conflicts as *cultural conflicts*, the Memoirist employs his own experiences to illuminate sociocultural currents that are much bigger than him. *God and Man at Yale* and *Harvard Hates America* both illustrate that personal experiences at institutions of higher learning can speak to the public interest, especially when the institution is a particularly prominent one to whose ideals and achievements many aspire. *See Church of Scientology v. Wollersheim*, 42 Cal. App. 4th 628, 650 (1996) ("Although matters of public interest include legislative and governmental activities, they may also include activities that involve private persons and entities, especially when a large, powerful organization may impact the lives of many individuals.").

Because any claims against the Memoirist would be subject to an anti-SLAPP motion (jurisdiction permitting), Would-Be Plaintiffs would need to demonstrate "a probability that [they] ... will prevail on the[ir] claim" in order to survive the motion. Cal. Civ. Proc. Code § 425.16(b)(1). They cannot demonstrate this, however, since they cannot even plausibly allege their claims, as explained earlier.

VII. Filing Attorneys and Their Clients May Be Subject to Rule 11 Sanctions

Additionally, filing attorneys may be subject to Fed. R. Civ. P. 11 sanctions (or state law analogues) if they fail to conduct a reasonable inquiry into the legal and factual bases of any libel allegations:

> An attorney is subject to Rule 11 sanctions, among other reasons, when he presents to the court "claims, defenses, and other legal contentions ... [not] warranted by existing law or by a nonfrivolous argument for the extension, modification, or reversal of existing law or the establishment of new law[.]" Fed. R. Civ. P. 11(b)(2). When, as here, a complaint is the primary focus of Rule 11 proceedings, a district court must conduct a two-prong inquiry to determine (1) whether the complaint is legally or factually baseless from an objective perspective, and (2) if the attorney has conducted a reasonable and competent inquiry before signing and filing it. As shorthand for this test, we use the word "frivolous" to denote a filing that is *both* baseless *and* made without a reasonable and competent inquiry.

Holgate v. Baldwin, 425 F.3d 671, 675–76 (9th Cir. 2005) (some internal quotes and citations omitted)

Given that any allegations of libel would be objectively baseless, as established herein, filing attorneys will be in violation of Rule 11 if they fail to conduct a reasonable and competent inquiry into the facts of the case and the governing law. Representative samples of the latter are compiled in this very Memorandum, disregard for which would be sanctionable. Because challenged statements must be read in the total context of the publication as a whole, filing attorneys must also demonstrate a reasonable comprehension of the Memoir in its entirety, including its intellectual dimensions, which they must consider in proffering their interpretations of the challenged statements. To the extent they are not personally qualified to investigate this, they may have to enlist expert assistance to escape Rule 11 sanctions.

The same holds true of the filing attorneys' clients. Rule 11 generally contemplates "that attorneys, as licensed professionals, should be held to a higher standard of conduct" than their clients. *Bus. Guides v. Chromatic Commc'ns Enters.*, 892 F.2d 802, 810 (9th Cir. 1989). But, in the instant case, Would-Be Plaintiffs clearly possess the legal sophistication to be held to the same standard as their attorneys—if not to a much higher one.

Memorandum of Law Concerning the Fair Use of Website Images

Introduction

Because the Stanford Law website images reproduced in exhibits C, D, and E ("the Images") are copyrighted, Stanford University would have a prima facie case of copyright infringement against the author, Rony Guldmann ("the Memoirist"). Any such action would be frivolous, however, as the Memoirist would readily prevail with a fair use defense, which like copyright itself promotes the progress in the arts and sciences of which *The Star Chamber of Stanford* ("the Memoir") is a prime illustration. This is not a close case. Federal copyright law provides:

> Notwithstanding the provisions of sections 106 and 106A, the fair use of a copyrighted work, including such use by reproduction in copies or phonorecords or by any other means specified by that section, for purposes such as criticism, comment, news reporting, teaching (including multiple copies for classroom use), scholarship, or research, is not an infringement of copyright. In determining whether the use made of a work in any particular case is a fair use the factors to be considered shall include—
>
> 1. the purpose and character of the use, including whether such use is of a commercial nature or is for nonprofit educational purposes;
> 2. the nature of the copyrighted work;
> 3. the amount and substantiality of the portion used in relation to the copyrighted work as a whole; and
> 4. the effect of the use upon the potential market for or value of the copyrighted work.

> The fact that a work is unpublished shall not itself bar a finding of fair use if such finding is made upon consideration of all the above factors.

17 U.S.C. § 107

As detailed in this Memorandum, all four factors weigh in favor of finding fair use: (1) The purpose and character of the Images' use are radically transformative and only minimally commercial. Whereas the original use was decorative, the new one is theoretical, and the Images are not exploited to market the Memoir. (2) The nature of the Images supports fair use because their contents are largely factual, only minimally creative, and are being used in their factual/historical aspect rather than for whatever modicum of aesthetic value they may possess. (3) The amount and substantiality of the copyrighted work used accrues to fair use because the Memoirist reproduces no more than is needed to effect his editorial purposes. (4) The use's market effect redounds to fair use because the use has no conceivable economic ramifications for the copyright holder.

Argument

I. Purpose and Character of Use Argue for Fair Use

In analyzing whether a use is fair, courts must examine "whether the new work merely 'supersede[s] the objects' of the original creation … or instead adds something new, with a further purpose or different character, altering the first with new expression, meaning, or message." *Campbell v. Acuff-Rose Music, Inc.*, 510 U.S. 569, 579 (1994) (citation omitted). If "the secondary use adds value to the original—if [the original work] is used as raw material, transformed in the creation of new information, new aesthetics, new insights and understandings—this is the very type of activity that the fair use doctrine intends to protect for the enrichment of society." Pierre N. Leval, *Toward a*

Fair Use Standard, 103 Harv. L. Rev. 1105, 1107 (1990). The "more transformative the new work, the less will be the significance of other factors, like commercialism, that may weigh against a finding of fair use." *Campbell*, 510 U.S. at 579.

A. Use of Images Is Transformative

Here, the Images' use is unambiguously transformative. They serve a vastly different purpose in appendix 1 of the Memoir than in their original use on the Stanford Law home page, where their function was aesthetic and decorative. There they served as visual embellishments to the home page's textual content by enabling visitors to favorably envision the Stanford Law experience and atmosphere. In contrast, the Memoirist introduces the Images as elements of his unique conflict with, and critique of, Stanford Law School. In enabling readers to visualize an aspect of his theorized gaslighting by law school representatives, the Images facilitate his cultural critique of Stanford and similar institutions, as detailed throughout the Memoir. *See Blanch v. Koons*, 467 F.3d 244, 252 (2nd Cir. 2006) ("The sharply different objectives that Koons had in using, and Blanch had in creating, 'Silk Sandals' confirms the transformative nature of the use.").

Where "the purpose of the challenged use is ... the same decorative purpose" of the original use, this "does not favor fair use." *Ringgold v. Black Ent't TV, Inc.*, 126 F.3d 70, 79 (2nd Cir. 1997). However, the Images as used in the Memoir serve no such purpose, and no reasonable reader could derive any aesthetic stimulation from them. The stimulation is, rather, intellectual and is provided by the commentary that surrounds the Images, not the Images standing alone, making their use transformative. *See Kelly v. Arriba Soft Corp.*, 336 F.3d 811, 818 (9th Cir. 2003) ("Kelly's images are artistic works intended to inform and to engage the viewer in an aesthetic experience. His images are used to portray scenes from the American West in an aesthetic manner. Arriba's use of Kelly's images in the thumbnails is unrelated to any aesthetic purpose.").

The Memoirist exhibits the Images not to promote or represent Stanford—their original use—but as pertinent historical artifacts from his time there, as the commentary details. The Second Circuit observed in an analogous case:

> ... DK's purpose in using the copyrighted images at issue in its biography of the Grateful Dead is plainly different from the original purpose for which they were created. Originally, each of BGA's images fulfilled the dual purposes of artistic expression and promotion. The posters were apparently widely distributed to generate public interest in the Grateful Dead and to convey information to a large number people about the band's forthcoming concerts. In contrast, DK used each of BGA's images as historical artifacts to document and represent the actual occurrence of Grateful Dead concert events featured on *Illustrated Trip*'s timeline.

Bill Graham Archives v. Dorling Kindersley Ltd., 448 F.3d 605, 609 (2nd Cir. 2006)

There is no legal daylight between *Bill Graham Archives* and the instant case. Both involve the transformation of the promotional into the historical. The Memoirist uses the Images not to promote Stanford but to "document and represent the actual occurrence" of events at Stanford.

The Memoir is not only social commentary but also a record of the Memoirist's experiences and career path. And courts recognize that biographies provide an appropriate context for the fair use of copyrighted materials. *See Warren Publ'g Co. v. Spurlock*, 645 F. Supp. 2d 402, 419 (E.D. Pa. 2009) ("What is particularly pertinent to this Court's analysis and conclusion is that the Gogos Book is appropriately characterized as a biography or a career retrospective."); *New Era Publ'ns Int'l, ApS v. Carol Publ. Grp.*, 904 F.2d 152, 156 (2nd Cir. 1990) ("Our cases establish that biographies in general, and critical biographies in particular, fit comfortably within these statutory categories of uses illustrative of uses that can be fair.") (internal quotes and citation omitted); *Bill Graham Archives*, 448 F.3d at 609 ("courts have frequently afforded fair use protection to the use of copyrighted material in biographies, recognizing such works as forms of historic scholarship, criticism, and comment that require incorporation of original source material for optimum treatment of their subjects.").

Stanford may object that the new use cannot be transformative because the Memoirist has failed to meaningfully embellish or otherwise alter the Images. That is of no moment where, as here, the new use serves a different purpose than did the old one. *See Perfect 10, Inc. v. Amazon.com, Inc.*, 508 F.3d 1146, 1165 (9th Cir. 2007) ("even making an exact copy of a work may be transformative so long as the copy serves a different function than the original work"); *Kelly*, 336 F.3d at 818–19 ("Kelly asserts that because Arriba reproduced his exact images and added nothing to them, Arriba's use cannot be transformative. ... Those cases are inapposite, however, because the resulting use of the copyrighted work in those cases was the same as the original use"). The personal narrative that the Images are used to advance transforms their meaning, as does the social commentary that intersperses and elucidates the narrative. Courts recognize that erstwhile aesthetic objects may be transformed into news or fodder for commentary, which the Memoir accomplishes. *See id.* ("By putting a copy of the photograph in the newspaper, the work was transformed into news, creating a new meaning or purpose for the work."); *Nunez v. Caribbean Int'l News Corp.*, 235 F.3d 18, 22 (1st Cir. 2000) ("Appellee reprinted the pictures not just to entice the buying public, but to place its news articles in context; as the district court pointed out, 'the pictures were the story.' ... Thus, by using the photographs in conjunction with editorial commentary, El Vocero ...

used the works for 'a further purpose,' giving them a new 'meaning, or message.'") (quoting *Campbell*, 510 U.S. at 579).

Courts are reluctant to find fair use when "the commentary has no critical bearing on the substance or style of the original composition, which the alleged infringer merely uses to get attention or to avoid the drudgery in working up something fresh." *Campbell*, 510 U.S. at 580. But the 135,000-word text that contextualizes the Images confirms that the Memoirist has in fact "work[ed] up something fresh" (as do the Memoir's two companion volumes, not yet published but freely available to readers in draft form). Courts have also "declined to find a transformative use when the defendant has done no more than find a new way to exploit the creative virtues of the original work." *Blanch*, 467 F.3d at 252. But in the instant case the creative virtues are entirely the Memoirist's. He reproduces the Images for the specific purpose of facilitating his commentary, by enabling readers to visualize its subject matter, and the Images can hold no interest for readers apart from that function.

Courts may reject a fair use claim where the new use fails to genuinely "criticize, 'expose,' or otherwise comment upon" the incorporated material. *Castle Rock Entm't, Inc. v. Carol Publ'g Grp., Inc.*, 150 F.3d 132, 142 (2nd Cir. 1998). But here, criticism and exposure are the Memoir's singular purpose from the outset. *See Blanch*, 467 F.3d at 253 ("Koons is, by his own undisputed description, using Blanch's image as fodder for his commentary on the social and aesthetic consequences of mass media. His stated objective is thus not to repackage Blanch's 'Silk Sandals,' but to employ it 'in the creation of new information, new aesthetics, new insights and understandings.'") (citation omitted). The Memoir imparts a new meaning to the Images because it argues that they have a clandestine significance that the naive observer would not naturally glean from them, as detailed from chapter 5 onward. Whether swayed or not, readers will reflect upon this thesis. Because the Images do not spur such reflection in their original use, the new use is transformative.

B. Use of Images Is Only Minimally Commercial

The Memoir is commercial only inasmuch as it is being sold at a profit, and the law is clear that this alone does not preclude a finding of fair use. "For a commercial use to weigh heavily against a finding of fair use, it must involve more than simply publication in a profit-making venture." *Nunez*, 235 F.3d at 22. If "commerciality carried presumptive force against a finding of fairness, the presumption would swallow nearly all of the illustrative uses listed in the preamble paragraph of § 107, including news reporting, comment, criticism, teaching, scholarship, and research, since these activities are generally conducted for profit in this country." *Campbell*, 510 U.S. at 584 (internal quotes and citations omitted).

The Images contribute to the Memoir's integrity by corroborating and illustrating some of its central claims, but they do not contribute to its commerciality. Though forming part of a for-profit venture, they are not exploited to advertise or otherwise market the Memoir. *See id.* at 585 ("The use, for example, of a copyrighted work to advertise a product, even in a parody, will be entitled to less indulgence under the first factor of the fair use enquiry than the sale of a parody for its own sake"). Indeed, readers are unlikely to learn of the Images' existence until after purchasing the Memoir, as they are tucked away in an appendix, where they need be accessed only once, when the narrative first turns to them. *See Haberman v. Hustler Magazine, Inc.*, 626 F. Supp. 201, 211 (D. Mass. 1986) ("*Hustler* did not exploit the value of Haberman's works in order to sell copies of its magazine. The works were reproduced as items inside the magazine in a regular feature section. In contrast to cases in which fair use was not established, their inclusion was not advertised on the cover, nor made evident to prospective purchaser[s] of *Hustler*."); *Kelly*, 336 F.3d at 818 ("Arriba was neither using Kelly's images to directly promote its web site nor trying to profit by selling Kelly's images ... Because the use of Kelly's images was not highly exploitative, the commercial nature of the use weighs only slightly against a finding of fair use.").

"The commercial/nonprofit dichotomy concerns the unfairness that arises when a secondary user makes unauthorized use of copyrighted material to capture significant revenues as a direct consequence of copying the original work." *American Geophysical Union v. Texaco Inc.*, 60 F.3d 913 (2nd Cir. 1994). However, the Memoirist cannot hope to capture significant revenue from Images with no commercial value. Even if the original Images had such value, the smaller, low-resolution, black-and-white reproductions in the Memoir certainly lack it. *See Kelly*, 336 F.3d at 818 ("the thumbnails were much smaller, lower-resolution images that served an entirely different function than Kelly's original images."). Any commercial reward the Memoirist reaps from the Images is indirect and entirely a function of the narrative and commentary through which he contextualizes them. He cannot be accused of appropriating the labor that went into producing the Images when that labor appears minimal in comparison with his own efforts.

Although the use of the Images may be commercial in the strict sense that the Memoir is being sold for a profit, the book cannot be fairly characterized as a commercial venture in light of the vast incongruity between the sum of the Memoirist's efforts and the wholly speculative financial returns on this investment. The Memoirist has spent a decade composing the Memoir and its companion volumes for what is likely to be a niche audience, sales to which cannot be expected to generate windfall profits. Given its educational and humanistic purposes, the Memoir is more akin to a nonprofit venture than to a properly commercial one, notwithstanding that the Memoirist may seek to capture whatever profits can be had at the end of the day. A minimally attentive reading of the Memoir immediately discloses that the Memoirist's underlying objectives are anything but commercial.

II. Nature of Copyrighted Work Argues for Fair Use

The second factor "calls for recognition that some works are closer to the core of intended copyright protection than others, with the consequence that fair use is more difficult to establish when the former works are copied." *Campbell*, 510 U.S. at 586. "A use is less likely to be deemed fair when the copyrighted work is a creative product." *Abend v. MCA, Inc.*, 863 F.2d 1465, 1481 (9th Cir. 1988). Correlatively, "fair use is more likely to be found in factual works than in fictional works." *Stewart v. Abend*, 495 U.S. 207, 237 (1990). For the "fact/expression dichotomy limits severely the scope of [copyright] protection in fact-based works." *Feist Publ'ns, Inc. v. Rural Tel. Serv. Co.*, 499 U.S. 340, 350 (1991). Accordingly, "greater leeway [is] allowed to a claim of fair use where the work is factual or informational." *Blanch*, 467 F.3d at 256.

Like photography generally, the Images have both factual and creative dimensions. The former are much more pronounced, however. While all photography is to a degree creative, the Images are conventional vignettes of university life of the kind found on any academic website and do not evince a distinctive artistic style or perspective. The photography is competent but not particularly original or expressive. Because the Images' original purpose was only to showcase the dedication of Stanford Law professors and earnestness of Stanford Law students, they fall on the factual end of the factual/creative spectrum, which supports a finding of fair use. *See Nunez*, 235 F.3d at 23 ("certainly, photography is an art form that requires a significant amount of skill; however, the photographs were not artistic representations designed primarily to express Nunez's ideas, emotions, or feelings, but instead a publicity attempt to highlight Giraud's abilities as a potential model.").

"[Even] within the field of fact works, there are gradations as to the relative proportion of fact and fancy. One may move from sparsely embellished maps and directories to elegantly written biography. The extent to which one must permit expressive language to be copied, in order to assure dissemination of the underlying facts, will thus vary from case to case." Robert A. Gorman, *Fact or Fancy? The Implications for Copyright*, 29 J. Copyright Soc. 560, 563 (1982).

Here, the Images are more akin to sparsely embellished maps than to elegantly written biographies. They convey only the bare fact that certain individuals were engaged in certain quotidian campus activities in or about the Stanford Law building at some undisclosed point in the past. They therefore do not evince the "pronounced creativity and investment of time" that would "weigh against a finding of fair use." *Haberman*, 626 F. Supp. at 211. Even if the Images were noteworthy artistically, the Memoirist reproduces them for their role in the events chronicled by the Memoir, not for their artistic merits, and this also redounds to fair use. *See Bill Graham Archives*, 448 F.3d at 612–13 ("even though BGA's images are creative works, which are a core concern of copyright protection, the second factor has limited weight in our analysis because the purpose of DK's use was to emphasize the images' historical rather than creative value.").

III. Amount and Substantiality of Portion Used Argue for Fair Use

The third fair use factor asks whether "'the amount and substantiality of the portion used in relation to the copyrighted work as a whole' … are reasonable in relation to the purpose of the copying." *Campbell*, 510 U.S. at 586 (quoting 17 U.S.C. § 107(3)). This factor weighs in favor of finding fair use because the Memoirist reproduces only a small fraction of the entire collection of photos that are or ever were available on the Stanford Law website. What photos he does reproduce he reproduces in their entirety. But "such copying does not necessarily weigh against fair use because copying the entirety of a work is sometimes necessary to make a fair use of the image." *Bill Graham Archives*, 448 F.3d at 613; *see also Kelly*, 336 F.3d at 821 ("This factor neither weighs for nor against either party because, although Arriba did copy each of Kelly's images as a whole, it was reasonable to do so in light of Arriba's use of the images. It was necessary for Arriba to copy the entire image to allow users to recognize the image").

However one characterizes the "amount and substantiality" of the Memoirist's reproductions, they are reasonable in relation to his transformative ends. Various sections of the Memoir elucidate the significance of "set 1," "set 2," and "the Preamble," and the Memoirist reproduces no more copyrighted material than is required to illustrate the subject matter of these discussions. *See Blanch*, 467 F.3d at 257 ("It seems to us that Koons's copying of 'Silk Sandals' was indeed reasonable when measured in light of his purpose, to convey the 'fact' of the photograph to viewers of the painting"); *Campbell*, 510 U.S. at 588 ("When parody takes aim at a particular original work, the parody must be able to 'conjure up' at least enough of that original to make the object of its critical wit recognizable.").

IV. Absence of Market Impact Argues for Fair Use

"The fourth fair use factor is 'the effect of the use upon the potential market for or value of the copyrighted work.'" *Campbell*, 510 U.S. at 590 (quoting 17 U.S.C. § 107(4)). Courts must "consider not only the extent of market harm caused by the particular actions of the alleged infringer, but also whether unrestricted and widespread conduct of the sort engaged in by the defendant … would result in a substantially adverse impact on the potential market for the original." *Id.* (internal quotes and citations omitted). Courts must furthermore consider the market impact on potential derivative uses, but this "includes only those that creators of original works would in general develop or license others to develop." *Id.* at 592.

While a fair use analysis must generally consider the cumulative effect of the alleged infringement's becoming widespread, this analytical prong is simply inapplicable to the instant case. Because the new use is self-evidently sui generis, it cannot become widespread or even be replicated a single time. That leaves only the Memoirist's own use considered in itself, which, owing to its transformative nature, cannot harm the copyright holder. No one would turn to the Memoir as a substitute for visiting the Stanford Law website to learn about J.D. admissions or to check course scheduling. Because the new use serves a new end, it cannot function as a market substitute for the old one. *See Castle Rock Entm't*, 150 F.3d at 145 ("The more transformative the secondary use, the less likelihood that the secondary use substitutes for the original."); *Campbell*, 510 U.S. at 591 ("when ... the second use is transformative, market substitution is at least less certain, and market harm may not be so readily inferred"). Because Stanford does not sell its website images, no one could be purchasing the Memoir in lieu of purchasing the Images directly from Stanford. Anyone who truly coveted Stanford Law imagery would simply take their own screenshots rather than purchasing the Memoir.

The Memoir also cannot impact any derivative market for the Images, given that Stanford University would not license them for a critique and exposé of itself—their use in the Memoir. *See id.* at 591–92 ("[A]s to parody pure and simple, it is more likely that the new work will not affect the market for the original in a way cognizable under this factor, that is, by acting as a substitute for it ... [T]he unlikelihood that creators of imaginative works will license critical reviews or lampoons of their own productions removes such uses from the very notion of a potential licensing market."); *Twin Peaks Prods. v. Publ'ns Int'l, Ltd.*, 996 F.2d 1366, 1377 (2nd Cir. 1993) ("In the cases where we have found the fourth factor to favor a defendant, the defendant's work filled a market niche that the plaintiff simply had no interest in occupying. Copyright holders rarely write parodies of their own works ... and are even less likely to write new analyses of their underlying data from the opposite political perspective").

V. This Memorandum Itself Weighs in Favor of Fair Use by Fairly Using the Images to Illustrate Fair Use

For all the foregoing reasons, this is a paradigmatic case of fair use. Additionally, the very presence of this Memorandum in the Memoir augments the transformative use of the Images, which are being fairly used to illustrate the fundamentals of fair use doctrine. In an age of social media, laypeople routinely encounter fair use issues without a precise understanding of the doctrine or the resources to consult an attorney. In making his fair use argument, the Memoirist provides readers with a practical introduction to some of the rudiments of copyright law, using the question of the Images' fair use—and hence the Images themselves—to illustrate fair use doctrine and give lay readers a checklist for working through their own fair use dilemmas. Because the Images do not serve this function in their original use, the Memoirist's very making of a fair use argument is itself a further argument for finding fair use.

NOTES

Introduction

1 Jean-Jacques Rousseau, *Discourse on the Science and the Arts*, trans. Ian Johnson (Vancouver, BC: Vancouver Island University, 2018), http://johnstoniatexts.x10host.com/rousseau/firstdiscoursehtm.htm.

2 Ashley Thorne, "LSU Campaign Retreats to Its 'Safe Space'" (blog), National Association of Scholars, October 10, 2008, https://www.nas.org/blogs/article/lsu_campaign_retreats_to_its_safe_space.

3 Timothy Burke, "Trump as Desecration," *Easily Distracted* (blog), May 26, 2017, http://blogs.swarthmore.edu/burke/blog/2017/05/26/trump-as-desecration/.

4 Thomas Frank, *What's the Matter with Kansas? How Conservatives Won the Heart of America* (New York: Henry Holt, 2005), 123.

5 Ernest Becker, *The Denial of Death* (New York: Free Press, 1973), 4-5.

1 The Beginning

1 Russell Jacoby, *The Last Intellectuals: American Culture in the Age of Academe* (New York: Basic Books, 1987), ix–x.

2 Mary Midgley, *Wisdom, Information, and Wonder: What Is Knowledge For?* (New York: Routledge, 1991), 52, 60, 64.

3 Friedrich Nietzsche, *Untimely Meditations*, ed. Daniel Brezeale, trans. R. J. Hollingdale (Cambridge: Cambridge University Press, 1997), 169.

4 Victor Davis Hanson, "Lord Obama," *PJ Media*, May 26, 2014, http://pjmedia.com/victordavishanson/lord-obama/.

5 Thomas Frank, *What's the Matter with Kansas? How Conservatives Won the Heart of America* (New York: Henry Holt, 2005), 119.

6 Thomas Nagel, *Mortal Questions* (Cambridge: Cambridge University Press, 1991), 24–38.

7 Bernard Williams, *Moral Luck: Philosophical Papers 1973–1980* (Cambridge: Cambridge University Press, 1981), 23.
8 Amy L. Wax, "The Conservative's Dilemma: Traditional Institutions, Social Change, and Same-Sex Marriage," *San Diego Law Review* 42 (2005): 1085.
9 Georg Simmel, *The Philosophy of Money*, ed. David Frisby, trans. Tom Bottomore and David Frisby (New York: Routledge, 1990), 448.
10 Ibid., 459.
11 Ibid.
12 Ibid., 460.
13 Ralph Waldo Emerson, "The American Scholar," in *The Essential Writings of Ralph Waldo Emerson*, ed. Brooks Atkinson (New York: Modern Library, 2000), 48.
14 Arthur Schopenhauer, *Essays and Aphorisms*, trans. R. J. Hollingdale (New York: Penguin Books, 1970), 91.
15 Michael Polanyi, *The Tacit Dimension* (Chicago: University of Chicago Press, 1966), 23, 75.
16 Charles Taylor, *A Secular Age* (Cambridge, MA: Harvard University Press, 2007), 81.
17 Ibid., 267.
18 Richard Hofstadter, *The Paranoid Style in American Politics* (New York: Vintage Books, 2008), 81.
19 Alvin W. Gouldner, *The Future of Intellectuals and the Rise of the New Class* (New York: Seabury Press, 1979), 84.
20 Nietzsche, *Untimely Meditations*, 175; Joel Kotkin, "Watch What You Say, the New Liberal Power Elite Won't Tolerate Dissent," *Daily Beast*, July 12, 2017, http://www.thedailybeast.com/articles/2014/06/07/watch-what-you-say-the-new-liberal-power-elite-won-t-tolerate-dissent.html.
21 Midgley, *Wisdom, Information, and Wonder*, 53.
22 Gouldner, *Future of Intellectuals and the Rise of the New Class*, 21.
23 Ibid., 85, 84.
24 Michel Foucault, *The Foucault Reader*, ed. Paul Rabinow (New York: Pantheon Books, 1984), 73.
25 Jonah Goldberg, *Liberal Fascism: The Secret History of the American Left from Mussolini to the Politics of Meaning* (New York: Doubleday, 2007), 404–5.
26 Peter Robinson with Andrew Klavan, "The World According to Andrew Klavan," Hoover Institution, September 8, 2008, https://www.hoover.org/research/world-according-andrew-klavan.

2 A Gathering Storm

1 Pierre Bourdieu, *Outline of a Theory of Practice*, trans. Richard Nice (Cambridge: Cambridge University Press, 1977), 82, 93, 87.

2 Jonah Goldberg, *Liberal Fascism: The Secret History of the American Left from Mussolini to the Politics of Meaning* (New York: Doubleday, 2007), 404–5.

3 Mary Midgley, *Wisdom, Information, and Wonder: What Is Knowledge for?* (New York: Routledge, 1991), 102.

4 Michel Foucault, *The Foucault Reader*, ed. Paul Rabinow (New York: Pantheon Books, 1984), 197.

5 Ibid., 195.

6 Russell Jacoby, *The Last Intellectuals: American Culture in the Age of Academe* (New York: Basic Books, 1987), 232–33.

7 Alvin W. Gouldner, *The Future of Intellectuals and the Rise of the New Class* (New York: Seabury, 1979), 44.

8 Michael Polanyi, *The Tacit Dimension* (Chicago: University of Chicago Press, 1966), 75.

9 John Rawls, *Political Liberalism* (New York: Columbia University Press, 2005), 61.

10 Lynch v. Donnelly, 465 U.S. 668, 688 (1984) (O'Connor J., concurring).

11 Friedrich Nietzsche, *On the Genealogy of Morals*, trans. Walter Kaufman and R. J. Hollingdale (New York: Vintage Books, 1989), 84 (essay II, sec. 16).

12 Norbert Elias, *The Civilizing Process*, trans. Edmund Jephcott (Hoboken, NJ: Blackwell, 1994).

13 George Lakoff, *The Political Mind: Why You Can't Understand 21st-Century American Politics with an 18th-Century Brain* (New York: Viking, 2008), 1.

14 Ibid., 10.

3 A Conspiracy Is Born

1 Pierre Bourdieu, *Homo Academicus*, trans. Peter Collier (Stanford, CA: Stanford University Press, 1988), 208.

2 Ibid., 95.

3 David Brooks, *Bobos in Paradise: The New Upper Class and How They Got There* (New York: Simon & Schuster, 2000), 151.

4 Ibid., 156.

5 Alvin W. Gouldner, *The Future of Intellectuals and the Rise of the New Class* (New York: Seabury, 1979), 19, 20.

6 David Gelernter, *America-Lite: How Imperial Academia Dismantled Our Culture (and Ushered in the Obamacrats)* (New York: Encounter Books, 2012), 82.
7 Bourdieu, *Homo Academicus*, 87.
8 Gouldner, *Future of Intellectuals and the Rise of the New Class*, 19.
9 Lawrence Lessig, "The Regulation of Social Meaning," *University of Chicago Law Review* 62 (1995): 943–1045.
10 Russell Jacoby, *The Last Intellectuals: American Culture in the Age of Academe* (New York: Basic Books, 1987), 146.

4 A Policy of Allusion, Intimation, and Ambiguation

1 "Cuts to hiring will affect growth, composition of faculty," *Stanford Daily*, June 4, 2009, www.stanforddaily.com/2009/06/04/cuts-to-hiring-will-affect-growth-composition-of-faculty/, last accessed April 28, 2011.

5 The Quid Pro Quo

1 Norbert Elias, *The Civilizing Process*, trans. Edmund Jephcott (Hoboken, NJ: Blackwell, 1994), 485.
2 Those pages no longer exist on the law school website. However, "Jim Gaither Honored," *Stanford Lawyer Magazine*, November 1, 2006, https://law.stanford.edu/stanford-lawyer/articles/jim-gaither-honored/, confirms that the fellowship could extend beyond two years.
3 Max Weber, "Science as a Vocation," in *From Max Weber: Essays in Sociology*, ed. and trans. H. H. Gerth and C. Wright Mills (Oxford: Oxford University Press, 1946), 132.

6 Theoretical Excursus

1 Michèle Lamont, *How Professors Think: Inside the Curious World of Academic Judgment* (Cambridge, MA: Harvard University Press, 2009), 140.
2 Karl R. Popper, *Conjectures and Refutations: The Growth of Scientific Knowledge* (New York: Routledge, 1963), 47–48.
3 Chris Mooney, *The Republican Brain: The Science of Why They Deny Science—and Reality* (Hoboken, NJ: John Wiley & Sons, 2012).
4 Angelo M. Codevilla, *The Ruling Class: How They Corrupted America and What We Can Do About It* (New York: Beauford Books, 2010), 20–21.
5 Lionel Trilling, *The Liberal Imagination* (New York: New York Review

of Books, 2008), xv; Richard Hofstadter, *The Paranoid Style in American Politics* (New York: Vintage Books, 2008).

6 Pierre Bourdieu, *Homo Academicus*, trans. Peter Collier (Stanford, CA: Stanford University Press, 1988), 19.

7 Ibid., 143.

8 Liam Gillespie, "Pierre Bourdieu: Habitus," *Critical Legal Thinking*, August 6, 2019, http://criticallegalthinking.com/2019/08/06/pierre-bourdieu-habitus/.

9 Karl Maton, "Habitus," in *Pierre Bourdieu: Key Concepts*, ed. Michael Grenfell (Durham, NC: Acumen, 2012), 54, 58.

10 Pierre Bourdieu, *Outline of a Theory of Practice*, trans. Richard Nice (Cambridge: Cambridge University Press, 1977), 72.

11 Ibid., 78; Pierre Bourdieu, *The Logic of Practice*, trans. Richard Nice (Stanford, CA: Stanford University Press, 1980), 94.

12 Dylan Riley, "Bourdieu's Class Theory: The Academic as Revolutionary," *Catalyst* 1, no. 2 (summer 2017): 112; Mathieu Hilgers, "Habitus, Freedom, and Reflexivity," *Theory & Psychology* 19, no. 6 (2009): 730; Robert N. St. Clair, Walter E. Rodríguez, and Carma Nelson, "Habitus and Communication Theory," *Intercultural Communication Studies* 14, no. 1 (2005): 143.

13 Bourdieu, *Outline of a Theory of Practice*, 72, 79.

14 Ibid., 18.

15 Alisdair MacIntyre, *After Virtue* (South Bend, IN: University of Notre Dame Press, 1984), 72.

16 Bourdieu, *Homo Academicus*, 89.

17 David Brooks, *Bobos in Paradise: The New Upper Class and How They Got There* (New York: Simon & Schuster, 2000), 152.

7 A String of Curious Irregularities

1 Martin Heidegger, *Being and Time*, trans. John Macquarrie and Edward Robinson (San Francisco: HarperSanFrancisco, 1962), 153–54.

2 Michael McConnell, "'God Is Dead and We Have Killed Him!': Freedom of Religion in the Post-Modern Age," *Brigham Young Law Review* (1993): 176.

8 More Curious Irregularities

1 Michael Shermer, "The Danger Is Real: Why We're All Wired for 'Constructive Conspiracism,'" *Quillette*, October 31, 2019, https://quillette.com/2019/10/31/the-danger-is-real-why-were-all-wired-for-constructive-conspiracism/.

2 Richard Hofstadter, *The Paranoid Style in American Politics* (New York: Vintage Books, 2008), 32.

3 Peter L. Berger and Thomas Luckmann, *The Social Construction of Reality: A Treatise in the Sociology of Knowledge* (New York: Anchor Books/Doubleday, 1967), 114, 115.

4 Ibid., 115.

5 Nomi Maya Stolzenberg, "'He Drew a Circle That Shut Me Out': Assimilation, Indoctrination, and the Paradox of a Liberal Education," *Harvard Law Review* 106 (1993): 581–667.

6 John Rawls, *Political Liberalism* (New York: Columbia University Press, 2005), 163.

7 Pierre Bourdieu, *Outline of a Theory of Practice*, trans. Richard Nice (Cambridge: Cambridge University Press, 1977), 94–95.

9 The End of an Era

1 Romer v. Evans, 517 U.S. 620, 652 (1996) (Scalia, J., dissenting).

2 Robert C. Post et al., *Prejudicial Appearances: The Logic of American Antidiscrimination Law* (Durham, NC: Duke University Press, 2001): 1–54.

3 Romer, 517 U.S. at 636.

4 Roger Scruton, *The Meaning of Conservatism* (South Bend, IN: St. Augustine's Press, 2002), 72.

5 For a critique of this view, see Richard T. Ford, *Racial Culture: A Critique* (Princeton, NJ: Princeton University Press, 2005).

6 Kenji Yoshino, "Covering," *Yale Law Journal* 111 (2002): 769–939.

7 Harvey Mansfield, *Manliness* (New Haven, CT: Yale University Press, 2007), 62.

8 Liam Gillespie, "Pierre Bourdieu: Habitus," *Critical Legal Thinking*, August 6, 2019, http://criticallegalthinking.com/2019/08/06/pierre-bourdieu-habitus/.

9 Larry D. Kramer, *The People Themselves: Popular Constitutionalism and Judicial Review* (New York: Oxford University Press, 2005).

11 Meditations on an Aftermath

1. Franz Kafka, *The Metamorphosis and Other Short Stories*, trans. Willa Muir and Edwin Muir (New York: Schocken Books, 1995), 148–50.
2. Peter L. Berger and Thomas Luckmann, *The Social Construction of Reality: A Treatise in the Sociology of Knowledge* (New York: Anchor Books/Doubleday, 1967), 165.
3. Ibid., 126, 127.
4. Ernest Becker, *The Denial of Death* (New York: Free Press, 1973), 5.
5. Carl L. Becker, *The Heavenly City of the Eighteenth-Century Philosophers* (New Haven, CT: Yale University Press, 2003), 34.
6. Christopher Lasch, *The Revolt of the Elites and the Betrayal of Democracy* (New York: W. W. Norton, 1995), 20–21.
7. Alvin W. Gouldner, *The Future of Intellectuals and the Rise of the New Class* (New York: Seabury, 1979), 59.
8. Jonathan Haidt, *The Righteous Mind: Why Good People Are Divided by Politics and Religion* (New York: Pantheon Books, 2012).
9. Charles Taylor, *A Secular Age* (Cambridge, MA: Harvard University Press, 2007), 102, 86.
10. Friedrich Nietzsche, *Beyond Good and Evil*, trans. Walter Kaufman (New York: Vintage Books, 1966), 158 (sec. 229).
11. Gouldner, *Future of Intellectuals and the Rise of the New Class*, 19, 60.
12. William Barrett, *Irrational Man: A Study in Existential Philosophy* (New York: Anchor Books/Doubleday, 1958), 5, 6.
13. Lasch, *Revolt of the Elites and the Betrayal of Democracy*, 20.
14. Plato, *The Republic*, trans. G. M. A. Grube, rev. C. D. C. Reeve (Indianapolis: Hackett, 1992), 186–87 (sec. 514).
15. Ibid., 187, 189 (sec. 515, 517).
16. Ibid., 189 (sec. 517).
17. Alan Bloom, *The Closing of the American Mind* (New York: Simon & Schuster, 1987), 257.
18. Harvey Mansfield, *Manliness* (New Haven, CT: Yale University Press, 2007), 56, 232.
19. Nietzsche, *Beyond Good and Evil*, 139 (sec. 213).
20. Friedrich Nietzsche, *Thus Spoke Zarathustra*, trans. R. J. Hollingdale (New York: Penguin Books, 1969), 78–79.
21. Nietzsche, *Beyond Good and Evil*, 137 (sec. 212).
22. Pierre Bourdieu, *Homo Academicus*, trans. Peter Collier (Stanford, CA: Stanford University Press, 1988), 4.

23 Michel Foucault, *Power/Knowledge: Selected Interviews & Other Writings 1972–1977*, ed. Colin Gordon (New York: Pantheon Books, 1980), 81–83.
24 Gouldner, *Future of Intellectuals and the Rise of the New Class*, 7.
25 Oliver Wendell Holmes, Jr., *The Common Law* (Cambridge, MA: Belknap Press, 2009), 3.
26 Ralph Waldo Emerson, "The American Scholar," in *The Essential Writings of Ralph Waldo Emerson*, ed. Brooks Atkinson (New York: Modern Library, 2000), 52–53.
27 Ibid., 58–59.

REFERENCES

Barrett, William. *Irrational Man: A Study in Existential Philosophy.* New York: Anchor Books/Doubleday, 1958.

Becker, Carl L. *The Heavenly City of the Eighteenth-Century Philosophers.* New Haven, CT: Yale University Press, 2003.

Becker, Ernest. *The Denial of Death.* New York: Free Press, 1973.

Berger, Peter L., and Thomas Luckmann. *The Social Construction of Reality: A Treatise in the Sociology of Knowledge.* New York: Anchor Books/Doubleday, 1967.

Bloom, Alan. *The Closing of the American Mind.* New York: Simon & Schuster, 1987.

Bourdieu, Pierre. *Homo Academicus.* Translated by Peter Collier. Stanford, CA: Stanford University Press, 1988.

———. *The Logic of Practice.* Translated by Richard Nice. Stanford, CA: Stanford University Press, 1990.

———. *Outline of a Theory of Practice.* Translated by Richard Nice. Cambridge: Cambridge University Press, 1977.

Brooks, David. *Bobos in Paradise: The New Upper Class and How They Got There.* New York: Simon & Schuster, 2000.

Burke, Timothy. "Trump as Desecration." *Easily Distracted* (blog), May 26, 2017. http://blogs.swarthmore.edu/burke/blog/2017/05/26/trump-as-desecration/.

Codevilla, Angelo M. *The Ruling Class: How They Corrupted America and What We Can Do About It*. New York: Beauford Books, 2010.

Elias, Norbert. *The Civilizing Process*. Translated by Edmund Jephcott. Hoboken, NJ: Blackwell, 1994.

Emerson, Ralph Waldo. "The American Scholar." In *The Essential Writings of Ralph Waldo Emerson*, edited by Brooks Atkinson, 43–59. New York: Modern Library, 2000.

Ford, Richard T. *Racial Culture: A Critique*. Princeton, NJ: Princeton University Press, 2005.

Foucault, Michel. *The Foucault Reader*. Edited by Paul Rabinow. New York: Pantheon Books, 1984.

———. *Power/Knowledge: Selected Interviews & Other Writings 1972–1977*. Edited by Colin Gordon. New York: Pantheon Books, 1980.

Frank, Thomas. *What's the Matter with Kansas? How Conservatives Won the Heart of America*. New York: Henry Holt, 2005.

Gelernter, David. *America-Lite: How Imperial Academia Dismantled Our Culture (and Ushered in the Obamacrats)*. New York: Encounter Books, 2012.

Gillespie, Liam. "Pierre Bourdieu: Habitus." *Critical Legal Thinking*, August 6, 2019. http://criticallegalthinking.com/2019/08/06/pierre-bourdieu-habitus/.

Goldberg, Jonah. *Liberal Fascism: The Secret History of the American Left from Mussolini to the Politics of Meaning*. New York: Doubleday, 2007.

Gouldner, Alvin W. *The Future of Intellectuals and the Rise of the New Class*. New York: Seabury, 1979.

Guldmann, Rony. "Determinism and Forbearance." *Social Theory and Practice* 32, no. 1 (January 2006): 97–135.

———. *Two Orientations Toward Human Nature*. New York: Routledge, 2007.

Haidt, Jonathan. *The Righteous Mind: Why Good People Are Divided by Politics and Religion.* New York: Pantheon Books, 2012.

Hanson, Victor Davis. "Lord Obama." *PJ Media*, May 26, 2014. http://pjmedia.com/victordavishanson/lord-obama/.

Heidegger, Martin. *Being and Time.* Translated by John Macquarrie and Edward Robinson. San Francisco: HarperSanFrancisco, 1962.

Hilgers, Mathieu. "Habitus, Freedom, and Reflexivity." *Theory & Psychology* 19, no. 6 (2009): 728–55.

Hofstadter, Richard. *The Paranoid Style in American Politics.* New York: Vintage Books, 2008.

Holmes, Oliver Wendell, Jr. *The Common Law.* Cambridge, MA: Belknap Press, 2009.

Jacoby, Russell. *The Last Intellectuals: American Culture in the Age of Academe.* New York: Basic Books, 1987.

Jaschik, Josh. "When Colleges Seek Diversity Through Photoshop." *Inside Higher Ed*, February 4, 2019. https://www.insidehighered.com/admissions/article/2019/02/04/york-college-pennsylvania-illustrates-issues-when-colleges-change.

Kafka, Franz. *The Metamorphosis and Other Short Stories.* Translated by Willa Muir and Edwin Muir. New York: Schocken Books, 1995.

Kotkin, Joel. "Watch What You Say, the New Liberal Power Elite Won't Tolerate Dissent." *Daily Beast*, July 12, 2017. http://www.thedailybeast.com/articles/2014/06/07/watch-what-you-say-the-new-liberal-power-elite-wont-tolerate-dissent.html.

Kramer, Larry D. *The People Themselves: Popular Constitutionalism and Judicial Review.* New York: Oxford University Press, 2005.

Lakoff, George. *Moral Politics: How Liberals and Conservatives Think.* Chicago: University of Chicago Press, 2002.

———. *The Political Mind: Why You Can't Understand 21st-Century American Politics with an 18th-Century Brain.* New York: Viking, 2008.

Lamont, Michèle. *How Professors Think: Inside the Curious World of Academic Judgment.* Cambridge, MA: Harvard University Press, 2009.

Lasch, Christopher. *The Revolt of the Elites and the Betrayal of Democracy.* New York: W. W. Norton, 1995.

Leong, Nancy. "Fake Diversity and Racial Capitalism." *Medium.com,* November 23, 2014. https://medium.com/@nancyleong/racial-photoshop-and-faking-diversity-b880e7bc5e7a.

Lessig, Lawrence. "The Regulation of Social Meaning." *University of Chicago Law Review* 62 (1995): 943–1045.

MacIntyre, Alisdair. *After Virtue.* South Bend, IN: University of Notre Dame Press, 1984.

Mansfield, Harvey. *Manliness.* New Haven, CT: Yale University Press, 2007.

Maton, Karl. "Habitus." In *Pierre Bourdieu: Key Concepts,* edited by Michael Grenfell, 48–64. Durham, NC: Acumen Publishing, 2012.

McConnell, Michael. "'God Is Dead and We Have Killed Him!': Freedom of Religion in the Post-modern Age." *Brigham Young University Law Review* (1993): 163–98.

Midgley, Mary. *Wisdom, Information, and Wonder: What Is Knowledge For?* New York: Routledge, 1991.

Mooney, Chris. *The Republican Brain: The Science of Why They Deny Science—and Reality.* Hoboken, NJ: John Wiley & Sons, 2012.

Nagel, Thomas. *Mortal Questions.* Cambridge: Cambridge University Press, 1991.

Nietzsche, Friedrich. *Beyond Good and Evil.* Translated by Walter Kaufman. New York: Vintage Books, 1966.

———. *On the Genealogy of Morals.* Translated by Walter Kaufman and R. J. Hollingdale. New York: Vintage Books, 1989.

———. *Thus Spoke Zarathustra.* Translated by R. J. Hollingdale. New York: Penguin Books, 1969.

———. *Untimely Meditations.* Edited by Daniel Brezeale. Translated by R. J. Hollingdale. Cambridge: Cambridge University Press, 1997.

Plato. *The Republic.* Translated by G. M. A. Grube. Revised by C. D. C. Reeve. Indianapolis: Hackett, 1992.

Polanyi, Michael. *The Tacit Dimension.* Chicago: University of Chicago Press, 1966.

Popper, Karl R. *Conjectures and Refutations: The Growth of Scientific Knowledge.* New York: Routledge, 1963.

Post, Robert C., K. Anthony Appiah, Judith Butler, Thomas C. Grey, and Reva B. Siegel. *Prejudicial Appearances: The Logic of American Antidiscrimination Law.* Durham, NC: Duke University Press, 2001.

Rawls, John. *Political Liberalism.* New York: Columbia University Press, 2005.

Riley, Dylan. "Bourdieu's Class Theory: The Academic as Revolutionary." *Catalyst* 1, no. 2 (summer 2017): 107–36.

Rousseau, Jean-Jacques. *Discourse on the Science and the Arts.* Translated by Ian Johnson. Vancouver, BC: Vancouver Island University, 2018. http://johnstoniatexts.x10host.com/rousseau/firstdiscoursehtm.htm.

Schopenhauer, Arthur. *Essays and Aphorisms.* Translated by R. J. Hollingdale. New York: Penguin Books, 1970.

Scruton, Roger. *The Meaning of Conservatism.* South Bend, IN: St. Augustine's Press, 2002.

Shermer, Michael. "The Danger Is Real: Why We're All Wired for 'Constructive Conspiracism.'" *Quillette,* October 31, 2019. https://quillette.com/2019/10/31/the-danger-is-real-why-were-all-wired-for-constructive-conspiracism/.

Sherwin, Katie. "University Websites: Top 10 Design Guidelines." Nielsen Norman Group, April 23, 2016. https://www.nngroup.com/articles/university-sites/.

Simmel, George. *The Philosophy of Money*. Edited by David Frisby. Translated by Tom Bottomore and David Frisby. New York: Routledge, 1990.

St. Clair, Robert N., Walter E. Rodríguez, and Carma Nelson. "Habitus and Communication Theory." *Intercultural Communication Studies* 14, no. 1 (2005): 135–50.

Stolzenberg, Nomi Maya. "'He Drew a Circle That Shut Me Out': Assimilation, Indoctrination, and the Paradox of a Liberal Education." *Harvard Law Review* 106 (1993): 581–667.

Taylor, Charles. *A Secular Age*. Cambridge, MA: Harvard University Press, 2007.

Thorne, Ashley. "LSU Campaign Retreats to Its 'Safe Space'" (blog). National Association of Scholars, October 10, 2008. https://www.nas.org/blogs/article/lsu_ campaign_ retreats_ to_its_safe_space.

Trilling, Lionel. *The Liberal Imagination*. New York: New York Review of Books, 2008.

Weber, Max. "Science as a Vocation." In *From Max Weber: Essays in Sociology*, edited and translated by H. H. Gerth and C. Wright Mills, 129–58. Oxford: Oxford University Press, 1946.

Wax, Amy L. "The Conservative's Dilemma: Traditional Institutions, Social Change, and Same-Sex Marriage." *San Diego Law Review* 42 (2005): 1059–1103.

Williams, Bernard. *Moral Luck: Philosophical Papers 1973–1980*. Cambridge: Cambridge University Press, 1981.

Yoshino, Kenji. "Covering." *Yale Law Journal* 111 (2002): 769–939.

ABOUT THE AUTHOR

Rony Guldmann is a New York attorney who has fought the good fight against the twin scourges of product mislabeling and unsolicited commercial texting, setting his crosshairs on purveyors of fraudulent manuka honey, diluted olive oil, and deceptively oversized food packaging, among other villains. He received his B.A. in philosophy from the University of Michigan, his Ph.D. in the same from Indiana University, and his J.D. from Stanford Law School, where he was the James C. Gaither Fellow after graduating. In a former life before the tribulations of *The Star Chamber*, Rony taught philosophy at Iona College, Hofstra University, and Fordham University in a bid to enlighten easily distracted young minds about human nature, ethics, and other lofty matters. He is the author of *Two Orientations Toward Human Nature*, published by Routledge and applauded in *The Review of Metaphysics* for doing "an impressive job of pulling together a considerable range of historical and contemporary reflection into a well-crafted, synthetically-rich, and engaging tour of human nature." He lives in Astoria, Queens. Learn more at ronyguldmann.com.

CPSIA information can be obtained
at www.ICGtesting.com
Printed in the USA
LVHW081341090422
715719LV00015B/464